T0309335

LEAPING INTO THE FUTURE

LEAPING INTO
THE FUTURE

China and Russia in the New World
Tech-Economic Paradigm

SERGEI GLAZYEV

Translated by Zhang Yumei

Books Beyond Boundaries
ROYAL COLLINS

Leaping into the Future: China and Russia in the New World Tech-Economic Paradigm

Sergei Glazyev
Translated by Zhang Yumei

First published in 2023 by Royal Collins Publishing Group Inc.
Groupe Publication Royal Collins Inc.
BKM Royalcollins Publishers Private Limited

Headquarters: 550-555 boul. René-Lévesque O Montréal (Québec) H2Z1B1 Canada
India office: 805 Hemkunt House, 8th Floor, Rajendra Place, New Delhi 110008

ISBN: 978-1-4878-1130-3

To find out more about our publications, please visit www.royalcollins.com.

Contents

PART V
RUSSIA GOING OUT OF THE PERIPHERY AND ENTERING THE WORLD ECONOMIC CENTER

PART VI
DEVELOPMENT OF THE EURASIAN ECONOMIC INTEGRATION STRATEGY

PART VII
BUILDING A GREATER EURASIAN PARTNERSHIP

Glossary

BRICS	Brazil, Russia, India, and China, and South Africa
GDP	Gross Domestic Product
WHO	World Health Organization
WTO	World Trade Organization
FES	Free Economic Society
MCP	Money-Credit Policy
EAEU	Eurasian Economic Union
EurAsEC	The Eurasian Economic Community
SCT	Single Customs Tariff
ECB	European Central Bank
EEC	Eurasian Economic Community
CES	Common Economic Space
MOEX	Moscow Stock Exchange
IMF	International Monetary Fund
ILO	International Labor Organization
MED	Ministry of Economic Development
WEP	World Ecnomic Paradigm
R&D	Research and Development
STP	Scientific and Technical Progress
CSTO	Collective Security Treaty Organization
MDUSMP	The Main Directions of the Unified State Monetary Policy
UN	United Nations
CU	Customs Union
TP	Technology Paradigm
RAS	Russian Academy of Sciences
FRA	The Federal Reserve System
CB	Central Bank
UNIDO	United Nations Industrial Development Organization

Introduction

This book calls for an objective understanding of the long-debated path of economic development.

The book presents the author's Theory of Long Cycles in economic growth, which considers the fundamental significance of scientific and technological progress, the cyclical process of constant technological and world economic paradigm change, and the ensuing long fluctuation cycles and long cycles of capital accumulation.[1] The theory reveals the objective reasons for the deep crisis and prolonged depression of the world economy, the outbreak of world wars, and social revolutions during the period of technological paradigm change. The world wars and social revolutions indirectly manifest the world economic paradigm shift. This theory enables us to explain the causes of the current world economic crisis and the expanding aggressive behavior of the US, whose ruling elite has launched a global hybrid war against China and Russia to preserve its global hegemony.

Based on the theory presented in the book, the author argues for practical suggestions that can both stop US aggression and form an effective management system for leapfrogging economic development. The theory includes a methodology for selecting priority directions for the development of key industries of the new technological paradigm and also presupposes that a mechanism for implementing the priority directions can be established by developing a corresponding system for the development of the new technological paradigm. The theory focuses the entire economic policy system on addressing system upgrading and shifting the system to a sustainable growth path based on the next technological paradigm leapfrogging.

All state regulatory bodies (including central banks and banking systems, government departments, enterprises, scientific research, and engineering organizations) must operate within the framework of a unified strategic planning system that includes two types of measures: a combination of private initiative and market mechanisms, as well as the implementation of government support for the common development plan. The planning should be developed based on the government-social capital cooperation model and provide for joint responsibility of the state administration and private enterprises to achieve jointly set goals. The modern experience of the Chinese economic miracle has established a management system model, which is highly relevant for Russia.

Unlike Russia's young reformists, who developed a "shock therapy" for the Russian economy based on the recommendations of the IMF, resulting in a systemic crisis for three decades, China's leaders have pursued a consistent policy of "reform and opening up" during these three decades, while insisting on systematic planning of China's social and economic development.

---

1. Глазьев С. Стратегия опережающего развития России в условиях глобального кризиса. М.: Экономика, 2010; Доклад ученых секции экономики ООН РАН 2011 г. / Под ред. С. Глазьева; Конкурентный потенциал России и пути его реализации для обеспечения национальной безопасности / Доклад С. Глазьева на заседании Совбеза России в 2015 г.

On August 24, 2020, Xi Jinping, General Secretary of the CPC Central Committee, said at a symposium of experts in the economic and social fields, "Since 1953, China has compiled and implemented 13 five-year plans, of which eight have been compiled and implemented since the reform and opening up. They have strongly promoted economic and social development, improved overall national strength, improved people's lives, and created a rare economy in the world. A miracle of rapid development and a miracle of long-term social stability. The practice has proved that the medium and long-term development plan can not only give full play to the decisive role of the market in the allocation of resources but also better play the role of the government."

The comprehensive economic and social development plan does not hinder the market-oriented transformation of China's economy but has moved it in an innovative direction. Rather than just a narrow privatization of state assets, market mechanisms have been skillfully embedded in governance to promote the well-being of society as a whole and ensure a progressive increase in the level of technological development and competitiveness of the Chinese economy. China's leaders have continuously improved the mechanism of combining state planning and the market, constructively using the market mechanism to achieve the set goals of socioeconomic development.

In the same speech, Xi Jinping presented to Chinese experts the ambitious goals of the country's economic development. He stressed that "The '14th Five-Year Plan' period will be the first five years when China begins its march towards the second Centenary Goal of building a modern socialist country, based on the successful achievement of the first Centenary Goal of building a moderately well-off society. Our country will enter a new stage of development. Forewarned is forearmed without prejudging the waste. We must have a long-term view, grasp the general trend, open the door to ask for ideas, brainstorm ideas, study new situations, and make new plans."

Xi Jinping called on experts to "look at the new opportunities and challenges of the new development stage with dialectical thinking." This creative approach to governance and economic reform is very different from the dogmatic approach of Washington's financial institutions (the IMF and the World Bank), whose agents recklessly destroyed the reproduction mechanisms of the Soviet economy and left it to be plundered by organized crime and corrupt officials.

Following the fantasy of a Utopian program of the rapid transition to a market economy, seeking overnight riches through the misappropriation of state property, and imagining the destruction of federal regulatory bodies to usurp unlimited power, the leaders of the Russian Federation and most post-Soviet republics had no qualms about destroying the reproduction mechanisms of a unified national economic system. This led to a rapid collapse of the complex "chain" of scientific and technical collaboration between production enterprises, scientific research institutions, design bureaus, and educational institutions. The scientific and productive potential was rapidly destroyed, the economy plummeted, millions of highly qualified specialists left the country, and capital outflows were estimated at more than a trillion dollars.

It is said that today only the blind or the cold-eyed refuse to recognize that the economic policy implemented in the post-Soviet period has led to the economic stagnation of Russia and other post-Soviet countries. Russia's technological level, productivity, human resources, and population's life quality have fallen below the world average and rank next to third world countries. China has maintained its socialist ideology and planning and has replaced the Soviet Union as the basis for a new world economic paradigm, establishing an advanced management system that has ensured the leapfrogging of its society and economy.

By combining the advantages of strategic planning with the mechanisms of market competition, combining state-owned infrastructure projects with private entrepreneurship, and regulating them based on the public interest to raise the level of social welfare, the Communist Party of China has created a fundamentally new system of production relations to meet the requirements of modern productive development. The sophistication of this system is reflected in the high rate of productivity growth and the rapid improvement of people's living standards. China has led the world economy with the help of an advanced system of production relations, leaving the capitalist countries far behind. The five countries of the South Central Peninsula (Thailand, Burma, Cambodia, Laos, and Vietnam), India, and Ethiopia have introduced economic management mechanisms similar to China's, and these countries are among the world leaders in terms of economic growth rates. Even before the Chinese economic miracle, elements of this management system had been adopted by the newly industrialized countries of Asia—post-war Japan and Western Europe.

In fact, the success achieved by all these countries has been due to the combination of socialist principles of economic activity subordinated to social interests, entrepreneurial initiatives based on private capital, and the unifying interests of the state based on the principle of uniting different groups in society in order to achieve the goals of growth in production and increased social well-being, based on socioeconomic development. Sorokin and the proponents of the theory of Economic Convergence foresaw the emergence of the system of integration half a century ago. The author believes that in terms of guaranteeing the development of productive forces, the integrated system combines the best parts of the socioeconomic system of socialism, capitalism, and communism.[2] The proliferation of this system of institutions, to some extent, guarantees expanded reproduction in China and other socialist market economies, transcends the boundaries of national systems and reaches an international level, forming a new world economic paradigm that will determine the future global economic system.

The new world economic paradigm differs from the current liberal globalization ideology in that the former respects national interests, recognizes the sovereign right of the state to limit any foreign economic activity, and adheres to the principles of mutual benefit, voluntariness, and common interest in international cooperation. In contrast, the latter considers only the high productivity growth of the US-centered multinational companies and the rapid improvement of people's living standards. The free movement of capital, goods, services, and people is not achieved by breaking borders and destroying national institutions but by combining the national interests of participating countries with institutional support for national development on the basis of common and mutually beneficial investments, which will be the guideline

---

2. Сорокин П. Главные тенденции нашего времени. М.: Наука, Российская академия наук, Институт социологии, 1997.

for the formation of a new system of world economic relations. If we use Perkins' terminology[3] to describe it, the new system of world economic relations is not built by economic killers but by experts who plan complex networks of creative cooperation. While economic killers represent the benefits gained by large transnational capital colonizing peripheral countries, these experts combine national competitive advantages in implementing co-investment projects to achieve multiplier effects. Thus, using Sorokin's definition, we call this new world economic paradigm an "integration system."

Technological and world economic paradigm change is a painful process accompanied by structural crises, economic depressions, and rising military-political tensions. Power-economy relations develop during the previous cycle of world economic evolution, and elites interested in perpetuating them and the institutions that serve them will use all means (including world wars) to preserve them. However, the victors of the wars are always the carriers of new leaders and more efficient systems of production relations, and the systems of the victors will then be emulated by other countries, spreading around the world and shaping a new world economic paradigm.

Thus, in the 20th century, Britain survived two world wars between the most threatening competing enemies to maintain its hegemony, but was unable to maintain its colonial system, which is now held by American multinationals. Currently, the US has already been organizing a hybrid world war to maintain its control over its peripheral countries. But the main result of this war is the strategic alliance between Russia and China and the consolidation of China's position as the leader of the New World economic and technological paradigm. Will this alliance be able to withstand US aggression and prevent a new world war? This book is written in detail about the strategy of the Russian-Chinese strategic alliance.

According to the objective laws of the long cycle of economic development, the world is shifting to a new technological and world economic paradigm. At the same time, a technological revolution is underway, and the system of institutions that determine the reproduction of national and world economies is changing. After the collapse of the Soviet Union, Russia and other post-Soviet countries found themselves on the "periphery" of the US-centered system of capital reproduction, which subordinated the economic development of post-Soviet countries to US interests. This book explains in detail the mechanism of subordination that has led to economic decline and a raw material-oriented economy in which the once-developed national economic complex fragmented into separate parts that served external interests. The US has gained from the Russian economy the "cash cow" of the US-centric financial system, capturing hundreds of billions of dollars of capital annually through a non-reciprocal chain of cross-border transactions.

After the collapse of the Soviet Union and the global socialist system it established, our social scientists, lost in their own illusions, followed the ideas of Western scholars and began to use vague notions of post-industrial society, post-modernism, post-Christianity, post-communism, and even post-humanism, abandoning dialectical logic and historical materialism. They confused themselves and their readers with

---

3. Перкинс Д. Исповедь экономического убийцы. М.: Претекст, 2005.

seemingly scientific inferences that could not provide any comprehensible theory of socioeconomic development.

With the return of the basic concepts of productivity, production relations, and factors of production, the analysis of objective data on the various effective models of transition to a market economy allows us to recover the understanding of the logic of socioeconomic development in a new technological paradigm. Unlike mainstream economic thought, the logic of socioeconomic development is not based on dogmatism, but on objective laws of economic development that explain the current structural changes in the world economy and the resulting crisis processes.

Currently, according to the objective laws of technology and world economic paradigm change, the US is losing its global dominance. Having lost the geoeconomic competition with China, the US is trying to improve its position by expanding its control over the peripheral countries of the global monetary and financial system, of which Russia is a key link. Following the "Anglo-Saxon" tradition in geopolitics, the US leadership has launched new wars in Europe, as previous wars have brought huge benefits to the US. To this end, the US groomed Ukrainian Nazis and pushed them into the mass murder and repression of Russians in southeastern Ukraine. This move is intended to plunge Russia into a military conflict to pit Russia against the Western world and trigger an economic disaster. This war, already waged on the information, diplomatic and monetary-financial fronts, is designed to destroy Russia, and Russians with foreign assets will not be able to avoid it. The US-controlled Ukrainian regime stipulates that Russians with foreign assets can only protect them by "betraying their country"; otherwise, their accounts will be "frozen," and their assets will be expropriated. The US leader issued the "Kremlin Report," an ultimatum to leading Russian businessmen and officials, allowing the US-controlled agencies to seize the assets of influential Russian citizens. The assets of those who do not serve the US interests and refuse to "cooperate" with US intelligence in the war against Russia will be confiscated.

This book shows from a scientific point of view that the macroeconomic policy pursued by Russia is outdated, wrong, and harmful. The danger of market fundamentalist ideology for Russia and other countries on the periphery of the financial and economic system centered on the US lies in a lack of understanding of the laws of technological and economic development, which precludes a proper policy of modernization and raising the economy to the level of advanced countries. If Russia "slumbers" in the next technological revolution based on nano- and bio-engineering technologies, it will repeat the failure of the Soviet Union to take advantage of the achievements of information and communication technologies of the previous revolution, which will lead to political risks, serious technological lag, and poverty of working people. To eliminate such risks, the book offers scientifically sound recommendations based on the basic laws of economic development and the successful experience of China.

The CPC Central Committee document cited earlier summarizes the implementation of the 13th Five-Year Plan, stating:

"The 13th 'Five-Year Plan' period was the decisive stage in building a moderately well-off society. Facing a tangled and complex international situation, the arduous tasks of reform, development, and stability, especially the severe shock of the COVID-19 epidemic, the CPC Central Committee, with Comrade Xi Jinping as the core, never forgetting its original intention and remembering its mission, shall unite and lead the entire Party and people of all ethnicities to forge ahead, blaze new trails of innovation, and work with enthusiasm and promise to advance the various undertakings of the Party and the State. Major breakthroughs have been made in comprehensively deepening reform, major gains have been made in comprehensively relying on the rule of law, and major achievements have been made in the comprehensive and strict governance of the Party. Progress in modernizing the national governance system and our governance capacity has been accelerated, and the advantages of the CPC's leadership and China's socialist system have been further demonstrated. Economic strength, scientific and technological strength, and overall national strength have leapfrogged to new levels, the overall operation of the economy is stable, and optimization of the economic structure continues. It is estimated that the 2020 GDP will surpass 100 trillion yuan (RMB). Poverty alleviation results have attracted the world's attention, as 55.75 million rural poor have been successfully lifted out of poverty. For five consecutive years, annual grain production has steadily remained above 1.3 quadrillions *jin* [650 million metric tons]. Pollution prevention efforts have been stepped up, and the ecological environment has improved significantly. Opening up to the outside has continued to expand, and joint construction under the 'Belt and Road' is bearing fruit. The people's standard of living has increased significantly. Higher education has entered the popularization stage, over 60 million new jobs have been created in cities and towns, and the world's largest social security system has been constructed. More than 1.3 billion people are covered by basic medical insurance, and nearly 1 billion people are covered by basic pension insurance."

There is no doubt that the following goals set by the CPC will be equally successfully achieved, "The 19th Party Congress has made a two-stage strategic arrangement for achieving the second centennial objective, that is, basically achieving socialist modernization by 2035, and establish China as a rich, strong, democratic, civilized, harmonious, beautiful modernized socialist world power by the middle of this century."

Scientists working on the "long" cycles of human development have identified the transitional nature of the present era, which is characterized by the alternation of different cycles in millennial civilizations.[4] It is very difficult to study the laws that govern these cycles, including the change of technology and world economic paradigms that have led to the current global economic crisis.

The current technological paradigm shift has led to a structural crisis in the economies of the world's leading countries, which is related to the exhaustion of the

---

4. Яковец Ю. Политическая экономия цивилизаций. М.: Экономика, 2016.

growth potential of the existing technological paradigm and the formation of a new technological paradigm growth trajectory. During the "birth" of the new technological paradigm, some countries could master the key industrial resources of the new paradigm ahead of time, while the former leaders would be caught in the stagnation of production and capital devaluation of the previous paradigm. In this way, post-war Japan and Western Europe achieved economic miracles and joined the ranks of world leaders led by the US and Russia. China and India are currently experiencing a similar leap.

Although the process of technological paradigm change has been well studied and a sixth change is underway, including a second one in the memory of contemporary leaders, few understand the logic of this change process. Developed countries, including Russia, have made the classic mistake of exacerbating the structural crisis by continuing to invest in expanding production in industries that do not hold promise and belong to the old technology paradigm that is about to be phased out, while delaying increased investment in the production of the new technology paradigm.

Even less is known about the theory of paradigm change in the world economy, which explains the logic of changes in the system of production relations and the system of reproduction of capital. The current increase in political tensions is typical of the world economic paradigm change, which until today has been accompanied by world wars.

According to the logic of this process, the "life cycle" of the US as the "core" of the financial monopoly world economic paradigm is coming to an end. The US is trying to maintain global hegemony by waging a hybrid world war to control its economic periphery, competing with China and other Southeast Asian countries that are forming the "core" of a new, integrated world economic paradigm. In his book, the author reveals the objective reasons for the US hybrid world war and the futility of the war.

The US has lost the war. China has outpaced the US economically, the Shanghai Cooperation Organization is ahead of the US politically, and the BRICS countries have formed an anti-war alliance ideologically. However, the US will continue to dominate the global monetary and financial system and the information space, and its ruling elites remain confident in their exclusive right to rule the world. This poses the risk of an escalation of US aggression, which for subjective and objective reasons is directed primarily toward Russia. Ignorance of the laws of the world economic paradigm shift leads to an underestimation of the risk of US aggression, which is seen either as a banal quest to weaken Russia and China, as the usual struggle against the US political system, or as a war against international terrorism. In reality, it is a war between the US ruling elite and the world to maintain leadership, which is slipping with the world economic paradigm that is retiring from the stage of history. The US cannot stop history, but it can disrupt the world. The US can easily overrun Europe, just as the British ruling elite did a century ago, when Britain launched World Wars I and II to maintain its global leadership as a colonial empire.

The dangerous resonance effects of two global cyclical crises caused by technological and world economic paradigm shifts have created economic and political crises. A similar resonance effect occurred in the 1930s when the catastrophe of the Second World War resolved the crisis phenomenon. This time, can the technological and geopolitical revolution that occurred with the change of world leadership take place without the resonance effect?

Theoretically, the BRICS countries and even the Shanghai Cooperation Organization could create an anti-war alliance if these countries could successfully form an alliance sufficient to stop the US aggression with the help of new technologies and the "wave" of growth of the world economic paradigm, and if they could reach a common position on the key issues of the new world economic paradigm.

The ruling elites of the advanced countries, having understood the laws governing the functioning of the contemporary world economic system, can reach a consensus on the harmonious future development of humanity. The author contends that the new world economic paradigm is developing into an "integrated system" that, according to the theory of evolution of civilizational cycles, will replace the capitalist system and become the basis for the transition to human intellectual civilization.[5] A large-scale transition is difficult to achieve, because the possibility of controlled development has emerged for the first time in human history.

---

5. Яковец Ю. В., Кузык Б. Н. . Цивилизации: теория, история, диалог, будущее. М.: Институт экономических стратегий, 2006. Т. 1; Яковец Ю. В., Акаев А. А. Перспективы становления устойчивого многополярного мироустройства на базе партнерства цивилизаций: Научный доклад. М.: МИСК, 2016.

PART I

BASIC LAWS OF ECONOMIC DEVELOPMENT

From the perspective of economic science, unlike traditional society, modern society is characterized by Scientific and Technological Progress (STP), which has become a principal consideration in economic growth. Among the factors influencing social production and welfare growth, STP accounted for 90%, and traditional factors such as labor, capital, and natural resources accounted for only 10%. Influenced by STP, those traditional factors themselves are constantly changing. The current situation was realized in the post-modernization era and even existed as early as the modernization era. We will embrace the Industrial Revolution as a historic milestone in determining the transition from a traditional society to a modern one. Thus, we believe that the period before the Industrial Revolution belongs to the economy of the past, while the new technological and world economic paradigms belong to that of the future. A transition to new technologies and world economic paradigms is underway.

Chapter 1

The Cyclical Changes of Technology Paradigm in the Development of Productive Forces

Since the Industrial Revolution, there have been five "long waves" (Kondratieff) of changes in economic growth (quotations). The rising stage of the life cycle of the corresponding technology paradigm has become the basis for long-wave replacement, that is, a renewable and complete technology-related industry system.

According to the author's definition, the technology paradigm is a technology-related industrial cluster separated from the economic structure. These industrial clusters are connected through the same type of technology "chain" and form a reproduction whole. Each paradigm has an internally consistent and stable composition, which carries out a complete macro production cycle within the framework of the paradigm, including the extraction and acquisition of initial resources, all processing stages, and a series of final products that meet the corresponding public consumption types.

Dynamically, a technology paradigm is a reproduction model[1] containing clusters of fundamental technologies developed synchronously and renewable for a new technology paradigm. In a static state, the technology paradigm can be defined as an industrial cluster with a similar technology level, that is, an economic level.[2]

The technology paradigm is characterized by similar levels of technology among industries that make up the paradigm. These industries are composed of similar resources connected vertically and horizontally, and at the same time, use labors commensurate with the technological level and rely on the same technological potential.

Technological paradigms have complex internal structures during their development. In this process, economic base innovation, which determines the "core" of the technological paradigm and innovates the economic and technological structure, plays a key role. Some industries use "core" products and play a major role when the technological paradigm spreads. It is these industries that constitute industrial clusters in key areas. The technology "chain" that forms the technology paradigm covers the technology-related industrial clusters (technology clusters) at all levels of resource processing and connects the corresponding types of non-productive demand. The latter forms the reproduction model of the technological paradigm and is also a great source of diffusion, thus ensuring the reproduction of the corresponding quality of labor resources.

The high requirements for consistency in the technological association process promote the strong connection between different industries that have entered the

---

1. Данилов-Данильян В. И., Рывкин А. А. Воспроизводственный аспект экономического развития и некоторые проблемы управления // Экономика и мат. методы. 1982. Т. XX, вып. 1.; Глазьев С. НТП и воспроизводственные структуры в народном хозяйстве. Препринт. М.: ЦЭМИ АН СССР, 1986.

2. Яременко Ю. В. Структурные изменения в социалистической экономике. М.: Мысль, 1981.

same technological paradigm. The rigid connection of technology cluster elements requires technical homogeneity (such as the same production technology level, product quality, raw materials and materials, labor qualifications, labor organization cultural level, and development according to established technological paths). There is a significant difference in technological level between industries within a technology cluster and industries that have not entered the technology cluster. Integrating industry into a technology cluster is usually a complex and completely economically unprofitable activity, because this activity either requires the transformation of the relevant production process (if the technology introduced is higher than the existing technological level of the industry in the cluster), or reduces the overall technology cluster's production efficiency and final product quality (when the introduced technology is lower than the existing technology level of the industry in the cluster).

The technical associations of the production process unite to form a technology cluster, which causes the simultaneous development of the technology cluster and the production process. The emergence, expansion, stabilization, and decline of the same technology cluster industry occurred simultaneously. Due to the internal integrity of the technology cluster, the formation of a new technological association process "chain" means eliminating the old chain. Therefore, any major technological innovation in the technology cluster can be reconstructed on the new technology platform, which marks the emergence of the next technology cluster.

Usually, technology clusters are closely connected, so that multiple specific technology chains are combined. These technology chains are not evenly distributed in the technology space but are connected in bundles within key technology clusters of the same type of technology chain. The homogeneity of the technology chain is manifested in the complementarity of finished products, unity of consumption types, similarity of resource quality, and consistency of production culture and production technology level. It is used as the same type of structural materials, energy carriers and transportation, and communication materials.

During its development, the associated technology clusters can adapt to each other. The needs of business entities for production stability make the cooperative relationship between technology clusters reproducible. Sustainable technology "chains" are emerging in the economy, and these "chains" can connect related technology clusters. These associated technology clusters can reasonably reallocate a series of fixed resources from mining to final product production.

The above explanation of the economic and technological structure allows us to describe the process of technological change as follows: the development of any technological system begins with the introduction of appropriate foundation innovations, while at the same time generating necessary supplementary innovations. Foundation innovation is completely different from the traditional technological environment. The effective operation of the technological system created based on foundation innovation requires the organization of new industries with similar technological levels. Therefore, the spread of foundation innovation is accompanied by the formation of new technology clusters. Conversely, only in a peer-to-peer production and technology environment (within the framework of the corresponding technology paradigm) can the effective operation of the technology cluster be ensured.

Each group of technologically interconnected industrial clusters formed by the connection of technological "chains" is more or less closely linked with other technological clusters. Therefore, on the one hand, changes in industrial clusters are restricted by the ability of related technology clusters to absorb these changes; on the other hand, the technology clusters themselves will also produce corresponding structural changes. It can be seen that the production and technology systems that constitute the technological paradigm have more or less synchronized transformation. The development and diffusion of technological processes are preconditions for developing clusters of related technological systems. Upward technological and economic development is achieved through new technological "chains," which are formed based on associated technological clusters and integrated into new technological paradigms.

The technological paradigm is formed within the entire economic system, covering all stages of resource processing and corresponding non-productive consumption types, forming a macroeconomic reproduction model. Therefore, each technological paradigm is a self-reproducing whole, and economic technological development must be realized through continuous technological paradigm replacement.

Therefore, the relationship between the technical paradigms that exist at the same time is contradictory: on the one hand, due to the development of the previous technical paradigm, the material conditions of the existing technical paradigm are formed; on the other hand, there is an inevitable competition for limited resources between concurrent technological paradigms. The technological and economic development of the new technological paradigm is based on the production potential created in the previous stage. The new technology paradigm can not only use the energy carriers, structural materials, raw materials, and mass consumption levels in the previous technology paradigm development, but it can also make the technology clusters meet their own needs and integrate these technology clusters into the reproduction model through transformation. However, the reproduction model of the new technology paradigm cannot be formed immediately. In the initial stage of the development of the new technology paradigm, the technology clusters generated due to the introduction of foundation innovation will not form a self-reproducing whole and will still be combined with those clusters of the previous technology paradigm for a period. A complete reproduction model of the new technology paradigm has gradually formed with the emergence of new technology clusters or the upgrading of traditional technology clusters. The formation of the new technological paradigm reproduction model is a long process, and it has two essentially different stages. The first stage is the emergence of the key factors and "core" of the new technology paradigm under the predominance of the former technology paradigm. The former technology paradigm objectively limits the formation of its successor products due to its own expanded reproduction needs. With the disappearance of the economic potential of this process, the second phase begins with replacing the dominant technology paradigm with a new one. It then continues in the form of another round of economic market "long wave." The period from the completion of the first stage to the beginning of the second stage showed the characteristics of economic depression, and the economic structure adjusted during the transition period. During this period, surplus capital, labor, and other resources flowed into the technology clusters of the new technology paradigm after the depreciation of obsolete industries. With the formation of the reproduction model, a new "long wave" of economic growth began.

Through empirical research on the dynamics of relevant indicators of technological and economic development, the reliability of the continuous process of technological paradigm and economic evolution and its life cycle replacement is confirmed. By measuring the results of technological changes related to the growth of various technological paradigms, it can be shown that the life cycle of a technological paradigm covers more than half a century, and its indicators have two obvious "peaks" and include the corresponding stages of technological and economic development.[3]

The cyclical change law of the technological paradigm is determined by the periodicity of scientific and technological progress. The interrelationship between technological progress and industry is constantly changing at different stages of the technology paradigm's life cycle. In different technological paradigms, these relationships are reproduced based on constantly changing technology. The production concentration based on integrated automation differs from that of the assembly line. However, in the past three centuries, the general mechanism for maintaining the periodic oscillations of the above relationship has remained unchanged in principle.

According to the logical growth curve,[4] the life cycle of any technology is limited. As we all know, the finiteness of the technology life cycle determines the mode of the technology paradigm life cycle, namely the stages of introduction, rapid growth, maturity, and decline. When the penultimate stage of the life cycle is reached, the return on investment in technology development diminishes, and the return on investment at the beginning of the recession stage shows negative growth. Because of the technological linkages among the industries that comprise the technology paradigm, these industries develop synchronously, resulting in models of the technology paradigm's century-long life cycle that resemble those of the logical growth curve. Figure 1-1 visually shows the life cycle of the technology paradigm, in which Kondratieff's long wave model corresponds to the "birth" stage of the new technology paradigm and the growth limit reached by the old technology paradigm. The figure shows that the life cycle of the technology paradigm is represented by two consecutive logical growth curves. The above figure reflects that the development of the new technology paradigm is in its infancy under the condition that the previous technology paradigm is dominant. The limits to growth of the previous technological paradigm mean that the economy is transitioning to downturns and downturns in the long wave cycle, which depresses not only existing industries but also new ones. Due to the overall deterioration of the economic market, the enthusiasm for investment and innovation is declining. The new growth of the economic market begins with the transition from the new technological paradigm to the growth phase, which is described by a larger-scale logical growth curve.

---

3. For the first time in the author's work, the law of periodic replacement of technological paradigm is used in detail: Глазьев С. Теория долгосрочного технико-экономического развития. М.: ВлаДар, 1993.

4. Львов Д. С., Фетисов Г. Г., Глазьев С. Ю. Эволюция технико-экономических систем: возможности и границы централизованного регулирования. – М.: Наука, 1992.

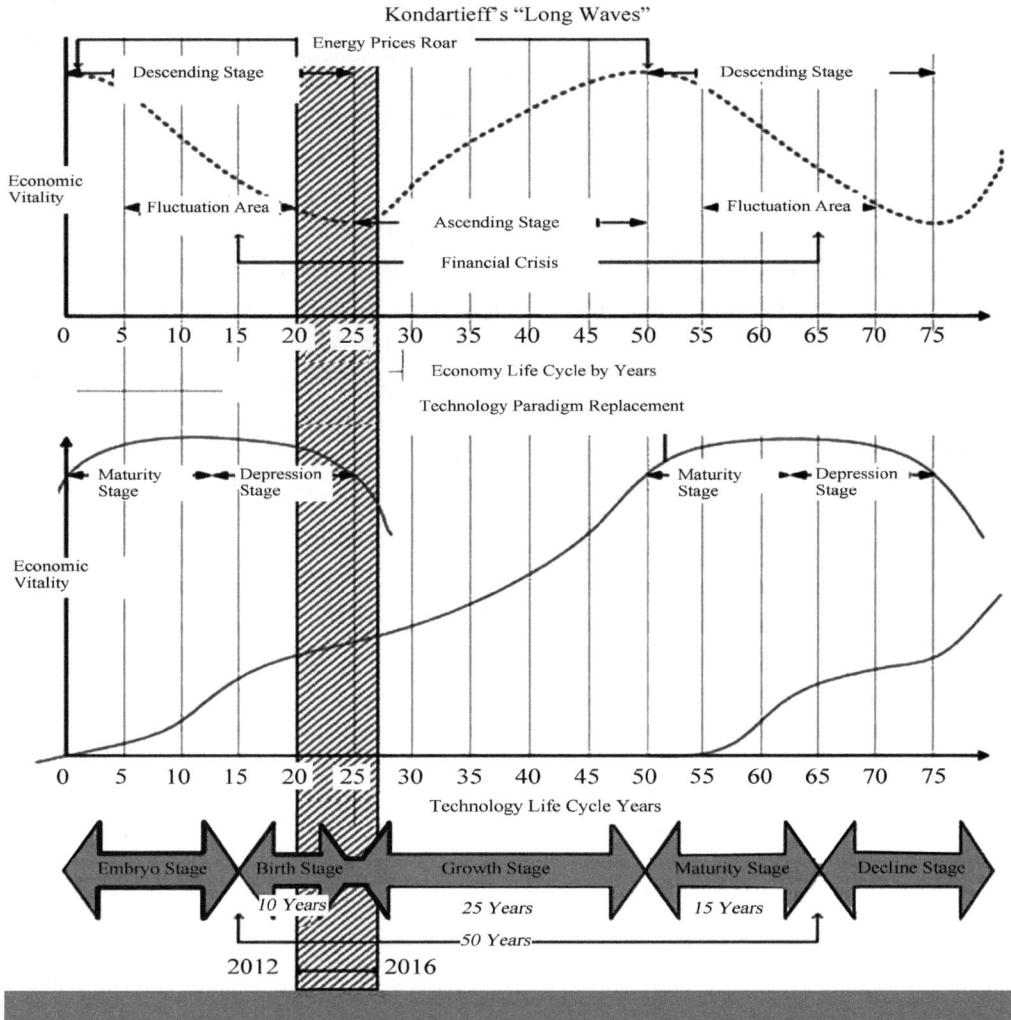

Figure 1-1 The Life Cycle of a Technology Paradigm

According to the above-mentioned regularity of technological and economic development and social capital reproduction, the life cycle of the technological paradigm on the surface of economic phenomena is reflected in the form of the corresponding phases of the "long wave" of economic market conditions. The depression period corresponds to the birth stage of the corresponding technological paradigm, the recovery period corresponds to the formation stage of the technological paradigm, the "long wave" rising period corresponds to the growth stage of the technological paradigm, and the recession period corresponds to the mature stage of the technological paradigm. The mature stage is characterized by further economic growth ability disappears, and the economy changes from further growth to a transition to a new technological paradigm.

The formation of the reproduction model has led to a rapid reduction in production costs. The new technology paradigm's growth phase is accompanied not only by a decrease in production costs, but also by economic evaluation reforms that are consistent with the reproduction conditions of the new technology paradigm. Changes in the price relationship help to improve the technical efficiency that constitutes the new technological paradigm. With the replacement of the traditional technological paradigm, the production efficiency of the entire society will also increase. The most obvious is that these changes are reflected in the cyclical fluctuations of energy carrier prices. As energy prices rise sharply, the efficiency of the dominant technology paradigm begins to decline, and new and more efficient technology paradigms begin to replace the old technology paradigm. The energy consumption of social production has decreased as a result of the development of the new technology paradigm, as has the demand for energy carriers and the prices of energy carriers, energy-intensive materials, and raw materials. This has created favorable conditions for the restoration of economic growth based on the new technology paradigm.

Figure 1-2 shows a chart released nearly 40 years ago that combines fluctuations in energy prices with deviations from global energy demand trends. We have not updated it to avoid getting into data related to the oil price surge in the year 2000, so as not to be suspected of data falsification. According to the law reflected in the graph, we timely predicted the inevitability of oil prices falling immediately after a sharp rise.

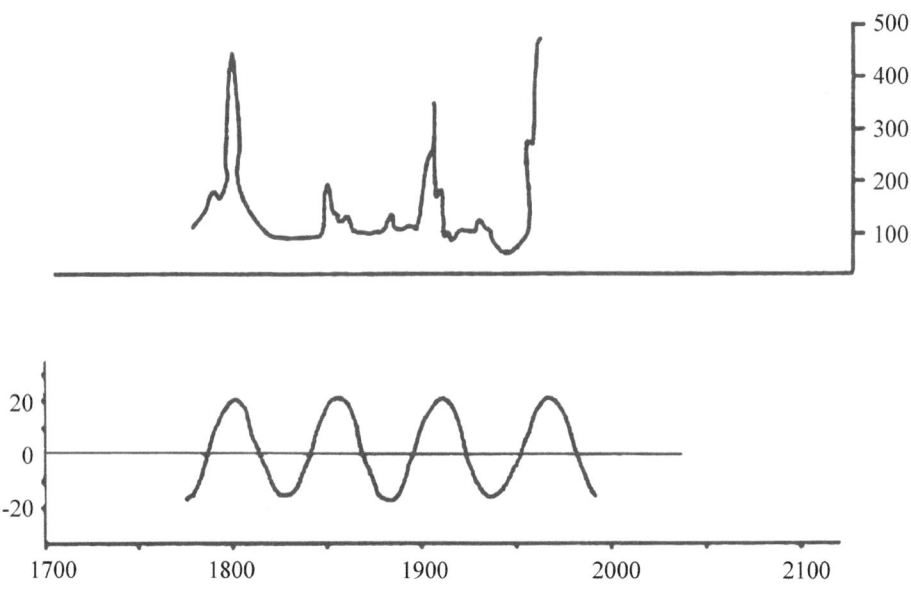

Figure 1-2 Energy Demands (Above) and Price Index (Bottom) Trends
Source: C. Marchetti, and N. Nakicenovic, "The Dynamics of Energy Systems and the Logistic Substitution Model," RR-79-13 / IIASA. Laxenburg, Austria, 1979.

With the development of the new technological paradigm, the corresponding social demand is saturated, the consumer demand and the price of its products fall, the technical ability to improve and reduce its production factors is exhausted, and the growth of social production efficiency has slowed down. The last stage of the life cycle of the previous technology paradigm coincides with the embryonic stage of the next technology paradigm. The growth rate and relative growth rate have further declined, and the social production efficiency in many fields has absolutely declined.

Due to the correlation between the industries that comprise the technological paradigm and the synchronization of their development, the decline in the efficiency of technological advancement has occurred almost simultaneously. The growth "contribution" indicator is declining. In the life cycle of the next technological paradigm, fluctuations in social production efficiency, various structural relationships, and proportions will occur again.

The regularity of the cyclical change of technological paradigm enables us to explain the imbalance and asymmetry of the economic development process caused by corresponding technological changes. When the previous technological paradigm still dominates the economic structure, a new technological paradigm will emerge, and its development will be restricted by a bad technological environment and socioeconomic environment. Only when the dominant technology paradigm reaches the growth limit and the profit rate of the dominant technology paradigm industry declines, will the large-scale redistribution of resources into the technology "chain" of the new technology paradigm begin.

The cyclical technological revolution confirmed the regularity of the cyclical replacement of technological paradigms. During this period, innovative activities increased sharply, production efficiency increased rapidly, and socioeconomic recognition of the potential of new technologies and price ratios changed according to the nature of the new technological system. The technological revolution is accompanied by large-scale devaluation and the reduction of obsolete capital. These capitals have been used in the outdated technology paradigm industry. The technological revolution is accompanied by the deterioration of economic conditions, the escalation of trade conflicts, and the intensification of social and political tensions. On the surface of the economic phenomenon, this period looks like a severe economic depression, accompanied by the deterioration of macroeconomic indicators—the growth rate of GDP and industrial production has fallen, and the unemployment rate has risen. Capital released from obsolete and unprofitable industries did not immediately flow into the new technological paradigm and remained stagnant in circulation for a period of time, exacerbating the financial bubble. According to Perez,[5] the transition to the next growth phase of the long wave of growth begins after the surplus capital depreciated in the bursting financial bubble has found a way out to invest in new technologies. This begins the growth phase of the new technology paradigm.

The changing law of technological paradigm can be confirmed by the following methods: periodic changes in social and institutional systems and production management systems. These changes can adapt the professional skills of members and managers of various organizations to the new conditions, thereby alleviating society. Pressure also helps to introduce technologies of new technological paradigms on a large scale, as well as consumption types and lifestyles that are compatible with the new

---

5. C. Perez, *Technological Revolutions and Financial Capital: The Dynamics of Bubbles and Golden Ages* (London: Elgar, 2002).

technological paradigms. After that, the rapid diffusion phase of the new technology paradigm began, which became the basis for accelerating economic growth and enabling the new technology paradigm to dominate the economic structure. In the growth stage of the new technology paradigm, most of the technology "chains" of the previous technology paradigm have been upgraded in accordance with the needs of the new technology paradigm. At the same time, the next latest technological paradigm appeared. This paradigm has been at its infancy stage until the dominant technological paradigm reaches its growth limit, after which the next technological revolution begins.

The technological paradigm change is reflected in the structural changes of the economic raw material base and is clearly reflected in the consumption of primary energy (Figure 1-3).

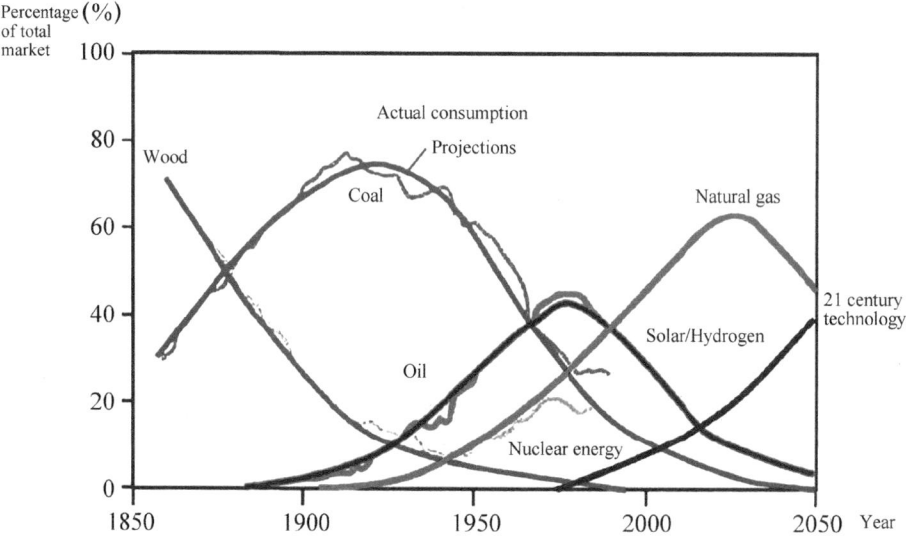

Figure 1-3 The Proportion of Energy Types in the Market since 1850 and the Forecast before 2050
Source: N., Nakicenovic, "Energy Strategies for Mitigating Global Change," IIASA, January 1992.

Each new technology paradigm first uses the existing transportation infrastructure and energy carriers in its own development, thereby stimulating their further expansion; at the same time, compared with the long-term trend, the rapid growth phase of the new technology paradigm is accompanied by GDP, consumption levels, and the cyclical increase in energy consumption. The limitations of the previous technological structure have been overcome with the development of the next technological paradigm, a new type of infrastructure has been created, and the transition to a new type of energy type has laid a resource foundation for the formation of the next technological paradigm.

In the process of technological paradigm change, the demand structure for scientific discovery and invention has changed. Because it is not adapted to the dominant technological paradigm of production and technological systems, many scientific inventions and discoveries have been left unattended for a long time. Only with the depletion of the growth potential of the technological paradigm, the demand for new technologies emerges fundamentally, and the competitive selection of new technologies has laid the foundation for the new technological path. The prerequisite for the emergence of the new technology trajectory is the semi-finished products that form the new technology trajectory in scientific research, trial production, and basic technology. When the traditional technological capacity for capital expansion is exhausted due to the saturation of the corresponding demand and the production efficiency reaching the growth limit, the above-mentioned prerequisites will be attained, and the potential capital investment method will become a reality.

Expressing long-term technological and economic development as a process of changing technological paradigms allows us to measure the process of long-term economic development. Measurement results using data from specific historical empirical studies of the world and the Russian economy revealed the formation and changes of five technological paradigms, including the current dominant information and electronic technology paradigms (Figure 1-4). These findings also reveal the structure of the new technological paradigm, and the development of the new technological paradigm will determine economic growth in the next 20–30 years.

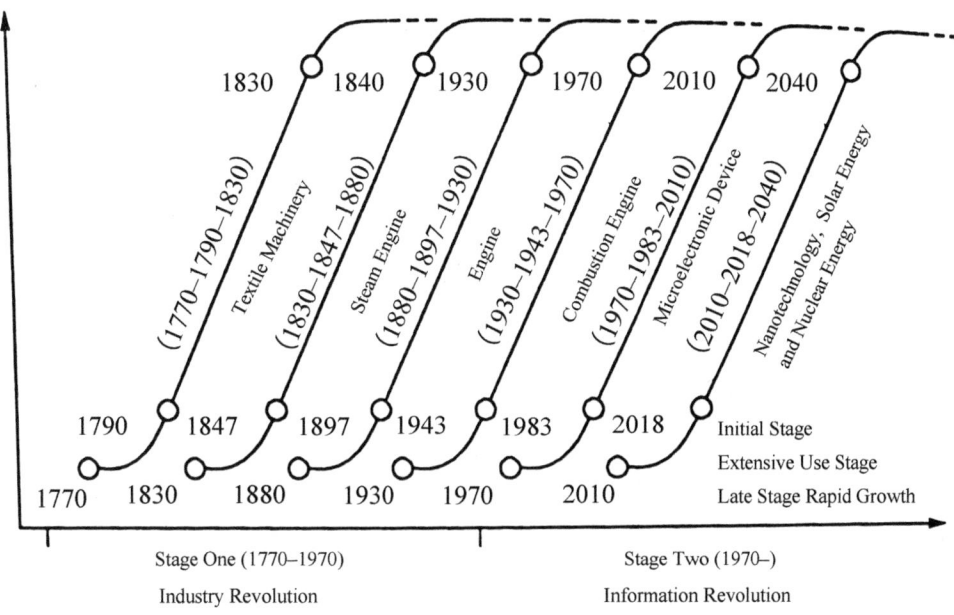

Figure 1-4 Technological Paradigm Change in the Process of Modern Economic Development (with Main Energy Conversion Technology)

The structural crisis of the world economy has caused a shift in the dominant technological paradigm. The main characteristics of the current structural crisis are the fluctuations in the price of energy carriers, the financial "bubble," and the economic depression.

The "surge" in the prices of petroleum and other energy carriers in 2000 indicated that the fifth technological paradigm had reached its growth limit. The discovery of the regularity of the cyclical change of technological paradigms makes it possible to predict the fluctuations of oil prices, the "inflation" and "collapse" of financial "bubbles," the slowdown of economic growth, financial crises, and depressions, which have swept the developed countries since 2008. Thanks to the growth of the new sixth technological paradigm, these countries are currently overcoming structural crises. By measuring the proliferation of key technologies, we can determine the progress of the new technology paradigm from the "birth" stage to the future growth stage. The new technological paradigm will soon dominate the economies of developed countries, thereby ensuring that developed countries leave the old "long wave" and transition to the new one of Kondratieff's.

The world's leading countries have successfully mastered nanotechnology, bioengineering technology, and additive manufacturing technology (3D printing technology). These technologies, together with information and communication technology (ICT), constitute a key factor in the growth of the new technology paradigm. The "core" of the technological paradigm is spreading at an annual rate of about 35%, forming a new "long wave" technological trajectory for economic growth[6] (Figure 1-5).

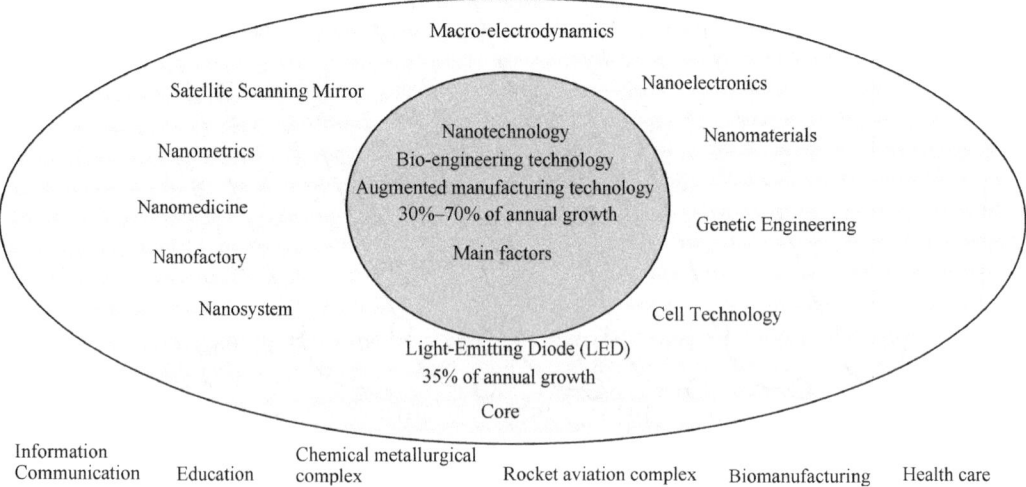

Figure 1-5 The Sixth Technology Paradigm Structure
Source: Russia's economic development strategy; academic report M.: National Development System, 2011.

The measurement results, the classification and description of technological paradigms, and the prediction of technological paradigm replacement related to technological change confirm that the periodic changes of technological paradigms discovered in the development of the world and the national economy are credible.

---

6. Нанотехнологии как ключевой фактор нового технологического уклада в экономике / Под ред. С. Ю. Глазьева, В. В. Харитонова. М.: Тровант, 2009.

This has laid a scientific foundation for the long-term prediction of technological and economic development processes, selecting priority areas for scientific and technological progress, and formulating national economic development strategies. The scientific and practical significance of discovering the law of technological paradigm development and replacement is as follows:

- Changing the concept of long-term economic development

If economic development is first expressed as a stable process of linear average around a certain equilibrium situation to improve efficiency, then with the discovery of the law of technological paradigm replacement, we can fundamentally understand the imbalance and asymmetry of the long-term economic development of the world and countries.

- Explaining the imbalance of economic development, cyclical depression, and severe economic crisis

In the long-term economic development of advanced countries, the period of an economic upswing (approximately a quarter of a century) and the period of economic restructuring (approximately fifteen years) are divided. An economic upswing is a period of growth based on the dominant technological paradigm. Economic restructuring occurs when the technological paradigm changes, accompanied by economic depression, economic crisis, financial turmoil, high uncertainty, and political tension.

- Proving that the limits of economic growth can be overcome under the change of technological paradigm

The long-term stable growth of the dominant technology paradigm has produced the illusion that economic development will not be a crisis. With the end of its life cycle, this illusion has become a feeling that economic growth has reached its limit. In fact, these growth limitations can be overcome by establishing a new technological paradigm. This new technological paradigm can exponentially increase efficiency, reduce energy and economic material consumption, increase labor productivity, and improve the population's life quality.

- Reliably predicting long-term technological changes in the world and national economies, and determining the direction of promising economic growth

At present, a new sixth technological paradigm is underway, and the key direction of long-term economic growth is gradually forming. The timely development of the key industries of the sixth technological paradigm can establish relative advantages, which will determine the geoeconomic competition until the middle of the 21st century. The key areas of the new technology paradigm have been identified: biotechnology based on molecular biology and genetic engineering, nanotechnology, additive manufacturing technology (3D printing technology),[7] artificial intelligence systems, global information networks, and integrated high-speed integrated transportation systems. Production automation, space technology, the production of structural materials with predetermined properties, the nuclear industry, and air transportation will be further developed. Since hydrogen energy is a clean energy carrier, the increase in demand for nuclear energy and natural gas can be eased by expanding the scope of use of hydrogen energy, and the utilization rate of renewable energy will increase significantly.

Most industries will transition to a sustainable innovation process, and most occupations will receive further education. The transition from a "consumer society" to a "smart society" will be completed, in which the requirements for quality of life and a comfortable living environment will be crucial. The manufacturing industry will shift to pure ecological and waste-free technology. In the consumption structure, information, education, and medical services to ensure the reproduction of human capital will dominate.

The next round of technological revolution is the transition to the sixth technological paradigm, which will greatly improve efficiency in key areas of economic development. Based on nanotechnology, the production and operating costs of computer technology will be reduced by another order of magnitude, and the usage related to miniaturization and adaptation to specific consumer needs will increase exponentially. Medical treatment will have technologies to fight disease at the cellular level. These technologies need to use the smallest amount of medicine and maximize the body's regenerative capacity to deliver drugs to the affected parts of the body accurately. Nanomaterials have unique consumption characteristics, which can increase the strength, abrasion resistance, and reliability of the finished products in a targeted manner. Genetically modified crops reduce costs exponentially and improve efficiency and the quality of pharmaceutical and agricultural production consumption. Genetically modified microorganisms will extract metals and pure materials from raw mineral materials, revolutionizing the chemical and metallurgical industries. In mechanical manufacturing, based on the "nanocomputer-nano operating device" system, automatic assembly equipment and 3D printers are created, which can "print" any macroscopic object based on the previously acquired or formulated network three-dimensional atomic distribution. With the development of nanomedicine robots and medical cell technology, preventive treatment capabilities have been greatly improved, and the human life span will be greatly extended.

---

7. Additive manufacturing ("to add" in English) is the process of synthesizing object materials layer by layer from the data of a 3D model: the product is actually grown from the material loaded into the printer. The name is the opposite of subtractive manufacturing technology. The advantages of additive manufacturing technology are the improved performance of finished products, the saving of large amounts of raw materials, and the ability to manufacture products with complex geometric shapes. About 600-650 industrial 3D printers are in use in Russia today, of which only about 10% are additive machines for processing metal powders, according to the Russian Ministry of Industry and Trade quoted in the 24th issue of Expert Magazine 2017 (article growth Technologies).

- Providing a scientific basis for the national economic development strategy, especially in the domestic economy-an advanced development strategy based on a new technological paradigm to accelerate growth.

Considering the transition from the new technological paradigm to the growth stage and the state of the Russian economy, an advanced development strategy has been formulated, which, based on activating the potential of existing science and technology (ST), puts forward the priority of the industrial development of the new technological paradigm. In the period of technological paradigm change, underdeveloped countries can jump to an advanced level of economic development. This requires resources to be concentrated in the production area of the new technological paradigm. To dynamically make up for industries that are far behind the world's advanced level, it is also necessary to stimulate innovation enthusiasm. Finally, in hopeless underdeveloped industries, it is necessary to implement an advanced development strategy that relies on introducing advanced technology and foreign investment. The implementation of this hybrid strategy of advanced development requires stimulating demand for new products, including financing the growth of new technologies through government procurement and long-term affordable loans.

- Determining the requirements for economic policies and macroeconomic policy systems

Priority should be given to the leapfrog growth of the new technological paradigm, the modernization of the Russian economy based on it, and the potential of the Russian economy. National policies should be formulated to realize the advanced development of the economy.[8] These include the deployment of strategic and indicative planning systems, long-term lending mechanisms for the growth of industries with promising new technology paradigms-models of government, and social capital partnership to achieve modernization and economic growth objectives based on advanced technology. In this case, management approaches that fit the new technology paradigm must be considered. Automated management of the entire product life cycle will be achieved through automated design systems as well as marketing and technology forecasting.

A compelling example of the successful implementation of this approach is China's economic development experience which has established an effective management system for STP. After studying the national development direction, China's leaders correctly identified economic and technological priorities, implemented strategic plans in conjunction with market competition mechanisms, and made timely adjustments according to the forecast of scientific and technological progress. This science-based approach forms the basis of China's economic and social development plan for the next five years. The Central Committee of the CPC has elaborated the relevant policy in the *Proposals*, using the special chapter of "Insistence on Pursuing Innovation-driven Development, Shaping New Development Advantages":

---

8. Глазьев С. Стратегия опережающего развития России в условиях глобального кризиса. М.: Экономика, 2010.

"We will adhere to the core position of innovation in China's overall modernization, have S&T self-reliance and self-improvement act as strategic support for national development, and be oriented toward the world's cutting edge in S&T, toward the main economic battlefields, toward the nation's major needs, and toward the lives and health of the people. We will deeply implement the strategy of reinvigorating China through science and education, the talent powerhouse strategy, and the innovation-driven development strategy, refine the national innovation system, and speed up the effort to make China into an S&T powerhouse.

Strengthening the nation's strategic S&T power. We will formulate an action agenda for becoming an S&T powerhouse, improve the new national system under socialist market economy conditions, successfully fight the tough battles for key and core technologies, and raise the overall effectiveness of the innovation chain. We will strengthen basic research, emphasize original innovation, optimize the layouts of academic disciplines and R&D deployments, promote the intersection and fusion of disciplines, and refine the supply system for common and basic technology. We will focus our aim on artificial intelligence (AI), quantum information, integrated circuits, life and health, brain science, bioengineered breeding, aerospace technology, deep earth and deep sea, and other cutting-edge fields, and carry out a set of major forward-looking and strategic national S&T projects. We will formulate strategic science plans and carry out strategic science projects, and promote an optimal allocation of scientific research power and sharing of resources among research institutes, universities, and enterprises. We will promote the construction of national laboratories and reorganize the national key laboratory system."

The *Proposals* also clarifies the priority direction of economic and technological development in line with the key elements of the new technological approach: "Developing strategic emerging industries. We will accelerate and expand industries such as new-generation information technology, biotechnology, new energy, new materials, high-end equipment, new energy vehicles, green and environmentally friendly products, and the aerospace and marine equipment industries. We will promote the deep integration of the internet, big data, AI, etc., in all industries, promote cluster development in advanced manufacturing industries, build a set of strategic and emerging industry growth engines with distinctive features, complementary advantages, and rational structures, and foster new technologies, new products, new industrial formats, and new models. We will promote the healthy development of the platform economy and the sharing economy, encourage enterprise mergers and restructuring, and prevent low-quality and redundant construction."

Chapter 2

The Cyclical Changes of the World Economic Paradigm in the Global Economic Structure

Although the research on the replacement regularity of the basic technological paradigm of production technology that constitutes Kondratieff's "long wave" theory is relatively sufficient and has been registered as a scientific discovery,[1] the cyclical process of the replacement of the world economic paradigm that forms the basis of the accumulation cycle system is still in the hypothesis stage. This chapter will provide a theoretical basis for this and analyze the relationship between technology and system changes.

In a historical study by Arrighi,[2] the evolution of capitalism can be divided into a series of accumulation cycles of the capitalist system. According to the names of the countries that are in the leading position in the corresponding cycle and present the structure of capital reproduction, Arrighi has divided the accumulation cycles of the Spanish-Genoa, Holland, the United Kingdom, and the US, each of which is about 100 years. This research does not show that there is a mechanism for the expansion of capital reproduction in each cycle of capital accumulation. The author is limited to describing in detail the historical conditions that formed each cycle of capital accumulation and the transition from one cycle to another, which was accompanied by the change of world leaders and the outbreak of world wars. He believes that the world is currently on the verge of a new capital accumulation cycle. After the US capital accumulation cycle, the focus of global economic development is shifting to Asia, especially the rising China.

To systematically describe the formation and change process of the world economic paradigm, we use the concepts of productive forces and relations of production in historical materialism. According to the traditional definition, productive forces refer to the laborers and material elements which are necessary to transform natural materials into products. Relations of production refer to the relations between people in the production, exchange, distribution, and consumption of material goods. However, the relations of production are often understood as a single economic relationship; the technical aspect of the production relations is directly related to production technology and labor organization. There is an inseparable internal connection between productive forces and production relations. Productive forces reflect the relationship between man and nature in the production process and constitute the mode of production, while production relations are the social form of production.[3]

---

1. Научное открытие «Закономерность смены технологических укладов в процессе развития мировой и национальных экономик» (свидетельство о регистрации №65 - S выдано Международной академией авторов научных открытий и изобретений под научно-методическим руководством Российской академии естественных наук).

2. G. Arrighi, *The Long Twentieth Century: Money, Power and the Origins of our Times* (London: Verso, 1994).

3. Nikolay Tsagolov ed., *Political Economy (2 vols.)* of *Economics* (1973), 59.

Marx's historical materialism reveals the dialectical relationship between productive forces and production relations; that is, the interaction between productive forces and production relations forms a contradictory movement between productive forces and production relations. When production relations conform to the nature of productive forces, they can promote the development of productive forces. But at a certain stage, the development of productive forces exceeds the existing production relations, and then the production relations will restrict the development of productive forces. There is a contradiction between productive forces and production relations. This contradiction is manifested in the aggravation of social and political contradictions and has become the root of social revolution. This social revolution destroys outdated production relations and replaces them with new ones, thereby providing space for developing productive forces. These revolutions embodied the law of production relations to adapt to the state of productive forces.[4]

On this basis, a theory of socioeconomic formation is produced, which divides the history of human society into five stages: primitive commune, slavery, feudalism, capitalism, and communism (socialism is the primary stage of communism). According to this doctrine, due to the need to adjust the relations of production regularly to keep them consistent with the level of development of the productive forces, they will be replaced by stages through the social revolution. The transition from socialism to communism will be an exception, and this transition will be carried out in a planned and conflict-free manner.

Putting aside the extensive criticism of the theory of socioeconomic formation in contemporary works, we use the concepts put forward by Arrighi to study the evolution and replacement mechanism of the accumulation cycle of the capital system that he revealed. At the same time, based on the modern understanding with regard to the law of productive forces development, it is considered that this is a process of continuous replacement of technological paradigms. At the same time, production relations are regarded as an institutional system that changes from one world economic paradigm to another. Fundamental changes occurred during the transition period.

Compared with the above-mentioned period of modern economic growth starting from the industrial revolution, the period of the capital system accumulation cycle is longer. With the emergence of banks and bourgeois urban republics in northern Italy, the germination of capitalism began to emerge, and the cycle of capital accumulation followed. It is preliminarily believed that the corresponding world economic paradigm is the basis of each capital accumulation cycle, that is, an interconnected institutional system that guarantees the expansion of capital reproduction and promotes national and world economic development during the corresponding capital accumulation cycle.[5] The systems of the world's leading countries are particularly important. These systems play a leading role in formulating and adjusting international standards for the world market and international economic, trade, and financial relations. Every world economic paradigm

---

4. Nikolay Tsagolov ed., *Political Economy* (2 vols.) of *Economics* (1973), 60.

5. Глазьев С. Закономерность смены мирохозяйственных укладов в развитии мировой экономической системы и связанных с ними политических изменений // Наука. Культура. Общество. 2016. №3.

has its development limit, determined by the internal contradictions accumulated by its system within reproduction framework. These contradictions will continue to develop until the international economic system, and political relations become unbalanced, and then the unbalanced relations will be resolved through a world war. Some countries that were dominant in the "outdated" world economic paradigm lost their dominant positions and resorted to organizing and provoking a world war to strengthen their control over the periphery of the world economy, as well as their competitive advantage, and also to weaken the position of potential competitors. However, there will always be a new leader among its competitors. The leader has a more advanced institutional system and production relations. It does not intervene in the war until the last minute, thus directly joining the camp of winners and seizing global leadership. With the replacement of world leaders, the new world economic paradigm system is expanding, so that the existing material and technological achievements can be preserved, and new opportunities are created to develop social productive forces.

Figure 2-1 is a schematic diagram of the capital accumulation cycle and the corresponding world economic paradigm, in which the world economic paradigm is named according to the dominant international economic and trade relationship system type at that time.

Granted, the types of international economic and trade relations proposed in the figure are very limited, and only superficially reflect the "sections" of the systems and production relations that determine the reproduction of the world's major economic systems. Below we will point out that the world economic paradigm differs not only in the types of international trade organizations, but also in production relations and systems. This allows leading countries to gain world advantages and determine the system of international economic and trade relations.

The use of the concept of "paradigm" aims to reflect the completeness of relevant reproduction factors: these factors are connected to the economic construction system (world economic paradigm) through production technology cooperation (technical paradigm). The combination of elements determines the synchronicity of its life cycle, at least in the mature and declining periods. In intermittent economic development, many factors change periodically simultaneously, resulting in a leap-forward technological revolution (when the technological paradigm changes) and a political revolution (when the world economic paradigm changes).

In the above discussion, the technological revolution reflects the qualitative change of the constituent elements of productive forces, and the political revolution reflects the qualitative change of the constituent elements of the relations of production. Although technological and political revolutions influence each other and are inherently consistent, they do not necessarily happen simultaneously. However, the inertia of production relations is far greater than the technological continuity of productivity. Therefore, the life cycle of the world economic paradigm is much longer than the life cycle of technology. Aivazov believes that one life cycle of the world economic paradigm contains two technological cycles.[6] We are currently in the crisis phase, where these

---

6. Айвазов А., Беликов В. Экономические основы цивилизационных волн развития человечества // Партнерство цивилизаций. 2016. №3 - 4.

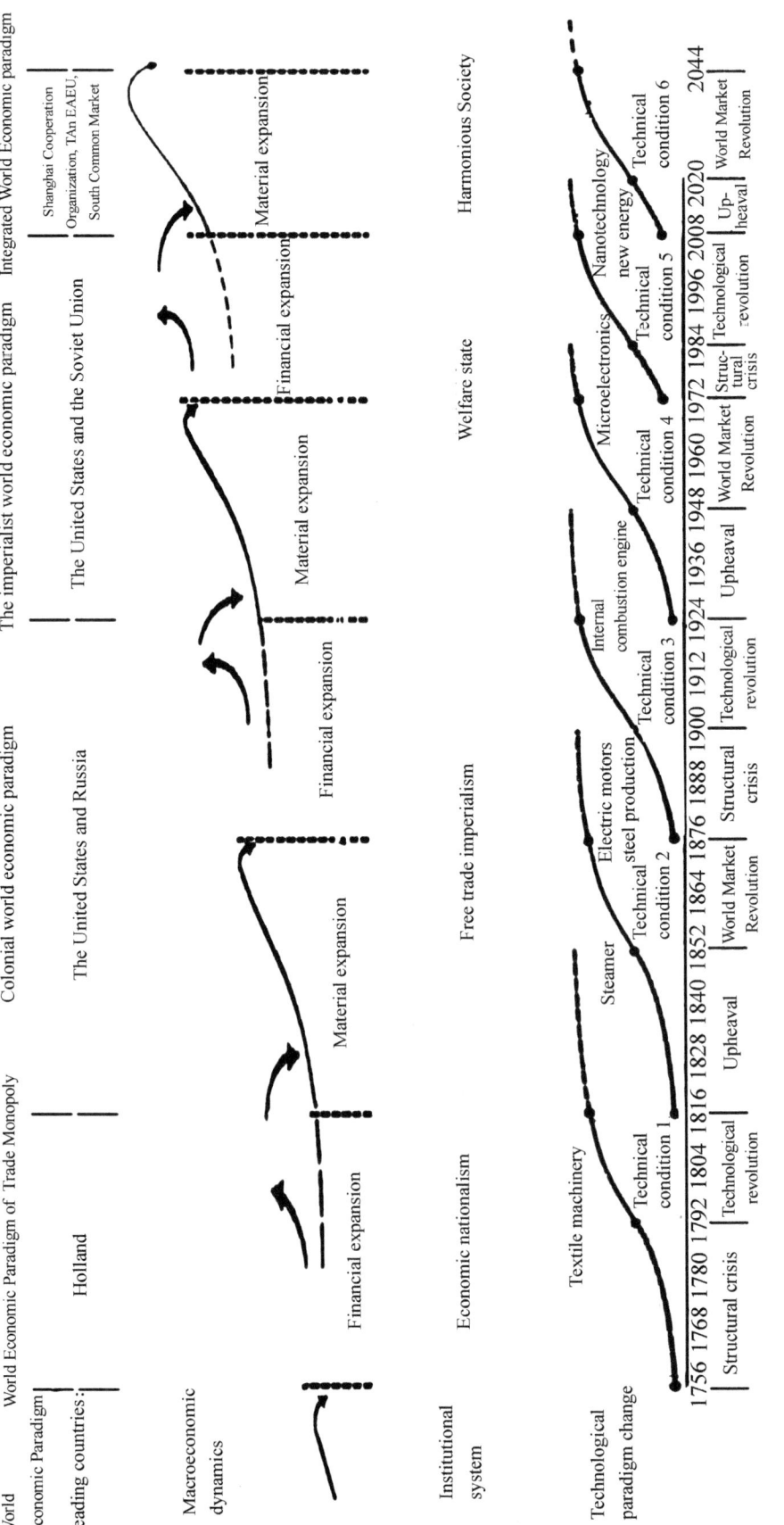

Figure 2-1 Cyclical Changes in the World Economic Paradigm

Source: Revised from Айвазов А. Периодическая система мирового капиталистического развития / Альманах? Развитие и экономика?. Март 2012. №2.

two cycles overlap. The overlap of the cycles causes dangerous resonance, which may destroy the entire world's economic and political system. During such a period, the system of international relations is turbulent, the old world order collapses, and a new world order takes shape. Based on the existing system and technical system, the potential for socioeconomic development has been exhausted. Therefore, some countries have encountered insurmountable difficulties in maintaining previous economic growth rates. Excessive capital accumulation in the old production technology complex has plunged the economy into depression, and the existing institutional system hinders the formation of a new technology chain. Some other countries that have emerged as leaders in economic development have mastered new technology chains and production organization systems.

The former leaders tried to maintain the dominance of the global market by strengthening the control of the "outer areas" of the geoeconomy, including through military and political coercive means. Usually, this will lead to major military conflicts and waste of their own resources, failing to achieve the expected results. Potential new leaders who are on the rise seek to adopt a wait-and-see attitude to maintain their own productivity and absorb the advanced ideas, capital, and wealth of war countries. When the warring opponent is weak enough, the new leader will have the opportunity to enter the world stage to win the fruits of victory.

The following turning points in world history have led to the replacement of global leaders. The first is the conflict between Spain and Britain. This conflict ended with the defeat of the Invincible Fleet in 1588, which allowed the Dutch bourgeoisie to break free from Spanish control. The continuing war led to the transition from the Genoa-Spain accumulation cycle to the Dutch accumulation cycle, and the corresponding change in the world economic paradigm based on trade, from the intercontinental trade of natural resources to the form of handicraft industry based on the trade of handicrafts. Based on the private property relationship between free handicrafts men and organized handicrafts men, Holland rebuilt its political system according to the needs of the existing capital reproduction system and established the most efficient economy at that time. By establishing the Dutch East India Company to create a joint-stock company, the company soon became the world's largest monopolistic business organization. It established the Amsterdam Exchange Bank and Stock Exchange.[7] Holland has rapidly expanded its business activities, providing opportunities to expand its entrepreneurial class. At that time, Holland had become a world leader in advanced technology, which enabled it to occupy a leading position in the formation of sailing fleets, waterway construction, and consumer goods production. Relying on its own competitive advantages, Holland created a global trade empire, connecting Europe with the rest of the world through conventional trade routes.

At this time in Europe, the West phalian System has begun to take shape, which is sufficient to satisfy the interests of the country's ruling elites protected by international law and the system of national sovereignty. Since the beginning of the 18th century, this system has provided a stable political environment for the reproduction of national capital.

---

7. Никонов В. Современный мир и его истоки. М.: Издательство Московского Университета, 2015.

From the perspective of international trade organizations, this world economic paradigm can be called the trade monopoly world economic paradigm, which reflects the leading role played by the world's first multinational company in the construction of international economic and trade relations at that time. The Dutch East India Company has become a model of the International Trade Organization. The stock exchanges and banks first established in Holland have become the prototype of the central regulatory agency for capital reproduction in all subsequent world economic paradigms. Still, its functions and the international economic and trade relations system have changed.

The trade monopoly world economic paradigm created the European colonial empire, and its national capital subordinated the world to its reproduction needs. There were constant conflicts among European colonial empires, and after the end of the Napoleonic Wars, a new world economic paradigm was formed. As a result, a pan-European economic and legal space was created, and a stable political system that satisfied the ruling elite's interests was established. At that time, the technology possessed by Holland had spread to other European countries. In the context of the rapid development of large European countries, the weak and small Holland could no longer maintain its leading position. To evade military and political threats from the European continent, Holland transferred the capital to Britain, which is closely connected with it, and brought advanced technology and methods of organizing production and trade to Britain. Britain rapidly developed its fleet, built canals, and expanded handicraft production in workshops. Under the protection of the monarchy, Britain imitated the Dutch East India Company and created the British East India Company, Virginia Company, and Plymouth Company. These companies became the largest industrial and commercial enterprises at that time.

The "qualitative change" of capital concentration created the conditions for the Industrial Revolution, which began in Britain at the end of the 18th century. During that time, the hydraulic loom came out. The factory system can be established by hiring many farmers who have been deprived of land use rights and land ownership as workers, as well as developing the corresponding production relations between capitalists and laborers. The rapid development of the machinery manufacturing industry and a large amount of cheap labor enabled Britain to complete the industrial revolution, master the production technology cooperation mechanism based on machinery manufacturing, and create the first technological paradigm of the industrial society. Britain made full use of the competitive advantages of the Napoleonic Wars, relying on the advanced technology and the international trade organization system at that time to complete its colonial rule in the mid-nineteenth century, ensuring its global leadership in the system of world economic relations.

Britain had formed an institutional system for organizing commercial, social, and political activities, creating opportunities for capital concentration of any size. Under the aegis of the British royal family, the Dutch East India Company and the Dutch West India Company became giant transoceanic monopolies, successfully mastering the huge resources of India, China, and the US. The judicial system, which focuses on the fair settlement of economic disputes, has ensured the rapid development of civil law based on protecting the interests of private enterprises, and has promoted increasingly fierce competition, which has created favorable conditions for capital accumulation. With the prevalence of joint-stock companies, capital accumulation has reached a higher level. The development of the private system, the shareholding system, and the state capitalist system have paved the way for constructing large-scale infrastructure and creating industrial enterprises. The disintegration of rural communes and the deprivation of land of farmers have provided cheap labor for construction sites and factories, thus creating conditions for the transition to the second technological paradigm. This technological paradigm is based on steam engines, coal industry, ferrous metallurgy, inorganic chemistry, and railways construction.

Under a democratic political system with limited voting rights, the dominance of private capital is deeply entrenched, which creates a favorable and stable environment for the expansion and reproduction of large amounts of capital. The leading position in technology has ensured the competitive advantage of the British economy, enabling the United Kingdom to realize economic reproduction in the world's largest free trade market for commodities.

The entire world was divided among the European colonial empires, which created a capital reproduction system protected by the suzerainty system in the colonial countries. Therefore, we call this world economic paradigm the colonial world economic paradigm. European empires competed for territories and communication lines to create favorable conditions for reproduction for their capitalists. The capital accumulation system established in the previous world economic paradigm strengthened the protectionist policies of the world's colonial empires. These empires themselves were built for global expansion, to maximize the country's capital reproduction space.

As V. Nikonov said: "Britain was in its heyday from 1845–1870. Britain's gross national product (GDP) at that time accounted for more than 30% of the world's, and its industrial output accounted for two-fifths." In the 19th century, the size and population of the British Empire increased by order of magnitude, reaching 11 million square miles, and the population increased to 390 million.[8] It should be pointed out that most of the population of the British Empire was deprived of citizenship and property rights.

The British turned a large number of people into living commodities and organized human trafficking on an unprecedented scale. Tens of millions were deprived of their property rights, turned into slaves, and forced to leave their places of residence and come to plantations in the New World. To maintain trade balance with China, Britain launched the Opium War and imported large quantities of opium into China to destroy the will of its citizens. At the same time, there was not much difference between the working class and the slave class in Britain. The peasants "liberated" from land ownership were forced to sell cheap labor and suffered ruthless exploitation. With the development of the labor market, the confrontation between capitalists and the proletariat has become a global feature.

Capitalists deprive labor of ownership and possess labor products, forming the basis of Marx's theory of surplus value, which explains the profit generated by

---

8. Никонов В. Современный мир и его истоки. М.: Издательство Московского Университета, 2015.

exploiting laborers' labor value.[9] According to this theory, it is concluded that there are inherent limitations in the development of capitalism. The trend of declining profit rates undermines the foundation of capitalist reproduction. In addition, there is a contradiction between the socialization of production and the private possession of the means of production in capitalism.

In the era of Marx, the potential of STP and the importance of human factors in it were not yet obvious. Marx explained the development of technology through the improvement of the organic composition of capital, and inferred the theory of the downward trend of the rate of profit from it. With the gradual exhaustion of the potential for industrial structure optimization, this trend will indeed occur in the life cycle of a technological paradigm. Marx created *Das Kapital* during the maturity and decline periods of the second technical paradigm, which is characterized by low-tech workers using giant steam engines and related machines to achieve centralized production. The second technological paradigm has limitations on the development of productivity. In the process of transition to the third technological paradigm, this problem was solved through economic electrification, which opened up a new path for improving production efficiency and developing productivity. In the third technical paradigm, the importance of staff skills and education has risen sharply, giving birth to corresponding national systems and causing major changes in production relations. A rigid institutional system focusing on protecting the privileges of the ruling class prevails in Britain and Europe. This system unlimitedly exploits the private property rights of labor. This world economic paradigm has begun to inhibit the development of productive forces.

At this time, the contradiction between productive forces and production relations intensified, and the communist movement emerged, which interpreted the technological and the world economic paradigm development limits as the end of capitalism. The communists suggested the implementation of ownership by the whole people, the realization of communism through the "deprivation of the deprived," the abolition of private ownership of the means of production, and the implementation of public ownership of the means of production to resolve the above-mentioned contradictions. They launched a class war against the capitalists, which is the proletariat's resistance in the face of oppression.

Socialist industrialization and collectivization made people rely on state-owned means of production; hence some observers called this production relationship a sign of state capitalism. However, unlike capitalism, the production goal of the Soviet Union was not to maximize profits, but to develop productive forces for the sake of communism. Profit has lost its meaning, and currency has become a tool for policy planning. The Communist Party of the Soviet Union (CPSU) did abolish the capitalist system. Still, it was unable to break away from this world economic paradigm based on coercive production relations until World War II.

The period when the European colonial empires partitioned the world mentioned above is called the colonial world economic paradigm according to the classification

---

9. Маркс К. и Энгельс Ф. Соч, т. 23. с. 10, 632. - М.: Государственное издательство политической литературы, 1960.

principle. If it had not been for Marx in the theory of historical materialism that the socioeconomic formation of ancient Rome had been defined as a slavery society, according to the types of production relations, this period could be called a slavery society. Although in the British capital accumulation cycle, the scale of slave labor cannot be compared with the trafficking and exploitation of slaves on a global scale. If we accept the Marxist interpretation of production relations and fully evaluate the degree of insult and exploitation of the working class by the European suzerainty, then we can definitely define this world economic paradigm as the classical capitalist world economic paradigm. Since then, after the abolition of slavery, the development of democratic systems, and the emergence of social legislation, racism, Nazism, and class ideology have disappeared.

From the end of the 19th century, with the emergence of the third technological paradigm, Britain's global leadership began to be impacted, and was soon chased by the Russian Empire. The Russian Empire's military strength and global political influence were not inferior to that of Britain. The Russian Empire retains the traditional system of monarchy and state religion to ensure political stability under the conditions of rapid industrial development, rapid education level, and rapid increase in social activities.

The abolition of serfdom and other reforms of Alexander II abolished many feudal systems that restricted the development of the market economy. It provided opportunities for the rapid growth of industrial production on the basis of the production relations of this world economic paradigm. From the end of the 19th century to the beginning of the 20th century, Russia moved from a catch-up development model to a transcendence development model. From 1860 to 1870, the output of the textile and paper industry doubled. With the increase in output during the first technical paradigm in Russia, the technical clusters of the second technical paradigm began to form rapidly (it is pointed out here that the second technical paradigm in the United Kingdom was formed from 1820 to 1840–1848). At this time, the country actively promoted the development of large-scale industrial investment and attracted large amounts of foreign investment and equipment based on technology imports. From 1860 to 1876, pig iron production increased by 30%, and iron production increased by 40%.[10] From 1875 to 1892, the number of steam engines in Russia doubled, the power tripled, and the output of smelted pig iron increased by 1.5 times in the 1980s. At this time, Russia's above-mentioned growth rate exceeded the United Kingdom's growth rate over the same period.

However, it needs to be pointed out that the "boom" of the Russian economy at that time was largely based on the expansion of the production scale in the second technological paradigm. This technological paradigm has been replaced by the third technological paradigm in developed countries. At the same time, with the strong support of the state, the power industry, inorganic chemistry, and power technology developed rapidly. The rapid development of the third technology paradigm basic technology cluster has narrowed the technology gap and created the prerequisites for Russia to enter the ranks of leading international countries. Compared with developed countries, certain industrial

10. Львов Д. С., Фетисов Г. Г., Глазьев С. Ю. Эволюция технико-экономических систем: возможности и границы централизованного регулирования. - М.: Наука, 1992.

sectors in Russia have competitive advantages, and the number of national engineers and technicians has increased rapidly, which creates good preconditions for Russia to integrate effectively into the international division of labor. However, the incomplete life cycles of the first and second technological paradigms and outdated political systems hinder the country's industrial development.

Promoting economic development with advanced technology may enable Russia to achieve world leadership. If it were not for the destruction of the revolution and civil war, Russia could have become a global superpower during the Great Depression in the 1930s. The Russian economy was not affected by the excessive accumulation of capital in obsolete technologies and was ready to make large-scale investments in producing new technological paradigms. Before World War I, Russia laid a solid foundation in the chemical, petroleum, metallurgical, automotive, aviation, and electric power industries, which became the driving force for its economic growth in the mid-20th century.

At the same time, during Bismarck's administration, Germany developed rapidly and became a global leader in the machinery manufacturing industry. By their respective institutional characteristics, Russia and Germany are in a leading position in terms of technological level and capital concentration. Germany relies on the rapid entrepreneurial activities of the educated citizen class, and Russia relies on abundant natural resources and human potential. Russia and Germany have successfully mastered the technology and production organization of the United Kingdom, thereby further promoting in-depth cooperation, and expanding the scale of production. Britain responded to the challenges of the aforementioned peripheral European countries through the First World War and skillfully made these two rising superpowers enemies.

The Russo-German alliance can form the strongest alliance at the time, becoming the dominant force in the world political landscape and saving the world from war. These two countries that have successfully developed in the new "long wave" of economic growth do not need this war. But Britain needs to maintain its leading position through war. Britain managed to destroy the Russian-German alliance[11] through a series of conspiracies to eliminate influential enemies so these two similar imperial countries had suicidal confrontations without major objective reasons. Neither the killing of the heir to the Austrian throne, the threat to Serbia's independence, nor the unreasonable desire to liberate Constantinople from the Turks and seize the strait cannot be regarded as a sufficient reason for a world war. Britain used diplomatic conspiracy and tricks to cause the First World War outbreak and create conflicts between rivals to maintain its global leadership.

The First World War destroyed Britain's main rival in the Old World, allowing Britain to maintain its global dominance until the middle of the 20th century. At this time, the American colonies got rid of the colonial oppression of European countries and established the US. The American system was initially established based on the interests of large private capital. Since there is no need to pay political rents for the monarchy and aristocracy, capital gains unlimited expansion opportunities. European

---

11. "The Treaty of Bjork" July 24, 1905, Tsar Nicholas II and Kaiser Wilhelm II met on the Royal Yacht Polaris outside Bjork Island (near Vyborg Bay) in the Baltic Sea, during which the Russian-German alliance was signed Secret treaty. Germany launched a diplomatic initiative to conclude the treaty, aimed at undermining the Russian-French alliance and preventing the establishment of the Allies. To this end, it is planned to turn the Russian-German alliance into a Russian-German-French alliance against Britain.

countries are faced with the problem of overpopulation in agriculture and military expenditure. The endless colonial wars have continuously flooded the population into the US, providing cheap and skilled labor for the development of American capitalism.

The fundamental difference between the institutional system formed after the Civil War in the US and the previous one is that it denies all the legal basis for classifying members of society into classes, groups, or hierarchies with different rights. Although the social status of a citizen is determined by the amount of his personal capital, all citizens are legally equal. Entrepreneurship and personal initiative have been vigorously promoted. Expanding production based on unrestricted capital concentration has unlimited prospects. This provides opportunities for engineers and scholars to create the most advanced industrial enterprises of various scales and technologies. By the end of the 20th century, the US had been at the forefront of industrial development. At the same time, Britain had also begun to form a third technological paradigm based on the power industry.

As Britain used diplomacy to promote the First World War, the US won the greatest victory. Just like Britain's involvement in the Franco-Prussian War, the US intervened in the war at the final stage and seized the main victory. The US not only participated in the division of the new world, but also gained advanced ideas, capital, and wealth that escaped from the First World War and the subsequent revolutions and civil wars of Russia, Germany, and Austria-Hungary. Engineers and scholars who emigrated to the US provided the latest technology to develop American capitalism. The US had become a leader in global technological and economic development. Based on the further development of the chemical and metallurgical industry, electrification and power engineering, railways, and shipbuilding, the US initiated large-scale construction of energy, engineering, and transportation infrastructure to meet the needs of the third technical paradigm.

American capitalism has more advantages than European colonial empires because it focuses on the institutional structure of capital concentration and the development of large-scale production industries. The talents and technologies of the European colonial empires continued to "flow" to the US, which promoted the rapid development of the American economy. Based on unrestricted private property, a system of expanded reproduction of capital was formed that laid the foundation for a new world economic paradigm which centered on multinational corporations. The establishment of the Federal Reserve (shortened as *The Fed*) in 1913 brought huge credit opportunities for American capitalism to achieve global expansion.

Soon after the rise of Soviet Russia, the US entered into a new "wave" of economic growth. The Soviet Union established a unified planning system and a production organization system on the ruins of the Russian Empire, concentrating resources on an unprecedented scale. The prescriptive planning system of the Soviet Union eliminated the limitations of private capital accumulation and subordinated currency circulation to the task of production growth for political purposes. Therefore, the system restrictions on economic expansion and reproduction were lifted, and reproduction could be carried out on a global scale. During the Great Depression, enterprises in capitalist countries faced the dilemma of insufficient demand and overproduction, proving the advantages of the unified planning and production organization systems.

Both the Soviet Union's unified planning system and the US' federal system can provide unlimited financial guarantees for global economic expansion. Although the two are carried out on an opposite owner relationship (in the Soviet Union, it is to provide funding for the national economic plan of state-owned enterprises, and in the US it is to refinance private enterprises), both have the basic ability of unlimited expansion of reproduction on a global scale. This was fully demonstrated after World War II. International Economic Organizations (WTO, IMF, World Bank) provided services for the expansion of the US capital reproduction system to achieve its global expansion; the Economic Mutual Aid Committee used the ruble as an international Currency to provide support for the world socialist system established by the Soviet Union. Therefore, we call this world economic paradigm the imperialist world economic paradigm to emphasize the global nature of its system and the expansion of reproduction mechanisms.

During the First World War, this world economic paradigm was at its infancy stage. With the establishment of the American and the Soviet models, the German model also emerged. Germany became the third empire with a national socialist ideology, dividing people into superior races and slaves according to race. It has the extreme characteristics of the colonial world economic paradigm. The colonial empires of the Western powers were built on racist ideology. Perhaps this is why German Nazism was treated calmly by the Western powers. Anglo-American capital has greatly contributed to the German economy's recovery and militarization.

In the 1930s, the Soviet Union and Germany made technological breakthroughs again, catching up with the US and the United Kingdom, which had fallen into the Great Depression. To contain the Soviet Union and Germany, the United Kingdom repeated its old tricks and provoked conflicts in its surroundings. Driven by American companies and British diplomacy, Nazi Germany was ready for war. Britain sacrificed two allies, Poland and France, and pushed fascist Germany towards the Soviet Union. The US succeeded again: just like in the First World War, the US intervened in the fighting in the final stage and seized the victory of the Western Europe and Pacific Wars. The European colonial empires collapsed, and the dominance of the capitalist world was transferred to American companies. At the same time, the socialist world came into being; it developed rapidly and quickly caught up with the US. Britain used diplomatic means to create a confrontation between the two systems, prompting the concentration of capital in the US. The US had seized technological leadership in forming the fourth technological paradigm, which was based on internal combustion engines, organic chemistry, and highway construction. In the next ICT paradigm based on software and microelectronics, the US technology leadership had been consolidated. This gave the US an advantage in the arms race, which caused damage to the diversified economy of the Soviet Union.

Due to the two world wars of the 20th century, the British dominance ended, the European colonial empire was destroyed, and the leadership of the capitalist world was transferred to the US After the US-Soviet "Cold War," with the disintegration of the Soviet Union, the US seized the global leadership position through its development advantages in the ICT paradigm and the US dollar's monopoly of world currencies. With the massive issuance of US dollars all over the world, American multinational corporations have completed the creation of this world economic paradigm, and liberal globalization has become the mainstream idea of this paradigm.

In the struggle between socialism and the capitalist world system, the life cycle of the imperialist world economic paradigm is coming to an end. The interaction between socialism and capitalism ensures the integration of universal values and global institutions. Slavery, racism, fascism, and the theories that divide humans into superior and inferior races, oppress or even eliminate the latter for the benefit of the former, all of which have disappeared in the long river of history. International law based on the principle of national sovereignty has begun to take shape, and the United Nations (UN) global system has emerged as the times require.

At the same time, within the framework of the imperialist world economic paradigm, the practical application of international law is still limited by the interests of global empires. If in the socialist world system, management is implemented according to the political decisions of the leadership of the CPSU, then in the capitalist world, international policies are determined by the views of American companies. To protect the interests of American companies, American intelligence agencies organized coups in neighboring countries and carried out political killings and repressive operations. The US Constitution places national laws above international obligations, and the US authorities regard it as a practice. After the disintegration of the Soviet Union, contempt of international law has become the norm of the US expansion policy. The US has established a global influence network in extra-legal space, completely disregarding national sovereignty and international treaties.[12]

To extend its jurisdiction to the entire world, the US has completed the life cycle of the imperialist world economic paradigm. The US has established a unified standard of popular culture, education, and ideology within its framework. It only uses dollars to measure the wealth created by human activities, suppressing the diversity of human culture, and inhibiting human development. The dystopian theory of Fukuyama[13] and Attali[14] proclaimed the "end of history" and the establishment of a new world currency dynasty, reflecting the completion of the American capital accumulation cycle. However, the US dollar worship established by the Federal Reserve aims to expand the wealth of private owners continuously. Due to the lack of cultural recognition, it cannot become the life principle of people in all countries. The completion of the life cycle of the imperialist world economic paradigm limits the further development of human productivity. Only by transitioning to the new world economic paradigm can this problem be solved.

In the previous evolution of productive forces and production relations, the prerequisites for the transition to the new world economic paradigm have matured. In the life cycle of the fourth and fifth technological paradigms, the importance of science and professional knowledge in organizational production has greatly increased with the development of productivity. Therefore, the importance of human factors in the process of capital accumulation and reproduction has increased. Since the second half

---

12. Филимонов Г. Культурно-информационные механизмы внешней политики США. Истоки и новая реальность. М.: Российский университет дружбы народов, 2012.

13. F. Fukuyama, *The End of History and the Last Man* (Free Press, 1992).

14. J. Attali, *Millennium: Winners and Losers in the Coming World Order* (New York: Random House, 1991).

of the 20th century, in advanced economies, investment in the reproduction of "human" capital (education and healthcare costs) has surpassed that in the reproduction of capital (housing, construction, machinery, and equipment). As a result, a new social welfare system was created, that is, through a corresponding increase in income tax to guarantee most of the expenditures used to expand the reproduction of human capital. Therefore, the development and replacement of the technological paradigm impact the formation of the social welfare system, creating prerequisites for forming an integrated world economic paradigm. These prerequisites gradually matured in the imperialist world economic paradigm, which entered a mature mode after World War II. All social systems based on dividing citizens into superior races and inferior races have collapsed. With the failure of fascism, European colonial empires no longer exist. Southeast Asian countries got rid of the Japanese occupation, and China moved on to the road of socialist construction. The Soviet Union was transitioning to advanced socialism, which eliminated forced labor and recognized all citizens' social rights and freedoms. With the competition between the capitalist and the socialist systems, the popularization of education was developed, the importance of creative and intellectual labor was elevated, workers were able to participate in production management and social management, and the political system was democratized. At this time, the theory of the convergence of these two systems emerged. Sorokin tried to prove that these two systems must be able to complement each other and converge into a new integrated system. The next chapter will discuss the transition to the new system in detail.

As far as this book is concerned, it is particularly important to analyze the evolution of the world economic paradigm. The global economy leader transitioned from a European colonial empire to an American multinational corporation. This change was achieved through two world wars and a cold war. With the end of each war, the world political system was fundamentally changed. The First World War led to the collapse of the monarchy, which hindered the expansion of the national capital. The Second World War brought down the colonial empire that restricted the international flow of capital. The subsequent Cold War led to the disintegration of the Soviet Union and the free flow of capital around the world.

But the story does not end. Contrary to the general view of Fukuyama's "End of History," American hegemony has been weakened due to unresolvable internal contradictions in the existing capital reproduction system. In theory, we can assume that due to the influx of foreign capital, these contradictions can be resolved, and the US can launch a new war to offset debts and encroach on the property of others. However, due to the nature of modern currencies, there are limits to using these mechanisms to maintain non-reciprocal international exchanges.

Chapter 3

Currency Evolution in the Process of Economic Development

The creation of credit currency (or fiat currency) is the most important institutional innovation of the imperialist world economic paradigm, ensuring that the leading countries in this life cycle have long-term competitive advantages. The issuance of credit currency does not have any actual value but uses relevant country and corporate bonds as collateral. Bonds can thus be "printed" without limit, at any interest rate, according to the interest of these countries and their capital.

Although the world's leading countries have used credit currency for a century, the process of creation and circulation of it is still unknown. Not only ordinary people but also rulers and merchants in many countries, and even economists who regard the dollar and other mainstream currencies as real gold and silver, are unaware of this process. The currencies of all countries in the world do not have value. Their nominal value is determined by the country, and purchasing power depends on a variety of factors, including convertibility, inflation, and circulation restrictions. Therefore, experts call it legal tender or credit currency to emphasize the difference between it and the following two currencies. One is the banknotes with the actual value of gold and silver currency in the previous circulation, and the other is the recent cryptocurrency with its value protected by a digital currency distribution trading system. To understand this issue, a brief analysis of the evolution of money and its role in the modern economy is required.

Stages of Currency Evolution

Currency has a system that embodies a series of complex economic relations, and it cannot be reduced to the basic functions of only value scales, means of payment, and means of storage—the nature of currency changes with changes in the world economic paradigm. Credit expansion must be realized to guarantee industrial development, and the credit currency system has become an inherent system of the imperialist world economic paradigm. The use of gold-backed banknotes to support economic and trade exchanges between underdeveloped countries or even lack of currency circulation through interconnected banking systems is a characteristic of the colonial world economic paradigm. With the transition to the integrated world economic paradigm, the digital currency has been produced and protected by coding and transaction methods under the new technological paradigm. The current digital revolution in currency circulation is of epoch-making significance. New types of currencies rarely appear, marking a new stage in the development of the currency industry and the entire economy.

Therefore, through the rise and development of banks, the transition from metal currency to paper currency began five hundred years ago, which opened opportunities for endless capital accumulation and international financial transactions. Otherwise, capitalism would not develop, the industrial revolution would not occur, industrial society would not be formed, urbanization would not be realized, and technological progress would stagnate. For over two centuries, the paper currency system has ruled the world, connecting billions of people in the endless production, circulation, and consumption of goods and services. Modern countries use paper currency issued by the country as the foundation of the national financial system, the main tool for controlling and distributing benefits, and a symbol of national sovereignty. Without paper currency, such a modern country cannot be formed.

The creation of computers and the application of computing and communication facilities in the financial sector have replaced banknotes with non-cash equivalents (digital records in bank accounts). This phenomenon occurred naturally and did not cause turmoil, because the circulation of non-cash currency occurred simultaneously with banknotes and bank issuing banknotes. Banks keep records of cash transactions and use records in bank accounts to ensure currency circulation. Before the computerization of banking, bank employees manually recorded on paper documents. With the advent of computers, records began to be stored in computer memory and copied onto paper documents for a certain period. With the development of software and data transmission equipment, salesmen have been replaced by computer technology, and paperless has been realized through backup systems and data protection systems. But in fact, the nature of these operations has not changed. The record on the bank account is the same as that on the paper document, except that it is no longer recorded by handwriting but automatically generated by computer algorithms.

The fundamental difference between the recent digital currency (encrypted currency) and the current currency is not in its paperless (electronic) form but in the lack of a bank as its issuer. In fact, this kind of digital currency is not banknotes (bank notes) but is issued through a computer algorithm that uses encryption to prevent the digital currency from being copied. If the non-cash currency related to the circulation of paper money is essentially nothing more than the bank account holder having the right to withdraw money, then the digital currency has a unique identification and is closely tied to its owner. The circulation of digital currency is not regulated by the bank but by a computer network (currently the Internet) to record all transactions (blockchain) in the distributed ledger multiple times. Each digital currency unit maintains its uniqueness in many transactions and is always identified by the computer's attribution relationship.

As an electronic form, each unit of digital currency has a unique number, which makes it look like paper money. However, the circulation of banknotes has the characteristic of being anonymous and can be stolen or forged, and any operation performed with digital currency is recorded by the computer. Under the condition of using standardized algorithms to organize currency circulation, digital currencies cannot be imitated or counterfeited.

Therefore, the new digital currency not only combines the advantages of current non-cash currency (easy to circulate and store) and cash currency (with serial numbers), but also has fundamentally distinctive features, making it a new type of currency. First, digital currency is not issued by banks but through computer algorithms. The further circulation and security of the currency have nothing to do with the issuer. Secondly, each unit of digital currency has a unique number, and it is still registered in the circulation process. Third, all transactions made with digital currency are recorded and stored on the network.

At present, all known digital currencies, including Bitcoin, are called encrypted currencies and are privately issued. Some market participants believe that this has the advantage of not being regulated by the government. In contrast, others believe that it is a tool to "inflate" the financial "bubble" and money laundering. Monetary authorities in all countries are vigilant against it, refuse to recognize it as currency, and generally do not allow it as a means of payment and settlement. But this situation will not last long, and more and more countries have announced the issuance of national cryptocurrencies.

The history of currency circulation shows that each new currency is first issued by private entrepreneurs, and then monopolized by the state. Therefore, the currency could be minted freely in ancient times and even in the Middle Ages. After that, the country began to mint currency, possessed the currency's issuance rate of return (seigniorage), and stipulated that only the currency was allowed to circulate in the controlled territory. Similarly, banknotes were originally issued by private banks, after which the country established its own currency, and the national (central) bank monopolized its issuance rights. Every currency nationalization will be resisted by its private issuers, but will be resolved by the state through forceful suppression and legislation. As a typical modern country, Russia stipulates in article 75 of the Russian Constitution that currency can only be issued by the Central Bank of the Russian Federation.

There is an exception to this rule. In the US, the US dollar is issued by the Federal Reserve, which was established by the US private bank more than a century ago. However, the Federal Reserve regulates the issuance of domestic currency in the US under legislative procedures, and its control method is mainly to purchase US Treasury bills. As a result, the US receives the largest share of seigniorage, and the US authorities use it to make up for a huge budget deficit equivalent to its military expenditures.

The Evolution of the Modern Monetary System

The modern monetary system was formed based on the state's monopoly issuing paper money. Paper money was originally issued by private banks in the form of bank notes, and holders could withdraw money at the bank by showing bank notes. The currency at the time was gold and silver coins. The state nationalized the right to issue banknotes. It established a state-owned bank for issuing banknotes to ensure that the banknotes could be converted into gold, and the corresponding gold reserves in the state-owned banks were concentrated. However, this situation did not last long.

On the one hand, private banks continued to operate and shifted to the domestic currency business. At the same time, private banks retained the function of issuing bonds. These bonds are currently issued in their own currency and automatically become national bonds. In this secondary banking system, the central bank acted as the lender of last resort, ensuring the safety of private bank depositors. But no matter how the country restricted it, private bankers always issued more currency than they received. Private banks, hidden under the guise of financial intermediaries, retained the ability to issue currency, albeit in a limited way. By increasing currency issuance, the gold reserves of the banking system could far exceed that of the central bank.

On the other hand, in the face of the irresistible need to expand spending, including emergency needs related to wars and other disasters, currency issuance exceeded the amount of gold reserves. Although other realizable assets had been added in addition to gold, including foreign bonds denominated in domestic currency, it was necessary to continuously increase currency issuance to make up for the budget deficits of major countries in the world.

As the gap between the total amount of currency issuance and the amount of gold and foreign exchange reserves of the central bank continues to expand, the domestic currency has become a fiduciary currency. In addition to gaining the trust of the operators and the public, it does not have any other guarantees. Its functions are guaranteed, and its purchasing power is maintained by state bonds, which is the case with currencies of all countries today. Even if the monetary base of a certain domestic currency does not exceed the central bank's gold foreign exchange reserves, modern countries do not undertake the obligation to convert the currency into gold at a fixed exchange rate. The US government assumed this obligation until 1971, when France required the Bretton Woods agreement to set the exchange rate and exchange its reserves for gold with US dollars. America's evasion of this obligation marked the end of the gold coin era. Since then, all currencies in circulation in the world have become fiduciary currencies. The issuance of credit currency does not have any actual value. Still, it uses the bonds of relevant countries and companies as collateral so that it can be based on the capital of these countries and their own countries. The interest is unlimited and "printing" of bonds at any interest rate.

The significance of credit currency to the development of the modern economy is equivalent to the discovery of the coveted golden stone by the medieval alchemist. The Middle Ages is different from the period of modern economic growth. The period of modern economic growth began with the first industrial revolution at the end of the 18th century. In the Middle Ages, technology was backward, lacking credit support, unable to finance the development of new technologies, and unable to advance funds for the expansion of production. At that time, they could only borrow money from usurers at super-high annual interest rates, which were as high as 50% and sometimes even 100%. Obviously, such loans couldn't be used to expand production (the profit rate of expanding production rarely exceeds 15%), nor could it be used to finance the development of production (the yield has fluctuated in the range of 3%–7% over the centuries, with an average of about 5%).[1] The national credit system creates unlimited sources of funds for the growth and development of production through the issuance of local currency, enables the successful operation of large-scale high-tech industries, and creates unlimited possibilities for technological progress.

Of course, the issuance of credit resources alone is not enough to promote economic growth. There is also a need for a system to ensure that credit is transformed into the expansion of production and investment, a need for technology and manpower that can guarantee engineering technology and organizational needs, and a need for a responsibility mechanism for the effective use and repayment of credit resources.

---

1. Пикетти Т. Капитал в XXI веке. М.: Ad Marginem, 2015.

Without the above mechanisms, it is impossible to develop a modern economy. If the mechanisms are not sufficient to support expanded reproduction, the economy will deteriorate. If the loan interest is too high, the economy will stop developing.

In essence, loans are a universal tool to promote economic growth, and loan interest should be regarded as a burden of economic growth. Loan interest is like taxation, but the collection of loan interest is not for the public interest, but for the personal interest of the banker. The author of *Theory of Economic Development*, J. Schumpeter, appropriately refers to interest as an innovation tax.[2] To reduce interest rates and promote production development, developed countries have implemented supervision over currency issuance to strengthen credit support for commercial activities with economic development prospects.

It should be noted that the creation of modern credit currency is the most profitable economic activity due to the issuance rate of return (seigniorage). The currency issuing country conducts the first transaction with the issuing institution that obtains the issuance rate of return (seigniorage).[3] This is the reason why private entrepreneurs initially tried to establish a central bank and bank supervision system. They attempted to obtain seigniorage in the issuance of local currency. This is achieved using "credit leverage," which allows the total amount of loans issued by commercial banks to exceed the sum of their deposits and own capital, as well as the number of commercial banks refinancing to the central bank. In this model, in addition to the interest collected by the central bank, the seigniorage in currency issuance mainly flows to commercial banks. However, the state relatively quickly took control of the distribution of seigniorage, trying to use seigniorage to promote the public interest, including financing budget deficits and providing loans to promote economic activities.

The Pros and Cons of the Credit Currency System

If the country does not control the production process of credit currency, the advantages of credit currency (free issuance and easy circulation) will soon become a disadvantage.

At the end of the 18th century, Hamilton tried for the first time in the US to use the national currency issued by the country to solve public interest issues, including the issuance of the national currency ("US dollars") to protect government expenditures. After some improvements, the initiative guaranteed the US currency demand until the beginning of the 20th century. Even after the privatization of the Federal Reserve's currency issuance, its purpose has remained unchanged until now. The purpose of issuing US dollars is to purchase national debt to make up for the national budget deficit, so that the US government can maintain huge expenditures on national defense, scientific research and experimental design, and economic and social development investment.

Since the end of the 19th century, Russia has often issued special loans to solve the financing problems of railway construction and other needs. Since then, credit issuance has become the foundation of the Soviet financial system, and all capital investment

2. Шумпетер Й. Теория экономического развития / Пер. В. С. Автономова. М.: Прогресс, 1982.
3. Отырба А., Кобяков А. Как побеждать в финансовых войнах. Альманах «Однако». Июнь-июль 2014 г. № 174.

has been linked to production and investment growth. In the post-war period, Japan (in accordance with the indicative plan to increase industrial production) and Western Europe (in accordance with the promissory notes of the production companies) implemented large-scale credit extensions.

The monetary authorities of the leading countries have learned how to create money based on national and corporate debts to finance the expansion of economic reproduction. Today, in the context of the structural crisis, these countries are investing in large-scale funding to stimulate investment in developing new technological paradigms. The main way is for the central bank to purchase low-interest treasury bonds to make up for the budget deficit. Under the "quantitative easing" policy, the Federal Reserve and the European Central Bank (ECB) also issue currencies to purchase large bank and corporate bonds. China and other successful developing countries follow the priorities set by the central government to "print money" for the investment plans of economic entities (Figure 3-1, 3-2, 3-3).

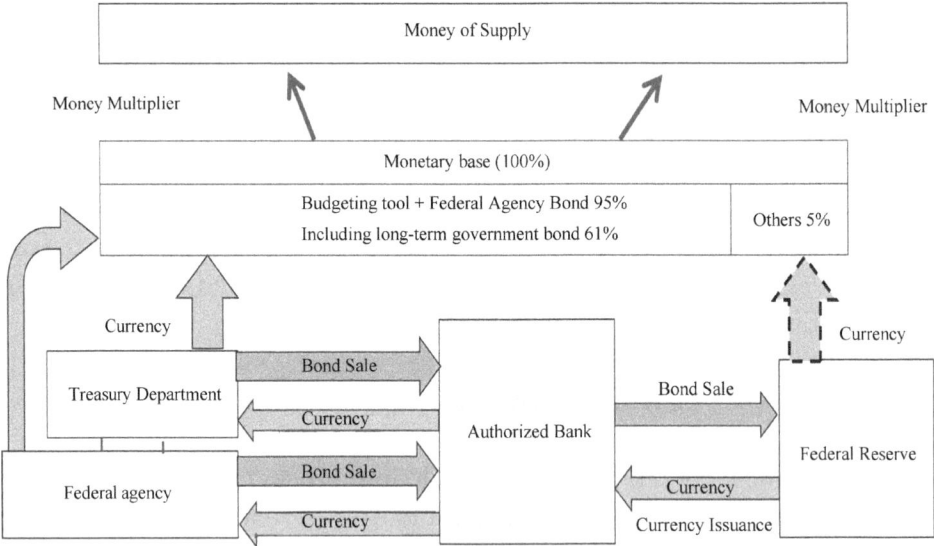

Figure 3-1 US Currency Issuance Plan
Source: Yershov, M. Based on Fed data.

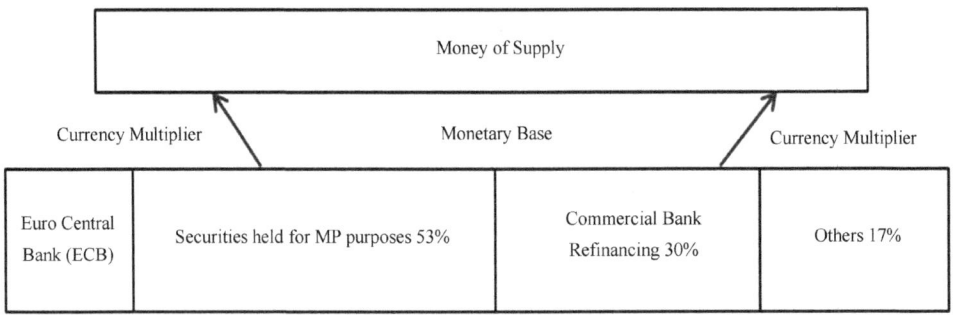

Figure 3-2 ECB Money Supply Mechanism
Source: Yershov, M. Based on ECB data.

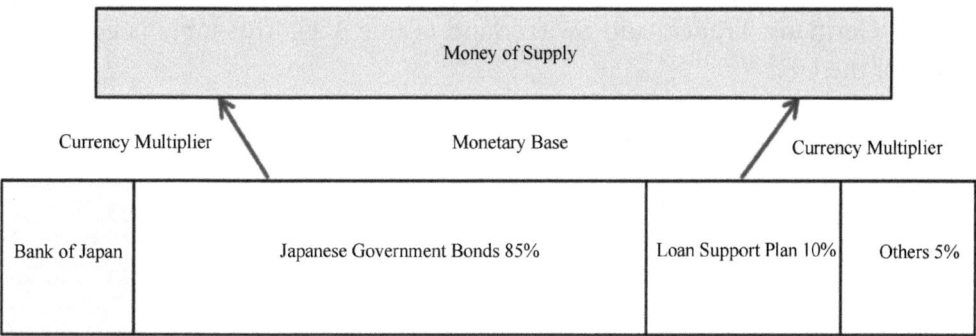

Figure 3-3 Bank of Japan Money of Supply Mechanism
Source: Yershov, M., based on Bank of Japan data.

Unlike Russian banks, the central banks of some reserve currency issuing countries provide a large number of cheap credit resources at quasi-zero interest rates (Figure 3-4). Since loans are used for investment in modernization and development of production, they will not cause inflation. They will eventually reduce costs and increase the supply of goods, increasing the purchasing power of money.

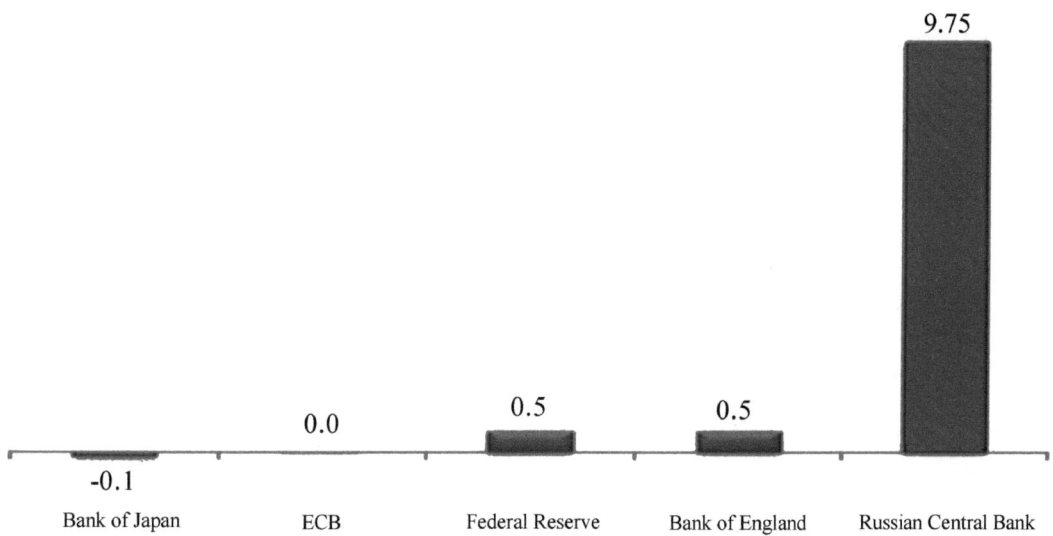

Figure 3-4 Benchmark Interest Rates of Central Banks in Some Countries
Source: Central Banks of Some countries.

At present, the main way for western countries to issue currency is through the central bank to issue currency to purchase national debt. For example, more than 90% of US dollars are issued in this way. But this does not prevent the Fed from issuing any amount of currency to support certain private banks when necessary. The Federal Reserve is "eliminating" the increasingly serious imbalances in the US dollar financial system by issuing currencies. These currencies are used not only to purchase Treasury bonds, but also to aid large private banks. During the 2008–2010 global financial and economic crisis, the Federal Reserve secretly issued 16 trillion US dollars to provide interest-free loans to systemically important private banks such as the US, the United Kingdom, Germany, France, and Switzerland (Table 3-1). This table is equivalent to the GDP of the US.[4]

Table 3-1 Banks Assisted by the Fed. (Unit: billion US$)

Bank	Country	Billion US$
Citigroup	USA	2513
Morgan Stanley	USA	2041
Merrill Lynch	USA	1949
Bank of America	USA	1344
Barclays Bank	UK	868
Bear Sterns	USA	853
Goldman Sachs	USA	814
Royal Bank of Scotland	UK	541
Deutsche Bank	Germany	354
United Bank of Switzerland	Switzerland	287
J.P. Morgan Chase	USA	391
Credit Suisse Group AG	Switzerland	262
Lehman Brothers Holdings	USA	183
Bank of Scotland	UK	181
BNP Paribas	France	175
Wells Fargo	USA	159
Dexia Group	Belgium	159
Wachovia Corp.	USA	142
Dresdner Bank	Germany	135

(Continued)

---

4. Смирнов Ф. Мировая финансово-экономическая архитектура. Деконструкция. М.: ООО «Буки Веди», 2015.

Societe Generale	France	124
Other Lenders	—	2639
In Total	—	16115

Source: Источник: Смирнов Ф. Указ. соч. 2015.

Following the Federal Reserve, other world currency issuing banks have also used currency "water injection" to stimulate their economic development (Figure 3-5). Similarly, under the "quantitative easing" policy, the ECB and the Bank of Japan used the excuse of stimulating economic growth to issue currencies to purchase stocks and bonds of certain financial intermediaries and companies.

In major Eastern countries, the main purpose of currency is to invest in areas with economic development prospects. The accelerated growth of the Chinese economy is one example. The funds for expanding investment mainly come from targeted loans issued through the refinancing of state-owned banks. The foreign direct investment attracted by the government to develop advanced technology and develop international production cooperation also played a certain role. With the increase in output in the future, residents' income and savings will also increase, leading to more funds flowing into new investment projects. At the same time, in accordance with the requirements of the central government, provinces, municipalities, and companies, to meet the investment needs of modernization and expansion of production, the People's Bank of China continues to increase credit supply through state-owned banks and development agencies. The financial investment platform established for this can reduce risks and ensure that the central bank allocates credit resources to industries with development prospects in accordance with national priorities.

Inflation is the main factor restricting credit currency. To avoid inflation, it is necessary to link the manufacturing industry's cash flow with the banking system's transmission mechanism. Otherwise, credit currency may become a hotbed of financial "bubble" and currency speculation, eventually leading to macroeconomic imbalances. China's experience also shows that targeted currency placement is highly likely to provide loans for development investment and production growth, which will not lead to inflation. From 1993 to 2016, for every 10-fold increase in China's GDP, investment, money supply, and manufacturing bank loans increased 28 times, 19 times, and 15 times accordingly. GDP growth per unit is almost accompanied by three units of investment growth, and about two units of money supply and loan growth. This illustrates the effect of China's economic growth mechanism: the growth of investment drives the growth of economic activity (measured by GDP), and most of the investment comes from the credit expansion of the national banking system. Although the growth of the money supply has surpassed production growth many times, China's inflation rate has remained within the range of 4%–7% during the entire period when the level of China's economic monetization has rapidly increased.

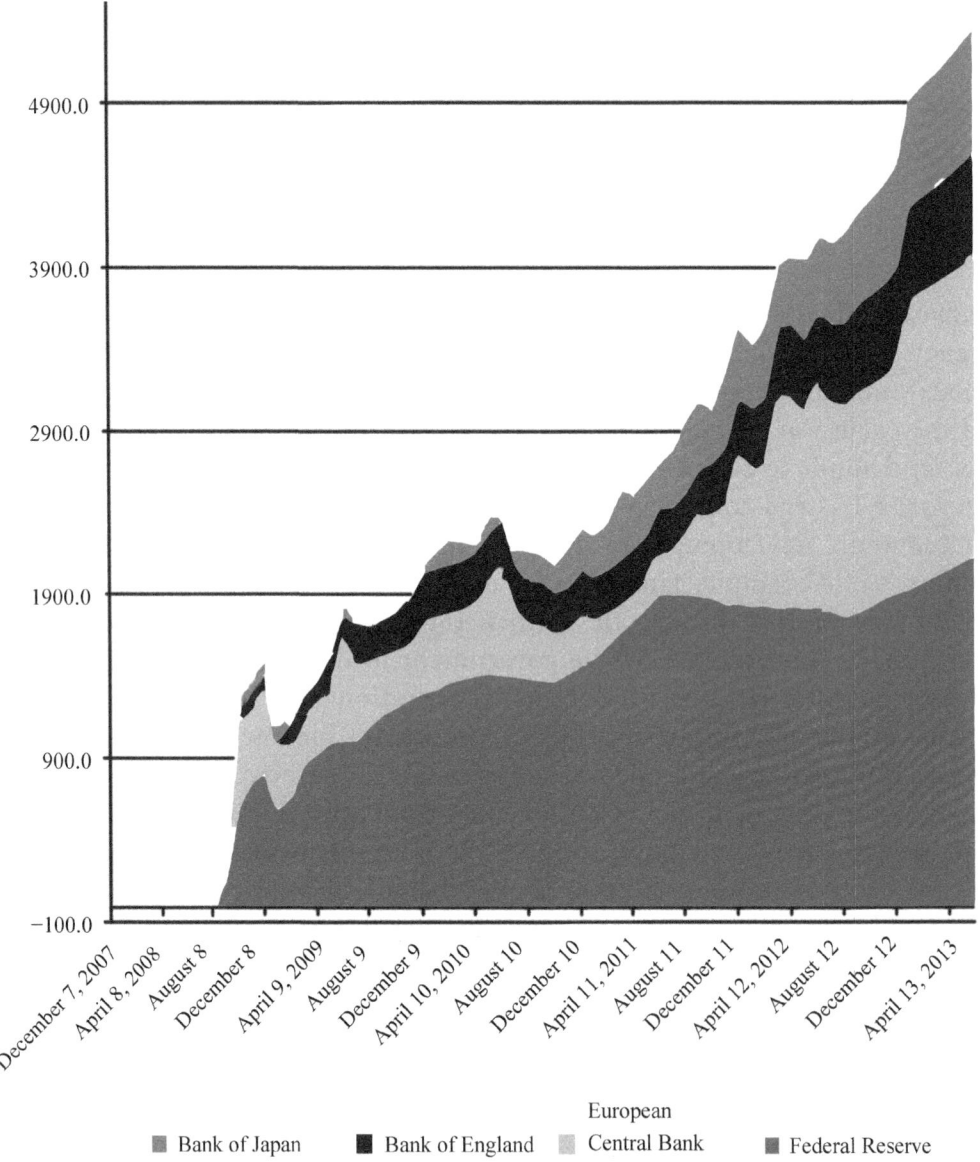

Figure 3-5 Growth of Central Bank Balances in Reserve Currency Issuing Countries
Source: Thomson Reuters Data Stream [Electronic Resource]/ Thomson Reuters Data Stream.

As the cash flow is maintained in the following loop, the production efficiency and output of goods are continuously improved, thereby ensuring low inflation. The loop is credit extension-investment growth-increased output and efficiency-reduced unit cost of produced goods, lower consumer costs, improved quality of goods-increased income-increased savings-increased investment. The realization of the above-mentioned loop requires national bank loans to provide guarantees for production and development investment projects, while maintaining currency restrictions on capital transactions, requiring national authorities to "implement" the responsibility of achieving production and investment targets and systematically combat corruption.

In Japan, India, Vietnam, South Korea, Malaysia, Singapore, and other successful developing countries, similar methods have been successfully adopted to promote investment growth by issuing credit currency to issue loans. Its characteristic is to increase targeted loans in advance to provide funds for investment projects per the country's priorities (Table 3-2).

Table 3-2 Increase of Accumulation Rate in the Period of Rapid Economic Growth

Year	Investment/GDP, %					
	Japan	South Korea	Singapore	Malaysia	China	India
1950	X	X	X	X	X	10.4
1955	19.4	10.6	X	9.2	X	12.5
1960	29.0	11.1	6.5	11.0	X	13.3
1965	29.8	14.9	21.3	18.3	X	15.8
1970	35.5	25.5	32.6	14.9	14.6	X
1975	32.5	26.8	35.1	25.1	X	16.9
1980	31.7	32.4	40.6	31.1	28.8	19.3
1985	27.7	28.8	42.2	29.8	29.4	20.7
1990	32.1	37.3	32.3	33.0	25.0	22.9
1995	27.9	37.3	33.4	43.6	33.0	24.4
2000	25.2	30.0	30.6	25.3	34.1	22.7
2005	23.3	28.9	21.3	20.5	42.2	30.4
2009	20.6	29.3	27.9	20.4	46.7	30.8
2010	20.5	28.6	25.0	20.3	46.1	29.5

Note: Russia's investment ratio/GDP is 16% (in 2017).
Source: Финансовые стратегии модернизации экономики: мировая практика / Под ред. Я. М. Миркина. М.: Магистр, 2014.

Therefore, in the case of low income and low savings of residents, the accumulation rate has increased sharply (Table 3-3). In all countries that have created economic miracles, targeted credit has always been the main source of capital for capital investment.

Table 3-3 Credit Volume during the Period of Rapid Economic Growth

Year	Domestic Credits/GDP, %				
	South Korea	Singapore	People's Republic of China	Hong Kong, China	India
1950	X	X	X	X	15,6
1955	X	X	X	X	18,9
1960	9.1	X	X	X	24.9
1963	16.6	7.2	X	X	25.8
1970	35.3	20.0	X	X	24.8
1978	38.4	30.7	38.5	X	36.4
1980	46.9	42.4	52.8	X	40.7
1990	57.2	61.7	86.3	X	51.5
1991	57.8	63.1	88.7	130.4	51.3
2000	79.5	79.2	119.7	136.0	53.0
2009	109.4	93.9	147.5	166.8	72.9
2010	103.2	83.9	172.3	199.0	76.2

Note: Russian credit ratio/GDP is 42% (2017), Bank credit ratio is no more than 5% of the investment.Source: Финансовые стратегии модернизации экономики: мировая практика / Под ред. Я. М. Миркина. М.: Магистр, 2014.

Experience with credit money over the past two centuries has shown its advantages and disadvantages. On the one hand, if credit currency is not issued for credit investment, it will not be possible to achieve modern economic development based on the continuous advancement of S&T. On the other hand, excessive issuance of credit currency will produce a financial "bubble" and cause inflation, undermining economic stability. There are many such negative examples in economic history.

Usually, in the case of wars and political crises, all countries are forced to issue "bottomless pit"-like credit currencies to finance current expenditures, and then immediately face hyperinflation.

From the historical experience of using credit currency, it is not difficult to find that all countries' governments strive to make the issuance and circulation of currency in line with the goals of expanding economic reproduction and social and economic development. For this reason, all developing countries have successfully adopted a comprehensive method to form a money supply mechanism with designated tasks, and rely on this mechanism to issue credit money. Developing countries achieve the above goals through indirect and direct currency issuance. The indirect method refers to refinancing under the guarantee of the state and repayable enterprises, and the direct method is state-owned asset financing, government credit guarantees, and development agency reserves. It is also a perfect mechanism to directly use credit currency to meet the country's needs through the purchase of national debt by the central bank.

However, the monetary authorities manage to ensure that the state controls the credit currency only within the scope of controlling the work of the banking system. The law stipulates the role of the central bank. Therefore, the main goal of the Federal Reserve is to consider the growth potential of production, maintain long-term growth in the total amount of money, maintain a moderate long-term interest rate, and promote employment. Under this circumstance, the Federal Reserve mainly issues US dollars by purchasing Treasury bonds. The monetary authorities of other Western countries have also tried to centrally control and regulate the issuance of credit currency, guide it through the national budget, and generate long-term credit resources under the conditions of the increased national debt. Developing countries have succeeded in controlling credit currencies by refinancing by national development agencies, no longer providing loans to the real economy, and switching to priority development areas.

The control of currency issued by private banks is much more complicated. The state can only adjust it indirectly through the reserve ratio and bank supervision. Although the state's supervision of private banks has become more and more stringent, private banks are striving to increase currency issuance by relying on the refinancing of the National Bank as the lender of last resort. In the context of the global financial crisis, this method is becoming an important channel for issuing currency. The actions of many American and European banks did not comply with the Basel Committee's rules. Many Japanese banks have been in negative equity for a long time. However, this does not prevent the monetary authorities of the world's major countries from increasing the issuance of currency to maintain the operation of commercial banks and refinance the expansion of reproduction and modernization of the national economy. The monetary base of the US dollar, euro, yen, and the Swiss franc is different from that of the Russian ruble. In the seven years since the outbreak of the global financial crisis, the monetary base of the US dollar, euro, yen, and Swiss franc has tripled (Figure 3-6). The main beneficiaries of many credit currencies are private banks and companies.

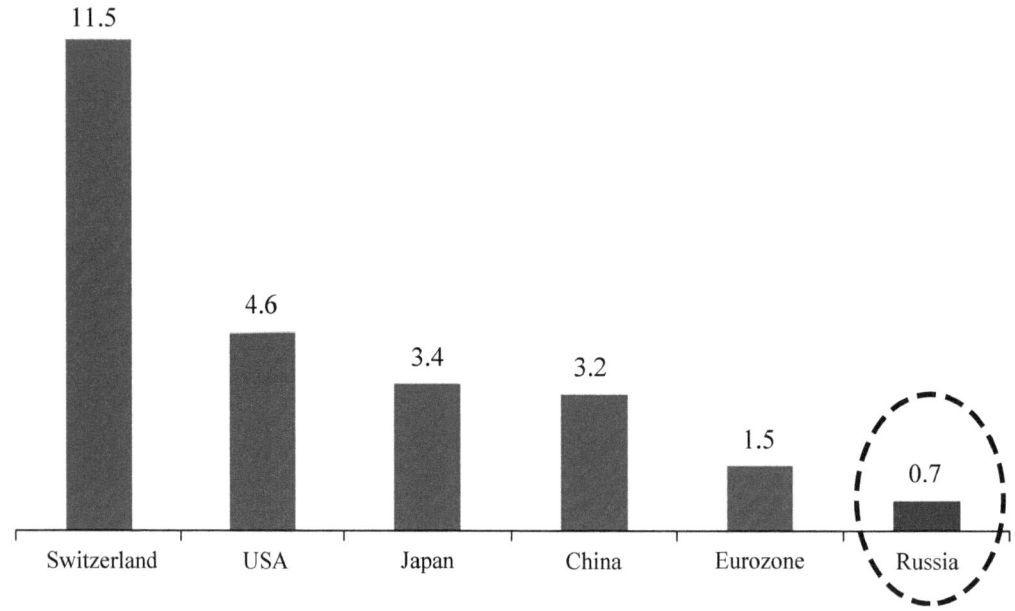

Figure 3-6 Growth of the Monetary Base by Country, 2007–2015
Note: The relevant exchange rate is in US dollars. Data is from 2007–June 2015.
Source: M. Yershov, data from Central Banks of Relevant Countries.

Due to the increase in the money supply, many cheap credit resources with quasi-zero interest rates have been produced. As long as money remains in the banking sector or is used for investment loans for modernization and production growth, it will not lead to inflation. As a result, costs will decrease, and the supply of goods will increase, which means that the purchasing power of money will increase. But the effect of "quantitative easing" MP is not perfect. Not all the issued currency flows to the physical sector. Most of the currency is thrown into the financial "bubble" by speculators. With the bubble's collapse, this part of the money also evaporates, which has an inflationary impact on the corresponding part of the financial market. But it does not affect consumer prices, and part of the loans that have been issued cannot be returned.

Formally, the issuance of credit currency means that the issuer (the country's central bank) legalizes a certain amount of digital currency, or the issuer grants a certain amount of digital currency status. But in fact, the issuance of credit currency is a phase of creating money supply and collecting seigniorage. This process consists of three main stages: putting money into the market and absorbing and writing it off. In this process, the stock market plays a major role as a mechanism, guaranteeing the absorption of the money supply during the inflation of the financial "bubble" and offsetting it during the bubble's collapse. In the stage of advocating a financial "bubble," when the stock market's return level greatly exceeds the indicators in other fields of activity, a large amount of currency flows into the stock market. When the financial bubble "collapses," these currencies will be offset. Only those who know the insider can win; that is, the international financial organization that controls all processes in the world's financial field.

As a stage of the cyclical process, sterilization provides currency issuers with the opportunity to continue their activities, so that currency issuers can generate income whether they are in the context of global economic growth or under conditions of currency and capital shortages caused by a crisis.

Today, this three-stage layout only applies to the US dollar, the universal reserve currency. Some secondary currencies are also recognized by the IMF as reserve currencies and can be used for international settlement within a certain limit. Still, due to the dominance of the US, the issuance of these currencies is restricted. In particular, the US dollar system has included all banks using the Euro, Japanese Yen, British Pound, and Swiss Franc. These banks are forced to use the US dollar as the universal equivalent currency and conduct international transactions through the US dollar proxy account with Bank of America.

The currency of financially underdeveloped countries is formally the national currency, but, in fact, it is a derivative of a high-level currency, which then constitutes a three-tier monetary system, including the Russian ruble. The creation and circulation of tertiary currencies are related to the formation of primary and secondary currency reserves, but the nature, function, and political and economic nature of these currencies are completely different. The tertiary currency is a tool financially developed countries can use to implement financial colonialism (neocolonialism) policies against the issuing country. The essence of this policy is a non-equal foreign economic transaction mechanism, through the sale of tangible assets to obtain primary and secondary credit currency, to form a reserve fund for issuing tertiary currencies. The IMF generally adopts the so-called currency board system, which stipulates that the issuance of tertiary currencies is closely integrated with the growth units of primary or secondary currency reserves. Therefore, to create a new unit of the national currency, it is necessary to obtain income from exports of goods and services or to attract loans or investments in primary or secondary currencies at the equivalent exchange rate. In other words, to obtain more loans, a country issuing a tertiary currency must first sell something to the country that holds the reserve currency. Therefore, the development of the national economy must conform to the interests of the country issuing the reserve currency. The issuing country of the reserve currency regularly executes operations to encroach on the assets of the dependent country.

To obtain seigniorage all the time, money issuing centers in financially developed countries regularly sterilize large amounts of money. But this process is only one stage in the cyclical process of creating money.

When the domestic currency depreciates and the prices of goods and assets are hit, the issuer of the world currency can create the amount of money needed without control and then buy it at a very low price. In every so-called "crisis" process, the issuers of world currencies have "devoured" part of global assets. Moreover, the global assets "swallowed up" have greatly exceeded the former every subsequent time.

Russian experts believe that the process of stock market crashes and financial and economic crises is spontaneous. In effect, this is a process that helps solve the problem of decoupling the market from the money supply. From this, a lot of seigniorage can be captured and another slice of the global economic pie. With the repetition of the above process, countries are constantly improving methods and technologies. It should be noted that sovereigns issuing tertiary currencies are trying to get rid of these colonial predatory financial mechanisms by conducting independent monetary policies and issuing money without reference to foreign exchange reserves. Demanded by a foreign exchange in current business, the issuance of tier 3 currencies is limited by the semiannual import financing criteria. In addition, the greater the ratio of the monetary base of the local currency to the number of foreign exchange reserves, the more opportunities to provide credit for domestic production and investment. However, to implement this sovereign policy, foreign exchange controls must be implemented to prevent capital outflows and prevent speculation.

However, in recent years, the cost of offsetting excess credit currency has been too high, and the global financial system is close to collapse. The global financial system has entered a stage of deterioration, characterized by the loss of stability of the financial system and the opening of a mode of volatility. The turbulence pattern has been established, with financial "bubbles" popping every seven years (Figure 3-7). When the crisis happened, the deposits of millions of savers who believed the financial system was stable disappeared. At the same time, the Federal Reserve is injecting large amounts of capital into selected banks, embezzling seigniorage from the US dollar issuance and encroaching on the property of bankrupt market participants. At the same time, the crisis began to spread in the core of the global financial system, with the depreciation of US dollar assets and the destruction of the stability of primary currencies.

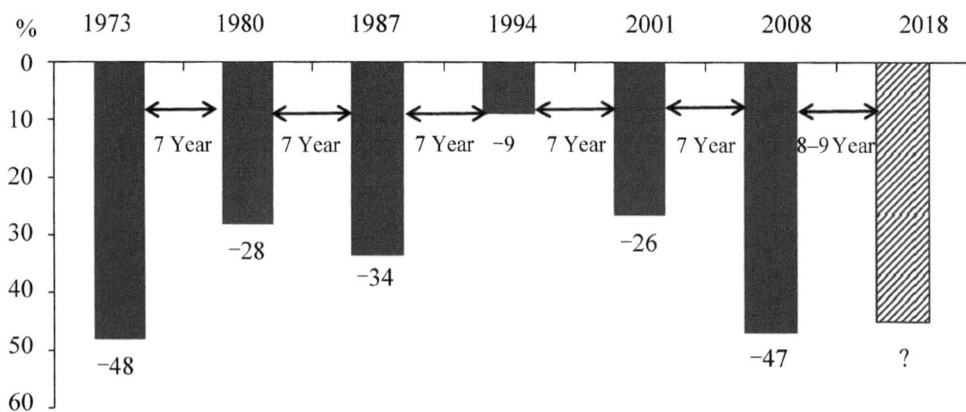

Figure 3-7 Cycles of Financial Bubbles and Crashes (US S&P 500)
Source: Yershov, M. Bloomberg.

The financial systems of Europe and Japan are also in bad shape. In the Eurozone, some countries' bonds have formed a financial "bubble." Cyprus had a serious financial crisis. Other countries try to "grab" money by cutting the budgets of insolvent countries. At the same time, the ECB is increasing credit to selected commercial banks to ensure that borrowers honor their commitments. Millions of citizens have seen their incomes and social benefits reduced, while bankers are getting more seigniorage for the euro.

In Japan, most commercial banks have negative profit margins and can only maintain operations through refinancing by the central bank.

All countries that issue international reserve currencies liquidate deposits of bankrupt bank depositors and reduce social welfare. Seigniorage is used to support selected private banks, while national wealth is spontaneously redistributed to the monetary authorities' cronies. Monetary authorities themselves are not subject to social control, neither elected by the people nor accountable to parliament.

The mechanism of subordinating the issuance of credit currency to the interests of the country issuing the reserve currency has failed. At the same time, the effect of issuing credit currency has dropped sharply. As mentioned above, only 1/5 of every US dollar issued by the Federal Reserve can flow into the real economy. The rest are "sucked in" by the financial "bubble," which is conducive to redistributing social wealth so that bankers close to the Federal Reserve can benefit. It should be added that the outbreak of the global financial crisis was linked to the excessive issuance of credit money by private banks. After the US Investment Bank lifted the restrictions on the absorption of deposits, the bank tremendously increased the issuance of US dollars, bringing the "credit leverage" to almost triple digits, which is a characteristic of the secondary banking system, that is, not fully controlled by the central bank.

In other words, the social benefits of the credit currency system have declined sharply in recent years. China is an exception among countries that issue an international reserve currency. Perhaps this is due to the non-convertibility of the current yuan in capital operations, which protects the Chinese financial system from speculative attacks from the outside world and enables it to remain stable despite the hyper-monetization of the Chinese economy. Another stabilizing factor is that Chinese commercial banks belong to the state, which excludes the possibility of voluntary currency issuance for private interests.

The Chinese government guarantees to provide long-term, low-interest-rate credit, and merchants promise to use it for specific investment projects in production development. The funds for the expansion of investment mainly come from directional loans issued through refinancing by state-owned banks (Figure 3-8). The foreign direct investment attracted by the government to develop advanced technology and develop international production cooperation also played a certain role. As production increases, residents' income and savings will increase in the future, allowing more funds to flow into new investment projects. At the same time, by the directive plan requirements of the government, provinces, municipalities, and companies to meet the investment needs of modernization and expansion of production, the People's Bank of China continues to increase credit supply through state-owned banks and development agencies. The financial investment platform established for this can reduce risks and ensure that the central bank allocates credit resources to industries with development prospects by national priorities.

The "excessive monetization" of the Chinese economy has become a financial reflection of China's economic miracle, which also confirms the general rule: the social-economic efficiency of creating credit currency is directly proportional to the state's ability to control its circulation and use seigniorage to promote social and economic development.

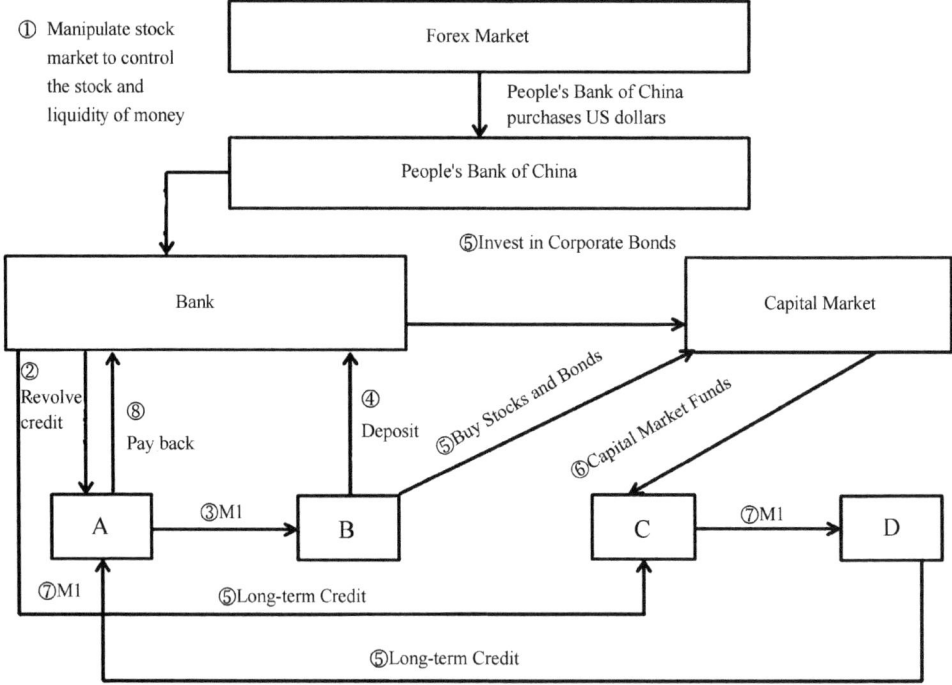

Figure 3-8 China's Money Supply Relationship
Source: Yu Yongding, 2017.

Much administrative control and indirect supervision methods have been adopted for the use of credit currency, but its effectiveness needs to be improved. On the contrary, the digital currency does not need to take similar measures. Initially, the issuance of digital currency was controlled by an algorithm, and all transactions would be recorded, thereby automatically controlling the circulation of digital currency.

It is not accidental that the Central Committee of the CPC proposed such a task in this programmatic document: "We will build a modern central bank system, improving the money supply control mechanism, steadily promoting digital currency research and development (S&D), and improving the market-based interest rate formation and transmission mechanism. We will also construct finance to support the real economy effectively. The system and mechanism of the company will improve the level of financial technology and enhance financial inclusiveness."

The Difference of Digital Currencies

Unlike conventional electronic money, the blockchain technology used in digital money is decentralized and does not require any central institution like a clearinghouse to process the data. Digital currency enables users to reliably control the flow of transaction funds, avoid the possibility of withdrawal of funds during the review or supervision process, and avoid the possibility of funds being stolen, abused, and converted into foreign currencies. These advantages are extremely attractive to countries that want to use digital currencies to meet their needs.[5]

Many member states of the EAEU have announced using currencies for public procurement, targeted credit, and investment. The use of digital technology in currency circulation can bypass the traditional bank information exchange system while ensuring that users better control the expenditure of target funds and ensure their safety. This method does not require bank guarantees and is not affected by bank risks, including risks caused by sanctions by third countries ("freezing" accounts, preventing transfers, disconnecting from the SWIFT system, etc.). Digital currency can enable users to significantly reduce transaction costs, lower interest rates, and raise the targeted credit necessary to carry out economic investment projects. The currency issued through digital technology will automatically flow to the final "link" of the use of credit resources: wage payment, dividend collection, and loan repayment.

The application of digital technology to use local currency for credit Issuance fundamentally differs from the issuance of private cryptocurrencies such as "Bitcoin." In the process of applying digital technology to use the domestic currency for credit issuance, the issuer is an organization authorized by the monetary authority, which controls the issuance of a "digital version" of the national currency and its exchange with ordinary currencies. The monetary authority determines the issuance amount, and the authorized issuer reserves the corresponding amount in the central bank's account. The central bank issues digital currency equivalently, conducts targeted credit investment, and expands production in activities prescribed by the state. Through this mechanism, loan interest can be reduced to a level acceptable to borrowers in the physical sector, and the existing scientific production potential can be used to increase production and promote investment. In addition, there is no need to control currency. Transactions can either use the national currency or use specially created tools. You can purchase other digital currencies by using your country's digital currency, and exchange them for ordinary credit currency and circumvent sanctions.

Interestingly, the proponents of digital currencies compare them with ordinary currencies. They usually refer to ordinary currencies as credit currencies. They indirectly emphasize that credit currencies also lack material protection. Like credit currency, the digital currency does not have any equivalent, but it has many of the above-mentioned advantages. Digital currency has all the functions of credit currency and can overcome the inherent shortcomings of credit currency. The digital currency can effectively prevent theft and robbery and reduce the insecurity caused by bank failures.

As Nobel Laureate Tobin suggested, the main objective of MP should be to create conditions that maximize investment and innovation, under the goals of socioeconomic development.[6] All developing countries follow this recommendation and use modern

---

5. On February 2, 2018, a high-level forum on "Digital Agenda in the Age of Globalization" was held on the sidelines of the EAEU Intergovernmental Council meeting. The purpose of the Forum is to promote global digitization in the Eurasian region and to strengthen partnerships in this field among participating countries. One of the key topics of discussion was national independent digitization, digitization within the framework of international organizations and partners, the regional strengths of the EAEU in this field, industrial digitization, technological entrepreneurship, and agricultural digital transformation

6. J. Tobin, "Liquidity Preference as Behaviour towards Risk." *The Review of Economic Studies*, no. 67 (February 1958).

international experience to issue currencies through multiple channels. Credit issuance in the US, the European Union, and Japan is mainly on the condition that the country issues bonds to raise funds for budget deficits, national planning, and development agencies. China, India, and other developing countries mainly issue credit to investors, and credit issuance is the main source of funds to ensure economic growth. The use of digital technology can tremendously improve the efficiency of currency issuance and circulation management, making it a reliable tool for increasing investment and production. Digital currency is most suitable for the integrated world economic paradigm because it can effectively use the country's monopoly on currency issuance to obtain credit investment to develop promising industries and other national priorities. This ensures currency circulation. Transparency fundamentally improves the quality of managing budget expenditures and controlling currency circulation. Therefore, it is not surprising that the countries forming the new world economic paradigm are planning to issue national digital currencies. For example, in 2017, China established a research group to study blockchain and big data technology. The Chinese authorities expect to develop and approve an algorithm that will enable the Central Bank of China to become the first regulatory agency in the world to issue its cryptocurrency to purchase any commodity. Similar processes have taken place in other fast-growing economies in the Asia-Pacific region, and we have listed these economies in the "core" of the new integrated world economic paradigm.

PART II

TECHNOLOGY AND MANAGEMENT CHANGE

The world is currently transitioning to an integrated world economic paradigm. China's communist system and India's democratic system have ensured that their countries' economies would not be seized by colonialists. The US's institutional system serves the financial oligarchy's interests, a parasitic product of the dollar as the world currency. By contrast, the institutional system of China, India, Japan, South Korea, Vietnam, Malaysia, Singapore, Iran, and other countries focuses on ensuring social benefits in social and economic development, aiming at coordinating the opinions of different social groups and strengthening cooperation, and establishing a partnership between enterprises and the country to achieve socially meaningful goals. The expansion of monetary capital is limited by national and international standards, which protect social interests and make the issuance of credit money subject to the regulation process of reproduction. The international law system established during the imperialist world economic paradigm is of great significance.

The modern development of productive forces requires new relations of production and the construction of a global economic system, which will guarantee sustainable development and defend the world against threats, including ecological and cosmic ones. Liberal globalization caters to the interests of multinational corporations, mainly British and American companies. In this context, there is still no solution to those problems that threaten the survival of mankind. Moreover, in the absence of democratic governance mechanisms, capital is excessively concentrated in the hands of hundreds of families. With their increase in global influence, their threat of world hegemony to ensure world oligarchy by oppressing all mankind is growing. Consequently, the risk of abusing world power is growing, and so is the risk of disaster for countries and the people of the world. The management framework of the integrated world economic paradigm must contain the world oligarchy and manage the global capital flow. With the rise of China, India, and Vietnam following Japan and South Korea, it is becoming increasingly clear that the transition to a new, integrated world economic paradigm will be accompanied by an entirely different system of institutions that serve the interests of sustainable human development. This transition needs to be achieved through a management change, which is based on digital technology. The application of digital technology can fundamentally improve the management quality of complex socioeconomic systems.

Chapter 4
Digital Transformation in Management System

Digitization, a hugely popular topic, didn't just appear today or even yesterday. People have begun to deal with numbers ever since they learn to speak and to describe the first character. In other words, the ability to speak and think distinguishes a rational man from an animal,[1] and the use of numbers has been around since ancient times. Numbers, like words, have been used for centuries to generate, transmit and store information, gradually forming a special mathematical language that has become the language of application in exact science and related technologies.

The emergence of the electronic computer is regarded as the beginning of the digital information revolution. Without human intervention, the electronic computer uses numbers to operate, receive, convert, and transmit data. Although people design programs and set tasks for computers, computers still use numbers to generate, store, and transmit new information independently. Without computers, human beings can't obtain all kinds of information independently. Computers are different from machines with automatic control systems that have been created and used by mankind since ancient times, from drainage boxes in bathrooms to modern CNC machines.

With the emergence of artificial intelligence systems, all large computers can independently design and complete tasks without manual intervention. Just as a literate child can read and write independently, modern computers can also read and generate digital information and transmit it to humans or other similar products. To communicate with humans, computers can convert numbers into sounds, words, and symbols to complete the transmission and reception of information between humans and computers. Computers can communicate information with similar products without human intervention through digital languages. Computers were originally programmed to implement certain functions or solve certain problems. In the Internet of Things or "smart home," computers can independently complete all tasks previously solved by humans and can complete tasks faster, more accurately, and more efficiently.

The first tube computer that appeared in the middle of the last century was bulky, consumed a lot of power, and required a lot of manpower to provide services. But at that time, no one might have guessed that the application range of computers would be so wide, and the number of applications would be countless. The boldest technological predictions were limited to computers in areas that required a lot of heavy computing, such as banking, the military, research, and state management. Today's computer can fit in a child's pocket, equivalent to a five-story building, ten employees, and a transformer more than half a century ago, and is now available to every family in the form of a mobile phone. Its widespread use in the fields of production, living, society, and state management has triggered the popular topic of the digital revolution.

---

1. Поршнев Б. О начале человеческой истории (Проблемы палеопсихологии). М.: Мысль, 1974.

Digital Information Revolution in the Context of Economic Paradigm Change

Now the digital revolution covers almost all fields and has drawn most people into its orbit. Since the first computer, the digital revolution has undergone three main phases. During this period, the world technological economic development has changed the technological paradigm twice.

The emergence and application of the vacuum tube computer occurred in the final stage of the third technology paradigm, the "core" of which was the electrical industry. At that time, the fourth technological paradigm was developing rapidly in the economies of developed countries, and its "core" was composed of the automobile industry, the organic synthesis industry, and new structural materials. One of the core elements is the production of semiconductors, which replaced electronic tubes in computers. Electronic tubes significantly reduced the cost of production and use of computers, expanding the scope of computer applications. But the real breakthroughs were the invention of integrated circuits and microprocessors, which laid the foundation for microelectronics in the 1960s and 1970s.

Microelectronics is a key element in the fifth technology paradigm, which has entered a stage of development since the early 1980s. The miniaturization of computers and the rapid reduction in the cost of producing and using them ensured the rapid spread of computer technology. The production automation was realized in the manufacturing industry based on the numerical control machine tool. The automated control systems are also used in technical and management processes. The emergence of the personal computer paved the way for the widespread use of computers in management, research, and consumption. The Internet and fiber-optic cables connect billions of computers to global information and communications networks.

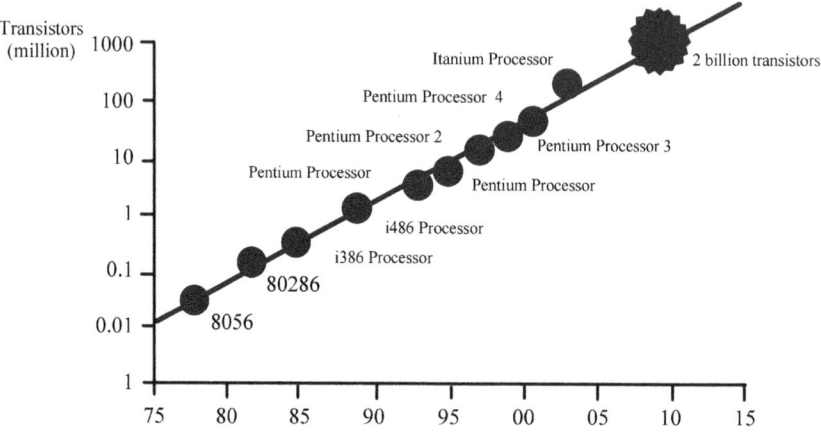

Figure 4-1 Dynamic Graph of the Growth of the Number of Transistors per Unit Area of IC

Source: Нанотехнологии как ключевой фактор нового технологического уклада в экономике / Под ред. С. Ю. Глазьева, В. В. Харитонова. М.: Тровант, 2009.

The "core" part of the fifth technology paradigm is the ICT complex, which was growing at about 25% a year until the early 2000s. Its rapid growth ensured continuous technological advances in microelectronics, where Moore's Law[2] (Figure 4-1) enabled us to reduce the cost of producing and using computers rapidly.

Computers are revolutionizing manufacturing, replacing manual labor with ubiquitous automation and industrial robots. On-board computers are widely used in the control of complex vehicles and vehicles. Mobile communications are booming, creating new, fast-growing industries in the consumer sector and dramatically improving people's quality of life.

Figure 4-2 The Dynamic Diagram of the Reduction in the Cost of Microcircuits with an Increase in Components
Source: Нанотехнологии как ключевой фактор нового технологического уклада в экономике / Под ред. С. Ю. Глазьева, В. В. Харитонова. М.: Тровант, 2009.

At the beginning of the 21 century, the development of the fifth technology paradigm was slowing down. Since 2008, the world has been affected by the financial crisis, followed by the reform of economic structure transitioning to the new sixth technology paradigm. Now, the transition process is nearing completion, and a new technology paradigm is entering a growth phase. As mentioned above, the information communication, nanoscale, bioengineering, and additive manufacturing technology

2. Gordon Moore's Law: The number of components that can be contained on an integrated circuit doubles every 18-24 months or so, and so does its performance. Based on this analysis, an assumption was made, which was subsequently confirmed, that the development of computer technology and its capabilities would increase exponentially.

complex, which is at the heart of the new technology paradigm, is expanding at a rate of about 30% per year, with its elements growing at a rate of 20% to 70% per year.

There is continuity between the fifth and sixth technological paradigms. Their key factor is information technology, based on knowledge of the basic material structure, information processing, and transmission algorithm (acquired through basic science). The boundary of the fifth and sixth technological paradigms lies in the degree of technological penetration into the material structure and the scale of information processing. The fifth technology paradigm relies on the application of microelectronics in operating systems for micron scale physical processes. The sixth technology paradigm is based on nanotechnology, which operates at billionths of a meter in size and can alter the structure of matter at the atomic and molecular level, fundamentally giving it new properties and improving it through the cellular structure of living things. Advances in nanotechnology and computer technology have allowed humans to create new structures of living and inanimate matter and grow them using self-replicating programs.

The Social and Political Components of the Digital Revolution

Clearly, the ruling elite is beginning to have a vague sense that they may eventually lose control of their citizens as the masses take over digital technology. But in fact, the spread of new technological paradigms has fundamentally changed the entire management system of global socioeconomic processes.

On the one hand, there are new opportunities to control citizens' behavior on a global scale fully. American intelligence is working aggressively in that direction, spying on millions of people around the world by listening in on phone calls and using chips built into computer technology to spy on social networks.

On the other hand, private transnational systems for managing economic, social, and political processes may arise to the detriment of States and institutions. Global social information and trade information networks, cryptocurrencies, the Internet of Things, and other anonymous transactions provide the basis for such systems, which take international financial trade out of national jurisdiction. Citizens can rely on the network to use blockchain technology and smart contracts to reject state systems to protect their interests.

National legal systems are clearly lagging behind the requirements of new technological capabilities. There is a lack of legal constraints not only on cybersecurity, e-commerce, and internet regulation, but also on biotechnology engineering, driverless vehicles, and 3D printers. Movies about out-of-control robots, modified humans, and human-robot monsters have caused public unease, businesses are luring consumers with smart homes, sound irons, and sound refrigerators, and forward-thinking architect advises the government to build a smart city …

At the same time, the informatization of management systems is still the most corrupt area, and management agencies are increasing their budgets without any obvious return. Recall that many governments have provided funds to address the YEAR 2000 pseudo-problem. Governments also force citizens to install unnecessary computer systems on their homes, cars, personal computers, and phones. Companies and government departments treat systems integrators as "cash cows," unnecessarily upgrading information technology and computer technology.

Let's try to understand the complex and realistic challenges of promoting digital technology. At the same time, let's consider the related changes in national, social, personal security, and human security.

Social Problems Brought about by the Digital Revolution

It is believed that due to job automation, management process automation, and the increasing popularity of 3D printers, the unemployment rate has risen, which poses a serious threat to social security. Although the problem is not new, nothing could be more distressing to society since the first Industrial Revolution than the Luddites who destroyed the motor movement in Britain more than two centuries ago, which still seems worrying today. Indeed, during the first large-scale automation, it can be expected that the unemployment rate of workers and employees in certain types of jobs and professions will increase significantly. But, as shown in the nearly 300 years of modern industrial development, this threat has been partially offset by other factors.

First, there is unemployment in some sectors, while others face labor shortages. During the technological paradigm change, the imbalance between supply and demand in the labor market deteriorated sharply. At this time, because the economy stopped expanding to various fields, the economy fell into a downturn, resulting in a decrease in production and investment in the main employment growth areas that guaranteed the two generations of labor. In areas with a large working population in the past, residents' income has undergone "shocks" and has fallen sharply. A large part of the residents will never be able to return to their original income levels. At the same time, the development of the new technological paradigm ensures the demand for labor in other professions. Those workers who are liberated from the old technological paradigm learn new skills and then are placed in new professions. The state can use subsidies for employee retraining programs and timely adjust the education system to meet the needs of new occupations, thereby vigorously alleviating labor market imbalances.

Second, just like the digital revolution, automation has been going on for a long time, destroying hundreds of millions of jobs across industries. Since the 1980s, production automation has covered many manufacturing industries with the development of new ICT paradigms of the time. Flexible production lines eliminate the need for millions of assemblers, packers, and machine tools. The high degree of automation in conveyor production has freed millions of people engaged in monotonous work and performing simple and repetitive operations. Advances in computer technology have eliminated millions of jobs for typists, punchers, examiners, designers, accountants, and other related jobs requiring routine calculations using established algorithms. Facts have proved that thousands of people have been replaced by automation and are in a difficult situation, but there has been no social disaster like the Great Depression. Enthusiastic young people have mastered new careers, such as programmers, operators, and debuggers, while the elderly retire early. Many people give full play to their talents in the service industry, and the rapid expansion of the service industry is one of the most obvious aspects of society's transition to a new technological paradigm. People are beginning to talk about the transition of society to the post-industrial stage of economic development. In fact, industry remains the foundation of the modern economy, and only in the labor markets of developed countries has the level of industrialization dropped to an average of 25%.

Third, for the Russian labor market, the adverse effects of economic policies will be more pronounced than the digital revolution for a long time. Russia carried out economic reforms in accordance with the IMF's plan, but it caused a sharp deterioration in the economy and destroyed an industry with millions of high-tech jobs. At the same time, contrary to global trends, Russia's production of modern technological paradigms that ensure global employment rates has fallen sharply. In the 1990s, the number of scientists, engineers, programmers, operators, debuggers, and other highly qualified employees decreased. Most of them were forced to engage in low-skilled jobs such as traders, ferry workers, and security guards. During the transition to the advanced economic development zone policy based on the new technological paradigm,[3] the Russian economy will face a severe shortage of engineering experts. The "recovery" of the Russian economy has been limited by the shortage of highly skilled workers and engineers.

In the end, the need for experts to create the digital economy's infrastructure in the future will be far greater than the number of regular jobs destroyed by the development of the digital economy. Indeed, this would be true if the digital economy were built on the nation's smart technology. If the country's policy in the field of information technology does not change and relies entirely on imports of hardware and software, it may have a significant negative impact. "White collar" workers freed from services, finance, and trade would have lost their jobs because of a lack of skills and foreign experts and equipment brought in to fill the needs of the Russian market.

So, the threat of a sharp rise in unemployment due to the digital revolution is greatly exaggerated. The threat could easily be offset by sound government economic policies. Until now, unsound economic policy, not the digital revolution, has been the main cause of the loss of millions of jobs and the decline in human capital. With the Izborsk Club's policy of advanced development zones in place,[4] the demand for highly qualified experts will far outweigh its reduced numbers. The problem is that there are large numbers of low-skilled and professionally restricted workers, and it will take a lot of effort to retrain them in order to accommodate them. Therefore, national policy is the decisive factor.

The use of digital technology in the realm of national regulation is indeed a political issue. For example, using blockchain technology, it will be impossible to falsify registration documents and licenses, and it will not be possible to "backdate"

3. Глазьев С. Стратегия опережающего развития России в условиях глобального кризиса. М.: Экономика, 2010.

4. К стратегии социальной справедливости и развития / Авторский доклад С. Глазьева Изборскому клубу. 2015 (3 августа); Встать в полный рост / Доклад Изборскому клубу / Под ред. С. Батчикова, А. Кобякова, С. Глазьева. 2014 (23 ноября).

a review certificate. The technology also eliminates a certain amount of unnecessary and expensive notary services. Smart contracts will eliminate corruption in state procurement. Forgery can be avoided by using electronic signatures and accurately identifying print and electronic media. The entire government system will become more transparent and open to public scrutiny. There will be less government corruption and less demand for supervisory officials. Perhaps this is why why developing national management systems has been so difficult, with so much money wasted on inefficient and repetitive routines.

The Challenge of the Digital Revolution to the Future of Mankind

Finally, let's address the last threat to humanity from the digital revolution. What excites me most is the imagination of sci-fi and dystopian screenwriters. Modern science has moved in the direction of technology that changes the nature of humanity, and there is a real risk that the digital revolution poses a threat to humanity. We will analyze them one by one according to the actual situation.

1. Using genetic engineering to create microorganisms that are harmful to humans. Genetic engineering has a long history, and national security agencies have clearly underestimated it. More than two decades ago, scientists acknowledged that genetic technology could be used to create viruses with selective functions that would target only people with certain biological characteristics. By combining the DNA of viruses that are human symbiotic with pathogens, viruses that cause disease in people of a particular sex, age, or even ethnicity can be synthesized. The transport of these viruses into the territory of an enemy country through food exports can then cause infectious diseases and spread widely in that country. In this sense, biological weapons are a double-edged sword. Obviously, research by American laboratories violates the rules prohibiting the development of biological weapons. In any case, some African leaders believe Washington is guilty of creating and spreading Ebola.

2. Clones with certain properties. Scientists have been discussing the threat of cloning humans since more than a decade ago, when experiments proved the practical possibility of cloning mammals and issued a power of attorney for cloning higher primates and humans. Now that the cloned dog industry has begun to commercialize, human cloning factories are theoretically possible.

3. Various computer-controlled devices have been implanted into human bodies. This is already a developed medical technology, with pacemakers, hearing AIDS, prostheses, and sensors widely used in the medical field. In theory, it is possible to transform people by giving them extra computing power to improve their senses, individual recognition, information transmission, and behavior.

4. Installing human organs and models in the robot equipment. This is the same as the fantasy in Belyayev's novel *Professor Dowell's Head*, in which professor Dowell's head remains alive after his death. The development of the human nervous system model is in full swing, and artificial intelligence robots with a human appearance will likely appear.

5. Loss of control over the bionic self-organizing robot system. In theory, the nightmare of a robot rebellion could become a reality shortly. Breakdowns in automated power systems have thrown big cities into chaos. If AI systems could organize themselves and make independent decisions, the consequences would be unpredictable.

All of the above threats to human existence are well known and have been discussed many times, but no real plan has been implemented to prevent them. Obviously, it is not realistic to stop scientific and technological progress, even with dangerous consequences for human beings, but it can be limited within the legal framework. To work well, these restrictions must be international and cover all countries with great scientific and technological potential.

The experience of concluding international treaties on the non-proliferation of missile and nuclear technology, on the prohibition of bacteriological and chemical weapons, and atomic weapons tests is encouraging. Although these treaties have no accountability mechanism for enforcement, most of the world does not normally violate them. The scope of such agreements will expand as countries move towards an integrated world economic paradigm based on mutual benefit, voluntary partnership, and strict compliance with international law.[5]

It also includes international treaties restricting countries from developing dangerous areas of digital technology. It provides that:

- Human cloning is prohibited;
- Development of viruses and other forms of biological weapons is prohibited;
- Implementing international standards for human device implantation;
- Monitoring the development of artificial intelligence systems to identify and eliminate threats to humanity;
- Experts trained in the field of information technology need to be globally certified;
- Internationally applicable technical regulations and procedures for the certification of intelligent robots shall be developed and implemented.

Russia can formulate and adopt an international convention on scientific ethics, which prohibits countries from researching in the fields of changing the nature of human beings, biological weapons, and programming to destroy bionic self-organizing robotic systems.

The digital revolution is far beyond people's imagination. It is a long process that has been developing for decades. Almost all information and financial fields are using digital technology. Digital technology has also become an important part of social production and permeates the life and business fields. The digital revolution has created opportunities and improved people's quality of life without much disruption to society. Numerous cases of using digital technology for anti-humanitarian and criminal purposes are related to human behavior, not to such technologies. At the same time,

---

5. Глазьев С. Экономика будущего. Есть ли у России шанс? М.: Книжный мир, 2017.

monopolizing digital technology under the pretext of private or state interests greatly increases the opportunities for these individuals to commit crimes and may threaten national security. These voices of the people should be addressed by law.

Harnessing the Power of the Digital Revolution in the Shifting Paradigm of the World Economy

Another problem involves the qualitative "leap" in human evolution. The digital revolution has greatly improved the ability to generate, process, transfer, store, and hold information. Computers will not forget anything, and the dissemination of information will not cost any money. Human beings can program any complex algorithm for everyday human activity and transmit it to a robot to perform it. The digital revolution has freed humans from drudgery and fatigue, not just manual labor, but boring office work. The digital revolution has freed up time previously spent making goods and services and opened up a new world of transition to fully creative activities. This is to the realm of freedom, exactly what the classic Marxist-Leninist writers dreamed of communism's "leap" from the realm of necessity.

Ironically, the digital revolution, which is unfolding in the wake of the collapse of the world's socialist system, can bring a qualitative "leap" to the effectiveness of national economic planning systems and a huge competitive advantage over capitalist countries. In the Soviet Union, STP could improve the welfare of citizens and extend free time in the human life cycle. In the postwar period, the amount of free time for people continued to increase with the development of the entertainment field. Although many residents drank in their leisure time, communist ideology dictated that citizens fill that time with personal self-improvement, creative work, education, and participation in social work, including state administration. So, it is no accident that the Soviet Union had the highest reading rate and the best mass education system in the world.

The CPC attaches great importance to the application of digital technology in the management of economic development. The Central Committee of the CPC, in the "14th Five-Year Plan Proposals," clearly put forward "Accelerating digitalization-based development. We will develop the digital economy, promote digital industrialization and industrial digitalization, promote the deep integration of digital and real economies, and create internationally competitive digital industry clusters. We will strengthen the construction of a digital society and digital government and raise the digitalization and intelligentization levels of public services, social governance, etc. For digital resources, we will establish basic property rights systems, trading and circulation, cross-border transmission, security, protection, etc. We will expand the orderly opening up of basic public information and data, construct national open platforms for unified data sharing, safeguard national data security and strengthen the protection of personal data, improve the digital skills of the whole people, and achieve full coverage of information services. We will actively participate in setting international rules and standards for digital fields."

For the capitalist system, in which companies maximize profits at all costs, the digital revolution poses unsolvable problems. On the one hand, the increase in labor productivity increases surplus value. On the other hand, freeing labor for productive activities means a corresponding reduction in demand, which limits the growth of production and the expanded reproduction of capital. Inequality is rising, and society is "splitting" between those who master key digital technologies and consumers who do not engage in productive activities. The entertainment industry strives to fill their leisure time, while actors, drug dealers, and publicists all make efforts. The information revolution has led to endless financial "bubbles" and pyramids as capital has poured into the financial sector, and society has gradually transited to unmanned production technologies.

The digital revolution has destroyed the usual rules of business. In the traditional sector, the more resources consumed, the higher the product price, but in the digital economy, the opposite is true: the more data you accumulate, the lower the cost of production. Neither the law of value nor marginal utility theory work in the digital economy. The accumulation of data can generate new data while reducing the cost of receiving other information. There is no material basis for the market valuation of Internet companies. As the scope of activities and market coverage expands, the marginal utility of investment increases rather than decreases as it does in the field of material production. The information revolution in the internet economy and finance makes the real sector a contributor.

The US-centric global economic paradigm is unraveling, and in the process, the digital revolution is creating more problems than opportunities for socioeconomic development. Even as the West "pulls" its economy with credit money, the lion's share of its money issuance is still "absorbed" by the financial sector, while the productive investment sector stagnates. The institutional systems of the US, UK, and other capitalist countries are centered on the interests of the digital economy's giants, rather than trying to mitigate the imbalances and eliminate the threats posed by the expansion of the digital economy. These problems hinder the productive use of new technologies and indicate that the existing world economic paradigm is not in line with the potential and needs of productivity development. This problem can be overcome by transitioning to a new world economic paradigm.

Chapter 5

From Empire to World Integration Economic Paradigm

As mentioned above, the growth potential exhaustion of the dominant technology paradigm has led to global crises and economic depressions that have swept the world's major countries in recent years. The world is currently in the "birth" stage of a new technological paradigm, with its economic performance characterized by financial turmoil. Accompanied by the formation and collapse of financial "bubbles," and economic depression, it is characterized by a drop in profit rate, output, income, and prices in traditional industries such as basic energy and structural materials. Only in the initial stage of the scientific research and production cycle can new technologies be rapidly popularized.[1]

The epicenter of the crisis process lies at the heart of the current world economic paradigm: the US financial system. The first "shock" of the global financial crisis hit major US institutions and the world's largest investment banks, the Lehman Brothers, JPMorgan Chase & Co., Bear Stearns Co., Deutsche Bank AG, Credit Agricole, Barclays, Credit Suisse ag, and BNP Paribas. Then the state institutions that guarantee the reproduction of capital, namely the insurance and mortgage institutions, collapsed. Although the US financial system survived thanks to a sharp increase in money issuance, imbalances have continued to grow since then, with the US National Debt surging to $21 trillion and derivatives of the financial "bubble" continuing to grow (Figure 5-1).

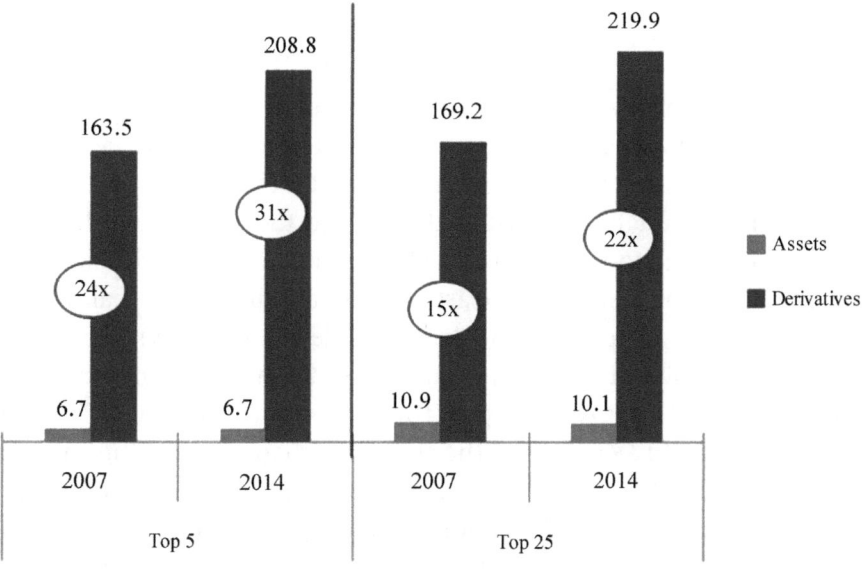

Figure 5-1 The Number of Derivatives, Assets (in Trillion Dollars), and Ratio (Times) of the Largest Financial Holding Companies in the US (Top 5 and Top 25), Namely Financial Derivatives Holders
Source: М.Ершов по данным Office of the Comptroller of the Currency. — Эксперт. — 2015, №36.

---

1. Глазьев С. О политике развития российской экономики / Доклад. М.: . 2013.

The increase in the issuance of US dollars has coincided with the rise in the number of US Treasury bonds and derivatives, suggesting that the dollar operates in a financial pyramid pattern, with short-term liabilities being paid back by issuing dollars. When the system loses stability and becomes vulnerable to external and internal "shocks," this mode worsens. All this proves that, within the framework of the imperialist world economic paradigm, the expansion of the capital accumulation cycle in the US has reached its limit, and the potential for economic development has also disappeared. Understanding this, the American ruling elites seized on the traditional "straws." To eliminate these threats, they embarked on the path of destabilizing and destabilizing the creditor countries, which were in chaos so that much of the US debt could be written off and the assets of the creditor countries could be expropriated.

In theory, the US can return to sustainable growth if the growth of the new technology paradigm is strong enough to generate income streams that offset the accumulated debt. However, the economic, financial, social, and technological development of the US is seriously unbalanced, and the institutional system that guarantees capital reproduction within the framework of the existing world economic paradigm is unlikely to return the US to a sustainable growth path.

The way out of the current slump will inevitably require massive geopolitical and economic changes. As before, "champion" countries cannot make fundamental institutional innovations, which can channel the funds released into restructuring the economic structure based on the new technological paradigm. The existing institutional system can continue to promote reproduction and truly serve the economic interests.

As mentioned above, the global economic structure is transitioning to a new technology paradigm based on nanotechnology, bioengineering, bioinformatics, information, and communication technologies. Soon, advanced countries will enter the "long wave" phase of their economic growth. The decline in oil prices marks the completion of the "birth" stage of the new technological paradigm. The rapid popularization of new technologies greatly improves resource utilization efficiency and reduces production energy consumption, making the new economic paradigm enter the stage of exponential growth. During a global technological paradigm shift, developing countries could make an economic "breakthrough" that brings them up to the level of developed countries, which are stuck investing too much in outdated production and technology complexes.

Today, China and the rest of Southeast Asia are making such breakthroughs. Over the past three decades, China has made remarkable achievements. China has vaulted from the edge of the world economic stage to leadership, ranking first in GDP and high-tech exports in 2014. Over the past three decades, China's GDP has grown 30-fold (from $300 billion to $9 trillion at the current exchange rate of the yuan against the dollar), its industrial output 40–50 times, and its foreign exchange reserves hundreds of times (from tens of billions to $4 trillion). In terms of economic development, China has moved from the list of the poorest countries to the top 30 high-income countries (middle income) based on per capita GDP.[2]

---

2. Перспективы и стратегические приоритеты восхождения БРИКС / Под. ред. В. Садовничего, Ю. Яковца, А. Акаева. М.: МГУ - Международный институт Питирима Сорокина-Николая Кондратьева - ИНЭС - Национальный комитет по исследованию БРИКС - Институт Латинской Америки РАН, 2014.

China is becoming a global engineering hub. In 2007, China accounted for 20% of the world's engineering and research workers, doubling from 1.42 million in 2007 to 690,000 in 2000. It is predicted that by 2030, there will be 15 million engineering, technical, and scientific workers in the world, of which 4.5 million (30%) will come from China.[3] By 2030, China's investment in S&T research and development will be the largest in the world, accounting for 25% of the global total.[4] Among the big countries, India, like China, is growing fast. Before the global financial crisis, Russia and Brazil were growing fast. The emergence of the BRICS on this basis reflects their shared interest in reforming the global monetary and financial system.

Since the emergence of the BRICS (Brazil, Russia, India, China, and South Africa) in 2001, their GDP has more than tripled and now accounts for 1/3 of the world's total. With the inclusion of the Republic of South Africa, the BRICS account for 29% of the land area (excluding Antarctica) and almost 43% of the world's population. In terms of purchasing power parity, BRICS account for 27% of the world's GDP. In 2012, BRICS contributed more than 47% to world economic growth.

The BRICS countries produce 1/4 of the world's high-tech goods and are expected to increase their share to 1/3 by 2020.[5] BRICS' spending on S&D is expanding and already accounts for nearly 30% of global spending. The economies of Brazil and Russia have stagnated because of the adoption of IMF advice. Still, thanks to the continued rapid rise of China and India, countries interested in transitioning to a new world economic paradigm have provided enough scientific and productive technology to enable technological "breakthroughs."

As the "core" of the capital accumulation cycle in Asia grows rapidly, the pace of growth in the "core" of the capital accumulation cycle in the US slows down, and the process is sustainable in the future. Table 5-1 only partially reflects this process, with the five Indochina countries (Thailand, Myanmar, Cambodia, Laos, and Vietnam), Iran, and Pakistan already joining the "core" of the Asian capital accumulation cycle, and the EAEU, Japan, and South Korea likely to join in the future.

Unlike the existing world economic paradigm, which focuses on the international financial and economic system as the basis for liberal globalization, the new world economic paradigm has a very diverse core. It is also reflected in the common values of BRICS countries, namely the free choice of development path, the denial of hegemony, and respect for the sovereignty of historical and cultural traditions. In other words, the BRICS represent a new model of cooperation that, as opposed to the unity of liberal globalization, respects diversity and is equally acceptable to countries at different stages of economic and social development.

---

3. Hu Angang, Yan Yilong, and Wei Xing, *2030 China: Towards Common Prosperity* (Beijing: Renmin University of China Press, 2011), 30.

4. Перспективы и стратегические приоритеты восхождения БРИКС / Под. ред. В. Садовничего, Ю. Яковца, А. Акаева. М.: МГУ – Международный институт Питирима Сорокина-Николая Кондратьева – ИНЭС – Национальный комитет по исследованию БРИКС – Институт Латинской Америки РАН, 2014.

5. Стокгольмский международный институт исследования проблем мира (СИПРИ), 2013.

LEAPING INTO THE FUTURE

Table 5-1 Comparison of Core GDP over Capital Accumulation Cycles in the US and Asia[6]

	1913	1950	1973	2000	2010	2020	2030
US and Euro	54.7	54.4	49.2	43.4	36.5	32.4	18.2
China and India	16.3	8.8	7.7	17.0	28.7	41.1	52.0
Japan	2.6	3.0	7.8	7.2	5.4	4.4	3.2
Russia	8.5	9.6	9.4	2.1	2.4	2.7	3.0

Key elements of BRICS cooperation:

- The shared desire of BRICS partners is to reform outdated international financial and economic systems that do not take into account the growing economic power of the emerging market and developing economies;[7]
- BRICS countries firmly support the unification of universally recognized principles and norms of international law and will not accept policies that impose military pressure and violate the sovereignty of other countries
- BRICS countries all face similar challenges and issues, namely the need for a large-scale modernization of economic and social life;
- Complementarity of BRICS economic sectors.[8]

The historic mission of BRICS countries as a community of civilizations is to propose a new paradigm for meeting the needs of sustainable development, considering ecological, demographic, and social limits of development, and preventing economic conflicts.[9] The BRICS shared principles of international organization are fundamentally different from the world economic paradigm shaped under Western European civilization, says Mr. Huntington: "The west won the world not through superiority of its ideas, values or religion, which few other civilizations converted to, but through superiority in organized violence. Westerners often forget this fact, but

---

6. GDP data are obtained using a purchasing power parity (PPS) measure. Data from 1820 to 2000 by A. Madison's. 2010-2030 data based on Madison's data by Chinese scientists. A. Maddison, The World Economy: Historical Statistics (Paris: OECD, 1995).

7. This reform may involve the establishment of a BRICS joint payment system while considering the BRICS payment system plans; Establishing the Joint Multilateral Investment Guarantee Agency; Development of international standards for ratings and the activities of rating agencies; Forming its own global payments system; Harmonize rules of action for national monetary authorities.

8. Please refer to "Vision for the Russian Federation's Participation in BRICS," approved by Russian President Vladimir Putin on 21 March, 2013.

9. Перспективы и стратегические приоритеты восхождения БРИКС / Под. ред. В. Садовничего, Ю. Яковца, А. Акаева. М.: МГУ – Международный институт Питирима Сорокина-Николая Кондратьева – ИНЭС – Национальный комитет по исследованию БРИКС – Институт Латинской Америки РАН, 2014.

non-Westerners never forget it."[10]

The BRICS countries have established a new world economic paradigm based on equality, mutual benefit, and consensus. These principles have led to the creation of regional economic organizations such as the Shanghai Cooperation Organization, the EAEU, Mercosur, and the CHINA-ASEAN Free Trade Area, as well as financial institutions such as the BRICS Development Bank and the BRICS Foreign Exchange Reserve Pool. The new world economic paradigm is different from the liberal ideas of globalization today: The former is based on respect for the interests of the state, admitting to national limits on any foreign economic activities of the sovereign rights, following the principle of mutual benefit, and the principle of voluntary and international cooperation principle of common interests; while the latter only considers the interests of big capital dominated by US-centred multinationals. The free movement of capital, goods, services, and people should not be achieved by breaking down borders and destroying national institutions. Instead, the national interests of participating countries should be combined with institutional support for national development based on mutual and mutually beneficial investment. This will be the guiding principle for forming a new system of world economic relations. To use the terminology of John Perkins,[11] the new system of world economic relations was built not by economic killers but by experts who planned complex webs of creative cooperation. Economic killers represent the benefits of large multinational capital colonizing peripheral countries. These experts, on the other hand, combine national competitive advantages to achieve synergies when implementing joint investment projects. Thus, using Sorokin's definition, we call this new world economic structure an "integrated system."

China is a model for Russia in choosing its economic development strategy. China is the largest neighbor and leader in establishing the new world economic paradigm and creatively applying the experience shared by China and Russia in building socialism.

---

10. Huntington. *The Clash of Civilizations and the Remaking of World Order*, 1996, one of the most popular geopolitical works of the 1990s. An article from the journal Foreign Affairs redefines the political realities of the entire planet's civilization and the predictions for global development. The publication includes Fukuyama's famous book, *The End of History*.

11. Перкинс Д. Исповедь экономического убийцы. М.: Претекст, 2005.

Chapter 6

China as the Center of the New World Economic Paradigm

The current global economic structure is transforming with technologial and world economic paradigm changes. China has become one of the leaders in the global economy, and the American ruling elite has upgraded global "hybrid war" to maintain the US hegemony. A new world order will be established in the struggle against these development trends. The outcome of the struggle will largely depend on the cooperation between China and Russia in building a greater Eurasian partnership, as both countries are seeking a peaceful transition to a new world economic paradigm.

New World Economic Paradigm in China's Economic Development Management System

Fully stimulating the vitality of investment and innovation is the key to the entire Chinese economic regulation system. The state economy plays an important role in the economic regulation system. The state economy mainly consists of the following aspects: the state banking system, which grants loans in accordance with guiding plans for investment and production growth; transport and energy infrastructure, to which national planning gives great importance; state-owned enterprises, concentrating their resources on scientific economic development, S&D and application of advanced technology. As John Ross has pointed out, government investment drives China's economy. Because of the guiding role of government investment, the risk of entrepreneurs investing is reduced, and the entrepreneurs also have access to the national infrastructure. Thus, as government investment grows, so does private investment. In addition, when private investment activity decreases, the state will adopt counter-cyclical policies to increase investment.[1]

Continuously increasing investment in promising areas of economic development can ensure the leap-forward growth of China's economy (Figure 6-1). Special loans are the main source of investment funds in economic development prospects. The government's policy of attracting foreign direct investment has played a decisive role in developing advanced technology and international cooperative production. In the future, as production increases, so will national income and savings, creating a flow of credit for new investments. At the same time, governmental, provincial, municipal, and enterprise guidance plans will clarify their investment needs for modernization and production expansion. The People's Bank of China will continue to increase credit supply through state-owned banks and development institutions based on specific investment needs. The financial investment platform created for this purpose, while reducing investment risks, can also ensure that the People's Bank of China provides

---

1. Росс Дж. Китай и новый период в мировой экономике // Экономические стратегии. 2017. №4. С. 40–53.

credit to promising industries according to national priorities.

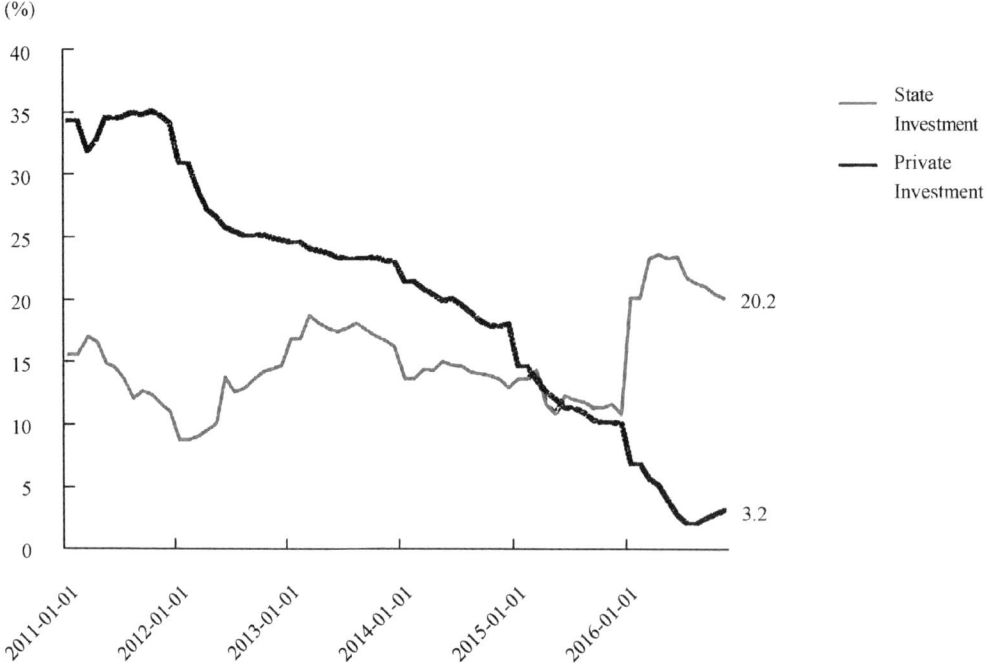

Figure 6-1 China's State Investment and Private Investment from 2011 to 2016
Source: Data from China Europe International Business School and National Bureau of Statistics of China, 2016.

The Leadership of the CPC has avoided ideological rigidity while continuing to build socialism. They prefer to formulate tasks related to "people's well-being" to eradicate poverty, build a moderately prosperous society, and raise people's living standards to world leaders. China's Communist party leadership tries to avoid excessive social inequality, ensuring that income is distributed according to work, economic regulation is geared toward productive activities, and long-term investment is geared toward developing productive forces.

When summarizing the completion of the 13th Five-Year Plan, the Central Committee of the CPC pointed out: "In the 14th Five-Year plan period, growth in people's incomes will basically be in sync with economic growth, and the distribution structure will be significantly improved. There will be a significant increase in equitable access to basic public services. The education level of the whole nation will rise continuously, the multi-level social security system will be more robust, and the health system will be improved. The results of the poverty alleviation campaign will be consolidated and expanded."

The CPC Central Committee's Proposals for formulating the 14th Five-Year Plan stressed the need to "Raise the people's income level. We'll: Adhere to distribution according to work as the main form, with multiple modes of distribution coexisting; increase the share of labor compensation in the primary distribution of income; refine the wage system, improve mechanisms for the reasonable growth of wages, strive to increase the income of low-income groups, and expand the middle-income group; refine the policy regime for distribution according to factors, improve mechanisms for market determination of compensation for factors of production, and explore increasing factor income in the incomes of low and medium-income groups by means of use rights and usufruct rights to land, capital and other factors; through multiple channels, increase the property income of rural and urban residents; refine redistribution mechanisms, increase the strength and accuracy of adjustment measures such as taxation, social security, and transfer payments, reasonably adjust excessively high incomes, and crack down on illegal income. We will fully utilize the role of tertiary distribution, develop charitable undertakings, and improve the distribution of income and wealth."

Against the backdrop of woefully underpaid modern Russia, workers produce three times as much per unit of pay as in the European Union. The Chinese government has been quite effective in adjusting income distribution in favor of workers, limiting the appetite of capitalists to reasonable standards. So, it's no surprise that average wages in China surpass those in Russia and all Soviet Union member states. And this was achieved without the labor shortage traditionally assumed by market theorists. At the same time, the Chinese government is implementing policies to reduce unemployment and increase employment.

The *Proposals* also put forward the following tasks: "Strengthening pro-employment policies. We should make every effort to stabilize and expand employment and adhere to an economic development-based employment orientation. We must enlarge employment capacity, raise employment quality, promote full employment, and safeguard the workers' treatment, rights, and interests. We will improve the employment public services system, labor relations coordination mechanism, and lifelong learning support and training system. We will place greater emphasis on relieving structural employment conflicts, accelerate the improvement of workers' skills and quality, refine the employment support systems for key groups, and comprehensively plan out the policy regime for rural and urban employment. We will also expand placement in public welfare jobs and help people with disabilities and members of zero-employment families find employment; refine systems that create jobs by encouraging entrepreneurship and offering multi-channel, flexible employment safeguards; support and regulate the development of new employment types; improve employment demand surveys and mechanisms for unemployment monitoring and early warning."

This is a common feature of the "core" countries in building the new world economic paradigm.

The rise of China has brought about changes in the world economic order and international relations. The "menu" of economic and social development planning, such as state regulation of the main parameters of capital reproduction, active industrial policy, cross-border capital flow regulation, and foreign exchange control, is restricted by financial institutions in Washington, DC and has become a common means of regulating international economic relations. Many scholars argue that the Beijing Consensus is more attractive to developing countries with large populations than the Washington Consensus. The Beijing Consensus is based on the principles of non-discrimination and mutual respect for the sovereignty and interests of cooperating countries. These principles are not designed to serve international capital, but to enhance the well-being of the people. At the same time, there could be new intellectual property protection and technology transfer regimes, new international trade standards in energy and resources, new international migration rules, and new treaties to limit harmful gas emissions. China's position in international political relations (refusal to interfere in internal affairs, opposition to the integration of armed forces and trade embargo) provides a viable option for developing countries, that is, to establish equal and mutually beneficial cooperative relations with other countries.[2] China firmly opposes the use of force, sanctions, and other means in foreign policy. In terms of relations with Taiwan, the mainland has always prioritized the expansion of cross-Straits economic and cultural exchanges and cooperation even though the Taiwan authorities have resisted them.[3]

Unlike the post-Soviet Union, China's market economy advocates pragmatism and innovative reforms. The construction of the market economy in China is based on the practice of economic management rather than ideological dogmatism, which is disconnected from the actual process of social economy. Just as engineers design new machines, China's leaders constantly improve new relations of production by solving specific problems, experimenting, and sifting for better solutions. China's leaders have worked patiently, step by step, to build their own socialist market economy, gradually perfecting the state's management system and selecting institutions dedicated to economic growth and social welfare. While maintaining the achievements of socialism, the CPC has incorporated the regulation of market relations into the state management system and added the private and collective economy to the country's basic economic system, so as to improve economic performance and benefit the whole people.

The state opens up infrastructure and natural monopoly services to enterprises at low prices, and enterprises are responsible for producing competitive products. To improve product quality, the state organizes and funds the necessary scientific research, experimental design, education, and personnel training, while entrepreneurs implement innovation and invest in new technological areas. The cooperation model between government and social capital is more in line with social interests, and can promote economic development and improve people's well-being and quality of life. Accordingly, the ideology of international cooperation has changed—the sustainable development model aimed at the benefit of all humanity has replaced the liberal globalization model aimed at the private capital interests of the world's leading countries.

In this regard, the *Proposals* is quite clear: "Promoting high-quality 'Belt and Road' development. We will: Adhere to the principle of extensive negotiation, joint construction and sharing of benefits; uphold the "green, open, and clean" philosophy, deepen pragmatic collaboration, strengthen safety and security measures, and foster common development; promote interconnectivity and interoperability of infrastructure, and third-party market cooperation; build a win-win production

---

2. J. Ramo, *The Beijing Consensus* (London: The Foreign Policy Centre, 2004).

3. Беседа В. Попова с П. Дуткевичем. 22 идеи о том, как устроить мир (беседы с выдающимися учеными). М.: Издательство Московского университета, 2014. С. 470 - 471.

chain and supply chain cooperation system, deepen international cooperation on production capacity, and expand two-way trade and investment; adhere to a market orientation in which enterprises are the mainstay, follow international practices and debt sustainability principles, and improve the diversified investment and financing system; promote the alignment of strategies, plans and mechanisms, and strengthen the linking together of policies, regulations and standards; deepen cooperation on public health, the digital economy, green development, and S&T education, and promote people-to-people exchanges."

For the new world economic paradigm, the structure of the economic regulation system should follow the principle that public interest is higher than personal interest. First, the state monitors the main parameters of capital reproduction through the planning mechanism, credit mechanism, subsidy mechanism, price mechanism, and enterprise operation mechanism. In such cases, the state is not so much a policymaker as a regulator, establishing mechanisms for social cooperation among major social groups. Instead of trying to lead entrepreneurs, officials are organizing the business, scientific, and engineering communities to work together to set common development goals and study ways to implement them. Likewise, the maximization of profits and wealth by entrepreneurs should be premised on the moral principles of safeguarding the interests of society. The enterprise activity mechanism should be aimed at achieving significant social results rather than maximizing profits. It should be expanded to establish and develop non-profit organizations, development agencies, and Islamic and Orthodox banks. The management of currency circulation should consider ethical standards and restrict illegal and unethical activities, and on this basis, establish a national economic control mechanism.

As a complete economic complex, enterprises that gather manpower, knowledge, equipment, raw materials, and fixed and flowing capital in expanding reproduction occupy the central position of economic development governance goals. No matter what form of ownership, enterprises that produce products needed by society and have good economic benefits can obtain government support. In this regard, the *Proposals* of the CPC Central Committee has described as follows:

> "Stimulating the vitality of various market entities. We will be unswerving in consolidating and developing the economy's public sector, and in encouraging, supporting, and leading the development of the non-public sector. We will deepen the reform of state-owned capital and enterprises and strengthen, optimize, and enlarge state-owned capital and enterprises (SOEs). We will accelerate the layout optimization and structural adjustment of the state-owned economy and utilize the strategic supporting role played by the state-owned economy. We will accelerate the refinement of the modern enterprise system with Chinese characteristics and deepen the mixed ownership reform of SOEs; improve the system of regulating state-owned assets primarily through capital management and deepen reform of state capital investment and operation companies; and promote marketization-based reform of competitive segments in the energy, rail, telecommunications, public utility, and other industries.

We will optimize the environment for private sector development, build cordial and clean relationships between government and business, and promote the healthy development of the non-publicly owned sector and the healthy growth of non-publicly owned sector individuals. We will also provide equal protection under the law to the property rights of private enterprises and the interests of entrepreneurs, break down various barriers constraining the development of private enterprises, and refine the legal environment and policy regime for facilitating the development of micro, small and medium enterprises, and sole proprietorships. We will promote the entrepreneurial spirit and accelerate the construction of world-class enterprises."

The Advantages of an Integrated World Economic Paradigm

The Chinese government continues to refer to China as a developing country humbly. Judging by the economic growth rate, China is indeed a developing country, but in terms of economic potential, China has reached the level of advanced countries in the world. In terms of the structure of production relations, China has become a model for many developing countries that want to replicate China's economic miracle and move closer to the "core" of the new world economic paradigm. The relations of production and social and political relations formed in China should not be regarded as transitional but as the most advanced social and economic system in the 21st century, i.e., the integrated world economic paradigm.

As early as 1964, Sorokin, a famous Russian thinker living in the US, foresaw this historic turning point and defined the main difference between the new and the old eras. The new era's dominant type of society and culture may be neither capitalism nor communism, but a unique type, which we call an integrated type. This type of order and way of life would be somewhere between communism and capitalism. This new genre absorbed many of the positive values of communism and capitalism while avoiding the fatal shortcomings of both. Moreover, the emerging type of integration may not be a simple compromise or fusion of the typical characteristics of communist and capitalist types, but an integrated system that combines the cultural values and social systems of the two, and is fundamentally different from capitalist and communist types."[4]

In essence, the system of production relations, institutions, and management methods established in modern China is an integrated framework. It has absorbed the Soviet socialist positive values (economic focus on meaningful goals, giving workers decent work, scientific and standardized management of the development of social infrastructure, MP subject to the task of manufacturing investment and financing) and those of American capitalism (entrepreneurial freedom, stimulating innovation, market competition conforming to the interests of the consumer). And there are no drawbacks, such as the chronic resource shortages inherent in command-planned economies and the recurrent overproduction crises peculiar to capitalist economies.

An example is an already quoted speech by Xi Jinping, General Secretary of the

---

4. Сорокин П. Указ. соч. С. 350.

CPC Central Committee, at a symposium with experts and scholars. He emphasized at the symposium, "We must give full play to the significant advantages of our country's socialist system in concentrating forces on major tasks and fighting for the key core technologies. Relying on our country's ultra-large-scale market and complete industrial system, we must create unique advantages that are conducive to the rapid and large-scale application of new technologies and iterative upgrades, accelerate the transformation of scientific and technological achievements into actual productivity, improve the level of the industrial chain, and maintain the safety of the industrial chain. It is necessary to give play to the main role of enterprises in technological innovation, make them a new force in the integration of innovative elements and the transformation of scientific and technological achievements, and create an innovation system that closely integrates technology, education, industry, and finance. Basic research is the source of innovation. We must increase investment and encourage long-term persistence and bold exploration so as to lay a solid foundation for building a strong S&T country. It is necessary to vigorously cultivate and introduce world-class talents and scientific research teams, increase the reform of scientific research units, maximize the enthusiasm of scientific research personnel, and improve the efficiency of scientific and technological output. We must persist in openness and innovation and strengthen international scientific and technological exchanges and cooperation."[5]

This orientation, which integrates all the effective mechanisms of social and economic development governance under various basic conditions, proves that its existence is the essence of the best government economic regulation design system in contemporary China. This can be proved by previous management experience. The first is the pragmatic line of Deng Xiaoping, who famously said: "It doesn't matter whether it is a yellow cat or a black cat, as long as it catches mice."

To eliminate the original and superficial interpretation of the CPC's economic management model transition, we might as well quote the report to the 18th National Congress of the CPC on building a moderately prosperous society: "Fresh progress has been made in social development. Basic public services have improved markedly, and access to them has become much more equitable. Education has developed rapidly, and free compulsory education is now available in all urban and rural areas. Marked progress has been made in developing the social security system; the basic old-age insurance system covering both the urban and rural population has been fully established, and a new type of social assistance system is taking shape. The whole population is now basically covered by medical insurance; the basic urban and rural healthcare systems are taking shape. Construction of low-income housing has been accelerated. We have strengthened and made innovations in social management and maintained social harmony and stability."

The report of the 18th National Congress of the CPC starts from the socialist ideological system. It summarizes the important achievements of the previous stage: "People's living standards have been significantly improved. Efforts to improve the people's well-being have been intensified; urban and rural employment has

5. Xi Jinping, "Speech at a Symposium of Experts in Economic and Social Fields," *People's Daily*, August 24, 2020.

continued to increase; individual income has increased rapidly; household assets have grown steadily; people's need for daily necessities such as clothing, food, housing, and transportation is better met; subsistence allowances for both urban and rural residents and the rural poverty line have been raised by a big margin; basic pensions for enterprise retirees have increased continually." The report's criticism of the accumulated problems in society, and the tasks it sets for party members to solve them, are more socialist in spirit. "On the other hand, we must be keenly aware that there is still much room for improvement in our work, and there are a lot of difficulties and problems on our road ahead. They include the following: unbalanced, uncoordinated, and unsustainable development remains a big problem. The capacity for scientific and technological innovation is weak. The industrial structure is unbalanced. Agricultural infrastructure remains weak. Resource and environmental constraints have become more serious. Many systemic barriers stand in the way of promoting development scientifically. The tasks of deepening reform and opening and changing the growth model remain arduous. The development gap between urban and rural areas and between regions is still large, and so are income disparities. Social problems have increased markedly. Many problems affect people's immediate interests in education, employment, social security, healthcare, housing, the ecological environment, food and drug safety, workplace safety, public security, law enforcement, administration of justice, etc. Some people still lead hard lives. There is a lack of ethics and integrity in some fields of endeavor. Some officials are not competent to pursue development scientifically. Some community-level Party organizations are weak and lax. A few Party members and officials waver in the Party's ideal and conviction and are not fully aware of its purpose. Going through formalities and bureaucratism, as well as extravagance and waste, are serious problems. Some sectors are prone to corruption and other misconduct, and the fight against corruption remains a serious challenge for us. We must take these difficulties and problems very seriously and work harder to resolve them." The report pointed out in summary: "Looking back at China's eventful modern history and looking to the promising future of the Chinese nation, we have drawn this definite conclusion: We must unswervingly follow the path of socialism with Chinese characteristics in order to complete the building of a moderately prosperous society in all respects, accelerate socialist modernization, and achieve the great renewal of the Chinese nation."

Efforts along this path have indeed yielded tremendous results. Not because of the market mechanism, but because it is guided by the socialist goal of improving public welfare. Many superficial observers compare China's economy to Lenin's New Economic policy of the Soviet Union. The Soviet state a century ago was rebalanced with the help of private enterprise. Then communists saw that policy as a temporary retreat from socialist construction. Today, the private economy has become a regular mechanism to achieve the goals of social and economic development within the framework of socialism with Chinese characteristics.

At the symposium, Xi not only pointed out the success of this path, but also pointed out the contradictions that must be resolved within the framework of socialist ideology. He said: "China has entered a stage of high-quality development. The main social contradiction has been transformed into a contradiction between the people's growing need for a better life and unbalanced and inadequate development. Our per capita GDP is now over US$10,000. With an urbanization rate of over 60% and over 400 million people in the middle-income bracket, the demand for good quality of life is ever increasing. We have many advantages for further development, including remarkable institutional superiority, improved administrative efficiency, sustained economic growth, rich industrial and labor resources, vast market volume, great flexibility, and a stable society. However, on the other hand, the lack of balance and sufficiency in our development is still outstanding. Our capacity for innovation is not enough to support the development of high quality. The agricultural base is relatively weak. The disparity of development and income distribution between rural and urban regions remains stark. There is more to be done in environmental protection, social security and social management."[6]

The collapse of Soviet socialism was that its institutional system was not flexible enough to guarantee timely resource redistribution, and it could not transfer resources from an outdated production technology system to a more effective new production technology system. The Soviet socialist system's understanding of the digital revolution was to automate the production process through special technical planning, so the Soviet Union created masterpieces for mass production, such as rotor automation production lines. But the planned economy remained "at the same level as before," serving the endless reproduction of the same technology. As a result, the national economy of the Soviet Union was only a mixed economy at the technical level. Outdated industrial technologies consumed too many resources, leaving the remaining resources insufficient to develop new technologies.[7] The strict hierarchical management system rejected the new opportunities created by the digital revolution. It continued the work method adopted during the First Five-Year Plan period, which was to increase production continuously. Unfortunately, excellent gross output eventually masked the flaws in the centralized planning system, where the marginal effect of investment in basic production tends to be zero.

The CPC has drawn the correct conclusions from the collapse of the centralized socialist economic management system and applied them to the self-organization mechanism of the market economy. At the same time, the centralized management system is retained in major fields such as finance and infrastructure to create conditions for the economic growth of enterprises. This revitalizes the economy, freeing management resources from rigid planning processes, focusing on strategic management, and coordinating socioeconomic interests to ensure economic reproduction for various social groups. Unlike the Soviet Union, China has transformed its economic management system from a technological and institutional perspective, weeding out outdated industries, stopping the supply of resources to inefficient firms, and helping advanced firms master the latest technology.

Deepening reform is the key to China's rapid transformation of its economic development mode. The core issue in economic restructuring is to strike a balance

---

6. Xi Jinping, "Speech at a Symposium of Experts in Economic and Social Fields," *People's Daily*, August 24, 2020.

7. Глазьев С. Теория долгосрочного технико-экономического развития. М.: ВлаДар, 1993.

between the government and the market, respect the rules of the market more, and better play the role of the government. At the same time, China unswervingly consolidates and develops the public ownership economy, implements multiple forms of public ownership, and deepens the reform of state-owned enterprises, improves various state-owned asset management systems. It promotes more state-owned capital investment in important industries and industries that are related to national security and the lifeline of the national economy. In key areas, the vitality, control, and influence of the state-owned economy have been continuously enhanced. China unswervingly encourages, supports, and guides the development of the non-public sector of the economy, ensures that economic entities under all forms of ownership have equal access to factors of production in accordance with the law, competes on a level playing field, and enjoys equal legal protection. China endeavors to improve the modern market system and institutionalizes macro-control of the objectives and policy instruments.

In view of the complexity of China's economic system, its policy is to continuously improve the socialist market economic system, enhance the basic economic system with public ownership as the mainstay and the common development of multiple ownership economies, and strengthen the distribution system with distribution according to work as the mainstay and multiple modes of distribution coexisting, and give full play to the fundamental role of the market in resource allocation and optimize the macro-control system.

At the same time, China attaches great importance to strategic planning and calls for strategic adjustment of the economic structure, which is the main direction of accelerating the transformation of the economic development pattern. It is pointed out that the focus should be on improving the demand structure, optimizing the industrial structure, promoting coordinated regional development, advancing urban development, and striving to solve major structural problems that hinder sustained and sound economic development. China will maintain the strategic focus on boosting domestic demand, accelerate the establishment of a long-term mechanism for expanding consumer demand, unleash the potential of individual consumption, maintain reasonable investment growth, and expand the domestic market size. China will firmly grasp the development of the real economy, which is a solid foundation that implements more policies and measures conducive to the development of the real economy. It will strengthen the demand guidance, promote the healthy development of strategic emerging industries and advanced manufacturing industry, speed up the transformation and upgrading of traditional industries, and promote the services sector, especially the modern service industry development, which is the reasonable layout of the construction of infrastructure and basic industries. China will build next-generation information infrastructure, develop a modern information technology industrial system, improve information security systems, and promote the widespread use of information network technologies. China will improve the core competitiveness of large and medium-sized enterprises, and support the development of small and micro enterprises, especially those based on S&T.

China's strategic plan for economic development considers the competition requirements in the international market and stresses the need to improve the level of openness of the economy comprehensively. To adapt to the new situation of economic globalization, it is imperative to adopt a more proactive strategy of opening up and improving the open economy that is mutually beneficial, diversified, balanced, secure, and efficient. It is demanded to accelerate the transformation of the pattern of external economic development and make opening up more structured, deeper, and more profitable. China endeavors to make innovations in opening up models, encourage coastal, inland, and border areas to draw on each other's strengths in opening up, form open areas that lead international economic cooperation and competition, and foster areas of openness that drive regional development. Equal importance is attached to export and import. China will strengthen coordination between trade and industrial policies, build new competitive advantages in export that focus on technology, brand, quality, and service, promote the transformation and upgrading of processing trade, develop trade in services, and promote balanced development of foreign trade. By increasing the overall advantages and benefits of utilizing foreign capital, China works to attract more investment, technology, and wisdom. Efforts are set up to go global, strengthen enterprises' ability to operate internationally, and cultivate a number of world-class multinational corporations. China coordinates bilateral, multilateral, regional, and sub-regional opening-up and cooperation, accelerates the implementation of free trade areas strategy, and promotes connectivity with neighboring countries. China enables itself to fend off international economic risks.

Against the backdrop of the deepening global economic crisis, Xi's remarks at a symposium of experts in the economic and social fields reflect the modern approach of Chinese leaders to developing international economic cooperation. In his speech, he pointed out the need to "be good at turning crisis into opportunities and strive to achieve higher quality, more efficiency, more fairness, and more continuous and safer development."[8] To this end, he called for "upholding and improving the system of socialism with Chinese characteristics and advancing the modernization of China's system and capacity for governance."[9]

From this point of view, the CPC Central Committee called for "upholding the multilateral trading system, actively participating in the reform of the WTO, and promoting the improvement of a more fair and reasonable global economic governance system. We will actively participate in multilateral and bilateral regional investment and trade cooperation mechanisms, promote the formulation of rules for economic governance in emerging areas, and enhance our capacity to participate in international financial governance. We will upgrade free trade zones and build a global network of high-standard free trade zones."

Compared with the Socialist system of the Soviet Union and the capitalist system of the West, the paradigm of the integrated world economy established by China is more efficient. China's achievements in the application of digital technology attest to this. Blockchain and other digital technologies are widely used in the country's economic circulation. China is still the world's largest manufacturer of robots.

---

8. Xi Jinping, "Speech at a Symposium of Experts in Economic and Social Fields," *People's Daily*, August 24, 2020.
9. Ibid.

Compared with the US and other core countries in the American capital accumulation cycle, China has established a more efficient economic development management system, which predetermines the leap-forward growth of the Chinese economy. China's GDP has surpassed that of the US. Importantly, China's economic growth has led to a wave of growth of new technological paradigms, which will ensure China's economic advance for the foreseeable future until the mid-21st century.

PART III

THE BATTLE FOR FUTURE ECONOMIC LEADERS

Chapter 7

The US's Strategy of Maintaining Global Dominance and the Threat of New World War

Due to the struggle for the dominant position of the global economic relationship system, world wars broke out many times during the 300 years of global economic development. By analyzing the capital accumulation cycle during the past 300 years and the corresponding world economic paradigm and the replacement of leading countries, we can find the objective reasons for the repeated outbreak of world wars. The current situation is the same as when the accumulation cycle changed in the past. The dominant country of the world economic paradigm gradually loses its influence, so it adopts coercive measures to maintain its dominant position. Due to pyramid schemes and excessive accumulation of capital in production, lack of product sales markets, and the decline in the share of US dollars in international transactions, the US seeks to rely on launching a world war to weaken its competitors and partners to maintain its dominant position. In terms of controlling major hydrocarbon resources and other important natural resources, the US has a more strategic advantage over the rising China by virtue of its control over Russia and its hegemony in Europe, Central Asia, and the Middle East. American control over Europe, Russia, Japan, and South Korea can ensure its advantages in creating new knowledge and developing advanced technologies.

The leading position of the US in technology, economy, finance, military, information, and politics is the foundation of its global hegemony. Technological advantages enable American companies to take possession of talent leases and use this to provide funds for scientific research and experimental design, thereby surpassing competitors in the broadest areas of scientific and technological progress. American companies monopolize the right to use advanced technologies. Therefore, they have advantages in the global market, both in terms of production efficiency and new product supply.

The US economic superiority lays the foundation for the dominance of the dollar. In addition, the US also maintains the dollar's dominance through military and political means. At the same time, it also relies on the issuance of world currency to obtain seigniorage and to make up for the national budget deficit caused by massive military expenditures. Now, the American military expenditure is ten times that of Russia, which is equivalent to the total military expenditure of the ten countries after the US (Table 7-1).

The ruling bloc of the US and its NATO Allies follows a liberal ideology that will not justify greater state economic intervention, except for defense needs. Therefore, when it is necessary to use national demand to stimulate new technological paradigms, leaders in the industry will escalate military and political tensions and use it as the main way to increase the purchase of advanced technology and equipment in various countries.

Table 7-1 Share of World Military Expenditure by Major Countries (Unit: %)

	Military Expenditure	**Nuclear Weapon**	**Arms Trade**
The USA	40.6	42.1	36.5
China	8.2	1.3	2.9
Russia	4.1	52.6	19.7
Britain	3.6	1.2	6.8
France	3.6	1.6	3.8
Japan	3.4	0	—
India	2.7	0.5	—
Germany	2.7	0	3.8
Brazil	2.0	0	—
The world	100.0	100.0	—

Source: Рогов С. Место России в многополярном мире / Доклад. М.: Институт США и Канады РАН, 2012.

The leading position in the above-mentioned fields has ensured the advantages of the US in the information field. The US then monopolizes the production and proliferation of information products, and controls the global information network and communication channels.[1] To control the public consciousness of people all over the world, the US controls the cultural information service market and establishes the value system and image system that America needs. Through monitoring global communication channels, the US can collect information on millions of people with national decision-making power and influence the decisions these people make. Monitoring the Global Information Network allows America to gather all the information useful to it from all parts of the world.

The dominant position in technology, economy, finance, military, and information can ensure the global political hegemony of the US. The global hegemony of the US is embodied in the following aspects: artificially monitoring the loyalty of political leaders and the ruling party of other countries to American values; utilizing the media to manipulate public opinion; using a large number of "road-paving" Non-Governmental Organizations to bribe and attract influential people; recruiting and extorting important figures from government agencies; and using force against people, social groups, and the state that disagree with their opinions.

The global competition under the world economic paradigm of the modern imperialism model (corresponding to the fifth technological paradigm) is not a competition among countries, but one among transnational reproduction systems. On

---

1. Филимонов Г. Культурно-информационные механизмы внешней политики США. Истоки и новая реальность. М.: Российский университет дружбы народов, 2012.

the one hand, each transnational reproduction system integrates the country's national education system, capital accumulation, and scientific research institutions. On the other hand, it unifies the production and financial structure of enterprises operating within the global market. These closely-connected systems determine the development of the global economy. After the collapse of the world socialist system, under the framework of global liberalism, the accumulation of capital in the US reached a new height. The result was the formation of a modern world order. In the modern world order, international capital and multinational companies refinanced by the Federal Reserve play a decisive role and constitute the "core" of the modern world economic paradigm. Countries that have not entered the "core" constitute the "periphery" of the modern world economic paradigm, and at the same time, lose their internal integrity and opportunities for independent development. The economic relations between the "core" countries and the "peripheral" countries of the global economic system are characterized by unequal exchanges. In this case, countries on the "peripheries" of the global economic system are forced to rely on natural resource rents and labor remuneration, exporting raw materials and low-tech goods and paying for the rental of imported goods and services.

By controlling the "peripheral" countries, the "core" countries possess the most high-quality resources of the "peripheral" countries-outstanding talents, scientific and technological achievements, and ownership of the most valuable part of the national wealth. The "core" countries rely on their technological advantages to force the "peripheral" countries to accept more beneficial standards and consolidate their monopoly in the field of technology exchanges. The "core" countries concentrate their fiscal potential, impose conditions on the capital flow of the "peripheral" countries and force them to use the currencies of the "core" countries, including the establishment of foreign exchange reserves. By establishing control over the financial systems of the "peripheral" countries, they distribute income within the global economic system. The "peripheral" countries are deprived of their main internal resources for economic development, and thus lose the opportunity to implement sovereign economic policies and manage their own economic growth and become an economic belt for the "core" countries of the world economic paradigm to obtain international capital.

Post-socialist countries have formed their own corporate structure and privatized the remaining production potential. Consequently, now the US and its G7 allies have lost the opportunity to plunder resources from post-socialist countries. To "implant" the US dollar into countries whose financial systems are not protected, the US, with the help of the IMF, evaluation agencies, and influential agencies that rely on the US dollar, forced these countries to accept monetary policies and engage them in financial wars, which in turn caused the US to suffer losses.

At the same time, countries that retain economic sovereignty (China, India) have not opened up their financial systems and can still maintain economic growth despite the global financial crisis. By opening the bilateral foreign exchange swap business, China has quickly established its own international settlement system. During the technological paradigm change, late-developing countries can "catch up"—saving the cost of basic research and exploratory research by imitating the achievements of advanced countries. In other words, advanced countries bear a greater burden because they invest a large amount of capital into the core technological production of the technological paradigm, which makes the technological production structure extremely inert. The late-developing countries have obtained the opportunity to "catch up" during the technological paradigm shift. These countries will focus their investment on the prospect of developing new technological paradigms. Today China, India, and Brazil are achieving technological leapfrog development in this way.

As the new technological paradigm evolves, the Federal Reserve's space for activities is rapidly shrinking. Due to the overproduction of the previous technological paradigm, the financial pyramid scheme, and the national debt crisis, the American economy had to bear the main impact of capital devaluation.

Scholars define the current US capital accumulation cycle as the "financial expansion" stage.[2] In 1980, the various financial sectors in the US brought 15% of profits to its industrial groups, and now these financial sectors bring more than 50% of profits to multinational companies.[3] This proves that under the current world economic paradigm, the development potential of productive forces has been exhausted. The existing technological paradigm limits the development of the new one because the elements of the technological paradigm in the financial pyramid scheme are connected to each other, and these elements will lose their value when the financial pyramid scheme "collapses."

The declining share of the US in the global market has undermined the economic foundation of its global hegemony. Today, the dollar's monopoly in the global monetary and financial system is the last advantage of the US. The share of the US dollar in the total currency in circulation globally is about 2/3.[4] As the economic foundation of the US as a global leader has been "eroded," to make up for the losses, the US attempts to exert military and political pressure on its competitors through violence. With the help of global networks such as military bases, information surveillance, electronic reconnaissance (intelligence), and NATO agencies, the US is trying to maintain global surveillance and stop individual countries from trying to get rid of their dependence on the US dollar. But the US is now finding it increasingly difficult to achieve this goal—America needs to carry out the necessary structural reforms to maintain its leadership. Still, inertia generated by outdated fixed-asset investments and a huge financial pyramid scheme involving private and state bonds has hampered reform. To get rid of the increasingly heavy burden as soon as possible and maintain the dollar's monopoly in the global monetary and financial system, the US hopes to write off its own debts. The best way to write off debts is to start a world war. Due to the risk of using weapons of mass destruction, it is impossible to start a world war conventionally. The US is trying to provoke a series of regional wars that will form a global hybrid war for the US and the world.

By organizing armed conflicts, the US creates "controllable chaos" in the world's

2. Айвазов А. Указ. соч. 2012.

3. К стратегии социальной справедливости и развития / Авторский доклад С. Глазьева Изборскому клубу. 2015 (3 августа); Встать в полный рост / Доклад Изборскому клубу / Под ред. С. Батчикова, А. Кобякова, С. Глазьева. 2014 (23 ноября).

4. Рогов С. Место России в многополярном мире / Доклад. - М.: Институт США и Канады РАН, 2012.

leading countries' natural resources, provokes them to get involved in conflicts, and then builds alliances against these leading countries, thereby consolidating its dominant position and legitimizing the outcome of the conflict. At the same time, America gains an illegitimate competitive advantage and uses it to isolate countries that are not under its control from prospective markets. The US also relies on "freezing" the dollar assets of the defeated countries to create opportunities for itself to reduce the national debt burden. At the same time, it defends its behavior of increasing national expenditures due to developing and promoting new technologies that are conducive to the growth of the US economy.

According to the theory of the accumulation cycle, the US cannot win the war it has started. But the accumulation cycle theory is not dogmatic, and it can only help us regulate our perception of historical processes. Unlike the engine's rotation cycle, the technological, social, political, and economic development cycles differ from each other considerably and are conditionally separated individually. The change of times is not a strictly cyclical process, and the cycle duration varies. However, the knowledge gained from the "long wave" theory and the accumulation cycle theory is sufficient to accurately reveal the crises and challenges in the next 20 years.

The era of American world hegemony is coming to an end. The institutional system proposed by the American accumulation cycle process cannot guarantee the sustainable development of productivity, and a new Asian capital accumulation cycle is about to come. With the establishment of the new world economic paradigm system, the system, production, economic, and technological centers of global economic development will also be transferred from the US to China and other "core" countries in the new world economic paradigm.

The global market has been unable to guarantee the operation of the expansion cycle reproduction system in the US. A new center has appeared in the "periphery" of the existing world economic paradigm. This new center will rapidly expand reproduction and surpass the US in commodity production. The US has established the Trans-Pacific Partnership (TPP), a Transatlantic Trade and Investment Partnership (TTIP), and has made itself the "core" of the partnership, hoping to increase its competitive advantage.[5] By trying to isolate the "core" countries of the imperialist world economic paradigm from the "periphery" countries, America is already showing a transition to decline. It is reminiscent of Britain's futile struggle a century ago to protect its domestic market by isolating its rival, the US, with tariffs. Just as a hundred years ago, the actions of the British became a signal to the elites of the American regime, telling them that the time had come to "break" the colonial world economic paradigm. The behavior of the US today is similar to that of Britain back then. The "core" countries of the emerging new world economic paradigm take it as a signal that the time to break the old-world economic paradigm has arrived. If the US hopes to rely on its hegemony

---

5. Imports from regions where the member states of the Intercontinental Military Alliance treaty are located account for the vast majority of world imports (approximately 85%). North American exports account for about 18% of the world's total exports, Europe accounts for about 36%, and Asia accounts for about 32%. Most of Russia's markets are also in these regions. EU countries' exports account for 53% of their domestic orders, and APEC member countries' exports account for more than 17% of their domestic orders.

plan to maintain its competitive position, it has lost the motivation to defend the US bond financial pyramid scam further. It must be understood that the financial pyramid scam is the foundation of the American capital accumulation cycle. China's decision not to increase its dollar reserves means that the conflict-free way to resolve the contradiction between the expansion of the reproduction of US bonds and the potential for global investment has reached its limit. After China, Russia no longer increases its dollar reserves. The process of expanded reproduction of US bonds will inevitably show an avalanche characteristic soon, which will lead to the collapse of the US financial system and the collapse of the existing world economic paradigm based on it.

Undoubtedly, the oligarchs of the American regime will try to hinder the development of the new global economic center. However, the US is likely to achieve this goal by conflict-free means, just like in 1985, when America artificially reduced the economic competitiveness of Japan by imposing the *Plaza Accord*[6] on it to contain the rising Japan, the precursor of the accumulation cycle in Asia. China is strong enough to fight unequal cooperation. India has been very sensitive to oppression from the Anglo-Saxons since ancient times. Putin's independence policy excludes the possibility of Russia being exploited, and Russia will no longer be at the mercy of the Americans in the 1990s.

Because it is impossible to measure the accumulation cycle accurately, it is necessary to link the various stages of its life cycle with typical geopolitical events, especially the life cycle and the world wars that indirectly show the change of the world economic paradigm. From Boris Dimitrievich Pankin's perspective, the period from 2014 to 2018 corresponds to the 1939–1945 World War outbreak. For this reason, the conflicts in North Africa, Iraq, Syria, and Ukraine can be regarded as the beginning of a series of interconnected conflicts that were triggered by the US and its allies. America and its allies hope to solve their own economic, social, and political problems with the help of the "controllable chaos" strategy. During World War II (called the "just war" by the US), Americans used this method to solve economic and socio-political problems.[7]

The US is trying to delay the collapse of its own financial system as much as possible and expects to jump into a new "long wave" of economic growth before it comes. For this reason, America is also trying to transfer its debt burden to other countries or completely offset it. To maintain control of the "petrodollar," they launched wars in the Middle East and Near East, throwing its former partners into chaos and helplessness. To control the "drug dollar," they invaded Afghanistan. But the main goal of American

---

6. In 1985, finance ministers and central bank governors of five developed countries (the US, The United Kingdom, Germany, France, And Japan) met at which the US persuaded the other four developed countries to implement a series of interventions in foreign exchange markets. These measures are aimed at weakening the dollar and boosting the value of other countries' currencies. The other four countries agreed to change their economic policies, interfere in the operation of foreign exchange markets, and devalue the dollar. Japan followed America's advice, raised interest rates and did what it could to make the yen's exchange rate "fully reflect Japan's favorable economic growth." The Japanese economy has been hit hard by the rapid rise of the yen, which has weakened the competitiveness of Japanese exporters in foreign markets. (There is even the argument that this contributed to Japan's decade-long recession.) On the contrary, the US economy grew, and inflation remained low after the agreement.

7. Пантин В. Циклы реформ-контрреформ в России и их связь с циклами мирового развития // ПолИс. 2011. № 6.

expansion and aggression is to control Europe. According to geopolitical traditions, the American oligarchs bet on the war between European countries and Russia, and they hope to again get rid of the current conflict as a victor of the war, as happened the previous two times. For this reason, American intelligence personnel launched a coup in Ukraine and established an anti-Russian right-wing regime in Ukraine.

According to Boris Dimitrievich Pankin's prediction,[8] the most dangerous stage for Russia will be in the early 2020s, when developed countries and China begin technological upgrading, and the US and other western countries will also benefit from the 2008–2018 economic depression and complete a new technological "leap." In other words, during the period 2021–2025, Russia's technological and economic development may once again obviously lag behind other countries, which will lead to a decline in Russia's defense potential, and the intensification of domestic social conflicts and ethnic disputes, as happened in the Soviet Union in the 1980s. Analysts from the CIA and other departments predict that Russia will disintegrate after 2020 due to internal conflicts. Those conflicts may be caused by external forces taking advantage of Russia's social and regional development imbalances, or by Russia's adoption of the macroeconomic policies recommended by the IMF, which results in a decline in the living standards of the Russian people.

Unlike World War II, there was no frontal conflict between the armed forces in the world war launched by the US this time. The new world war mainly relies on "soft power," that is, the use of modern information technology and financial and monetary technology, while restricting military power to punish opponents who have lost resistance. To undermine the internal stability of the "victim country," US will use the following methods: destroying the social consciousness of the "victim country" through subversive concepts, undermining the stability of the social and economic situation of the "victim country," cultivating various opposition forces; bribing the elite to weaken the state power, thereby overthrowing the legitimate government, and then transferring the power to the puppet government.

Such wars are called "hybrid wars": the leaders of the "victim country" will not feel threats from their opponents till the last moment, the political will of the "victim country" will be restrained by endless negotiations and consultations, and the nation will be suppressed by deceptive propaganda, and at the same time, opponents actively carry out actions to destroy the national security system of the "victimized country." If it is suppressed by an opponent's armed forces at a critical moment, the security system of the "victim country" will be destroyed. It was in this way that America successfully defeated the Soviet Union during the Cold War and launched a coup in Russia in 1993. Now the US has created "vortexes" in strategically important regions such as the Near East and the Middle East, which has aggravated the chaos in these regions. The US also tried to forcibly implant the puppet government into the former Soviet Socialist Republic, thereby regaining control of the post-Soviet region.

With its monopoly on world currency issuance, the US launches hybrid wars on many fronts. This allows the Americans to rely on the US bondholders, including

---

8. Пантин В. Наиболее вероятный прогноз развития политических и военных конфликтов в период 2014–2018 гг. / Аналитический материал. URL: newsdon. Info, 12 июля 2014 г.

the "victims" of American aggression, to raise funds for launching, propagating, and organizing wars and other military expenditures for the country. The US launches such a war on the principle of self-financing. The US invades the mining areas, infrastructure projects, and domestic markets of the "victimized countries" and transfers them to American companies. The Federal Reserve controls currency circulation and binds domestic currency issuance to another manifestation of national bonds, that is, the growth of foreign exchange reserves. The funds for the activities of the US to invade the regime of other countries are paid by the people of the "victimized country," and the people of that country are also forced to conduct pseudo-elections to legitimize the US puppet regime.

The existing world economic paradigm was established under the influence of the US. Therefore, within the existing world economic paradigm framework, the US has an advantage regardless of conflicts with any opponent. Based on the technological system of the current world economic paradigm, the US can engage in an effective hybrid war with half of the world. On the financial front, Americans have an overwhelming advantage in controlling the issuance of world currencies and the IMF. The IMF can determine the rules by which the world's money markets and those of most countries, including Russia, operate.

The currencies of Japan, the United Kingdom, and the European Union also occupy a certain position in the global currency market. These countries are geopolitical alliances of the US. Together with the US, they control most of the world's currency and financial markets and have a great say in the international financial system.

On the information front, the global hegemony of American media enables it to create public opinion and influence voters' preferences with the help of public opinion, thus controlling the political situation in most democratic countries. The US also has obvious advantages on other fronts of hybrid warfare, namely, culture, ideology, food, energy, and communications.

Under the current world economic paradigm, no country with an open economic system and a democratic political system can defeat the US in a hybrid war, and no country can be immune from American aggression. Only countries with closed financial, information, and political systems can effectively resist American aggression. However, self-reliance will lead to technological backwardness and economic recession, which in turn will lead to a decline in people's living standards and a country's internal political crisis. In fact, only a timely transition to the new world economic paradigm, readjustment of the global financial information system's main functions, and establishment of a responsibility mechanism that conforms to international law can contain American aggression.

The elites of the US regime still dream of regaining control of the "peripheral" countries that are no longer subject to them, not clearly recognizing the limitations of their own capabilities. This limitation arises not only because the new world economic paradigm is more efficient, but also because the "core" countries of the new world economic paradigm can implement independent policies. In addition, these countries have sufficient military strength to use necessary resources and domestic markets to safeguard national sovereignty and achieve the goal of expanding reproduction. However, due to its "peripheral" position in the imperialist world economic paradigm, each of the above-mentioned countries still cannot get rid of the dependence on the American capital accumulation cycle mechanism. To this end, these countries should establish alliances, which should also become the strategic core of Russia's international economic and political relations.

The US launched a hybrid war against Russia, which is definitely not coincidental with the conflict that broke out in Ukraine. On the contrary, the Ukraine conflict is only part of American policy, which seeks to give the US an advantage in the global leadership battle with China by launching a war against Russia in Europe. Like the aggression in the Middle East, the American aggression in the post-Soviet region is also manipulated by the elites of the US regime to maintain global hegemony and self-interest during the long cycle of world economic evolution.

With the help of the right-wing extremist who usurped Ukrainian power, the US instigated the European Union against Russia, thereby weakening the power of the EU and Russia and making it easier for the US to monitor them. In the EU, the US has aggravated the internal conflicts in the European Union by creating an immigration crisis. In Russia, the US has made Russia the next country to be divided by destabilizing the domestic political situation in Russia and organizing a national coup. In this way, the US can exercise control over Central Asia. The US forces most countries in the Eurasian region to enter the American interest circle, thereby strengthening its own power and weakening China's power. American geopoliticians hope to use this to maintain US global leadership. Therefore, the strike against Russia plays an important role. The use of Ukraine has enabled the US to achieve a win-win situation. All actions are achieved through the hands of other countries, and all losses are borne by Russia, which is gradually becoming self-destructive.

At the beginning of the Ukrainian coup, the US intelligence personnel instructed the Ukrainian leaders who established the extreme right-wing regime to organize a war against Russia, bringing NATO European countries into the war. During the four years of potential occupation of Ukraine, the US had been preparing personnel, armed forces, and industry to achieve the following goals:

- During the military operations in Donbass, hundreds of thousands of young people conducted military training and psychological training;
- Establishing a combat-capable armed force controlled by the Pentagon, and gradually carrying out modernized weaponry transformation;
- Establishing training camps and training young people in military operations, including sabotage operations, through the training camps;
- Rebuilding the military industry in accordance with NATO standards;
- Infiltrating public opinion with anti-Russian sentiment and controlling the media by US spies;
- Being the ruling party or the opposition party, all of them were controlled by American spies.

The President of Ukraine and members of the government are both puppets of the US, and the powerful departments are managed by the US. The control of the fiscal revenue department and important strategic departments, including the integrated agro-industrial system and the integrated system of fuel and energy for the defense industry, is gradually transferred to the American capitalists.

The prediction of Ukraine's collapse of the anti-Russian regime is not without reason. Under the leadership of the Central Intelligence Agency of the US, the Ukrainian Security Agency used a large number of political persecutions to suppress protests and intimidate the Ukrainian people. Millions of professional and technical personnel who are dissatisfied with the Ukrainian government have immigrated to other countries. The remaining people have adapted to the ever-changing environment, learned to work in accordance with the requirements of the new owner, and gradually transformed the technological productivity of Ukraine to meet the needs of the Western market.

Don't expect the West to tire of Ukraine's endless requests for help. The encroachment policy formulated by American intelligence agencies operates on the principle of self-financing: part of the funds for the militarization of Ukraine comes from taxpayers of Ukrainian state-owned property, and the other part comes from businessmen in Russia and Donetsk. The US buys these businessmen's companies at low prices and puts them under the control of American companies. Under the order of the US, Ukraine handed over natural resources and infrastructure projects, nuclear power plants used American fuel, and farmers were forced to plant Monsanto's genetically modified crops. Ukrainian companies and entrepreneurs serving the interests of the US have earned more income. In contrast, Ukrainian companies related to the Russian market are declining. The severance of ties between Ukraine and Russia caused huge losses. Most of these losses were borne by the Russian people working in the economically developed regions of the southeast. At the same time, the Russian economy has suffered a lot of losses. The losses in bilateral cooperation alone amounted to US$75–150 billion. (In terms of economic cooperation between Russia and Ukraine, Russia's losses due to other factors amounted to US$400 billion).[9]

If the relationship between Russia and Ukraine continues to be negative in the future, and Russia also indirectly recognizes the legitimacy of the anti-Russian government in Kiev, then the situation will only be more unfavorable for Russia. The US and NATO are building military bases and infrastructure on a large scale in order to invade Russia. The size of Ukraine's armed forces continues to expand, reaching 3 million people in a special period. At that time, the Ukrainian region will become a military base for the anti-Russian war. Western countries will rely on Ukraine's economic and demographic potential to launch this anti-Russian war and bring the greatest harm to Russia at the least cost to western countries. According to the officially announced plan, the purpose of the new right-wing regime is to destroy the Donetsk People's Republic and Luhansk People's Republic, and then use the "liberation" of Crimea as an excuse to launch armed aggression against Russia. The longer-term goal is to occupy Kuban and destabilize the Volga region and other regions.

Although the military pranks of the Ukrainian right-wingers may seem absurd, it should be pointed out that these pranks are just a portrayal of the real American plans.

---

9. Косикова Л. Новейшие украинские шоки российской экономики (о воздействии «постмайданного» кризиса в РУ на воспроизводственные процессы в РФ) // Российский экономический журнал. 2017, №4. С. 69–82.

For the Americans, what matters is not the result, but the fact of the Russo-Ukrainian War. To ignite the war between Ukraine and Russia, the US can fabricate any nonsense that can inspire fanatical right-wing extremist anti-Russian sentiment. We should not rule out the threat of the use of nuclear weapons. Ukrainian atomic energy experts may have created nuclear weapons. Although the US has publicly declared that it will not allow Ukraine to restore its nuclear power status, the US may have secretly helped Ukraine manufacture nuclear weapons.

The extreme right-wing regime has passed a bill on the main points of national policy on the Donbass issue. With this bill, the extreme right-wing regime legally transformed "counter-terrorism operations" into "wars against invaders to liberate occupied territories."

Before fighting with the Ukrainian regime, to undermine the anti-Russian aggression plan, Russia must seize the initiative. To this end, the following measures should be taken:

1. The legalization of the extreme right-wing regime is based on international law and Ukrainian law. The extreme right-winger usurped the power of the Verkhovna Rada and carried out a series of illegal actions, including holding elections, thereby realizing an illegal coup. Therefore, the extreme right-wing regime is illegal by its very nature.

2. To file charges against the leaders of the extreme right-wing regime for crimes committed against the people of Donbass, including genocide, war crimes, political persecution, and killing opponents. Some representatives of the Kiev regime committed crimes against humanity, and their list should be made public. The Ukrainian refugees and the people of Donbass should accuse the activists of the extreme right-wing regime in Kiev, and the people's court investigate the crimes of the Ukrainian Nazis. At the same time, institutions such as the International Human Rights Organization, the International Criminal Court, the European Court of Human Rights, the UN platform, the Organization for Security and Co-operation, and the Council of Europe Parliamentary Assembly are used to expose the nature of the crimes of the extreme right-wing regime.

3. Recognizing the Donetsk People's Republic and Luhansk People's Republic (they may form the Ukrainian Federation) as the legal successors of the Ukrainian Soviet Socialist Republic and post-Soviet Ukraine. This is not only the basis for restoring the status of the Donetsk People's Republic and the Luhansk People's Republic as sovereign states, but also the restoration of the treaty legal system between Russia and Ukraine before the coup in Ukraine in February 2014 (including the Russia-Ukraine Free Trade Area Agreement). In addition, other areas of Ukraine are legally invaded by right-wing extremists and cannot establish a legal regime.

There is another reason for the recognition of the status of the Donetsk People's Republic and the Luhansk People's Republic: the extreme right-wing regime passed the bill on Ukraine's abandonment of its non-aligned status and the bill on "decommunization." These bills led to the political aspects of the *Minsk Agreement* cannot be realized. If the *Minsk Agreement* is implemented, these republics can use the incompetence of the current Kiev authorities as an excuse to declare independence.

It should also be announced that other regions of Ukraine have voluntarily returned to the Ukrainian Federation. In this way, legal conditions can be created for the liberation of Ukraine and the dissolution of the extreme right-wing regime.

The US political elites cultivate anti-Russian right-wing extremists, with their help to launch anti-Russian aggression and "provoke" wars in Europe, to maintain the US global hegemony by destroying Russia and consolidating its dominant position and control in the European Union, Asia, the Caucasus, the Near East, and the Middle East. Provoking a world war to maintain control of "peripheral" countries is typical behavior of world leaders in the period of technological paradigm and world economic paradigm change. According to the Anglo-Saxon geopolitical tradition, Russia was once again selected as a victim of the next world war. Control of Russia is necessary for maintaining global hegemony and weakening China's power. The occupation of Ukraine and the utilization of Ukraine's population and natural economic potential are the main political strategies adopted by the American ruling elite in a hybrid war to maintain global hegemony. But the main front of the hybrid war lies in the economy. American spies have successfully dealt a devastating blow to the Ukrainian economy.

Chapter 8

The Response of the CPC to American Pressure

The main goal of the US in launching a hybrid war is to maintain its global leadership under the condition that China has ranked first in the fields of industrial scale, knowledge-intensive product exports, and economic modernization investment. To undermine China's rapid economic development, the US has used all legal means to violate the norms of international law established by the WTO (as recognized by the WTO itself) in national legislation. Its actions include unilaterally raising import tariffs, imposing an embargo on advanced technology exports, pressuring US companies to move production back, banning the use of Chinese smartphone apps, and imposing selective financial sanctions.

In addition to the three rounds of sanctions imposed by the US on Chinese imports (the total value is estimated to be between US$400 billion and US$500 billion since 2018), the fourth round of discussions on anti-China trade and economic and financial restrictions continue. Once these measures take effect by imposing 25% tariffs on a wide range of goods, China's losses may increase by US$300 billion yearly.

Such economic pressure from the US will not have as big an impact on China's economy as expected, but will have a major impact on all global supply chains without exception, analysts said. The US doesn't care, or at least claims to bring back the production capacity as the ultimate benefit and localize it. In this context, China has a lot of room to maneuver, especially with the US accounting for about 20% of its exports, EU countries accounting for the same amount, and Asia (ASEAN) accounting for more than 50% of its exports. Facing the increasing pressure of sanctions from the US, China can rely on its inherent thoroughness to deepen industrial cooperation in the Asia-Pacific region and even the broader Eurasian continent, so as to reduce its dependence on the US market by at least half. And the US, which has transferred a large amount of production capacity to China, is experiencing a severe shortage of manufactured goods and intermediate goods, severely weakening its industrial base and reducing the possibility of mitigating the impact of inflated public debt.

It must be admitted that the US government (persistently) underestimated China's ability to deal intensively with this pressure. China has not only introduced countermeasures that have caused serious damage to the US market, but it has also made tremendous efforts to strengthen its own scientific and technological capabilities. The prerequisites for this have been prepared, so China not only effectively resisted the pressure of the US in trade, but also realized the substitution of American imports in the high-tech field. If the US share of high-tech exports in 1999 was almost 20% and China's was less than 5%, by 2015, China had substantially increased the development and production of high-tech products in accordance with the goals of the 17th and 18th National Congress of the CPC. According to World Bank data, by 2015, the share of high-tech exports from the US had fallen to 7%, and China had increased eightfold to 26%. For example, the mainland of China, Taiwan, China, and South Korea are now producing almost all parts of smartphones, computers, and televisions, such as flash memory chips, liquid crystal, plasma displays, semiconductor lasers, and solid-state sensors.

US intelligence agencies have crossed the red line of the international security system and used the development of biological weapons to exhaust all relatively legal means to undermine China's economic development. The US is the only country in the world that continues to conduct scientific research and experiments in this field and refuses to sign the *Convention on the Prohibition of the Development, Production and Stockpiling Bacterial (Biological) and Toxin Weapons and on Their Destructions*.

But China is also prepared to deal with the threat. China has seized and made good use of this important period of strategic opportunities for development, worked hard to overcome a series of major challenges, and pushed socialism with Chinese characteristics to a new stage of development. China has continued to deepen reform and opening-up and accelerated development. Taking the opportunity of its accession to the WTO, China has turned pressure into a driving force and challenges into opportunities to unswervingly advance the process of building a moderately prosperous society in all respects. China has carefully reviewed its development practices and accurately grasped the characteristics of its development at different stages, thus opening up broad space for economic and social development. After 2008, the international financial crisis confronted China with serious difficulties in its development. However, China took the lead in stabilizing and recovering its economy through scientific judgment, decisive decisions, and a series of major measures. It gained important experience in effectively coping with external economic risks and maintaining steady and rapid economic development.

In the context of the growing geopolitical and economic tensions in the world at present, China's economic reproduction is facing external challenges. It is more realistic to overcome these challenges by vigorously promoting socialism with Chinese characteristics. The combination of strategic outlook on development, creative thinking, and state structural liberation to achieve inclusive social development allowed China to benefit during and after the 2008 global financial crisis and overcome the "sudden outbreak of SARS" without causing major losses. There is no doubt that biological weapons, banned at the end of the first decade of the 21st century, were used as a tool to suppress the economic growth of a rising China. Today, the US accuses China's COVID-19 outbreak is not a "zero" infection, and it is further spreading to the west, attempting to sabotage the rapid development of China in various aspects, including economy (investment and growth in GDP), society (state of guarantee of equal wealth for all workers), and politics (to expand China's political and diplomatic agenda to areas of the world that the Americans have not touched).

However, Chinese leaders withstood this test, effectively contained the spread of the pandemic, and resumed production, trade, and foreign relations with greater enthusiasm. By strengthening the discipline of all social groups, the carrying structure of the new world order has been strengthened; resources have been mobilized; joint responsibility and power credibility have been strengthened and improved. China's will is unwavering.

The fight against the epidemic has strongly promoted the development of China's medical and health undertakings. The 14th Five-Year Plan of the Central Committee of the CPC specifically addresses this issue: "Comprehensively promoting the construction of a Healthy China. We will put the protection of people's health in a strategic position for priority development, adhere to the prevention-first directive, deeply implement the Healthy China initiative, refine national health promotion policies, weave a strong web for national public health defense, and provide comprehensive, full life cycle health services for the people."

As China curbed the spread of the COVID-19 infection after the decline in GDP in the first quarter of 2020, the Chinese economy began to grow in the second quarter. Restrictive measures in EU countries vary widely, from a total lockdown in Italy to partial restrictions in Sweden. In this regard, the impact on the economy is also different, with the most restrictive countries having the most economic impact. With the unprecedented support of the US economy, social tensions have intensified and caused riots, thereby complicating the recovery process. The question of which measures are effective will not be answered until the end of the pandemic.

Some international organizations predict that only China, among the major world economies, can avoid a decline in GDP in 2020. By 2021, most developed countries will not be able to reach the level of 2019, and most Asian countries will be able to surpass them. Therefore, the trend of Southeast Asia's fast-growing economies playing an increasingly important role in the world economy will be strengthened in the short term. Macroeconomic policies will play an important role in this process. Monetary instruments in developed countries have been exhausted when interest rates are close to zero, and liquidity growth in emerging economies may still provide a huge impetus to economic growth.

Countries around the world have taken similar measures to deal with the decline in economic activity caused by the implementation of quarantine due to COVID-19. On the one hand, actions were quickly taken to strengthen the health system's response to the epidemic; on the other hand, families, and businesses received support to maintain their financial stability. Governments and central banks around the world have formulated and implemented a wide range of financial and administrative support programs. These measures laid the foundation for economic recovery after the crisis.

There are two main economic models in the world, which take different measures to stabilize their respective socioeconomic conditions, namely the "Western" model and the "Eastern" model. The "Western" model is mainly the US and European Union countries, and the "Eastern" model is mainly China and other Asia-Pacific countries. The "Orient" or "China" model is characterized by large projects that support export-oriented industries. The "Western" model is characterized by expanded funding for existing programs, including government (health services, support for socially vulnerable groups, small and medium enterprise development) and central bank programs (securities buybacks).

Due to the high level of economic management, the epidemic in China and other Asian countries was quickly reduced in the first half of 2020. At the same time, "western" countries, due to a greater degree of social "democratization," were slower to adopt restrictive measures, resulting in high morbidity and rapid spread of the epidemic. Thus, while eastern countries, mainly China and South Korea, gradually began to lift restrictions on certain economic sectors, the incidence rate in western countries had not yet reached its "peak," affecting the speed of recovery from the "first wave" of the epidemic in these economies. In addition, the European Union and the US were affected by a "second wave" of the epidemic in the third quarter of 2020, and Asian countries, due to their own national specificities, were able to ensure that economic activity was maintained, and the outbreak contained within their territories.

The experience of the current and 2008–2009 crises shows that Russia and other EEU countries are in a more vulnerable position. This has to do with the excessive looseness of exchange controls that have made financial markets dependent on international speculators. American hedge funds and related speculators manipulate the countries' money markets by destabilizing their currencies' exchange rates. This caused enormous damage to mutual trade and co-investment and destabilized the macroeconomic situation. It is worth following that China's experience of including the RMB in a basket of world reserve currencies without allowing free cross-border capital account trading.

In the past ten years, China has successfully resisted other more traditional tools of aggression by the US, such as cyber-attacks by American intelligence agencies (attempts by its controlled media, and some bloggers manipulating public awareness, standing up to destabilize politics in Trump's trade war), and fending off monetary and financial threats. Washington's sanctions on Chinese high-tech companies have forced them to demand that their S&D departments build a national technology base. As a result, China's innovation activities have ranked first in the world.

In conclusion, it must be acknowledged that China has beaten back the COVID-19 outbreak and is on the counter-offensive, providing medical care, protective equipment, and disinfection assistance to the affected countries. Thus, as in previous times, China has used its achievements to reverse the offensive direction of the enemy's weapons and neutralize Washington's ideological and political initiatives. At the same time, the US's stubborn attempt to discredit China as the source of the epidemic was defeated by the evidence of the artificial origin of the virus in the US biological laboratory.

With a firm attitude to overcome any form of external pressure and the phase of hybrid war, China will undoubtedly continue to carry out its own Belt and Road international cooperation projects, the core of which is the implementation of joint investment projects to improve the competitiveness of participating countries and the well-being of their people. In constructing just six economic corridors, China plans to invest about $900 billion in 900 projects in 60 countries; the projects are also being financed by the Asian Infrastructure Investment Bank and the Silk Road Fund. In the new world economic pattern, the main motive of international integration is not the market liberalization of TNCs and foreign investors, but the realization of industrial growth through joint investment and joint ventures combined with the competitive advantages of cooperative countries. Under China's "command," mutual respect for national interests, the inviolability of sovereign rights of states to pursue independent policies, mutually beneficial principles of international trade and financial and economic relations, and norms of international law have been restored. Under China's initiative, the Shanghai Cooperation Organization, ASEAN, and the EAEU countries are forming a new world economic order attractive to all developing countries. With its inclusion in the larger Eurasian partnership, a new world order is being established.

Generally speaking, to prevent the recurrence of such global destructive phenomena and events, it is necessary to form a Eurasian grand partnership and a new integrated world economic order, and to make active efforts to build an anti-war alliance based on mutual respect and in the spirit of constructive and mutually beneficial cooperation. Only then can a concerted coalition of nations be a real deterrent to the US and its Allies. Because they are continuously engaged in hybrid warfare by any means and at any cost.

In addition to the case already made for a broad alliance of States advocating a harmonious world order, the non-acceptance of any intention to impose on others, including the open international investigation of the sources of COVID-19 by inappropriate means, could serve as a starting point for the establishment of such a coalition. Thus, states parties to the *Convention on the Prohibition of the Development, Production and Stockpiling of Bacteriological (Biological) and Toxin Weapons and on Their Destruction*, which entered into force in 1975, could have accused the US of violating the Convention by refusing to accept the 2001 Protocol providing for a mutual verification mechanism. As part of that claim, data on a network of secret bioengineering laboratories set up by US intelligence agencies in countries on every continent could be requested. Investigations could also complement the Protocol by imposing sanctions on States that conceal their activities in this field.

As noted above, developing a set of cybersecurity measures can also be a substantive setting for coalition-building, since this area is another of the most important battlegrounds for US dominance. China takes practical "quarantine" steps at the national level to protect it from social networking sites, parts of the internet, and some telecommunications technologies. In the fight against COVID-19, these measures have averted widespread panic through their cognitive impact.

The book explains why China and Russia are willing to form an anti-war alliance. This is related to the need to maintain long-term peace and promote economic development within the framework of the new world economy. If China has already mastered the basic system, the complete (as opposed to the decaying American central empire) order, successfully used the proposed tool to solve the economic reproduction of the target, then Russia, squeezed by dogma imposed by the Washington consensus, has not yet able to overcome its liberal inertia, and become the subject of an international initiative on a wide range of global issues, based on the law of modern technological economic development, economic transformation is carried out to become the vanguard of new technological order.

China has successfully solved technical problems by applying the experience of national economic development. Russia started to build a new country after 1991, and China started a new development policy at the same time.

As John Ross says, "China's socialist model is overtaking capitalism," and the fastest-growing economies since the 1989 Washington Consensus (except for oil producers or countries with populations of less than 5 million) are not followers of the IMF/World Bank model advocated. They (China, Vietnam, Cambodia, and Laos) followed or were heavily influenced by a completely different Chinese "socialist development strategy." In China and Vietnam, both self-defined socialist countries, poverty has fallen by 85%.

Ignoring scientific advice, common sense, and international experience, Russia fell victim to the idol of market fundamentalism in citizens' savings, high-tech industries, and natural rents. Hundreds of billions of dollars of oil were used to pile up the dollar financial pyramid, and its domestic scientific and productive potential was deprived of necessary modernization resources. The research and production complex was emasculated by privatization. Instead of gradually developing market competition mechanisms and carefully transforming socialist economic giants into competitive companies, a national financial and investment system oriented towards long-term loans for modernization projects was established.

Let's look at the main differences between China's experience of economic reform and Russia's, which have put China at the forefront of scientific and technological development.

1. China has established an optimal economic model of a reasonable combination of private and state economies. What the West does not like to recall is that the Soviet Union was competing not with a market economy but with a mixed and regulated economy. In the US, Europe, and Japan, the economic systems included elements of socialism introduced after the Great Depression, resulting in high growth in GDP (as high as 9–10% a year) and living standards. After the collapse of the Soviet Union, major Western countries began to move away from mixed-regulated economies. Neoliberal myths that justify dismantling state regulatory institutions, privatizing the public sector, and abandoning protectionism for liberal globalization in the interests of big capital began to take root. As a result, the reproduction of the real sector became subordinate to the interests of the financial oligarchy, and growth in production and living standards slowed. Western countries that have simplified their economic regulation systems are losing ground to China, complicating their mixed economy principles.[1]

2. Party leaders, mindful of the dismal experience of the Soviet Central Committee, can contain the crisis at the highest levels of politics. After the reform and opening up in 1978, the CPC ensured power stability. China embarked on a path of confident development. Deng Xiaoping played a crucial role in the success of China's reform by applying the theory of integration that combined the best features of capitalism and socialism to the construction of New China.

3. Chinese leaders have eradicated the western countries' attempts to interfere in their internal affairs. The role of external influences in economic reform decision-making is translated into the recommendations of research scientists and experts, which are filtered with "Chinese characteristics." American hopes that China would collapse or be transformed into a junior partner in Brzezinski's concept of "China-America" have been dashed. At the same time, China has managed to capture a significant portion of the US market, attracting large amounts of investment and acquiring advanced technology.

---

1. Макаров В. Л. Социальный кластеризм. Российский вызов. -М.: Бизнес Атлас, 2010. - 272 с.

From the perspective of scientific knowledge, the two different theories were compared and tested in practice, and the results were completely opposite. The main indicators of Russia's S&T potential and investment have declined more than twice. The economy is in serious recession and falling to the raw material "periphery" of the world economy; China's economy is growing, deeply modernizing, and accelerating based on a new technological order.

Therefore, the new world economic order established by China; namely, the combination of state planning and market mechanism, the state's control over the basic parameters of economic reproduction and free enterprise, and the thought of common interests and individual initiative, has made China's economic development management highly efficient. At the same time, as the originators of the "convergence theory" pointed out half a century ago, China has indeed managed to combine the powerful attributes of socialism and capitalism, avoiding the negative characteristics of each.

On the one hand, by introducing a market competition mechanism that disuses outdated and inefficient production, China eliminated the unbalanced characteristics of the Soviet policy planning model from the unbalanced levels of technological diversification, overproduction, and long-term lack of high-quality consumer goods. On the other hand, due to flexible strategic planning and maintenance of the financial system, basic economic sectors, and infrastructure under state control, China has managed to avoid the abuses of the capitalist system, such as excessive social inequality, overproduction crises, and financial bubbles, and protect its economy from capital outflows and speculation from abroad.

At the same time, Chinese leaders have truly succeeded in combining the strong characteristics of socialism (i.e., concentrating resources in key areas of development, prioritizing the development of social infrastructure, and guaranteeing the provision of basic consumer goods, free education, and health care) and capitalism (entrepreneurship, aspirations for innovation, selection of best economic practices and the optimal use of resources in competition). The CPC has learned to use the energy of private enterprises to grow public welfare. As a result, Chinese leaders have ensured the modernization and expansion of production in China's traditional economic sectors, as well as accelerated the pace of new development, by flexibly changing the priorities of social and economic development, employing advanced technology, and concentrating resources to solve social priorities and promising areas of economic growth. Production in the technical field has created conditions for innovation, entrepreneurship, and technology import.

At the same time, socialist values, such as improving public welfare, caring for the people, creating conditions for the potential of individual creative activities, and educating the younger generation, are still key components of the economic reform policy set by Chinese leaders. The *Proposals* emphasizes:

> "We must insist on taking the realization, defense, and development of the fundamental interests of the overwhelming majority as the starting point and objective of development. As far as our strength allows, we must do our best to improve the basic public service system, refine the social governance system of joint construction, joint governance, and sharing

of benefits, and firmly promote shared prosperity. We must continuously enhance the people's sense of gain, happiness, and security, and promote all-round human development and comprehensive social progress."

"Constructing a high-quality education system. We will fully implement the Party's educational policy, adhere to cultivating people of character, strengthen the building of teachers' ethics and dedication, and cultivate people to build and carry on the legacy of socialism who are fully developed ethically, intellectually, and physically in the areas of aesthetics and labor education. We will improve collaborative education involving schools, families, and society and increase the competence of teachers in teaching and educating; enhance students' civilizational literacy, awareness of social responsibilities and practical skills; emphasize the physical fitness and mental health education of youth; adhere to the principle of education for the public good, deepen educational reform, promote educational fairness, promote balanced development of compulsory education and rural-urban integration, refine mechanisms for universal preschool education, special education and professional education, and encourage the diversified development of schools at the high school level; increase investment in human capital, make vocational and technical education more adaptive; deepen collaboration of ordinary and vocational high schools, integration of industry and education, and cooperation between schools and enterprises; explore an apprenticeship system with Chinese characteristics, and vigorously cultivate technically skilled talents; increase the quality of higher education, construct world-class universities and world-class curricula category by category, and accelerate cultivation of talents in short supply in the science, engineering, agricultural and medical professions; raise the quality and level of education in ethnic minority regions, and intensify efforts to popularize the national common language and writing system; support and standardize development of private education, and regulate extramural training institutions; take full advantage of online education, refine the lifelong learning system, and build a learning society."

Chinese wisdom is commendable. One year before the outbreak of the global financial crisis, based on the modernization of traditional industries, the CPC solved the problem of balanced economic growth and set the goal of bringing the economy onto the path of innovative development promptly, emphasizing the urgency and importance of strengthening the process of forming an innovative country. The successful operation of the national innovation system requires not only strong science and education, but also a set of other institutional conditions, which highlight: As the main promoter of innovation, the existence of a competitive business sector; as a necessary condition for the development of the country's high-tech sector, integrating into the global innovation field; giving priority to public policies in the development of education, S&T, and creating favorable conditions for the growth of innovation. China implements an innovation-driven development strategy, regarding technological innovation as a strategic support for improving social productivity and overall national strength and placing it at the core of the overall national development; China adheres to the path of independent innovation with Chinese characteristics, plans and promotes innovation with a global perspective, and improves original innovation. China integrates innovation and the introduction of digestion, absorption, and re-innovation capabilities, emphasizing collaborative innovation. At the same time, China continues to deepen the reform of the S&T system, promote the close integration of S&T and the economy, accelerate the construction of a national innovation system, strive to build a technological innovation system that is enterprise-oriented, market-oriented, and combine production, education, and research. China endeavors to improve the knowledge innovation system, strengthen basic research, cutting-edge technology research, and social welfare technology research, improve the level of scientific research and the ability to transform results, and seize the commanding heights of scientific and technological development strategies. China implements major national S&T projects to break through major technological bottlenecks; accelerates the development and application of new technologies, new products, and new processes and strengthens technology integration and business model innovation; improves scientific and technological innovation evaluation standards, incentive mechanisms, and transformation mechanisms; implements intellectual property strategy and strengthens intellectual property protection; promotes the efficient allocation and comprehensive integration of innovation resources; condenses the wisdom and strength of the whole society to innovation and development.

China promptly transitioned from extensive growth to innovative development in the era of technological system reform. Although developed countries are in crisis and economic activities have been stagnant for a long time, China has concentrated its resources on key growth areas of new technologies and provided unlimited support for private innovative companies to master advanced technologies. To this end, the aforementioned "window of opportunity" opened for developing countries during technological change is used. By correctly choosing the priorities for the development of the new technological order and intensively investing in the rise of its important industrial sectors, China has achieved a new wave of long-term economic growth, putting its economy into the world's leading ranks.

Hu Angang, a well-known Chinese economist, believes that in forming the national innovation system, the continuous improvement of technology and technological production is the most important factor in China's transition from an extensive to an intensive economic growth model. As a latecomer to industrialization, China boasts a "late-mover advantage" (the potential for "dynamic catch-up"), mainly in the possibility of catching up quickly and cheaply with developed countries through imported agricultural technologies and import-based domestic R&D. Chinese scientists proposed three sources of technological innovation: importing new technologies through foreign trade, including copyright transfer, and licensing, and importing high-tech production materials; acquiring foreign technologies and technologies in the process of foreign direct investment; and their own technological innovations derived from national S&D increase in expenditure.

In 2006, the State Council of China passed the *National Medium and Long-term Program for Scientific and Technological Development (2006–2020): An Outline*, establishing the direction of innovation-driven economic construction for the first time. The essence of an innovative country is to enable S&T to contribute to economic and social development and national security, combine basic scientific and advanced technology research, and obtain world-leading scientific and technological achievements. Since the implementation of this plan, Chinese leaders have continued to pursue a positive innovation incentive policy. In the autumn of 2020, the Central Committee of the CPC proposed new ambitious goals in formulating the 14th Five-Year Plan for National Economic and Social Development and Social Development and the Long-Range Objectives Through the Year 2035. The most important content is to increase innovation:

> "Refining S&T innovation institutions and mechanisms. We must deeply promote the reform of S&T institutions, improve the national S&T governance system, optimize the national S&T planning system and operating mechanisms, and promote the integrated allocation of projects, bases, talents, and funds in key fields. We will improve S&T project organization and management methods and implement mechanisms such as announcing lists of outstanding professionals; refine S&T evaluation mechanisms and optimize S&T incentive programs; accelerate the reform of scientific research institutes and expand the autonomy of such institutes; strengthen intellectual property protection, and greatly increase the effectiveness of transfer and conversion of S&T achievements into practical applications; increase R&D investment, improve investment mechanisms in which government investment is predominant but with multiple social investment channels, and increase support for basic and cutting-edge research. We will refine the financial support system for innovation and promote the commercialization and scaled-up application of new technologies; promote the scientific spirit and the spirit of craftsmanship, strengthen science popularization efforts, and create a social atmosphere in which innovation is revered and championed. We will also improve the S&T ethics system, promote open S&T collaboration and study and establish globally oriented scientific research funds."

At the same time, it is also very important to strengthen the innovation capabilities of enterprises as the mainstay of economic development. The *Proposals* puts forward:

> "Improving the technological innovation capability of enterprises. We will enhance the mainstay status of enterprises in innovation and promote the aggregation of various innovation factors among enterprises; promote the in-depth integration of industry, universities, and research institutes and support enterprises taking the lead in forming innovation consortia and undertaking major national S&T projects; fully utilize the important role that entrepreneurs play in technology innovation, encourage enterprises

to increase R&D investment, and introduce tax incentives for corporate investment in basic research. We will fully utilize the leading and supporting roles of large enterprises, support the growth of micro, small and medium-sized enterprises into major innovation seedbeds, enhance the construction of common technology platforms, and promote innovation based on synergy, resource integration and collaboration among large, medium and small enterprises in the industrial chain—upstream, midstream and downstream."

Judging from history, we can say that China's grand plan for economic, scientific, and technological transformation has been successful in a short time. China has built a modern and mature innovation-oriented economy that makes innovations based on the rational use of advanced foreign technology. Private enterprises have become the core driving force in establishing the national innovation system. The government has no restrictions on the loans it offers and ensures that all the necessary resources are provided to enable companies to complete innovation. The widespread of this innovative approach has ensured a rapid rise in China's economic competitiveness. So, as experts say, a real breakthrough in technology development strategy has been achieved.[2]

Entering a new stage of development, Chinese leaders have taken stimulating scientific and technological innovation of scientists and engineers as a necessary condition for building their own scientific and technological base, moving from introducing new technologies to developing independently. The Central Committee of the CPC pointed out in the *Proposals*:

"Stimulating the innovative vitality of talents. We must implement policies that respect labor, knowledge, talent, and creation, deepen the reform of talent development institutions and mechanisms, comprehensively train, introduce and utilize talents, create more world-class technology talents and innovation teams, and cultivate a reserve force of young technology talents with economic competitiveness. We will: Improve the S&T talent evaluation system oriented toward innovation capability, quality, practical results, and contributions; strengthen the construction of the academic atmosphere and uphold academic integrity; deepen reform of the academician system; improve innovation incentive and support mechanisms, construct revenue distribution mechanisms that fully reflect the value of innovation factors such as knowledge and technology, and refine mechanisms for sharing the rights and benefits of inventions achieved by scientific research employees. We will strengthen the cultivation of innovation-oriented, application-oriented, and skills-oriented talents, implement knowledge-updating projects and skills-upgrading activities, and expand the ranks of high-level engineers and highly skilled personnel. We will support the development of high-level research universities and

2. М.: Институт Дальнего Востока РАН, 2009.

strengthen the cultivation of basic research talents. We will implement more open talent policies and build bastions of research and innovation that attract outstanding domestic and foreign talents."

Chinese President Xi Jinping delivered a speech at a forum of experts in economic and social fields in 2020 and proposed "catalyzing new development momentum through technological innovation. To achieve high-quality development, it is necessary to achieve connotative growth driven by innovation. We must also vigorously improve our independent innovation capabilities and make breakthroughs in key core technologies as soon as possible. This is a major issue related to the overall situation of my country's development, and it is also the key to forming a major domestic cycle."

It should be pointed out that when"Chin'se leaders determine economic development tasks, they fully realize the importance of the economic development cycle mentioned in the book's theoretical viewpoints. Xi Jinping said, "We must advocate the new development paradigm featuring dual circulation, in which domestic and overseas markets reinforce each other, with the domestic and overseas market as the mainstay." He was referring to the transformation of China's economic development towards solving domestic problems and expanding domestic demand.

Xi Jinping said at the symposium, "Since the 2008 international financial crisis, China's economy has been shifting towards a major domestic cycle. The ratio of current account surplus to GDP has dropped from 9.9% in 2007 to less than 1%. Domestic demand has an impact on the economy. The growth contribution rate exceeded 100% in 7 years. In the coming period, the feature of the domestic market's domination of the national economic cycle will be more salient, and the domestic demand potential of economic growth will continue to be released. We must adhere to the strategic direction of supply-side structural reform, twist the strategic basis of expanding domestic demand, make production, distribution, circulation, and consumption more dependent on the domestic market, improve the adaptability of the supply system to domestic demand, and create a higher-level dynamic equilibrium where supply and demand boost each other."

The failure of the US to Impose an"emba'go on the export of advanced technologies to prevent the rise of China's technology proves that the Chinese economy has achieved self-sufficiency in its innovation and development. Let us give some compelling examples to illustrate China's leadership in the new technological order, such as telecommunications and renewable energy.

On October 31, 2019, China launched the 2020 5G global plan. At the same time, three local mobile operators began to provide fifth-generation network access in 50 cities across the country, which not only enabled China to lead the world in the application of new technologies overnight, but also strengthened the position of Huawei, which has been sanctioned by the US. As a result, China has become the world's largest new network user. Since the US does not use Huawei's solutions, fifth-generation communications services can only be provided in certain areas of some cities. However, Shenzhen in China's Guangdong Province has become the world's first city with complete coverage of a new generation of 5G communications. According to data from the China Academy of Information and Communications Technology, a total of 93.7 million 5G smartphones were sold in China from January to August 2020. It is worth pointing out that more than 90% of China's smartphone supply comes from local manufacturers.

Another example is China's leading role in the development of hydrogen energy. In June 2019, the China Hydrogen Alliance published a white paper on China's hydrogen energy and fuel cells, stating that in the short term (from 2020 to 2025), the output value of the hydrogen industry will reach US$148 billion, and the number of fuel cell vehicles will reach 50,000. The infrastructure includes 200 hydrogen filling stations. From 2026 to 2035, industrial production is expected to increase to US $740 billion, the number of hydrogen vehicles will reach 15 million, and the number of hydrogens refueling stations will reach 1,500. By 2050, hydrogen will account for 10% (US$60 million) of China's energy consumption. Hydrogen production revenue will reach US $1.5 trillion.

In the first seven months of 2019, although government subsidized for new energy vehicles have ceased, China's hydrogen fuel cell installed capacity increased by 642.6% (45.9 MW) over the same period in 2018. The production and sales of hydrogen fuel cell vehicles have increased by 7.8 times (1,106). By 2030, China plans to produce 2 million hydrogen fuel cell vehicles (HFCV).

According to Bloomberg News, by 2023, China's investment in hydrogen fuel transportation will exceed US$17 billion, of which US$7.6 billion will come from China's National Heavy Truck Company. The funds will be used to produce hydrogen cars at a factory on the east coast of Shandong province. It will also establish large-scale fuel cell production and build a high-tech gas station network and supply chain.

Shanghai plans to build a world-class "hydrogen energy port" in the Jiading district to create a reliable production chain for hydrogen fuel cell vehicle transportation. Based on the hydrogen energy port, an industrial cluster with an area of 2.15 square kilometers will be formed, and the annual income will reach US$7.2 billion. Wang Gang, who led China to achieve breakthroughs in the field of electric vehicles, was commissioned by the CPC to lead the development of the hydrogen industry.

By 2025, China will transform Wuhan, the capital of Hubei Province, into a leading hydrogen center in China. In the first phase, 20 gas filling stations are planned to provide services for about 3,000 hydrogen vehicles. By 2025, the largest companies in the field of fuel cell production and more than 100 hydrogen-related companies will be concentrated in the city. The number of gas filling stations will increase from 30 to 100, and the total investment is estimated to be around US$1.7 billion.

Chinese President Xi Jinping delivered a speech at the National Conference on S&T Innovation, the 18th Meeting of Academicians of the Chinese Academy of Sciences, the 13th Meeting of Academicians of the Chinese Academy of Engineering, and the Ninth National Congress of the Chinese Society of S&T, confirming that China will become one of the innovative countries by 2020 and a leading innovation country by 2030. In 2049, China will celebrate the centenary of the founding of the People's Republic of China and become a world power in S&T.

Chapter 9

Seven Options for the Future

As mentioned above, according to the internal and external factors of the Sino-Russia-US trilateral relationship, Russia's future development plan can be determined. If in the new world economic paradigm, the relationship between Russia and China remains the status quo and forms a new center of the global economic system soon, then there are two situations in which Russo-American relations will develop.

The first situation is that the US policy remains basically unchanged. The US government still maintains the US's global hegemony along the lines of the past, continues to launch a hybrid war against Russia, and at the same time, curbs China's development. The second situation is that the US government turns to reasonable policies, acknowledging the fact of a multi-polar world and the inevitability of transitioning to a new world economic paradigm. The latter requires fundamental reforms by the American ruling elite and is therefore even more impossible to achieve.

Russia's development plan depends on domestic economic policies. The first situation is that Russia keeps its current economic policies unchanged. This means that Russia's economic and technological development continues to lag behind. At the same time, its competitiveness is declining, and its ability to develop independently will be completely lost. Eventually, the Russian economy will decline. The second situation is that Russia adopts the author's reasonable suggestions in this book and other monographs, and turns to the advanced development zone policy based on the new technological and world economic paradigm. This requires the implementation of an independent MP and the development of a mixed-ownership economy, that is, increasing investment; accelerating catch-up in areas where the technology gap is relatively small; and in areas where development is seriously lagging, introducing modern technology to achieve catch-up.

Therefore, the following options can be considered:

1. Maintaining the status quo. China, Russia, and the US continue to develop in accordance with existing policies. This means that Russia lags behind not only the central country of the new global economic system, but also the central country of the old global economic system. This will lead to a weakening of Russia's military and technological strength, and a decline in people's living standards and social support. The decline in social support will also lead to intensified US aggression against Russia, including the increase of provocative military activities in Ukraine, which is planned by the new extreme right-wing regime controlled by the US; terrorist activities in the Caucasus and Volga regions will be escalated; the stability of the socio-political situation will be destroyed in the capitals of the member states of the EAEU. At the same time, China will increase its economic influence in Russia and the countries of the EAEU. Under such circumstances, the economies of Russia and the EAEU may not be able to withstand the pressure, and Eurasian integration will also

withstand the test of the old and new global economic centers. The Russian economy will become some weakly interconnected enclaves and serve all areas of the world market.

2. American colonies. When Russia's social and economic problems are getting worse, the pro-American power of its domestic politics is recovering. The Russian side made concessions to pressure from the West to lift the sanctions. This will lead to the continuous strengthening of the US aggression against Russia until the establishment of a puppet regime in Russia. America will manipulate the puppet regime to achieve Russia's nuclear disarmament, which will lead to Russia's disintegration. Russia will lose its sovereignty at that time, and the EAEU will no longer exist.

3. Under the conditions that Russia's economic situation is backward and deteriorating, the strategic partnership between Russia and China will be of practical significance. With China's funding, the docking project between the EAEU and the Silk Road Economic Belt" initiative will be implemented. At the same time, China will vigorously invest in Russia's energy and fuel industry, agro-industrial complex, and transportation industry, all of which are adjusted in accordance with the needs of the Chinese market. The development direction of Russia's military-industrial complex will also be consistent with the external defense objectives of the Collective Security Organization and the Shanghai Cooperation Organization. The remaining potential of Russia's high-tech industry will be jointly tapped by Sino-Russian joint enterprises. Russia will maintain independent political sovereignty and develop an equal military and political partnership with China.

4. Isolation and interference. This is the worst plan for Russia. Russia will lose its foreign exchange reserves and foreign sales markets and will be completely isolated. While maintaining the current economic policies, the quality of life of the Russian people will drop sharply. At the same time, the stability of the social and political environment in Russia will be undermined. The EAEU is very likely to disintegrate. The instability of Russia's domestic social and political environment will lead to external aggression. Russia will be split into two world economic centers, the old and the new, within the different spheres of influence of China and the US.

Fortunately, the strategic partnership between China and Russia and the high consensus of the two heads of state based on mutual trust will exclude the fourth option. But geopolitical conspiracies from the West have been trying to divorce the relations between China and Russia. If the leadership of China and Russia changes, or a coup occurs in either of the two countries, then the Western conspiracy is likely to succeed.

Based on the achievements in economic and social development, the Chinese government can coordinate the interests of all social groups. While safeguarding socialist values and national sovereignty, the Chinese leadership has embarked on enhancing the people's well-being and achieving economic development by leaps and bounds. This is a manifestation of their wisdom. Unlike the naive politicians under Gorbachev and Yeltsin, China's leadership will not over-trust

"Western partners." China's political tradition derives from its traditional moral values and pragmatism and is not mixed with the cynicism and pathological lies of Anglo-Saxon geopolitics.

The macroeconomic policy recommended by the Federal Reserve is based on the Washington Consensus Principle. If Russia continues to adopt the above macroeconomic policy, the risk of instability in Russia's political situation will gradually rise. The continued implementation of macroeconomic policies will lead to the following consequences: a raw material-oriented economy, a fragile Russian economy, capital and brain drain, the processing industry and declining social infrastructure continuing, population poverty, and extreme social inequality. Because of Russian President Vladimir Putin's firm stance on the Sino-Russian strategic partnership of cooperation, the possibility of such a situation is currently zero. However, the enormous influence of American agents in Russian businesses, media, and financial and economic institutions should not be ignored. The comprador oligarchs will own a lot of property by manipulating the ruble exchange rate and earning natural resource rents by exporting natural resources. With the accumulation of the wealth of the comprador oligarchs, the power of the network of relations centered on Washington continues to increase. At the same time, as the Russian people's living standards decline, this network's scope of influence will gradually expand. If the independent foreign policy insisted on by the Russian President is opposed, and the suicidal macroeconomic policy advocated by the Federal Reserve is retained, the possibility of this plan will increase dramatically.

5. Isolation and mobilization. Under the global anti-Russian front, if Russia still has the development potential of scientific research and production, military technology, natural resources, and human resources, Russia can continue to survive and develop independently based on the global economic integration mobilization model. This model supports the offshore economy and advocates using gold as the main component of foreign exchange reserves, controlling currency funds, restricting cross-border capital transactions, and implementing a compulsory foreign exchange settlement and sale system. In addition, it is necessary to review the results of privatization, implement a progressive tax system on income and property, and nationalize natural resource rents. Otherwise, it will not be able to mobilize public awareness and restore the people's trust in the impartiality of the government. Monetary and credit policies should aim at modernization and the development of productive forces. State-owned enterprises, banks, and various departments should carry out their work in accordance with the indicative strategic plan and assume their due responsibilities. But the current ruling elite cannot do this in principle. Therefore, all personnel in state power institutions and commercial institutions should be replaced.

6. China-Russia strategic partnership of coordination. The Sino-Russian strategic partnership will be implemented when Russia establishes a new world economic paradigm mechanism and transitions to an advanced development zone policy. China and Russia jointly implement development plans and

large-scale joint investment projects. Substantial progress will also be made in the docking project between the EAEU and the "Silk Road Economic Belt." The greater Eurasian Partnership is being established. Russian high-tech products enter the Chinese market. Russia has entered the "core" zone of the new center of world economic development. In this scenario, Russia's economy is growing the fastest, with its GDP growing by 10% every year and investment by 20%. Russia, China, and preferably India, jointly establish an anti-war alliance. At the same time, Russia's political elite will also be replaced.

7. Sino-Russian-US partnership. To achieve this plan, China, Russia, and the US need to jointly assume the responsibility of protecting the world and recognize the inevitability of the transition to a new world economic paradigm. At the same time, the US lifts its sanctions against Russia and establishes friendly relations among China, Russia, and the US. Therefore, the possibility of implementing this program is now very slight. In fact, the condition for realizing this plan is that the US ceases its aggression against Ukraine and Russia. This situation is most beneficial to Russia, but its realization depends on the effectiveness of Russian economic policies, so this situation is unstable. If the current economic policy is maintained, the development of the matter may be "off track" and return to the fourth option.

If Putin remains the president of Russia, both the fourth and second options can be ruled out. Only in the event of a "color revolution" or a national coup will these two scenarios happen.

Under current circumstances, the sixth option is the first choice for Russia. In fact, Russia can get rid of the influence of the US through this program, use cooperation with China to cast off the threat of the US, and simultaneously maximize rapid economic growth. The seventh option is most conducive to Russia's development, but the prerequisite for the seventh option is to implement the sixth option.

Chapter 10

Transition to a New Global Economic Development Management Thought: The Concept of Social Conservative Integration

The theory of market fundamentalism is the ideological basis of liberal globalization. This theory holds that state intervention is not conducive to economic development, and removing state regulation is more helpful to the free flow of capital. Market fundamentalism is aligned with the interests of large American capitals that are part of the institutional system of the American capital accumulation cycle. The New World Economic Paradigm is completely alien and incomprehensible to the American social elite and its allies. But scientific refutation of the doctrines of market fundamentalism,[1] as well as those espoused by American elites and their allies, can weaken the bonds of America's cyclical institutional system of capital accumulation, and contribute to its disintegration.

Market fundamentalism does not recognize the rationality of national economic regulation. The theoretical basis of this idea is a virtual market equilibrium model. Market fundamentalists try to argue that in the absence of national government intervention, free market competition can automatically rationalize existing resources and achieve virtual self-sufficiency. This theory is later proved to apply only to protecting private property, competition, and national defense. Although none of the principles based on these models has been proven to achieve market equilibrium, this does not prevent the regime elite, most officials, business people, and experts from loving the theory.

If there is a necessary condition in any economic reform, it must be scientific and technological progress. The progress of S&T can guarantee the continuous development of productivity, and the continuous improvement of labor productivity and production efficiency. In the current stage of economic development, STP's contribution rate to advanced countries' GDP reaches 90%.[2] The advancement of S&T is the main factor in improving production efficiency and reducing production costs. When increasing investment in developing new technologies, advancement in S&T can also reduce inflation. For this reason, market fundamentalism based on the economic equilibrium model is not in line with reality. Therefore suggestions based on market fundamentalism are not helpful and are often even disadvantageous.

In the main areas of modern industry and the service industry, the sustainable innovation process has not brought the economy to a balanced state, and the

---

1. Глазьев С. Уроки очередной российской революции: крах либеральной утопии и шанс на экономическое чудо. М.: Экономическая газета, 2011.
2. Глазьев С. Экономическая теория технического развития. М.: Наука, 1990.

economy has always been characterized by imbalances. The main reward of market competition is the availability of talent leasing. Talent leasing is obtained by relying on technological advantages, which are protected by intellectual property laws and can obtain excess profits through more efficient production or higher quality products. To pursue technological advantages, advanced enterprises constantly change a variety of technologies and the productivity of factors of production. Still, in theory, advanced enterprises cannot find a technological balance point. The development limit of the existing technology determines that an economic attraction zone will appear in reforming the economic system. Economic attraction zones are temporary in nature, so as new technologies emerge, they fade away and are replaced by new economic attraction zones.

A new economic development model has emerged in modern economics, which studies the complex, unbalanced, nonlinear, and uncertain economic development process.[3] The new economic development model has laid the foundation for the ideology of the new world economic paradigm.

The theory of market fundamentalism and equilibrium serves the imperialist world economic paradigm ideologically. The imperialist world economic paradigm will give way to the integrated world economic paradigm, the ideology of which is based on the system approach and sustainable development theory. The systematic approach harmonizes the interest relationships of social groups through the development of social welfare. From this point of view, the optimal economic management methods that market fundamentalists call "mysterious science" are groundless. It also illustrates the absurdity of doomsday talk in the context of a liberal model of globalization centered on the US. In fact, the development of the model has reached its limit and will enter the stage of self-destruction under the influence of internal contradictions.

The core of the world economic integration order is the strategic planning oriented to the growth of social welfare, which requires a truly scientific understanding of the laws of social and economic development. As the experience of the collapse of the Soviet Union has shown, modern society can critically perceive any dogma that has not been confirmed by practical experience. Today, people believe more in scientific understanding than religious evangelism and ideological propaganda. In this sense, China's economic reform policy is also significant. In contemporary China, development is the overriding principle, and accelerating the transformation of the growth model is a strategic choice that bears on China's overall development. In response to domestic and international economic changes, China proposes to speed up the creation of a new growth model and ensure that development is based on improved quality and performance. It is also proposed to fire all types of market participants with new vigor for development, increase motivation for pursuing innovation-driven development, establish a new system for developing modern industries, and create new favorable conditions for developing the open economy. This will make economic development driven more by domestic demand, especially consumer demand, by a modern service

3. Эволюционная теория экономических изменений / Под ред. Р. Р. Нельсона, С. Дж. Уинтера. М.: Дело, 2002; Глазьев С. О новой парадигме в экономической науке // Экономическая наука современной России. - 2016. - №3 (С. 7–17) - №4 (С. 10–22).

industry and strategic emerging industries, by scientific and technological progress, by a workforce of higher quality and innovation in management, by resource conservation and a circular economy, and by coordinated and mutually reinforcing urban-rural development and development between regions. Taking these steps will enable us to sustain long-term development.

The scientific methods implemented in economic policies based on socialist values have always been the basis for Chinese leaders to formulate social and economic development plans. The Central Committee of the CPC proposed in the development plan for the next five years: "We must adhere to the guiding position of Marxism in the ideological arena, have firm cultural self-confidence, adhere to cultural construction led by socialist core values, and strengthen the construction of socialist spiritual civilization. We must focus on the mission of raising our banners, rallying public support, fostering new generations with sound ethical values, revitalizing Chinese culture, and presenting a positive image. We must also promote the meeting of people's cultural needs in unison with increasing the people's spiritual strength and promote the building of China into a socialist cultural powerhouse."

The *Proposals* puts forward an ambitious system goal: "Raising the level of social civilization. We will promote the formation of new ideological concepts, mental attitudes, cultural currents, and behavioral norms that respond to the needs of the new era. We will carry out study and education on Xi Jinping Thought on Socialism with Chinese Characteristics for a New Era, and promote research and construction projects in Marxist theory."

Xi Jinping talked about the need to constantly promote theoretical innovation, proposing that special attention should be paid to innovation in "development philosophy, ownership, distribution system, government functions, market mechanism, macro-control, industrial structure, corporate governance structure, people's livelihood security, social governance, and other major issues."

As Sergetsev said,[4] the oligarchy centered on the US is in a leading position in the world, which reflects the value system based on the image of the US as a superpower. The main idea of this system comes from the post-modernism theory of liberating human minds and imposing moral constraints on human beings. The absolute degree of human dogmatism will eventually change into power, which is reflected in the behavior of the American oligarchy. They attempt to monopolize the right to issue the world currency and thus control global resources at will. Only a higher-order value system based on the limitation of human free will can put an end to such arbitrariness. Only the objective laws recognized by rational thinking and the supreme and inviolable religious moral precepts can override the will of people and society. The objective laws recognized by rational thinking are based on the scientific paradigm of sustainable development, and the religious moral precepts should be regarded as the axioms of the global legislative system.

All great religions limit arbitrary human freedom by adhering to moral codes. Modern Western civilization in the post-Christian era (referring to the declining

---

4. Сергейцев Т. Падение мировой сверхвласти: крымский рубеж. М.: Однако, июнь-июль 2014. №174..

influence of Christianity on American political culture) does not accept the absoluteness of these norms, interpreting them as relative or outdated norms that can be violated if circumstances require. When international conditions permit, the American oligarchy has a chance of global dominance. The global dominance of the American oligarchy can be reversed by limiting the US by expanding the opportunities and potential of its competitors. Within the existing world order framework, it is possible to achieve such changes through a world war. To avoid the occurrence of world war, it is necessary to rebuild the world order, that is, to impose absolute limits on the arbitrary actions of individuals and any community (including states and the alliance of states), so as to eliminate the foundation of superpower threatening human security in the imperial world economic system.

The idea of socialist conservative thought (a combination of socialist and conservative ideas), which combines the value systems of world religions with the achievements of the social welfare state (German "Sozialstaat"), socialist ideology, and the scientific paradigm of sustainable development, can be the ideological foundation of the new world order.[5] This thought can serve as an administrative program for establishing an international anti-war coalition and provide clear principles for the orderly and harmonious development of sociocultural and economic relations worldwide.

Only by relying on the basic values recognized by the major cultural and civilized communities can the harmonious development of international relations be achieved. The principle of non-discrimination (everyone is equal) and the principle of loving your neighbor as yourself proclaimed by all religions fall into this category of values. In this sense, such values are expressed as fairness and justice, responsibility, and citizens' enjoyment of legal rights and freedoms. In addition, regardless of religious beliefs, nationalities, class attributes, and other attributes, the basic values of human beings and the equal rights of everyone should be recognized by various religious beliefs and national ideologies. If in terms of modern secular ideology (socialist ideology, bourgeois ideology), this issue can be resolved at the constitutional level, then as far as the relationship between traditional sects is concerned, the issue of unifying values remains to be resolved by itself.

Believing in only one god is the basis of monotheism. The various doctrines of monotheism indicate that to realize the way of salvation for the right to exist, people must believe in and obey the only god. As Davidov, the outstanding modern thinker, pointed out, it is impossible to force one person to believe in another person's ideas, just as it is impossible to replace one to eat and then force him to satisfy. Based on this understanding, violent conflicts between religions and ethnicities can be eliminated, and conflicts can be transformed into people's free choice of ideology. It is necessary to formulate relevant laws for religious participation in social life and the resolution of social conflicts. This will undermine one of the most destructive American strategies in the world's melee, which is to use the contradictions between different sects to provoke armed conflicts between religious groups and ethnic groups, and escalate conflicts into civil wars and regional wars.

Religious participation in international political construction will provide moral

---

5. Глазьев С. Социалистический ответ либеральной глобализации. М.: АПН, 2006.

and ideological support for preventing ethnic and racial conflicts, create prerequisites for transforming contradictions among ethnic groups into constructive dialogue, and eliminate conflicts with the help of various national and social planning methods. At the same time, religious participation in the formulation and implementation of social policies will provide an ethical basis for national decision-making, which will help curb the wanton and unethical behavior of the privileged classes in developed countries and arouse the authorities' re-understanding of social responsibility. Current unstable values in the country are strongly supported by ideology. At the same time, all political parties must recognize the importance of the basic moral constraints that safeguard the foundation of human existence. All these help political leaders and major countries realize their global responsibility for the harmonious development of international relations and promote the successful establishment of anti-war alliances.

The socialist conservative thought (the thought that combines socialism and conservatism) is based on the principles of fairness and justice, mutual respect for national sovereignty, and mutual benefit. It provides an ideological basis for the reform of international monetary and financial relations and international economic relations. To implement reforms, it is necessary to fundamentally restrict the free role of market forces (i.e., supply and demand forces). The free play of market forces often leads to inequality in wealth and income for most citizens and countries. The socialist ideological system with national characteristics adopted by China is an excellent example of this method.

Deng Xiaoping used the term "Socialism with Chinese characteristics" to describe the combination of a socialist planned economy and a market economy under the leadership of the Communist Party. To this day, China's top leader quoted Deng Xiaoping's 1992 speech as saying: "If you do not adhere to the leadership of the CPC, do not adhere to socialism, do not reform and open up, do not develop the economy, do not improve the people's livelihood, there is only a dead end."[6]

The party's leadership and tens of millions of members of the ruling party united to rectify the order of government agencies, encourage the people to speed up the construction of a well-off society, and lay the foundation for a new leap in the economy. This was later called the "Peaceful Rise of China." Initially, GDP growth was achieved, and then the annual GDP growth rate exceeded 10%.

In addressing the key issue of choosing the optimal economic model, Xi Jinping, President of the People's Republic of China, made the following judgment on the vitality of the national economy in November 2013:

> "China faces huge contradictions and challenges in its development. China has encountered considerable difficulties and problems on the road of development, such as unbalanced, uncoordinated, and unsustainable issues in development. China is not strong enough in scientific and technological innovation, and its industrial structure is unreasonable. So far, most fields still adopt extensive methods. The development model, urban and rural development levels, and the gap between the income

---

6. *Chronology of Deng Xiaoping, 1975–1997* (Central Party Literature Press, 1998), 459.

levels of different classes of people continue to grow in the fields of education, employment, social security, medical care, housing, ecological environment, food and drug safety, safe production, public security, law enforcement, etc. Many problems closely related to the vital interests of residents have accumulated. Social conflicts have intensified, and the lives of subsistence residents are struggling. There are outstanding problems in formalism, bureaucracy, hedonism, and luxury. In some weaker areas, Corruption cases and other negative phenomena are constantly being exposed, and the anti-corruption struggle is still severe and complicated. To solve the above problems, we must deepen reforms."

The deepest reforms being pursued by Xi Jinping and his comrades are called the "New Normal," "New Standard," or "New Norm."

The meaning of "New Normal" in the economy is as follows: The era of China's rapid development at the expense of the environment and the interests of residents, resulting in the imbalance of economic development ratio, is passing. The time has come to build a high-quality economic structure, maintain a balance between industries and regions, improve the utilization of capital, energy conservation, and emission reduction. The days of total reliance on external markets to attract foreign investment at all costs are passing. The time has come to meet domestic demand, greatly improve the living conditions of urban and rural residents, and narrow the gap between urban and rural areas. The era of pumping cheap labor into the world's production chains and pouring money into the US-controlled financial system is ending. The time has come for China to rely on its own scientific and technological achievements to produce high-end competitive products, create an independent financial system and secure its global trade interests.

The economic indicators in the first five-year plan to realize the "Chinese Dream" (13th Five-Year Plan) are upbeat, and for a good reason. Even after economic policy changes, inevitable losses from the closure of backward companies, and the release of millions of workers, GDP growth averaged 7.2% a year. For China, this means that the goal of building a moderately prosperous society in all respects will be achieved by 2020. A GDP growth rate of 6.5% is enough to achieve the goal of building a moderately prosperous society. Other indicators are equally impressive, with inflation at 2% and unemployment at 5%. The per capita real disposable income of Chinese residents was 23,821 yuan in 2016, an increase of 7,311 yuan from 2012. This means China's per capita real disposable income rose 7.4% yearly. By autumn 2017, only 43 million people were living below the poverty line (2,300 yuan per year), 55.6 million less than in 2012. Since the mid-2000s, China has shaken off the trend of weak economic development and entered the track of stable development.

The success of the first Five-Year Plan (the 13th Five-Year Plan) to achieve the Chinese Dream is not only because the Party and the state have identified an inspiring long-term plan, which set out very practical medium-term guidelines for the foreseeable future. The drafters of the plan kept filling in specific strategies etc., proposing the "New Normal" in the economic field, the "Rule of Law" in the social life field, and the "Belt and Road" initiative in the international economic relations field. The initiative and other strategic guidelines complement each other and gradually develop into a complete innovation system. The achievements of this innovation system are impressive, and the experimental "Chinese Dream" has a chance to be a big success.

The "reform and opening-up" policy proposed by Deng Xiaoping in 1978 first developed into "socialism with Chinese characteristics." At a new level of development, China has entered a new era, namely the era of "the Great Renewal of the Chinese nation" or "Socialism with Chinese Characteristics for a New Era."

Far from departing from socialist ideals, Xi's innovative ideas return more explicitly to them after three decades of balancing liberalism and market axioms. At the National Congress of the CPC, Xi said the CPC takes realizing communism as its highest ideal and ultimate goal. Xi Jinping, the party leader, has strengthened the leadership of the Communist Party, preserving the planning system for developing the national economy and even implementing long-term plans (typically ten years or more) for developing the national economy instead of five-year plans. While he promoted competition between big and private companies and stimulated public-private partnerships, he kept key sectors of the economy firmly in state hands.

The report of the Congress of the CPC pointed out that it is necessary to uphold and improve China's socialist basic economic system and distribution system, unswervingly consolidate and develop the public sector of the economy, also unswervingly encourage, support and guide the development of the non-public sector of the economy, so that the market can play a decisive role in allocating resources, and better play the role of the government. President Xi Jinping, at the end of the report, concluded by focusing on realizing socialist ideals, such as getting rid of poverty, building a moderately prosperous society and bringing the poor into the middle class.

Experts from the Brookings Institution estimate that China's middle class will reach 850 million by 2030, accounting for more than 70% of the country's population. No one is lucky or unlucky all his life; as the old saying goes, after a storm comes a calm. For this reason, a "safety net" should be set up in advance, and a nationwide social security system and pension system should be established. To maintain the principle of social fairness and justice, the huge gap between the "upper class" and the "lower class" should be narrowed, a relatively fair society should be built, and the government should actively fight against corruption.

It is most suitable to describe the future state of Chinese society in terms of Confucianism's "Great Unity" and "Great Unification." The term embodies the affluent and just society in people's ideals praised by generations of philosophers, poets, and dreamers. Xi Jinping, General Secretary of the CPC, said at the 19th National Congress of the CPC that a great cause should be pursued for the common good.

Socialism with Chinese characteristics for the New Era not only means that China will become prosperous and strong, but also heralds common prosperity with its near and distant neighbors. For this reason, the "Belt and Road" initiative has become indispensable to realizing the "Chinese Dream." The 19th National Congress of the CPC agreed to include the promotion of the "Belt and Road" construction into the party constitution, strengthening open cooperation in innovation capabilities and forming an open pattern featuring land-sea internal and external linkages and mutual assistance between the east and the west. Building a community with a shared future for mankind gives the "Chinese Dream" a new global positioning. In the foreseeable future, building a community with a shared future for mankind will become the theoretical basis of China's foreign policy.

Under the leadership of the CPC, the "Reform and Opening up" policy has been implemented in China for 40 years. Socialism with Chinese characteristics and socialism with Chinese Characteristics for the New Era have become one of the largest and most meaningful attempts in the world. Socialism with Chinese characteristics has gone through many stages, and has been on the brink of collapse more than once. However, the 70 years since the founding of New China and the 40 years of Reform and Opening up prove that socialism meets China's urgent needs. Practice is the sole criterion for testing truth, and it is clear that China's experiment was successful and that no force can reverse the historical trend of socialist development. The Chinese once again made great contributions to the development of human civilization and paved the way for mankind to realize a "Great Harmony" society.

Liberal globalization has undermined the state's control over national income and wealth distribution. Multinational companies gain the right to transfer unregulated assets previously controlled by the state. Therefore, the country is forced to lower the people's social security level to maintain the attractiveness of its economy to investors. At the same time, the benefits of national social investments have declined, and consumers of social investments are not restricted by nationality. Because the US-centered oligarchs take the gains generated in the world economy for their own use, people's living standards in countries with open economic systems have fallen, the gap in civil welfare has widened, and social inequality has once again intensified. To prevent these destructive trends, it is necessary to change the overall structure of international financial relations by restricting capital flows. On the one hand, it is necessary to prevent capital flows from avoiding the possibility of social responsibility, and on the other hand, to balance the country's social policy costs.

It is necessary to reduce the scope of capital evasion of social responsibility, including abolishing offshore jurisdictions that allow capital to evade tax liability, and recognizing the state's power to supervise cross-border capital flows. Equalizing social costs across countries requires global minimum standards to accelerate improvements in social protection for people living in poorer countries. In view of this, an international mechanism aimed at improving people's living standards should be established, and related financing methods should be created.

Social conservatism sees the formation of a global social security system as part of a new (integrated) world economic paradigm. For example, a tax equivalent to 0.01% of the transaction value can be imposed on foreign exchange transactions to ensure that activities are carried out under a global social security system. Tobin, a representative of modern monetary theory, argued that the tax was a reasonable deterrent to financial speculation that undermined sustainable economic development. Such taxes should be collected within the framework of national tax laws and in accordance with relevant international agreements, and the taxes collected should be used by authorized international organizations. Authorized organizations include The Red Cross (which aims to prevent and overcome the consequences of humanitarian disasters caused by natural disasters, wars, epidemics, etc.); World Health Organization(WHO) (prevention of epidemics, reduction of child mortality, vaccination of the population, etc.); The International Labor Organization(ILO) (to establish a global system for monitoring the implementation of technical safety and compliance with accepted norms of labour law, including the payment of a minimum standard of the living wage and the prohibition of child labour, forced labour, and labour migration); World Bank (for social infrastructure such as water supply, roads, sewerage, etc.); UN Industrial Development Organization (which provides technology transfer to developing countries); and UN Educational, Scientific and Cultural Organization (supporting international cooperation in science, education, and culture, protecting cultural heritage, etc.). The expenditure of funds shall be based on the relevant budget, which is recommended for authorization and approval by the UN's General Assembly.

Relying on the investment of enterprises that have polluted the environment to establish a global environmental protection system is another direction of the world economic paradigm integration system. To this end, it is recommended to sign relevant international agreements, introduce general environmental pollution penalties, and use the fines for environmental protection activities in accordance with national legislation and under the supervision of authorized international organizations. Part of the funds raised should be used to hold global ecological activities and organize environmental monitoring. Expanding and activating the *Kyoto Protocol* mechanism can establish an alternative mechanism based on emissions allowance trading.

Establishing a global system that eradicates illiteracy and ensures access to information and modern education for all citizens of the planet is the most important orientation of the integrated system of the new world economic paradigm. This global system must set minimum requirements for universal primary and secondary education and subsidize the implementation of these requirements in underdeveloped countries by the levies collected. There should also be a system of higher education services provided by leading institutions in developed countries, in which global citizens can participate. Mainstream universities in developed countries can allocate their own places to accept foreign students recruited in international competitions (tuition is provided by mainstream universities). At the same time, participating universities should set up a global system of distance learning services that provide free secondary education to all citizens of the planet. It recommends building and maintaining a corresponding information infrastructure, and entrusts UNESCO and the World Bank to raise funds from participating universities.

The integrated world economic paradigm calls for a plan to stabilize the global economy, based on the principles of reciprocity and fair competition, aiming at optimizing global financial relations and avoiding monopolizing certain functions regulating international economic exchanges in pursuit of personal or national interests. The widening gulf between rich and poor countries threatens the survival and development of humanity, and the US and its allies have appropriated many functions of international economic exchange for their own benefits. These countries monopolize the right to issue the world's currency, using equity premiums to provide unlimited access to credit to their banks and companies for personal purposes. They monopolize the setting of technical standards while maintaining the technological edge of their industry. They have imposed favorable international trade rules on the world, forcing other countries to open their domestic goods markets and severely limiting the competitiveness of their national economies. They force most countries to open their capital markets, create conditions for their financial oligarchy's monopoly position, and give the oligarchy the monopoly right to issue the world currency without limit.

Ensuring that the social economy successfully achieves sustainable development means eliminating the monopoly and differential treatment of international economic exchange functions for personal or national interests. For this reason, it is recommended to implement restrictive measures at the global and national levels.

In particular, urgent measures must be taken to prevent a global financial catastrophe, to eliminate the appropriation of global equity premiums for personal or national interests, based on the reciprocal exchange of national currencies, and to form a new secure and effective international monetary and financial system. Commercial banks serving international economic exchanges shall conduct their business in their own currency. At the same time, exchange rates shall be determined in accordance with procedures agreed upon by national banks within the framework of relevant international agreements. If necessary, gold, IMF Special Drawing Rights or other international settlement currencies can be used as general equivalents. It is suggested that super-sovereign digital currencies, which were originally created based on regional integration structures, be treated as general equivalents.

In view of this, the functions and management system of the IMF should be changed. The role of the world currency issuing countries in providing emergency credit in the event of temporary deficits in the balance of payments of individual countries and their banks is clearly defined in the system for monitoring the exchange rates of their currencies, to prevent regional and world monetary and financial crises and create conditions for stable international economic exchanges. Together with the Basel Institute for Economic Studies, the IMF could perform its global banking supervision function by setting the necessary standards for all commercial banks that serve international economic exchanges. To this end, it is necessary to democratize the IMF's governance system, and all its members must enjoy equal rights.

To equalize opportunities for socioeconomic development, developing countries need to be provided with free access to new technologies, if they do not use the technologies acquired for military purposes. Countries that agree to this limit and disclose information about their military expenditure are exempt from international export control regimes. There is also a need to help developing countries gain access to new technologies essential to their development. To this end, the United Nations Industrial Development Organization (UNIDO) and the World Bank must promote active activities, including forming corresponding information networks. The IMF shall provide credit facilities issued by the World Bank for long-term financing of investment projects in developing countries for developing modern technology and establishing infrastructure. International regional development banks can also access these funds under the same refinancing conditions.

To ensure fair competition, international mechanisms should be established to prevent TNCs from abusing their market monopoly position. It is proposed that the WTO be given a relevant role in antitrust policy through international agreements to which all members must adhere. The international agreement should provide that the subjects of international economic exchanges have the right to demand the elimination of the abuse of market monopoly position by TNCs and to compensate for the losses caused by TNCs by adopting appropriate sanctions. Among the abuses of power by TNCs, in addition to overestimating or underestimating prices, falsifying product quality, and other typical examples of unfair competition, are the payment of wages below the regional minimum standard of living established by the ILO. Reasonable price control procedures should be established for global and regional natural monopolies.

In the case of unequal economic exchanges, the state must ensure that it can freely regulate the national economy to achieve the goal of balancing the level of social and economic development. In addition to the mechanisms adopted under the WTO framework to protect the domestic market from unfair external competition, the tools of state freedom to regulate the national economy include various mechanisms to stimulate scientific progress and state support for innovation and investment activities, establishing state monopoly over natural resources, implementing currency controls to limit capital exports and eliminate speculative attacks on the national currency, maintaining state supervision over the most important sectors of the national economy, and improving national competitiveness in other ways.

In the field of information, including the mass media, it is important to create favorable conditions for fair competition. All the world's inhabitants have access to the global information space as consumers and providers. To keep the market open, strict antitrust restrictions should be adopted to restrict any country or related group from occupying a monopoly position in the global information space. At the same time, groups of different cultures should be ensured free access to information services markets. UNESCO can provide important support through foreign exchange transaction tax revenues and the payment of user fees for limited information resources. At the same time, international standards must be adopted to cut off the dissemination of information that is not conducive to social stability.

If the US and EU refuse to re-order the world economy along these lines, countries that want to make a rapid transition to the new world economic paradigm should prepare to set up their own international institutions to replace the IMF, World Bank, and Basel Institute for Economics. This can be achieved by a united stand of BRICS countries.

The expansion of the new centers of global economic development limits the reproduction of the current world economic paradigm, which was designed to protect the interests of American capital. The idea of financial oligarchs voluntarily giving up their global dominance is naive. Financial oligarchs are likely to wage world wars to protect their dominance, forcing the US military and political machine to destroy the economic "periphery" beyond its control.

Chapter 11

Forming an Anti-war Alliance for the Transition to a New World Economic Paradigm

To prevent war in time, the aggressor must be convinced that its goal cannot be achieved. To this end, an international alliance must first be established so that the aggressors objectively cannot win the war. Second, the alliance members should have a unified understanding of threats and a common vision for the future. It is important to reach a consensus on social and economic development laws. Lastly, the alliance members need a common goal and a plan to unite the member states. Of course, measures should be taken to weaken the aggressor and punish him for violating international law.

The international anti-war alliance for the transition to the new world economic paradigm should include the following members:

- The member states of the EAEU and the Collective Security Treaty Organization (CSTO), whose historical destiny and national interests are closely linked to Russia.
- SCO countries that fully understand the dangers of Western aggression.
- BRICS countries whose economic recovery may be disrupted due to the turmoil in the US.
- Some countries in the Central South Peninsula that are unwilling to deteriorate relations with Russia (namely Myanmar, Laos, and Cambodia). Some countries in the Middle East maintain their sovereignty because the world war means an escalation of their own regional conflicts.
- The countries of the Bolivarian Alliance of America. The direct invasion of the US will promote the escalation of a new world war.
- The members of the Group of 77. These developing countries are the successors of the Non-Aligned Movement. They oppose wars launched in pursuit of a just world order.
- Certain European countries. The political elites of these countries can serve their national interests, and they are totally unable to accept that a world war would happen again on European territory.

The reason for the formation of the Anti-war Alliance is that the US has launched hybrid world wars and posed a common threat to the alliance members. As mentioned above, an important condition for the success of the alliance is the denial of the US ideological monopoly in the ideological sphere by constantly being revealed the anti-human consequences of its armed intervention in other countries, such as the mass killing of civilians and the devastating results of puppet regimes arranged by the US in various countries. The myth of American perfection must be debunked to expose the audacity and deceit of American leaders. The disastrous consequences of their double-standard policy and the incompetence and ignorance of American officials and politicians must be demolished.

Religious organizations can be powerful allies in the anti-war alliance because they help prevent recklessness and moral depravity and support the spread of family and other shared human values. Religious organizations would help the members of the alliance organize their work and present a new unified ideology to the world, starting from the restoration of arbitrary moral restrictions on mankind. In addition, international humanitarian organizations and anti-fascist organizations should be given a constructive role. Potential allies should also include the world scientific and expert community, which should take a common stand and develop concrete sustainable development projects.

The goal of the Anti-war Alliance is not only to expose and destroy America's political advantage, but also to destroy its political and military power, which is supported by the US dollar as an international currency. The members of the Alliance should refuse to use the dollar in their trade cooperation and refuse to link the dollar to gold and foreign exchange while the US continues its aggressive actions to provoke a world war.

The Anti-war Alliance must follow the principles of mutual benefit, fairness and justice, and mutual respect for sovereignty and formulate a positive plan for the stability of the global financial and economic system. In other words, an agreement needs to be reached based on establishing a new world economic paradigm. To avoid global disasters in the increasingly chaotic situation of hybrid warfare, it is necessary to reach a consensus on key issues of the world economic system, such as climate, energy, finance, food, water, population, and waste disposal.[1]

The necessary measures to be taken to solve this problem have been introduced above, including stabilizing the financial system, improving the efficiency of supervision of financial markets, banks, and investment intermediaries, promoting the development of new technological paradigms, carrying out gradual structural changes, and establishing relevant new institutions.

The implementation of the above measures to solve the main causes of the global financial crisis, the most important reasons are as follows:

- The lack of supervision on the issuance of reserve currencies in the world has caused the issuing countries to abuse their monopoly position out of their own interests, at the expense of aggravating the imbalance of the global financial and economic system and tending to collapse.
- The existing banking and other institutional business control mechanisms cannot ensure that the country's financial system is protected from the following conditions: speculative attacks aimed at destabilizing the financial system, excessive risks of cross-border speculative capital flows, and the formation of financial bubbles, etc.
- The development of mainstream technology has reached its limit, and the conditions for establishing a new technology paradigm are not yet mature,

---

1. Кьеза Д. Что вместо катастрофы. М.: ИД «Трибуна», 2014.

including the lack of investment to widely introduce clusters that constitute the basic technology of the new technology paradigm.

The Anti-war Alliance should propose active measures to get rid of the global financial crisis, including eliminating the causes of the global financial crisis, creating stable conditions for the world financial market and mutually beneficial international monetary and financial transactions, and developing international production cooperation and world commodity and technology transactions. The above conditions will help the national monetary authority to provide financing for producing new technological paradigms and economic modernization and stimulate innovation and business enthusiasm in the economic direction with growth potential. For this reason, the world's reserve currency issuers must ensure the stability of the world's reserve currency by complying with certain restrictions on government debt and balance of payments and trade deficit. In addition, the issuing countries of the world reserve currency should abide by relevant international standards, ensure the transparency of the national currency issuance mechanism used by them, and guard that all assets in the issuing country can be traded in that country's currency without hindrance.

The important requirement for the issuing countries of the world reserve currency is to observe the principle of fair competition and non-discriminatory access to the domestic financial market. In addition, other countries that comply with similar restrictions need to create conditions for partner countries to enable partner countries to use the country's currency as a foreign trade and currency financial exchange tool, including as a reserve currency. For national currencies that seek to play the role of world reserve currencies or regional reserve currencies, currency classifications should be made according to the country's compliance with the requirements of stability and convertibility.

While setting requirements for the world's reserve currency issuing countries, it is necessary to strengthen the control of capital flows to prevent speculative attacks that damage the world and national monetary and financial systems. To this end, the Alliance countries need to prohibit their residents from transacting with offshore areas, and not allow banks or companies established by offshore companies to participate in refinancing programs. If the issuing country does not comply with the established requirements, then the use of that country's currency should be restricted in international settlements.

The use of digital technology in currency circulation can greatly simplify the solution to the above tasks. If anonymity is not adopted, the national and supranational digital currency will automatically meet most of the requirements for the world's reserve currency issuers.

To clarify the requirements imposed on the world reserve currency issuers and monitor their compliance, it is necessary to deepen the reform of the international financial mechanism to provide fair representative institutions for participating countries in accordance with objective standards. The objective standards should consider each country's share of the world's production, trade, finance, natural potential, and population. According to the same standard, it is possible to create a currency basket, issue a new international settlement currency, and determine the exchange rate of all national currencies, including world reserves, to the new international settlement currency. In the initial stage, the currencies of the alliance countries that agree to comply with the relevant stipulated obligations will enter the currency basket.

The implementation of such a large-scale reform requires corresponding legal and institutional guarantees. In the specific implementation process, the international obligations of countries intending to participate in the reform can be established by issuing resolutions. The actual work can also be carried out with the help of UN agencies and authorized international organizations.

To encourage the popularization of the important achievements of the new technology paradigm on a global scale, it is necessary to deploy a global socioeconomic strategic planning system, which includes the formulation of long-term forecasts of scientific and technological progress, the determination of the development prospects of the world economy, regional organizations and major countries, and the exploration and elimination of existing imbalances. The state's capabilities include eliminating the gap between developed and underdeveloped countries, as well as selecting priority development directions and indicative activity plans for international organizations.

Obviously, the US and the G7 member states will oppose the implementation of the above-mentioned recommendations on reforming the global monetary and financial system. The implementation of the above-mentioned recommendations will undermine their uncontrolled monopoly on issuing world reserve currencies. Developed countries are very satisfied with the current economic activities and factor exchange mechanisms between developing and developed countries. Western countries obtain huge profits by issuing world reserve currencies and introducing new restrictions to restrict capital, technology, and labor from entering their own markets.

The policies implemented by the US show that, rather than reforming the world financial system based on fairness, mutual benefit, and respect for sovereignty, the US prefers to provoke a chaotic world war to maintain its dominant position. For this reason, to become a truly effective anti-war alliance, it should have sufficient defensive capabilities to repel aggressive acts and destabilize attempts initiated by the US anywhere in the world. To this end, the scale of the CSTO should be expanded to attract countries such as China, Vietnam, Syria, Cuba, Uzbekistan, Turkmenistan, Azerbaijan, etc. A partnership mechanism that supports peace should be established in cooperation with India, Iran, Venezuela, Brazil, and other countries threatened by US aggression. If they believe in the importance of the intention to create a superpower, they will be interested in participating in this alliance.

The balance of power between the US and the Anti-war Alliance largely depends on the positions of European countries. As a result of joining NATO, European countries closely follow the foreign and military policies of the US At the same time, the hybrid war launched by the US against Russia goes against the interests of European countries, and the American aggression against Ukraine poses a serious threat to the security of European countries. The sanctions against Russia initiated by the US made the economic status of European countries the first to suffer. For this reason, Russian President Vladimir Putin's efforts to explain to the leaders of European countries the harmfulness of the US policy towards Ukraine are very important.

Even without European powers, the Anti-war Alliance has military, political, and economic strength that rivals NATO, and can resist conflicts initiated by the US. Regardless of the wishes of the US, for the sustainable development of the world economy and all national economies, the anti-war alliance will begin to reform the global financial and monetary system. If the G7 rejects the reform of international financial management institutions, then the anti-war alliance will fully cooperate to establish an alternative global management institution.

It is recommended to start with the issue of ensuring economic security and form an alliance during the transition to a BRICS-based world economic order, including:

- Establishing the BRICS universal payment system and issuing the BRICS universal payment card that connects China UnionPay, Brazil ELO, India RuPay, and Russian payment systems;
- Establishing a banking information exchange system independent of the US and the European Union, like the SWIFT system;
- Switching to using the alliance's own rating agency.

The way to resolve the contradiction between the issuer of the world's reserve currency and the other member states of the G20 is to launch large-scale global innovation projects. They allow the excessively issued world reserve currency to be invested in investments that guarantee the conditions for the sustainable development of all mankind. The above situation can ensure the transition to the new technological paradigm and guarantee the real balance of interests of the world's leading countries. However, this has not been achieved until now. The global financial crisis (just like the current financial crisis) was resolved through disasters. The financial crisis in the 1930s through 1940s was eliminated by the Second World War, and the financial crisis in the 70–80s was eliminated through the external space arms race, which led to the economic decline of the Soviet Union.

The rising military and political tensions of the last decade are typical of a period of technological change, in which the world powers attempt to maintain their dominance through economic restructuring and modernization at the expense of others. On the one hand, the surge in military spending can finance the creation of key industries in new technological paradigms. On the other hand, resources necessary for key industries of new technological paradigms are obtained from dependent countries according to various unequal mechanisms of foreign economic exchange.

Under the current conditions, the mechanism that has existed so far to solve the structural crisis of the global economy through economic militarization and military and political confrontation will bring catastrophe to all mankind. Existing mechanisms should be replaced with those open to all countries to develop reciprocal global projects, where joint implementation will enable advanced countries to leverage their strengths in establishing new technology paradigms. In contrast, remaining countries can reap tangible benefits by participating in new technology paradigms. But creating such a mechanism requires global institutions with the capacity to harmonize interests and formulate and implement mutually beneficial development plans. The G20, as a dialogue club for the world's largest economies, is the best platform for setting up such a mechanism, including:

- Developing global sustainable development goals, including the elimination of threats to human security;
- Developing and approving global development plans;
- Establishing financing mechanisms for global development programs.

Until now, global sustainable development programs have been based on mutual constraints. The reluctance of some big countries to abide by these limits has led to the failure of many mature initiatives. For example, no global mechanism has been established to limit greenhouse gas emissions, which is the main threat to climate change, because of disagreements between China and the US. In terms of actual results, the International Symposium on Climate Change and Sustainable Development did not produce any results.

With its experience as a world leader, Russia can give impetus to the pooling of resources to achieve the goals of human survival and development based on mutual benefit and equitable distribution of benefits and costs among member States. It is easy to agree that the initial goal is to select solutions that eliminate significant threats to human security. Addressing this problem requires massive sums of money in S&D and creating new technology paradigm production industries.

The global Planetary Prevention System is one of the projects that formed the Anti-war Alliance. At the end of the 20th century, science confirmed the possibility of asteroids and comet nuclei with huge kinetic energy colliding with the Earth. Such a collision would have wiped out humanity instantaneously or set it back hundreds of years in development. Therefore, the asteroid threat in space must be viewed as a challenge for the entire human race by national and international security organizations. The Working Group on Risk and Safety under the RAS and the Federal Council of the Russian Federation believe that the threat of space asteroids should be considered a national security priority. The Russian Ministry of Emergency Situations has included the development of space asteroid threat prevention measures in the work plan to reduce the risk of accidents caused by natural and man-made disasters.

Examples of this threat include:

- The Tunguska asteroid crash of June 1908 and the Brazil asteroid crash of September 1930 with an explosion equivalent to one million tons of TNT.
- In February 2009, asteroid 2009DD45, 50 meters in diameter, passed the Earth at a speed of 10 kilometers per second at a distance of 70,000 kilometers, and was discovered only three days before the event.
- On December 11, 2012, asteroid 2012XE54, 40 meters in diameter, passed by Earth at 13 kilometers per second, about half the distance between Earth and the moon, and was discovered only a week before the event.
- The asteroid Apophis (2004MN4) is predicted to pass at a distance of 35,000 km (12.6 km/s at impact time) in 2029. It is not yet possible to predict whether the asteroid will pass close to Earth in 2036.
- The asteroid 2007VK184, 130m in diameter, is predicted to approach earth in 2048 with a probability of 0.0005 (impact speed of 19 km/s).

If the last two predictions come true, they could have fatal consequences for the contemporary biosphere and the intellectual sphere of the planet. Although the probability of such events is 1%, asteroids are extremely frequent in earth's vicinity, and their appearance is usually unpredictable.

The measure to deal with asteroids' harm is establishing an international planetary defense system. The Soviet Union, the US, and other countries all had established the basic components of the international planetary defense system, including rocket space technology, nuclear weapons, and communication tools, which demonstrates the feasibility of building an international planetary defense system. Russia today has all the basic components of an international planetary defense system and an important scientific and technological foundation in this field. However, in contrast to the US and Western Europe, which occupy a leading position in scientific research and implement programs to detect dangerous celestial bodies with strong national support, Russia and the CIS countries lack unified coordination in the field and work mainly based on the initiative. The reason is that the related departments and enterprises responsible for it negatively affect inter-departmental and inter-disciplinary issues.

Facing the mission's complexity, the US considered the possibility of using the equipment being developed to defend against asteroid hazards in the military. At the same time, it organized a series of activities to improve the coordination of work in this field. In January 2016, the National Aeronautics and Space Administration (NASA) established the Planetary Defense Coordination Office. NASA created this department to learn from the fall of the Chelyabinsk meteorite and the asteroid approaching the earth during Halloween.

The BRICS countries have also paid attention to the issue of preventing asteroid hazards. Russia can work independently or with BRICS countries to propose a plan to jointly build a global planetary defense system with other members of the G20 and build an effective mechanism for financing and coordination in the corresponding agreement. Effective coordination is a key mission in establishing a global partnership for planetary defense, because many of the results that have been achieved in the establishment or development of planetary defense system components may be used in the military. For example, using ground-based and space-based telescopes for detecting dangerous celestial bodies also poses a threat. The reason is that if the information obtained through it is monopolized by a country or an alliance of countries (such as NATO), then these countries or organizations may conceal the information about the fall of celestial bodies from other countries. This situation has been confirmed to exist. The US has expressed the need to conceal the information about detecting dangerous celestial bodies, and the US has indeed done so. For example, on January 13, 2004, American astronomers discovered an asteroid named 2004AS1. According to preliminary assessments, it may fall into the northern hemisphere. However, they did not inform other countries of this danger, but continued to observe. Therefore, the key point is to consider the military strategic significance of various celestial bodies approaching/flying over geographic location information.

The foundation for establishing a planetary defense system is the concept of a "castle" international planetary defense system formulated by Russia. The development of the plan is mainly based on Russian technology. Still, considering this is a global issue, the planetary defense system should be created with the best results for mankind. To this end, it is necessary to carry out a lot of search and application research in the promising scientific and technological development field, which will inject a strong impetus into the construction of a new technology paradigm. The core of the new technology paradigm is nanotechnology, biotechnology, information communication technology, and additive technology. The development and creation of the necessary technical means to eliminate the threat of asteroids will promote the development of the above-mentioned technologies, and then apply and promote them to other fields, thereby promoting the economy's transition to a new technological paradigm. The basic elements used as a defense threat system are various technologies in the field of military technology: detecting targets, creating high-energy pulse energy and its delivery methods, etc., while considering their scale. The military-industrial complex has received many orders for manufacturing and developing new technologies, which will prevent militarization from becoming a means of transition to a new technological paradigm. International experience gained in technological breakthroughs confirms that it is entirely reasonable to invest large amounts of resources in major scientific projects, even if the initial goals of these projects are not recognized.

The scale of this task requires the integration of global knowledge, technology, and information resources. This task can only be solved by combining the scientific and technological strengths of Russia, the US, and other world-leading countries based on corresponding international plans. The development of extensive international cooperation based on such a large-scale plan will strengthen countries' trust and prevent the development of confrontational trends. Implementing this type of project will create conditions for the incidental resolution of important tasks to ensure human safety, such as establishing a world anti-missile system for unapproved missile launches.

An anti-war alliance can be formed by concluding an international cybersecurity convention.

Cyber threats from the US pose serious security issues to Russia, China, India, Iran, and other countries that have suffered hybrid wars launched by American authorities. Due to resource constraints, it is difficult to solve this problem by Russia alone. Due to the decline of the electronics industry and the increasingly backward development of nanotechnology and ICT, it is impossible for Russia to use domestic production to replace imported technology in any field. The issues involved are only defense industries, intelligence agencies, and national management systems. So far, the national management system mainly uses imported computer platforms and software to carry out its work. Many of the authorizations put forward by national leaders on this issue have not been implemented, and the operating system independently developed by Russia has not been promoted.

The key way to solve the above-mentioned problems is to sign a broad international cybersecurity agreement, which requires the contracting parties to impose collective sanctions on countries that refuse to join the agreement.[2] These measures include:

2. Глазьев С. Информационно-цифровая революция / Доклад Изборскому клубу // Журнал «Изборский клуб». 2017. №8.

- A country can be identified as a cyber intruder if its intelligence agencies are found to have hacked into or damaged databases, websites, servers, data centers, administrative systems of state authorities, defense and strategic facilities, state-owned enterprises, banks, transportation, communications and energy facilities, and other life support systems.
- For countries identified as cyber intruders, banning the import of computer technology, software, and equipment needed by the state and state-owned companies, cutting off social network connections, shutting down television broadcasts, and stopping bank settlements.
- Taking collective action to maximize the losses caused by sanctions imposed on cyber-invading countries. These actions include developing and implementing a unified import substitution scheme, joint development of software tools, a unified social and information network, and an interbank settlement system.

It is recommended that the SCO member states first sign a treaty on collective response to cybersecurity threats. This will inject strong impetus into the development of the electronics industry of the SCO member states and the production of software products and complicated technical system management complexes. The declaration of such an international treaty that excludes the US may itself be a warning to the US, and we can establish a global cyber security system. If the system is established in most parts of Europe and Asia, then this problem can be solved smoothly. Establishing a Eurasian cybersecurity system can automatically deprive the US of its leadership in the world's information space, computer technology equipment, and software production. After losing important offensive weapons, Americans should stop launching world-class hybrid wars, including aggression against Russia soon.

If the task of ensuring international cybersecurity at the national level is solved, then eliminating threats from individual criminal groups, extremist organizations, or individuals will become a technical problem. To deal with this problem, the national systems of the parties to the international treaties should be used and coordinated to monitor and implement a unified action plan jointly. If the US refuses to sign an international cybersecurity treaty, it is recommended that the state parties build an international alliance against cyber threats. The alliance's mission also includes combating cyber threats from the territories and jurisdictions of third countries.

Despite the current liberal globalization, the leaders of the new and old-world economic orders are far less capable of understanding each other than before. Suppose the accumulation cycle of the Dutch, British, and American systems is based on the common Anglo-German civilization and Protestant ethics that uphold individualism and competition. In that case, China, Japan, South Korea, Russia, and India belong to another civilization that prioritizes collectivism and solidarity.

In the entire era of capitalist development after the fall of the Byzantine Empire, the center of global capital accumulation was within the framework of Western European civilization. After the collapse of the Soviet Union, Western European civilization turned the rest of the world into its own marginal zone. The capital accumulation cycle in the 20th century was built by this civilization. It has a unique idea of capital accumulation and coercive means. In the American system, this idea of the accumulation cycle has evolved into advocating omnipotent money power. Personal value depends on the amount of capital owned by an individual.

The Asian Integrated world economic order is based on another civilization. Although the foundation of this civilization has complex characteristics, the core country's traditional values are to reject violence as the main way to identify relationships, seek harmony between mankind and nature and society, condemn greedy behavior, and pursue cooperation and balance of interests. In international relations, the above values can be expressed as mutual respect for national sovereignty and the pursuit of cooperation while maintaining national diversity and formulating a unified development strategy. In the economic field, they criticize the current world economic order as unfair, since it exploits other countries through unequal foreign economic exchanges to ensure the prosperity of "Golden Billion" countries (US$1 billion: refers to relatively wealthy people in industrialized countries or western countries). There is no aggression and violence in the above-mentioned values, but they cannot prevent aggression from maintaining American global leadership. The only way to eliminate this aggression is to establish an alliance of nations whose members are the potential core countries in the accumulation cycle of the new century, and the accumulation cycle is formed by the institutions of the integrated world economic order.

The Anti-war Alliance must be strong enough to cope with the above-mentioned principled changes in international relations. The Alliance will be resisted by the US and other G7 countries, because they will derive huge benefits from it by virtue of their monopoly position in the global market and international organizations. To maintain the privileged position of the US, these countries are launching a world melee to punish all countries that disagree with the abuse of privileges in the global financial and economic system. To win this war and rebuild the world economic order with the goal of harmonious development, the Anti-war Alliance must be prepared to impose sanctions on countries such as the US that refuse to recognize that international obligations are higher than their own national laws and regulations. The most effective way to force the US to cooperate is to refuse to use the US dollars in international settlements.

The paradigm of sustainable development that replaces confrontation and competition advocates collaboration and cooperation as a mechanism for integrating various resources in the most promising areas of scientific and technological progress. As the scientific basis for the management mechanism that forms the new technological paradigm, this paradigm clearly exceeds the arms race. Moreover, the main consumers of products in the new technology paradigm are the health, education, and cultural sectors, which are rarely affected by military expenditures. At the same time, in the short term, the output value of these non-production sectors, together with the scientific field, will reach half of the GDP of developed countries. Thus, it is necessary to shift the focus of national defense S&T from national defense to the humanities, starting with biomedical research. Since more than half of state expenditures are spent on health, education, and science, this shift can promote planned work in managing social and economic development.

The countries that play leading roles in building the Anti-war Alliance are Russia and China. Because the two countries are in a weak position, they will not be able to win the world war against them if they do not do so. If Russia and China do not propose to build this organization soon, then the US and its NATO allies will vigorously threaten other countries, including our partners in the SCO and the BRICS, to destroy or prevent potential allies from participating in the construction of anti-war alliances.

Russia's historical experience as a leader in world politics is no less than that of the US. Russia has the required spiritual authority and sufficient military technology. The national economic system formulated by the Soviet Union systematically removed the restrictions on expanded reproduction. This is an important new measure, and the starting point for building an integrated world economic order. In its short life cycle, the Soviet Union became a bridge from a colonial world economic order to an integrated world economic order. At the same time, it completed unprecedented industrialization and protected the world from the threat of German fascists trying to colonize the world. Otherwise, German fascists could stop human development grow for a long time.

To gain leadership, Russian society needs to shed a series of inferiority complexes instilled by the pro-Western media during the Perestroika Gorbachevian era and the pro-American Yeltsin era. There is a need to restore Russian pride in a civilization that has been built over centuries of hard work, bringing together many peoples and cultures; and, more than once, saving Europe and humanity from the brink of destruction. Recall that from the era of Kievan Rus to the modern Russian Federation, which became the successor of the Soviet Union and the Russian Empire, Russia's role in creating the culture of all mankind has a historical inheritance. Against this background, the Eurasian integration process should be put forward and transformed into a global program to re-establish a unified space of development in which people from Lisbon to Vladivostok and from St. Petersburg to Hanoi live, cooperate, and prosper together for generations.

PART IV

REASONS FOR RUSSIA'S ECONOMY LAG

The Middle Ages differed from the modern period of economic growth (beginning with the first industrial revolution at the end of the 18th century) when there was a lack of S&T and investment loans to guarantee the development of new technologies and the expansion of production. These investment loans had to be obtained from loan sharks, which provided loans at 50% annual interest rates and sometimes even at 100% annual interest rates. Obviously, this type of loan could not be used to expand production, and its profit rate rarely exceeded 15%, let alone to ensure the investment in production and development. The average rate of return had fluctuated in the range of 3%–7% for centuries, about 5%.[*] As mentioned above, this is the reason for creating the national credit system, which provides unlimited sources of funds for the development and expansion of production through the issuance of the national currency. It also creates conditions for establishing large-scale and high-tech industries and provides the possibility to promote scientific and technological progress. In essence, credit is a universal tool to promote economic growth, and interest is a tax burden. To lower interest rates and open up prospects for production development, advanced countries have adopted effective monetary policies for two centuries to regulate the amount of credit issuance to ensure effective and stable economic growth.

The Russian monetary authorities resolutely refuse to adopt a special credit policy to support economic growth, resulting in economic growth relying on external loans. To a large extent, it has determined the decline of Russian economic growth and the specialization of raw materials, thus falling into a neocolonial mode of operation. European and American

---

[*] Пикетти Т. Капитал в XXI веке. М.: Ad Marginem, 2015.

sanctions have prevented Russia from obtaining external loans, and the Russian economy has returned to the period when it relied on loan sharks to develop in the Middle Ages. The severe lack of loans is destined to degrade the economy further. Due to high-interest rates and the redistribution of bankrupt borrowers' assets, commercial banks with state support can obtain excessive monopoly profits. This is precisely the result of the MP being controlled by the Russian monetary authorities for many years.

This chapter studies the complexity of Russia's current macroeconomic policies by analyzing the theory of monetarism from a practical perspective, summarizing the results of applying the theory of monetarism in Russia, explaining the reasons for the continued application of the theory of monetarism, and predicting the impact of the continued application of the theory of monetarism.

Chapter 12

The Insufficiency of Macroeconomic Policy Theory and Economic Development Practice[*]

Under the dogmatic framework of the Washington Consensus, and almost throughout the post-Soviet period, Russia's macro policies have been implemented under the slogan of continuous reform. The essence of the Washington Consensus, led by the American oligarchs, is to eliminate the state's economic control system to fully realize the free flow of foreign capital (mainly the US) and make the consensus serve the interests of the oligarchs. The requirements of the Washington Consensus include:

1. abolishing economic controls, realizing the liberalization of the financial foreign exchange market and foreign trade, reducing state expenditures, and improving the service level of external loans;
2. reducing the country's social obligations, reducing labor income, and reliance on pensions;
3. bundling the issuance of Russian rubles with the acquisition of US bonds denominated in US dollars, thereby increasing foreign exchange reserves, which will artificially limit the amount of foreign currency acquired by the country to the actual money supply, and economic development is subject to external demand;
4. increasing the tax burden of producers and reduce food consumption;
5. implementing high-interest rates that hinder industrial development; refusal to support private producers, which will cause losses to the entire national economy;
6. complete privatization, including natural monopolies.

To ensure the free competition of market forces, Russian reformers focus on "fighting" against inflation, using simple monetarist "recipes" as weapons. According to the "recipe," the macro policy should be based on the automatic operation of the market's self-organization mechanism, use available resources in an optimal way, and reduce inflation by restricting the money supply. Monetarists firmly believe that reducing the scope of state intervention in the economy by controlling the money supply can provide a stable macroeconomic environment for the free operation's expansion. This free operation is based on a competitive mechanism to ensure the maximum efficiency of economic activities.[1] From a monetarist point of view, this is enough to make the economy develop successfully.

---

[*] This chapter is based on the article titled "Poverty and the Glory of Russian Monetarists" published in the 2–3 issue of *Modern Russian Economic Science* in 2015, and has been updated and supplemented.

[1] M. Friedman, "Guantity Theory of Money," in *The New Palgrave*, eds. J. Eatwell, M. Milgate, and P. Nevoman (1998).

This view is in sharp contrast with the general principles of management theory. Any student who understands management theory knows that the ability to select a management system must correspond to the various states of management objects. It contradicts both common sense and scientific opinion to reduce the objective parameter of such a complex management system as the national economy to the growth of consumer prices and to regard the determination of money quantity as a universal tool. Based on modern systematic management methods and synergy as a leading scientific paradigm, monetarism is more like a religion than a science. From an ideological point of view, it is a kind of obsoletism, a relic of a religious worldview. It is committed to simplifying all the complex phenomena of social and economic reality into a simple entity-money. The monetarist policy is like the medieval practice of treating any bleeding disease: modern monetarists attribute every macroeconomic problem to an excess of money, medieval doctors attributed the cause of all disease to an excess of "bad blood," and in the end, their treatment resulted in the end of the patient's life due to the extreme weakening of the body's organs, even if the disease was not fatal.

The Bankruptcy of MP Theory

Half a century ago, monetarism flourished following criticism of the dominant Keynesianism, which could neither foresee the crisis of the world capitalist economy in the 1970s nor explain the premises on which it occurred. The emergence of monetarism can also be attributed to New Keynesianism itself because it accuses the state of over-regulating the economy. The collapse of the socialist system in Soviet Eastern Europe was a victory for monetarists, from which the danger of state intervention in the economy was clearly seen and truly confirmed. The IMF regards monetarist theory as a key element of the Washington Consensus Theory, which has become the basis of economic policies in most countries with economies in transition. The monetarist theory is predominant in the Russian ruling establishment, obsessed with privatizing state property and monetizing national wealth, and constantly exporting capital abroad.

However, just as Keynesianism was powerless in the face of the crisis of the 1970s, the monetarist theory could neither explain the disastrous consequences of applying the theory in Russia and other post-Soviet republics, nor the Asian crisis of 1998 and the global financial crisis of 2008. The major capitalist countries that issued the world's reserve currencies quickly abandoned the theory of monetarism and began to get rid of economic crises by issuing currencies uncontrollably. This is different from monetarism, which will not lead to a "surge" in inflation, but it is also different from Keynesianism, which cannot guarantee economic growth. For western economics, the world crisis is unusual. None of the mainstream schools of economics, including monetarism, Keynesianism, and neoclassical synthesism, was, or is, able to foresee any kind of world crisis.

To find the reasons for the unforeseen future crises within the framework of the "mainstream" economics, we should turn to the basic premise of the neoclassical paradigm, which is based on the "mainstream" of economics. As we all know, the neoclassical paradigm is based on several axioms: treating all diversified business entities as the subject of economic activities to maximize current profits; assuming that these entities operate rationally, possess all existing technological capabilities, and compete freely in an institutional "vacuum." Bringing markets to equilibrium through the most efficient use of resources is still the explanation of neoclassical economic behavior.

None of the above-mentioned axioms correspond to economic reality, and many well-known scientists have paid attention to this reality many times. Back in 1971, the president of the American Economic Association (AEA) and Nobel laureate in economics, Leontief, spoke of this in his official annual address. In 1972, his successor, D. Tobin, another Nobel Laureate in Economics, also discussed this topic. In 1980, R. Solow, the author of the classic book on economic growth theory, officially announced the crisis of neoclassical economics. Since then, there have been many books on the flaws of neoclassical theory, which explain many economic phenomena resulting from the inadequacy of neoclassical axioms.

Empirical research on the behavior of enterprises in the physical market shows that the motivation of business entities is by no means limited to the pursuit of profit maximization or other economic performance indicators. Facts have proved that the market conditions and technical information available to business entities are incomplete, and there are even information transaction costs and other related expenses related to obtaining such information. And the idea of artificially achieving economic balance has also been questioned. However, the axiom of the rationality of the business entities' behavior in the market has been seriously questioned. Many studies on corporate behavior have determined that business entities have limited analytical capabilities when making the best choice. In the concept of limited rationality developed half a century ago, the goal of a company is not to make the best choice, but to make an acceptable choice for its behavioral variants.[2]

However, until now, criticism has not prevented the neoclassical paradigm from gaining a place in the thinking of political and economic power groups. Worse, the development of mainstream economics has become increasingly simplified and isolated from reality through abstract mathematical structures. In monetarist theory, this process has reached its logical end. Just as V. Naydenov and A. Smenkowski wrote about the essence of monetarism in their profound and persuasive book, supplementing the unrealistic axioms of the neoclassical market equilibrium theory. M. Friedman, the founder of monetarism, also made a premise that was completely out of touch with the real economy[3]:

1. Constant population;
2. Fixed market entity style and preference;
3. A fixed amount of physical resources;
4. Constant labor productivity;

---

2. Herbert S., *An Administrative Behaviour: A Study of Decision-Making Processes in Administrative Organizations* (Glencoe: Free Press, 1960).

3. Найденов В., Сменковский А. Инфляция и монетаризм. Уроки антикризисной политики. Киев: ОАО БЦКФ, 2003; Фридмен М. Количественная теория денег. М.: Эльф пресс, 1996.

5. Stable social structure;
6. Free competition;
7. Stable capital goods without loss;
8. Unable to buy or sell capital goods;
9. Prohibition of lending;
10. Only money for services and services for money are allowed, i.e., barter is prohibited;
11. Free pricing;
12. Keep only cash (coins and notes);
13. A fixed cash amount.

Friedman used the premise that the economy was in equilibrium to analyze the economy. Within the framework of these assumptions, he analyzed the consequences of discrete growth of nominal money. He concluded that as the purchasing power of money decreased, prices would rise proportionally, and economic equilibrium would gradually recover. Friedman believed that the quantity of nominal money was determined by its supply, the quantity of real money was determined by its demand, and the quantity of demand remained unchanged in his "fixed society" model. Based on this, he concluded that an increase in the amount of currency in circulation would lead to a proportional increase in prices and a decrease in the amount of personal and social wealth. He argued that by virtue of the law of self-organization of markets, prices would automatically enter a new equilibrium state. He concluded that the main condition for monetary stability was to restrict the money supply.

Friedman wrote: "The theory of money supply stability is the closest to the optimal policy.… The short-term goal of this policy may be to stabilize resource prices. If the elasticity of real money demand were the same as the elasticity of demand income, the US would need to increase the money supply by about 1% a year, given population and labor force growth. If the elasticity becomes greater as in the last century, the money supply can grow by about 2% yearly."[4]

This conclusion of Mr. Friedman is in sharp contrast with the actual monetary policies of all world reserve currency issuing countries: in recent years, these countries have expanded their monetary bases by a greater order of magnitude. L. Lehmann gave an accurate guess about Friedman's neoclassical dogma. He believed that neither Friedman's calculations nor the "growth of population and labor force" could prove the argument. D. Camp added that the US needed a gold standard like that before 1933, which explained the increase in gold mining in those years.[5] As the convertibility of the US dollar to gold recovers, inflation will disappear. In their extraordinary and persuasive research, V. Najdenov and A. Smenkowski concluded,[6] "this, in effect, is how Friedman and other monetarists used to determine the 'optimal' amount of money in circulation. Monetarism reproduces quantitative monetary theory in the age of metal coins. This chapter builds on the work of V. Naydenov and A. Smenkowski

---

4. Фридмен М. Если бы деньги заговорили… М.: Дело, 1998.
5. Kemp J., *An American Renaissance: A Strategy for the 1980s* (N.Y., 1979).
6. Найденов В., Сменковский А. Инфляция и монетаризм. Уроки антикризисной политики. Киев: ОАО БЦКФ, 2003.

and the analysis of Friedman's article, who objectively describe monetarism as "a vulgar variation of the classical quantitative theory of money."[7]

Based on the quantitative theory of money, monetarists believe that the main factor of inflation is the change in the amount of money in circulation. In their view, the actual production volume does not directly depend on changes in the money supply. Still, it is determined by the supply of existing production factors in the economy, such as the scale and productivity of labor, equipment, land, and technology. In this case, they support Fisher's hypothesis about currency "passivity" (the size of the transaction depends on other factors, not the amount of currency[8]), and monetarists coarsely ignore Fisher's condition that an increase in the money supply positively affects trade.

Since Fisher's equation of exchange has become a basic doctrine of monetarists, it is necessary for us to study its meaning in depth. Fisher formulated the exchange equation as early as 1911: $MV = PQ$, where M is the money supply, V is the velocity of circulation, P is the price, and Q is the quantity of goods. In fact, this equation is an identity because one of its variables—the velocity of money circulation—is usually determined by other variables, namely $V = PQ/M$. Moreover, this equation violates the theoretical frequency in practice, replacing the quantity of goods with GDP, and explaining the price as changes in consumer prices, which is called inflation.

This identity is not verifiable and is regarded as an axiom from which the most important assumptions of the quantity theory of money can be derived. On this basis, according to the direct proportional relationship between the increase in the amount of money and the rate of inflation,[9] recommendations on macroeconomic policies were put forward.

Contrary to monetarist beliefs, prices may rise and fall if all other variables (including money supply) remain the same. In addition, the increase and decrease of commodity supply may depend on the dynamic process of economic changes. Introducing new technologies leads to a decrease in prices, and the fraudulent behavior of monopolists leads to an increase in prices. Changes in one set of commodities' prices will never be compensated by the opposite changes in another set of commodities' price. Moreover, this compensation may only occur when commodities' supply and demand prices (this price is consistent with speculative behavior) are inelastic, which is not included in Friedman's axioms.

The monetarist's identity reflects a static picture, which can theoretically be copied as a certain market equilibrium state in an abstract mathematical model. When the dependency relationship that reflects the real economic process is introduced, the variables of this identity can be changed independently of each other. In fact, the economy will never regain balance, and at any time, it will enter a new state with the value of the variable of the currency identity.

The contradiction of the quantity theory of money, ignoring the main factors of economic growth, such as STP and the inverse link between the money supply and

7. Найденов В., Сменковский А. Инфляция и монетаризм. Уроки антикризисной политики. Киев: ОАО БЦКФ, 2003.

8. Фишер И. Покупательная сила денег. М.: НКФ СССР, 1926.

9. Глазьев С. Нищета и блеск российских монетаристов // Экономическая наука современной России. 2015, №2–3.

the expansion of production, rendered meaningless all the practical conclusions and recommendations of the theory, including those drawn up by Friedman and other economists, such as the monetarist favorite creed put forward by the representatives of the "Chicago School" in the late 1950s: the root of difficulties and crises-external factors and government intervention in the economy. Therefore, the country's regulatory role must be minimized; the main mechanism of economic regulation should be the monetary and credit policy; an important part of the macroeconomic policy should be to restrict wages, because it has a decisive impact on prices.

The superficial conclusions drawn by monetarists' mechanical reasoning cannot withstand any criticism. A. Okun deduced the inverse relationship between unemployment and production based on the "Phillips Curve," which means that for every 2% decrease in the gross national product (GNP), below the potential gross national product, the unemployment rate will increase by 1%. As pointed out by V. Najdenov and A. Smenkowski, if the conclusions of Phillips and Okun were combined, there would be a direct relationship between inflation and production. Some monetarists concluded that to reduce the inflation rate by 1%, it is necessary to sacrifice 5% of the annual GDP or 2.5% of the employment rate.[10] Although the Phillips curve is unreliable and has not been confirmed since the 1970s (even throughout the period after World War II, McConnell and Brue's research showed that this hypothesis could not be verified by the regression analysis of US macroeconomic indicators[11]), it is still used in the mathematical models of commodity currency exchanges of the IMF and even the Bank of Russia.

Therefore, when the monetarists' advice was put into practice, it led to disastrous results, and they made a pseudo-scientific explanation for this. They interpreted the decline in production and the increase in unemployment caused by the "shrinkage" of the money supply as reasonable consumption to reduce inflation. Before the disastrous results caused by this policy, G. Mankiw called the severe drop in production due to falling inflation "shock therapy." However, if inflation falls because of reduced demand, it will usually not last long. The "shrinkage" of the money supply will lead to stagflation. In the case of rising inflation and unemployment, production and investment will fall at the same time. In post-socialist and advanced capitalist economies, many studies have failed to reveal a significant relationship between the growth of the money supply and the increase in inflation. However, a stable and statistically confirmed link can be clearly found between the decline in the money supply and the decline in production and investment.[12]

Practical Flaws in MP

There is an obvious negative correlation between the application of monetarism theory and economic growth rate. The IMF (IBM) is considered the most authoritative and influential "defense lawyer" of this theory. Therefore, to evaluate its effectiveness, we

10. Мэнкью Г. Макроэкономика. М.: Из-во Московского университета, 1994.

11. Макконнелл К., Брю С. Экономикс: принципы проблемы и политика. М.: Республика, 1992.

12. Обучение рынку / Под ред. С. Глазьева. М.: Экономика, 2004.

can simply compare the economic development results of those countries that have adopted and have not adopted the IMF recommendations. It can be seen from Figure 12-1 that the average economic growth rate of countries that have not adopted the IMF's recommendations is approximately twice that of other countries.[13]

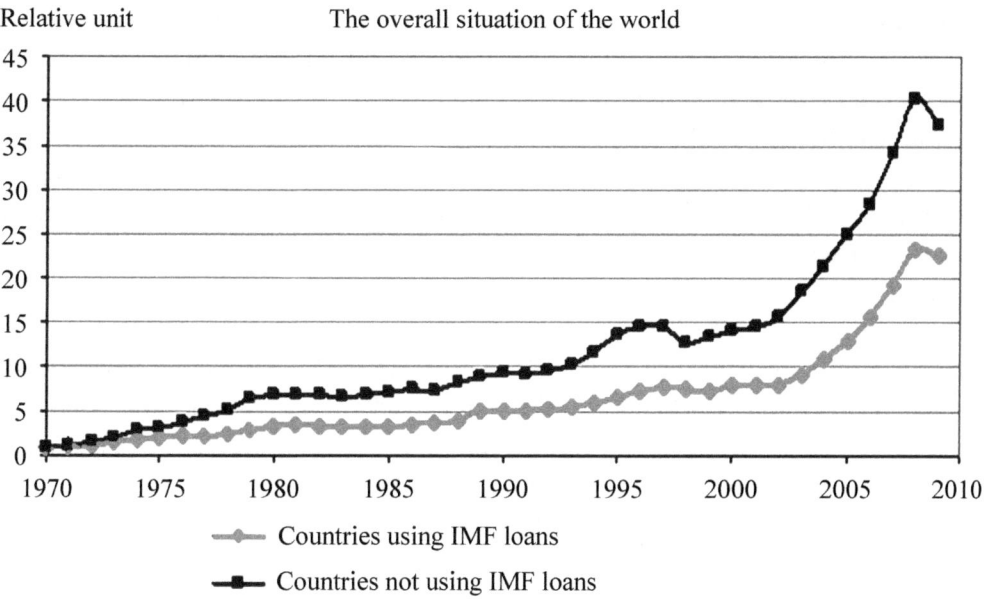

Figure 12-1 Relative unit / The overall situation of the world

— Countries using IMF loans
— Countries not using IMF loans

Figure 12-1 GDP of Countries That Have (Not) Borrowed from the IMF

Please note that developed countries have never adopted the recommendations of the IMF, nor have they seen them as a tool for universal neocolonial policies against dependent countries. It is no coincidence that the IMF is supervised by the US Government's Deputy Treasury Secretary responsible for cooperation with foreign countries. The recommendations of the IMF are just based on these developed countries. This double standard has always existed and has repeatedly led to large-scale crises in developing countries. The IMF's recommendations focus on serving the US capital interests related to the Federal Reserve, which issues world currencies. In developing countries, the leaders of American capital interests are comprador elites, who use Western capital to develop their own natural resources and population potential. The division of society into super-rich "elites" and poor people controlled by authoritarian regimes is one of the consequences of monetarist politics. The growth index of capitalization and the number of billionaires (usually used to prove the currency's success) expose the beneficiaries of the policy and hide the victims, including the majority of people who are exploited because of national monetarism.

L. Erhard's policy is an intuitive positive case against neoclassical dogma. He created the economic miracle in Federal Germany after World War II. Regarding the

13. Политическое измерение мировых финансовых кризисов / Под ред. В. Якунина, С. Сулакшина, И. Орлова. Центр проблемного анализа и государственно-управленческого проектирования. Век глобализации. 2013. Выпуск №2 (12).

monetarist's suggestion, he wrote: "Currency has a priority status that the economy does not have. The first and only thing we should pay attention to is economic welfare. They are reasonable only when monetary and technical measures really serve to achieve this goal. Money is not at the same level as the economy, but one of its auxiliary mechanisms."[14] He believes that in the case of insufficient utilization of existing productivity, it is necessary to increase credit to expand production growth. In addition, he knows the limits of increasing credit. That is, there is no causal relationship between inflation and the amount of money in circulation. Inflation occurs only when income is obtained in the medium-term plan or from business activities[15] (which do not bring real benefits to the economy).

J. Cairns described the relationship between the money supply and the dynamics of production: "When the employment of the factors of production is insufficient, the degree to which the factors are used will change in proportion to the quantity of money; when employment is sufficient, the price will alter in proportion to the quantity of money."[16]

Therefore, the absurdity of the Bank of Russia's current policy is that the actual money supply is reduced when the industrial capacity load is about 60%. In addition, contrary to the facts, the Bank of Russia claims that the productivity utilization rate of the manufacturing industry is still high. However, infrastructure and institutional constraints still exist. All these limits the growth rate of potential GDP, and without modernization and labor productivity improvement, the possibility of a non-inflationary production increase will also be limited.[17]

Economy-mathematical structures (simple extrapolation of observed indicators, Philips curves, production functions, and other artificially constructed dependencies traditionally used by monetarists, despite mismatches in the real relationship between production dynamics and money supply) demonstrate that this claim contradicts official statistics. It seems that the existing simple economic and mathematical tools of the Bank of Russia are only tailored to the doctrine of monetarism.

The most important of all macroeconomic policies is to reduce inflation. This is an assumption that has not been confirmed by statistical studies and is not found in Friedman's work or that of other prominent monetarist theorists. Still, it is considered an IMF axiom that the lower the inflation rate, the higher the growth rate of production is likely to be, and vice versa.

At the same time, P. Samuelson, a classic writer of modern economic theory, pointed out: Does anyone worry about inflation? Will resource use efficiency or actual GNP be higher or lower? The answer to these two questions is: no. Inflation is balanced and predictable and will not affect actual output, efficiency, or income distribution.[18] Later, V. Polterovich used many examples to prove that moderate inflation (up to 20%

14. Эрхард Л. Полвека размышлений. М.: Руссико-Ордынка, 1993.

15. Эрхард Л. Полвека размышлений. М.: Руссико-Ордынка, 1993.

16. Кейнс Дж. Избранные произведения. М.: Экономика, 1993.

17. Основные направления единой государственной денежно-кредитной политики на 2015 г. и период 2016 и 2017 годов // Вестник Банка России. №106 (1584) от 1. 12. 2014.

18. Самуэльсон П., Нордгауз В. Макроэкономика. К: Основы, 1995.

per year) will not hinder economic growth.[19] At the same time, inflation exceeding 40% will have a negative impact on economic growth.[20] Under the leadership of R. Nyzhgorodtsev, he conducted research on data from more than 30 countries and clarified the relationship between inflation and economic growth.[21] According to the obtained model, it can be determined that for most countries, if the upper limit of the maximum inflation rate within the allowable range is not exceeded, the steady growth of GDP can be maintained. Moreover, as the author pointed out, the reasonable range allowed for changes in key macroeconomic parameters must vary from country to country, and its value should be determined according to the specific economic dynamic trajectory.

Like Friedman, the Russian monetarists believe that inflation is a monetary phenomenon everywhere and must only be fought with restrictions on monetary credit policy—the second doctrine. At the same time, half a century ago, even in the monetarist model (especially L. Harris and F. Keygen),[22] it was determined that there was a possibility of inflation without a corresponding increase in the money supply. The typical behavior of business entities in the modern economy clearly shows the unreliability of the above-mentioned dogma. Monetarists divorced from reality can see neither the field of production nor the progress of S&T in their speculation theory. Therefore, they cannot understand that the monopolist's pricing policy is the main factor of inflation in the real economy of most countries (such as Russia). The main factors in reducing inflation are the reduction of parity costs and the improvement of product quality. Both are defined by scientific and technological progress. In turn, STP relies on loans for investment and innovation.

Based on many statistics, through the analysis of the relationship between money supply and GDP and inflation, any illusions about the successful realization of macroeconomic stability by restricting money supply have been dispelled. In this regard, Japan and China are the leaders, where the amount of money supply exceeds 1.5 to 2 times of GDP.[23] During the period of economic growth, the money supply grows by 20%%–40% every year, accompanied by deflation.

Research conducted by experts from the World Bank also refuted this dogma and pointed out that there was a very clear inverse relationship between currency circulation (money supply as a percentage of GDP) and inflation: according to the comparison of data from various countries, the smaller the circulation, the higher the inflation rate.[24] This fact contradicts the usual monetarism, and the specific explanation is as follows.

19. Полтерович В. Механизмы «ресурсного проклятия» и экономическая политика // Вопросы экономики. 2007. №6.

20. Найденов В., Сменковский А. Инфляция и монетаризм. Уроки антикризисной политики. Киев: ОАО БЦКФ, 2003.

21. Нижегородцев Р., Горидько Н., Шкодина И. Институциональные основы теории финансов: современные подходы. М.: ИНФРА-М, 2014.

22. Харрис Л. Денежная теория. М.: Прогресс, 1990.

23. Обучение рынку / Под ред. С. Глазьева. М.: Экономика, 2004.

24. Бузгалин А. В., Колганов А. И. Введение в компаративистику (Исследование и сравнительный анализ социально-экономических систем: методология, теория, применение к переходным экономикам). М.: Таурус-Альфа, 1997.

According to the logic of the actual relationship between enterprises, the restrictive MP aimed at reducing the monetary base is not so much a reduction in the quantity of the money supply, as it is a reduction in the quality of the money supply. The interconnected production cooperative enterprises compensate for insufficient funds by issuing currency substitutes (various bonds), thus alleviating the debt crisis. For example, it is estimated that in the mid-1990s, the total amount of "quasi-money" circulating in Russia reached half of the total money supply. In some areas, it accounted for 80%–90%[25] of the total operation of Russian enterprises. Substituting currency substitutes for money does not guarantee sufficient funds for reproduction and investment, leading to an intensified economic recession. Coupled with the increase in the risk of arrears, inflation will also increase.

In 2013, the inverse relationship between inflation and the level of economic monetization was convincing: the higher the amount of money in the economy, the lower the inflation, and vice versa.[26] Not only the post-Soviet countries, but also European countries (Bulgaria and Romania) that had imposed the most stringent restrictions on circulation encountered the most serious problems in terms of inflation and curbing the decline in production. Afterwards, most of these countries used the expansion of currency issuance to stimulate economic growth, contrary to the monetarist dogma of financial stability.

The latest research by R. Nizhegorodtsev and N. Goritko shows a U-shaped relationship between money supply and inflation.[27] According to the empirical data of many countries, they clearly confirmed that the excess and shortage of money supply are equally dangerous to the stability of currency circulation. The excess and shortage of money supply hinder the effective management of the inflation process to the same extent. In other words, the stability of the money market requires that the money supply is not less than the supply necessary for simple economic reproduction, nor should it be more than the supply necessary for expanded reproduction based on available resources. Because in both cases, inflation will inevitably increase. When the amount of currency in circulation is maintained at a moderate level, the inflation rate is extremely low.

Therefore, the relationship between inflation and money supply is not only nonlinear but also non-uniform. Inflation will increase when the amount of money exceeds the optimal level of expanded reproduction or is insufficient (Figure 12-2).

Finally, the third dogma and the conclusion of monetary theory boil down to opposition to government intervention in economic activities in any form, because according to Friedman, government intervention in economic activities threatens the consensus reached on income distribution, the moral foundation of a free society.

---

25. Яковлев А., Глисин Ф. Альтернативные формы расчетов в народном хозяйстве и возможности их анализа методами субъективной статистики // Вопросы статистики. 1996. № 9. С. 21–31.

26. Якунин В. Сулакшин С., Орлов И. Указ. соч. 2013.

27. Нижегородцев Р., Горидько Н. Критика формулы Ирвинга Фишера и иллюзии современной монетарной политики / Материал к обсуждению на научном семинаре кафедры теории и методологии государственного и муниципального управления ФГУ МГУ, 2016; Глазьев С., Горидько Н., Нижегородцев Р. Критика формулы Ирвинга Фишера и иллюзии современной монетарной политики // Экономика и математические методы. 2016. №4. С. 3–23.

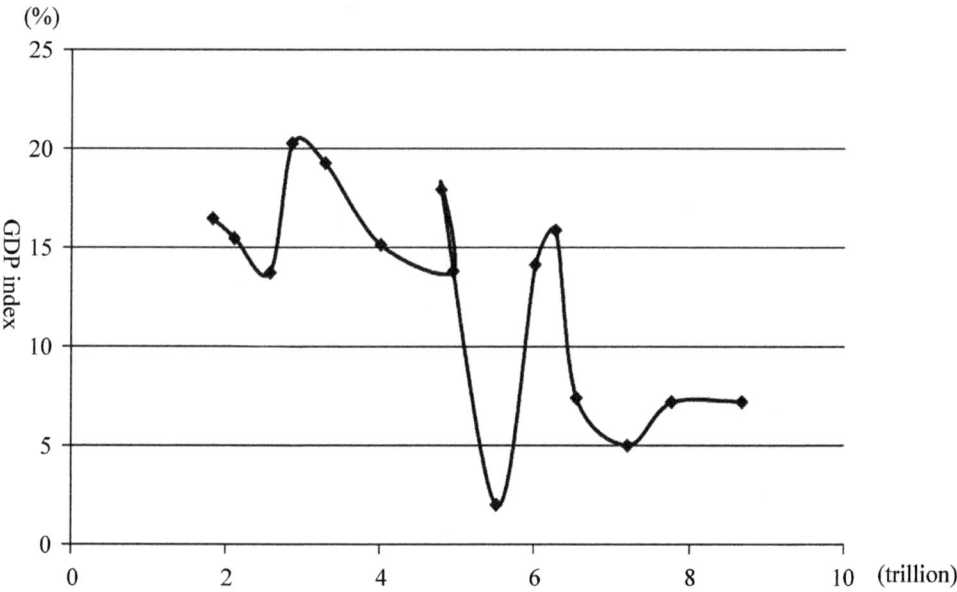

Figure 12-2 The Relationship between Russia's Money Supply and Inflation from 2001 to 2015
Source: Нижегородцев Р. М., Горидько Н. П. Управление монетарной сферой и перспективы экономического роста: уроки кризиса, модели, прогнозы. В кн: "Экономическая безопасность современной России: уроки кризиса и перспективы роста" / Под ред. В. А. Черешнева, А. И. Татаркина, М. В. Федорова. Екатеринбург: Институт экономики УрО РАН, 2012. Т. 1. С. 831–877.

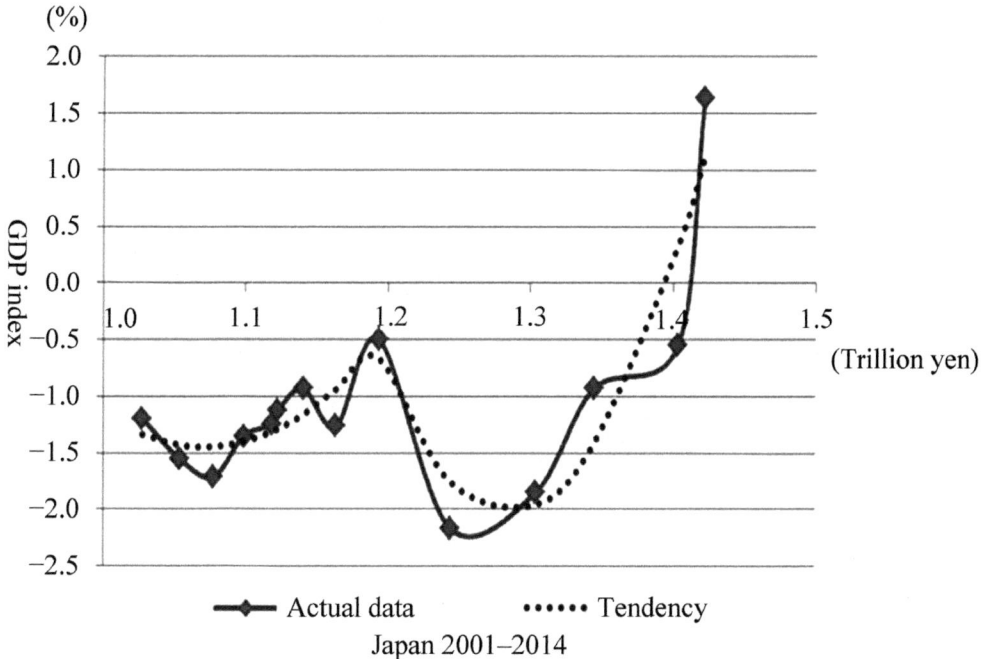

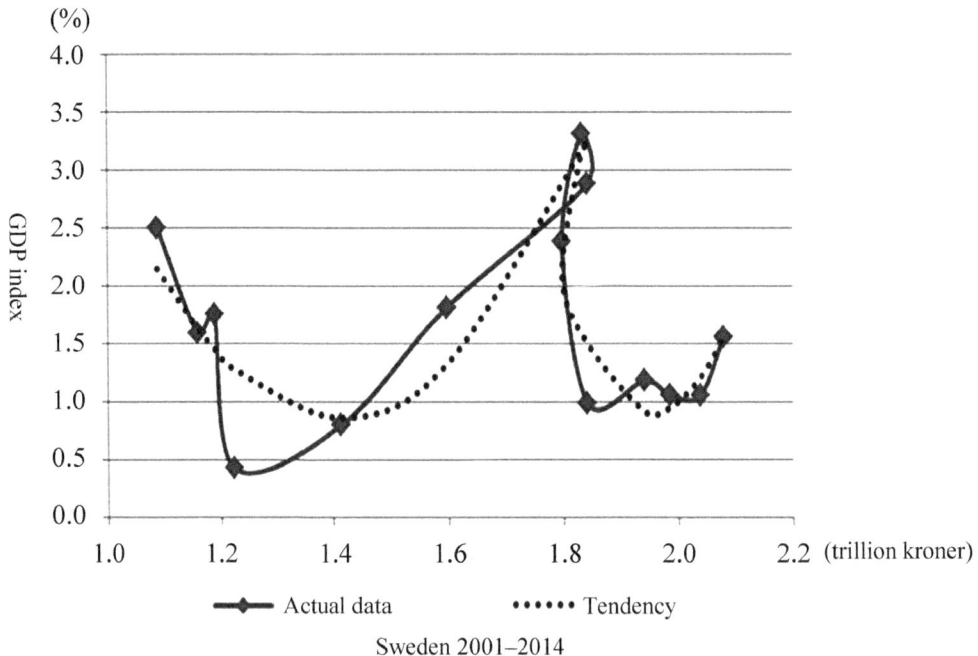

Sweden 2001–2014

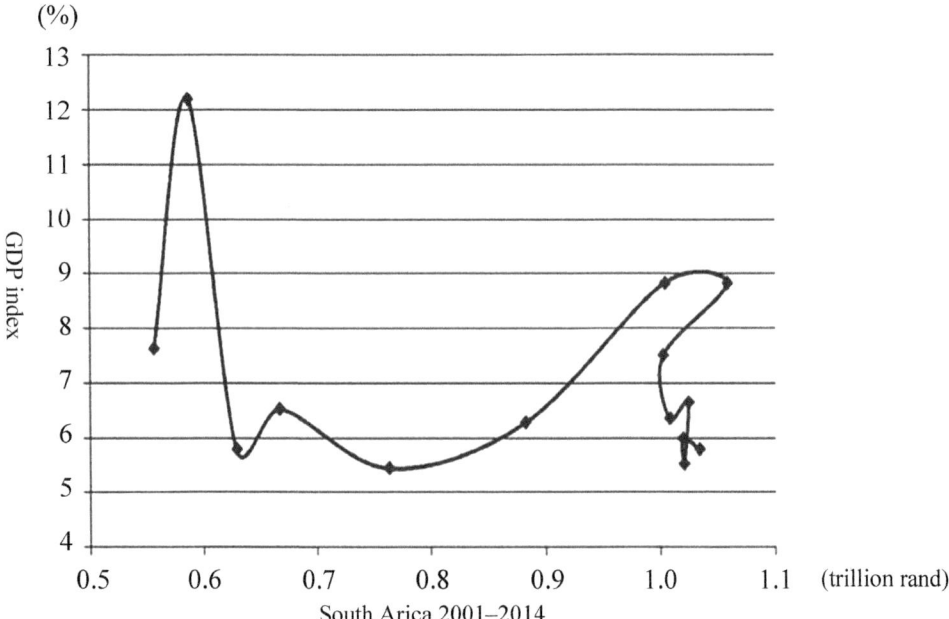

South Arica 2001–2014

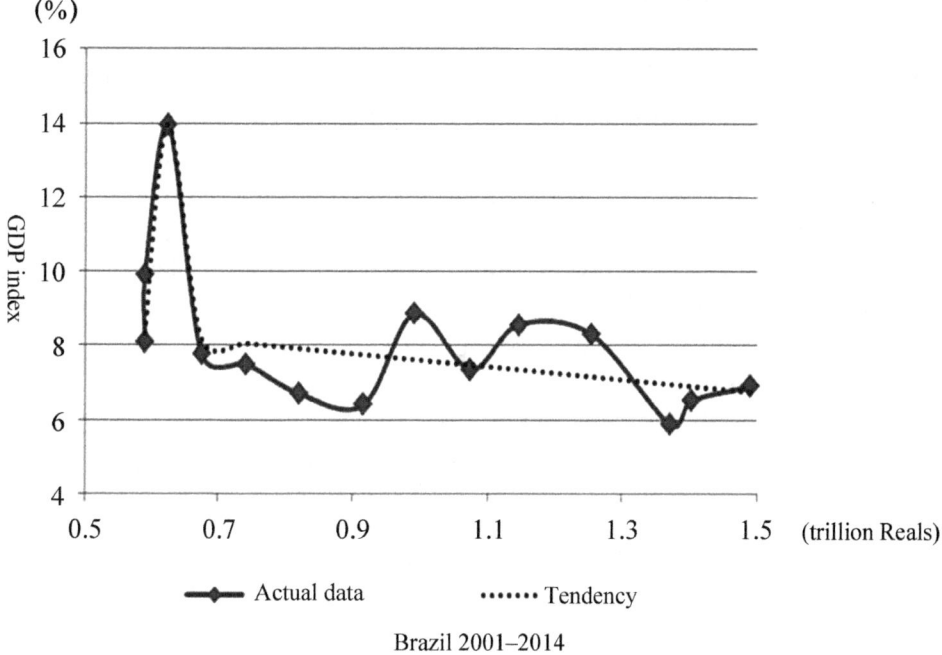

(%)

GDP index

Brazil 2001–2014

Figure 12-3 Relationship between Inflation Rates and Money Supply in Countries around the World

However, this does not prevent monetarists from proposing "income policies" to limit wage growth, thereby ensuring what they believe is low inflation. The result of Russia's implementation of this policy is that real wages, pensions, and social welfare levels have dropped significantly. Essentially, that means genocide: under normal fertility conditions, the potential population has decreased by 12 million compared to the 1990s.[28] This dogma is supplemented by proposals to reduce budget expenditures and oppose issuing agencies to make up budget deficits. Monetarists believe that funds should only be raised from illegal channels to make up for budget deficits: internal and external loans in financial markets.

On the contrary, in the US, the European Union, and Japan, national bonds are issued to make up for budget deficits. And national bonds are the basis for ensuring the safety of major currencies in the world. Essentially, this means that monetarists try to prohibit other countries from issuing currencies according to their own needs to force them to bear the debt obligations of the US and other countries that issue reserve currencies. Raising funds for the budget deficit through external loans and using the currency reserves of the borrowing country as a guarantee for repayment can be seen in the monetarist's attempt. If domestic loans are not supported by the corresponding currency issuance, then investment will be reduced to raise funds for the budget deficit, which will automatically lead to a slowdown in economic growth. Facts have proved that monetarists use their advice to force national monetary authorities to manipulate

---

28. Glazyev S., *Genocide* (Terra, 1998).

budget deficits and provide loans to world currency issuing countries. These countries pursue a policy that is the opposite of their recommendations-unlimited currency issuance.

China's approach differs from the dogmatic economic policies prevailing among Russian leaders. The most important lesson of China's development path is to boldly promote theoretical innovation on the basis of practice and put forward a series of closely connected and seamless flows of new thoughts, new viewpoints, and new conclusions on upholding and developing socialism with Chinese characteristics. Xi Jinping's thought on Socialism with Chinese Characteristics for the New Era is the latest achievement of the theoretical system of socialism with Chinese characteristics, the crystallization of the collective wisdom of the CPC, and a powerful ideological weapon that guides all the work of the CPC and the country. This thought is the product of combining Marxism with contemporary Chinese reality and the characteristics of the times, raising the understanding of the laws of socialism with Chinese characteristics to a new level, and opening up a new realm for developing contemporary Chinese Marxism.

The Central Committee of the CPC reiterated in the *Proposals* for the 14th Five-Year Plan that it is necessary to focus on the real economy and develop industrial cooperation: "We must adhere to making the real economy the focal point of economic development, resolutely build China into a manufacturing powerhouse, a quality powerhouse and a cyber powerhouse, build a digital China, promote industrial base upgrading and production chain modernization, and boost the economy's quality, efficiency, and core competitiveness."

> "Raising the levels of the production and supply chain modernization. We will keep manufacturing's share [of GDP] basically stable, and bolster the foundation of the real economy. We will adhere to independent controllability, security, and high efficiency, do well at supply chain strategic design and targeted policies for different industries, and promote optimization and upgrading of whole production chains. We will forge production chain and supply chain strengths, rely on China's industrial scale advantages, supporting advantages, and first mover advantages in some fields, create new and emerging production chains, promote the upscaling, intelligentization, and green transformation of traditional industries, and develop service-oriented manufacturing."

According to the understanding of Chinese leaders, macroeconomic policies, including MP, cannot exceed the goals of productive development and infrastructure. The 14th Five-Year Plan of the Central Committee of the CPC recommended the following tasks.

"Improving macroeconomic governance. We must improve the macroeconomic governance system, taking national development planning as the guide and fiscal and monetary policies as the main tools, in close coordination with employment, industrial, investment, consumption, environmental protection, and regional policies, and with optimized objectives, a reasonable division of labor, and efficient collaboration."

It proposed "strengthening overall planning of fiscal resources, strengthening medium-term fiscal planning and administration, and increasing financial support for major national strategic tasks." It listed the tasks for infrastructure development as follows:

> "We will: Build modern infrastructure systems that are complete, efficient, practical, smart, green, safe, and reliable; systematically lay out new infrastructure, and accelerate the construction of 5G communications, the industrial internet, big data centers, and other facilities; accelerate the construction of China into a transportation powerhouse, refine comprehensive transport corridors, comprehensive transportation hubs, and logistics networks, accelerate rail transit networkization of urban agglomerations and metropolitan areas, and increase the penetration of transportation access into rural and border areas. We will promote the energy revolution, refine the energy production, supply, storage, and marketing systems, strengthen domestic oil and gas exploration and development, accelerate the construction of oil and gas storage infrastructure and national backbone oil and gas pipelines, construct intelligent energy systems, optimize power generation and distribution channel layouts, boost new energy consumption and storage capabilities, and improve the ability to transmit and distribute power to remote regions. We will strengthen the construction of water infrastructure and improve capacity for optimally allocating water resources and defending against floods and droughts."

Of course, Chinese leaders have never forgotten that the ultimate goal of economic policy is to increase social well-being. The *Proposals* also emphasizes:

> "Persist in being people-centered. We will adhere to the mainstay status of the people and the direction of common prosperity, and always practice development for the people, development by the people, and sharing the fruits of development by the people. We will protect the people's fundamental interests, inspire the enthusiasm, initiative, and creativity of all the people, promote the well-being of the people, and continuously realize people's aspirations for better lives."

It can be concluded from the above that half a century ago, American subjects used the monetary theory formulated by the US exclusively for external consumption. In modern terms, it is used by the US monetary authorities as a cognitive weapon. This weapon touches the consciousness of the elites of the affiliated countries, thereby strengthening the economic policies they need. But in Russia, only the beneficiary countries (and influential countries) through the theory of monetarism can strengthen the economic policies they need.

The monetarist paradigm dominates the thinking of government economists, with the ruling elite firmly convinced that monetarism was infallible, and the poor utterly disillusioned that only money could solve everything. In this situation, Russia will complete its transition to a market economy. But in the current state of social cognition, the country can hardly be expected to develop successfully.

The next chapter will explain the cost of Russia's MP.

Chapter 13

Losses Resulting from Implementation of IMF Recommendations

Economic policy is not neutral in terms of economic interests. It often comes from the dominant and most influential groups for their interests, which do not always correspond to the national interest groups. The IMF, for example, has imposed the "Washington Consensus," for the sake of international capital, on developing countries and economies in transition against their national interests.[1] We also observed the consequences of this policy in Russia in the 1990s, when the actions of Russian banks stifled high-tech industries while bringing unprecedented profits to foreign (mainly American) financial capital.[2] Something similar is happening now.

Given the intensification of external pressures and the isolation of Russian borrowers from global capital markets, higher rates would increase the cost of credit and increase the risk of default by borrowing companies. Russian banks have created mechanisms to replace external credit with internal resources, not so much to make up for the credit shortage caused by the sanctions as to aggravate the credit resources shortage. While maintaining a system of free capital operations, Russian banks have facilitated the export of capital, amounting to about $80 billion a year. Stopping illegal capital outflows could eliminate the negative effects of sanctions, the central bank could take all possible measures. However, Russian banks refuse to adopt the exchange control guidelines necessary to end "capital flight" and instead continue passively to follow the doctrine of "free movement of capital."[3]

In Russia's first year of the monetarist policy, GDP fell by 15%, and real wages fell by more than 30%. Industrial production in 1992 fell back to 12 years earlier. Between 1991 and 1998, Russia's productivity fell by 42%, more than in any other G7 country, half as much as in India, and three-quarters less than in China. Overall, Russia's share of world GDP almost halved, from 5.5% in 1990 to 3.0% in 1995 and 2.7% in 2001. Fixed-asset investment shrank even more, falling by almost four-fifths in the first few years of the reforms and still running at half its pre-reform level.

Throughout the monetarists' "shock therapy" policy, the volume of productive activity, fixed asset investment, and economic efficiency indicators declined steadily until the late 1990s. Russia's production structure has deteriorated considerably compared with other successful developing countries that have increased the production of high-value-added goods. Russia's GDP growth is mainly sustained by energy exports and increased trade in imported goods. The share of the fuel and energy complex and the chemical and metallurgical complex in the industrial production mix has increased sharply, while the share of machine manufacturing has been declining.

The most serious deterioration was seen in high-tech industries, investment and

---

1. Перкинс Д. Исповедь экономического убийцы. М.: Претекст, 2005.
2. Глазьев С. Центральный банк против промышленности России // Вопросы экономики. 1998. №1–2.
3. Годовой отчет Банка России за 2013 г. URL: http://www.cbr.ru/publ/God/ar_2013.pdf.

agricultural machinery manufacturing, light industry, and production of industrial consumer goods, among which the level of industrial production and even applied science fell by order of magnitude. Moreover, if Russia's GDP (at purchasing-power parity) falls to one-seventh of America's, its production of technology-intensive goods will fall to less than 1/100 of America's.

Producers of final products experienced extremely painful process due to the monetary policies, costs rising sharply as decades of partnerships were destroyed, and importers were fiercely competitive. Production declined in proportion to its complexity and value-added in each field. Those sectors likely to be the basis of a market-oriented economy and the drivers of economic growth, which safeguard the link between domestic production growth and demand, fell the most. A rational transition to a market economy would increase its efficiency and expand production, avoiding excessive unemployment in technology-intensive and manufacturing-intensive areas and making them the "vanguard" of economic growth and employment growth centers.

The simplification of the economic structure was accompanied by the degradation of almost all economic areas, manifested in the decline of labor productivity, the increase of energy consumption, and the decline of the utilization of fixed assets. The destruction of the reproduction mechanism led to the cessation of investment activity and the beginning of a transition to a mechanism that consumes previously accumulated potential. Except for trade, the financial sector, and telecommunications, the aging of fixed assets, declining efficiency, and deterioration of the structure of output were seen in all sectors of the economy.

So far, 25 years after the start of radical reforms, almost all indicators of economic productivity in Russia today are not comparable to the Soviet model of 1990. Many researchers who have been able to find temporary links and establish causality have been forced to acknowledge the obvious: Russia's economic disaster is the result of monetarist policies. The white papers on reform, which are regularly published, contain much factual material on the dynamics of objective indicators to produce physical goods and the investment in social infrastructure.[4]

In the post-Soviet era, there have been many attempts to stem the decline and return the economy to a sustainable growth path. The first attempt was made by the supreme Council, the highest authority, which announced the impeachment of then-President Boris Yeltsin in September 1993. The government staged a coup and seized power from criminal groups that had looted the country's wealth with the strong support of the US and its NATO Allies. In a second attempt to pull Russia out of its self-destructive rut, the Primakov-Maslyukov-Grashchenko government quickly stabilized the macroeconomic situation. It resumed production, with industrial growth growing at a record rate (more than 1% per month). After he was elected as president, Putin began to maintain political stability and end the country's division, guaranteeing the positive trend of national development and forming a vertical power separation from the oligarchs. However, during this period, oil prices and state tax

4. Кара-Мурза С. Г., Батчиков С. В., Глазьев С. Ю. Белая книга. Экономические реформы в России (1991–2001 гг.). - М.: Изд-во ЭКСМО. - 2003.

revenues (which seek to recover most of the natural resource rents from hydrocarbons exported) began to rise, weakening the momentum for the transition to economic development policies.

Comprador oligarchs not only continued to make super-profits from exploiting Russia's national wealth, but also maintained their way of doing business offshore, exporting a large share of national income abroad. Although the country eliminated the burden of foreign debt and reduced its dependence on American financial institutions, the government supervision had not changed and still focused on serving the interests of the world capital. Russia's offshore economy became the "periphery" of the world capital. This undeveloped growth continued until the global financial crisis, accompanied by further deterioration of the domestic economy and the intensification of technological lag.

The global financial crisis of 2008 provided another opportunity for the transition to development policies. However, the complacency of Russia's ruling elites played a deadly role. They relied on oil and gas rents, indulged in the illusion that Russia, the "Island of Stability," had a greater appeal to international capital. They dreamed of a transition to innovative development as academic and applied sciences collapsed. Of all the G20 countries, Russia suffered the largest economic loss in terms of GDP and the highest cost of anti-crisis measures. Economic stability was achieved through subsidies from banks and businesses controlled by the ruling elite, many of which had gone bankrupt and cut back on production. Worse, the monetary authorities mastered mechanisms to manipulate the rouble to make excessive profits by depreciating the savings and incomes of law-abiding citizens and businesses and enabled monetary financial speculators to profit from the crisis. Russia missed an opportunity to put its economy on a development path. Today, Russia's regulatory system is more subordinated to the ruling elite's interests, which continues to operate offshore and extract more than $100 billion a year from Russia.

The paradox of Russia's monetary and credit policy will go down in history as a ridiculous joke. It is like explaining to a reasonable person that under what circumstances, the greater the foreign exchange earnings from oil exports, the fewer monetary resources Russian companies have at their disposal. The wider the scope of foreign capital inflows, the narrower the potential for domestic savings. The bigger the budget surplus, the higher the country's domestic debt.

These paradoxes are due to the operation of money supply programs themselves. Until the 2008 financial crisis, money supply programs were essentially reduced to annual money supply growth programs due to the goal of limiting inflation and vague proposals to change the velocity of money circulation. After setting a benchmark for money supply growth, the monetary authorities withdrew more money from the market than this amount. Moreover, the recipients of the issued currency were mainly exporters, foreign creditors, and investors. The withdrawal of "surplus" currency was carried out in the budgetary system through lower wages and socioeconomic development expenditures.

Figure 13-1 shows the currency-issuance program that was operational until recently, with the main channels of income (foreign loans and investment) blocked following the imposition of sanctions. To support economic growth, jobs, and investment, Russia issued money differently from developed countries as government and corporate debt grew. Russian banks' currency issuance techniques generally ignored these objectives, limiting themselves to short-term liquidity balances in the banking sector and meeting the needs of foreign lenders and investors in the Russian market.

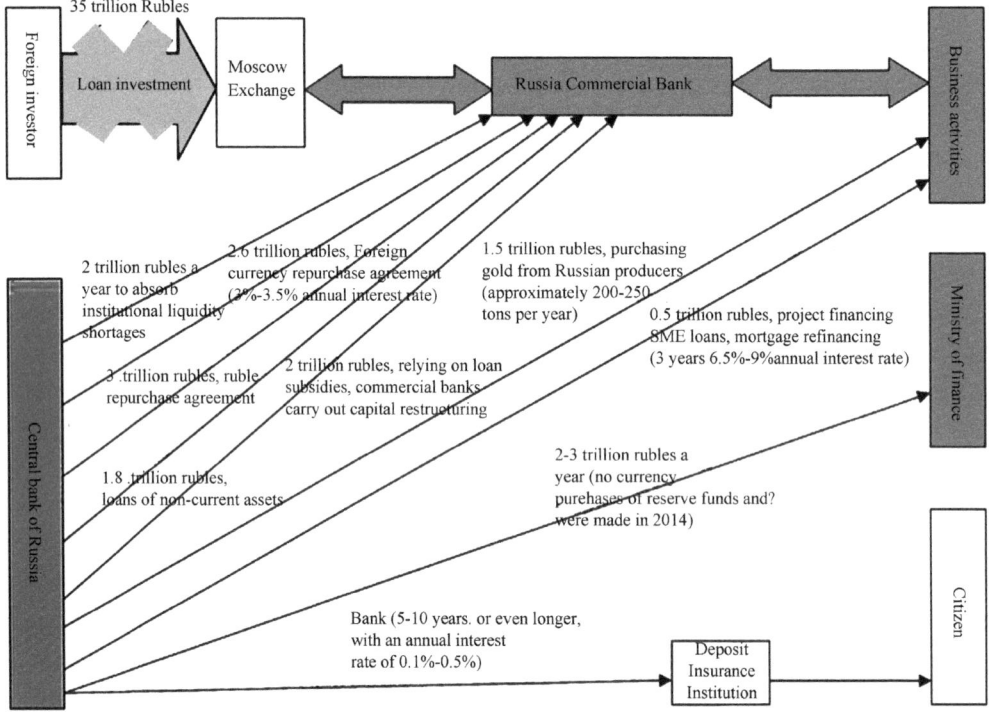

Figure 13-1 Currency Issuing Mechanism Used in Russia (2014–2017)
Source: Глазьев С., 2017.

After the financial crisis, Russian banks abandoned money-supply plans in favor of a policy of refinancing commercial banks using interest rates as a regulatory parameter. Until 2013, the policy provided loans of about 9 trillion rubles to the economy to ensure the maintenance of economic activity in the face of a reduction in foreign exchange inflows due to the deterioration of the external economic situation. But then, at the mercy of the IMF, the Central Bank decided to raise the refinancing rate, which soon exceeded the profitability of most of the real sector. The Central Bank renamed the refinancing rate the key rate, raising it to a level excluding loans for investment in production projects. Commercial banks, deprived of solvent borrowers, began to repay loans they had previously received from the Central Bank. By the end of 2017, Russian banks had withdrawn almost all their previous loans from the economy and began siphoning money out of it by opening deposits and issuing bonds. In effect, since 2014, Russian banks have returned to their previous policy of withdrawing money from the economy under bad conditions. If earlier the monetary authorities had banned some of the money supply growth caused by foreign currency inflows, the money could have been recovered by reducing lending to real sector liquidity and investment in the event of falling oil prices.

Indirect losses (twice the cumulative capital outflow) from Russian banks' actions, combined with insufficient funds to refinance domestic investment, put the total losses in the country's financial system at more than $1 trillion. Moreover, as a result of the Bank of Russia's policy in the 1990s, industrial production fell by half, and there was a 1/3 drop in underinvestment in economic development compared to the 2000s. The policy implementation led to three financial market deteriorations in 2008 (a record by world standards) and a national bankruptcy in 1998. These disasters could have been avoided if the country had implemented sound monetary and credit policies focusing on achieving national socioeconomic development goals rather than the interests of foreign capital. If the central bank had developed internal sources of credit for the development of the national economy, Russia's GDP would have increased by 1.5 times, living standards would have doubled, and cumulative investment in production modernization would have increased by five times.

The monetary authorities carried out monetary policies according to the instructions of the American financial organization and dragged the domestic economy into the "trap" of stagflation. Therefore, shortly after the first anti-Russian sanctions were imposed, Russian banks followed the advice of the IMF mission (they were in Moscow on October 1, 2014):[5] "The Bank of Russia is justified to continue its tight monetary and credit policy and to raise interest rates to reduce inflation, while continuing to work towards its own inflation target with exchange rate flexibility; a tight monetary and credit policy is needed to reduce inflation. In recent months, the Bank of Russia has taken appropriate measures to raise interest rates and resume the transition to greater exchange rate flexibility. However, underlying inflation has accelerated, and further tightening monetary and credit policy is needed to stabilize and control inflationary expectations; higher interest rates will also help to limit capital outflows."

Oddly, the IMF made the opposite recommendation to the US, that raising rates too soon would lead to tighter financial conditions or destabilize financial stability, which would hamper economic growth…[6] The duality of the IMF's advice exposes political shady and the vainglory of its position. Russia's suicidal monetary and credit policy threatens "stagnation" and another reproduction collapses like that experienced by the country in the 1990s. Meanwhile, the IMF is forcing Russia to accept this policy as the only option. The continuation of this policy will lead to a decline in citizens' production, income, and standard of living, an avalanche of bankruptcies of banks and enterprises, the destruction of scientific and technological potential, and Russia's credibility loss and the destruction of the Eurasian integration process. The Central Bank's policy has expanded NATO sanctions against Russia to weapons of mass destruction, killing all sectors of economic activity that officials do not protect, from small businesses to large machine makers to construction and agricultural firms.

Migaev said that after the global financial crisis, the policy of using monetary means to achieve macroeconomic stability (to fight inflation by reducing the money supply and reducing government expenditures) was resumed, which would lead to an

---

5. URL: http://www.imf.org/external/np/ms/2014/100114.htm.
6. "2015 Article IV Consultation with the US of America Concluding Statement of the IMF Mission," IMF, May 28, 2015.

intensified economic recession and paralysis of the banking system, only to pursue economic development by increasing foreign debt scale, which is the inevitable result.[7]

In the first phase of the 2008–2009 global crisis, Russia lost 1/3 of its foreign exchange reserves, industrial production fell by more than 10%, investment fell by 15%, the stock market fell by 2/3, confidence in its currency was lost, and inflation jumped to 18%. Tens of thousands of citizens with foreign-currency loans, including consumer and mortgage loans, were facing bankruptcy and increased unemployment. Corporate financial performance plummeted by two-thirds, and solvency declined sharply. Serious problems arose in the repayment of foreign debts by Russian banks and companies. In 2009, the amount of expenditure in this area was 136.1 billion US dollars. In 2010, it was 86.7 billion US dollars, and after 2010 it reached 274.8 billion US dollars.[8] Russia's economic crisis was obviously more severe than other major countries in the world and most CIS countries.

In this context, Russia adopted a costly anti-crisis policy. According to the Federal Audit Office, the total spending to defuse the crisis amounted to 10 trillion rubles (considering credit resources), 25% of GDP in 2008. If the $200 billion allocated from the Central Bank's reserves to support the rouble is included, the figure will rise to 16 trillion rubles, 40% of GDP in 2008. Other big countries spent 13% of GDP in China and 20% in the US. As Dmitrieva[9] pointed out, the results of the global financial and economic crisis are still to be worked out. Here are a few reasons. The first is the "inverted" structure of resources employed. According to government reports and the Federal Audit Office, 85%–88% of these resources went to supporting the financial system, the functioning of the stock market, and saving the "oligopoly," while only 12%–15% went to support the real economy. In addition, commercial banks converted most of the anti-crisis loans obtained from the Central Bank of Russia into foreign exchange assets and withdrew circulating funds, resulting in the rouble facing great pressure in the foreign exchange market.

The second reason is the wrong choice of anti-crisis support form and its specific priority direction, and the implementation of the latter budget mechanism is inefficient.[10]

Unfortunately, Russia failed to recognize the negative impact of this measure. It mistakenly rated this anti-crisis plan as a successful plan and implemented it repeatedly in a more destructive form. The main source of funding for anti-crisis measures in 2008–2009 was Central Bank credit issuance. The implementation of those measures relied heavily on budgetary funds, thus squeezing other expenditures that are more important for socioeconomic development. Bank subsidies replaced budget spending on state purchases and investment, which was important for reviving production, and much of the bank subsidies were also used for currency speculation.

7. Митяев Д. А. О динамике саморазрушения мировой финансовой системы (сценарии и стратегии). Возможности адаптации и выбор стратегии для России / Сценарно-игровой доклад. 2009.

8. Маевский В. И. Реальный сектор и банковская система. (URL: http://www.econorus.org)

9. Дмитриева О. Еще раз об измененном бюджете-2009 и правительственной антикризисной программе // Российский экономический журнал. 2009. №5.

10. О внешних и внутренних угрозах экономической безопасности России в условиях американской агрессии / Научный совет РАН по комплексным проблемам евразийской экономической интеграции, модернизации, конкурентоспособности и устойчивому развитию. 2014.

The Russian bank quietly became an "anti-Central Bank," misperforming its main function. After all, the point of a Central Bank is to ensure that the state monopolizes the circulation and issuance of money to establish and maintain favorable conditions for economic development. In addition to monetary stability, these conditions include the availability of credit, mechanisms to accumulate savings and convert them into long-term investments, and stable refinancing for expanded reproduction. Instead of developing the money supply to finance growth, the central bank had been working to remove money from the economy and artificially limit its growth.

Unprecedented in economic history, Russia's monetary authorities turned the state's monopoly on the money supply from the most important economic engine to a brake stop. In this absurd macroeconomy, only businesses that exported and borrowed from abroad, not relying on the monetary authorities, survived. Almost all manufacturing sectors focused on the domestic market, without foreign credit funds, continued to slump until painful extinction.

From the perspective of common sense, Russia's MP seems utterly preposterous. If Russia abandoned its Central Bank and currency, entered the Euro zone, and stopped accumulating foreign reserves, the currency would triple, inflation would fall by 2/3, and borrowing costs would be halved. But from the perspective of the interests of fund managers (including the state), this is idealism because the loan interest rate can be increased to obtain excess profits and seize the property of bankrupt debtors. That is why state-backed bankers have in various ways supported and continued to praise the activities of the monetary authorities. To obtain excess profits, the country missed the opportunity for economic growth, resulting in lower citizens' income.

In the context of restricting the money supply, binding currency issuance to the growth of foreign exchange reserves led to the outflow of monetary funds from most of the manufacturing industry that focused on the domestic market. Without loans, the domestic market was forced to seek development by lowering wages. Most sectors in manufacturing, construction, and agriculture were threatened by a sharp decline in production and prolonged depression as a direct result of MP.[11] Credit remained inaccessible or economically meaningless for most economically active citizens and businesses. These citizens and businesses were being asked to borrow at their own disadvantage at inflated interest rates and short-term collateral. The vast majority of enterprises could only rely on their own funds to develop, and bank credit accounted for less than 1/10 of the financing of large and medium-sized enterprises. The underdeveloped commercial lending system, with almost no mechanism for long-term lending to manufacturing, is a direct consequence of the persistence of the monetary authorities, which fail to play a major role in the supply of credit in a market economy.

The petrodollar did not power the Russian economy in the 2000s, the money flowed abroad, and the monetary authorities did not crack down on capital outflows but promoted them. Foreign exchange controls were abolished, and "oil revenues" were drained abroad to buy US debt. MP boils down to lending oil and gas money to finance spending by the US and other NATO governments.

---

11. Глазьев С. Центральный банк против промышленности России // Вопросы экономики. 1998. №1–2.; Глазьев С. Кудрявая экономика. М.: Политический журнал, 2006.

Let us take a closer look at the paradox of the above-mentioned monetary and credit policies pursued by Russian banks.

Under this MP, rising incomes and exports become useless for economic growth. According to the budget rules proposed by the monetary authorities,12 the more foreign exchange revenue flows into the country, the more rubles are issued by the central bank (to meet the foreign exchange revenue), and the higher the hedge. To the extent that oil and gas companies receive foreign exchange earnings and pay export taxes, the state budget and the banking system allocate funds to keep them contained in the stabilization fund and central bank liabilities.

Foreign investment also proved useless under the policy because, according to monetarist logic, the more capital foreign investors used to buy shares in Russian companies, the higher the increase in foreign exchange reserves and currency issuance, and the more money the monetary authorities had for currency hedging. It has been proved that the massive influx of speculative foreign capital into financial markets has led to an increase in the use of the fiscal system to carry out currency hedging and the outflow of capital from the real economy. Thus, as speculative foreign capital drives asset inflation, the Russian economy's capitalization deepens, and the real economy's financial situation deteriorates further. The paradox of this opposite trend will inevitably lead to financial disaster. The higher the degree of financial market "bubble," the greater the financial crisis, which will promote the degree of the economic capitalization in line with the value of the real economy.

The banking system cannot develop properly under such circumstances. The combined assets of all Russian commercial banks are a fraction of those of any large bank in the US, the European Union, or Japan. The "lightweight" of Russian commercial banks is predetermined by monetary authorities' policies. Because the Central Bank strictly limits the money supply and has not established a refinancing system for commercial banks, their development in Russia is strictly restricted by the money supply growth regulations of the monetary authorities. Therefore, commercial banks cannot meet the growing loan demand, and the high-quality customers of these banks have to turn to foreign loans.

The central bank purposely shrinks the money supply. It keeps the refinancing rate above the rate of profit of the internally oriented economy, limiting the demand for money through short-term speculation and ultra-profitable industries. The policy of the Central Bank forces competitive enterprises to obtain loans from abroad, thus destroying the development opportunities of the domestic banking system and financial market, which creates the premise for foreign capital to encroach on the Russian financial market.

It is easy to calculate the effect of this strange macroeconomic policy. In the 2000s, the Russian government lent Russian taxpayers' money to foreign borrowers at 4%–5% interest rates, while Russian borrowers were forced to borrow from foreign borrowers

---

12. Since 2012, the "Financial Budget Rule" has gained official status (relevant laws have been passed). According to this rule, Russia's budget deficit should not exceed 1% of GDP, except for "excess" funds (income from energy sales exceeding the established limit) into the reserve fund. In 2014, oil prices fell sharply, and the ruble exchange rate also fell sharply. The "budget rules" designed to limit budget expenditures lost their meaning (super high income disappeared). This rule was suspended in 2016.

at 8–15% a year. After the global financial crisis, rates fell to 1%–2% and 6%–9%, respectively, but there is still a big difference between them. The losses caused by such absurd financial transactions are estimated at tens of billions annually. Russia lends to the US and Europe at low-interest rates, but the US and Europe lend at high-interest rates. At the same time, the more foreign exchange flows into the country, the less demand for loans from the national banking system, and the more actively Russian companies borrow from abroad.

With less credit available at home, solvent Russian companies have been forced to borrow from abroad to finance the expansion of production. Despite the sanctions, Russia's external debt is around $500 billion. The Russian financial system is suffering losses and is paying off these loans with huge amounts of money, with an investment income deficit of about $50 billion annually. The side effects of external dependence are the offshore economy and the transfer of Russian property under the aegis of the foreign jurisdiction, since offshore companies can easily obtain foreign loans through collateral. Offshoring, in turn, leads to capital outflows and a lot of tax evasion. Russia is at war with the US and the European Union, whose financial system subsidies are hardly in its national interest.

The experience of the 2008 economic crisis shows that the Russian economy is highly vulnerable in the global financial market. There are some unreasonable aspects in Russia's domestic regulatory policies, including lowering the credit rating, making illegal requirements for opening the domestic market and complying with financial restrictions, and imposing non-equivalent foreign economic exchange mechanisms. To sum up, for the above reasons, Russia loses about $100 billion a year, of which about $50 billion flows out of the country in the form of a deficit in foreign loans and investment and about $50 billion in the illegal capital outflow. This illegal capital outflow has accumulated as much as $500 billion, and when combined with foreign direct investment by Russian citizens, the total outflow has reached about $1 trillion. State budget revenues are losing about 1 trillion rubles yearly due to capital outflows. State budget revenues are losing about 5 trillion rubles a year due to high levels of offshore economy, capital outflow, and other tax evasion activities.[13]

It is well-known in economic science that there are reasonable limits to foreign investment. When foreign investment hits the "red line," further development of foreign investment will become an obstacle to economic development because the amount of money being repaid for these investments increases too rapidly. Judging from the trend of rapid growth in foreign debt payments, foreign investment has already exceeded the limit (Figure 13-2), and foreign investment repayments have exceeded income. At the same time, about 70% of foreign investment is Russian enterprises' offshore investment. As it turns out, the relationship between Russia's financial system and the rest of the world is largely made up of the recycling of Russian capital, which is tax free abroad and only partially repatriated.

---

13. Петров Ю. К формированию новой экономической модели: рестрикция бюджетных расходов или повышение собираемости налогов? // Российский экономический журнал. 2013. №4.

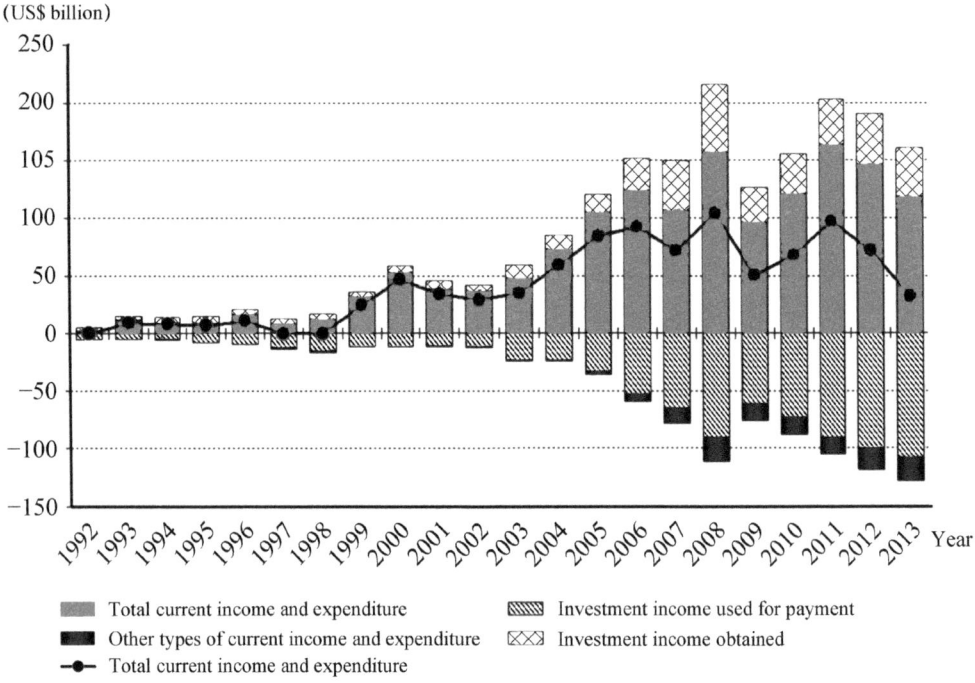

Figure 13-2 Revenue Loss Due to Offshore Business 1992–2013
Source: Yu. K. Petrov, "The Formation of a New Economic Model: Limiting Budget Expenditures or Increasing Taxes?" *Russian Economic Journal*, no. 4 (2013).

Objectively speaking, the lack of funds in the Russian reproduction system is not the reason for Russian economic entities seeking external loans. This is illustrated by Figure 13-2, which clearly shows that external borrowing has grown in tandem with capital outflows. If Russian citizens did not hide their income offshore and deposit money in the Russian banking system, there would be no need for external loans to balance supply and demand in the credit market. But Russian banks artificially raise interest rates to force companies to borrow abroad, and the proceeds are used to repay those loans. This breaks the cycle of capital appreciation and capital shortage created by the Central Bank, because the cheap currency flows out of Russia via offshore companies without paying taxes, while the currency flows back with interest payments and profit sharing (Figure 13-3). At the same time, about half of those who left Russia have settled abroad after buying high-end property and acquiring foreign citizenship, further burdening the process of reproduction of the Russian economy, which has, in effect, become a cash cow for foreign lenders. The Bank of Russia's policies has encouraged further offshoring of Russian business, leaving businessmen who do not use outside capital in trouble.

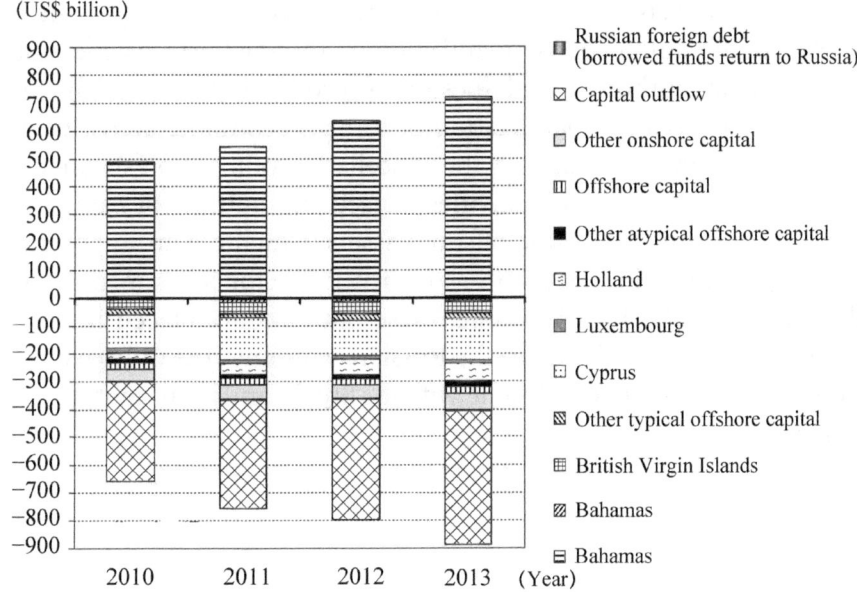

Figure 13-3 Russian Foreign Debt and Outward Direct Investment Funds from Russia

Source: Петров Ю. К формированию новой экономической модели: рестрикция бюджетных расходов или повышение собираемости налогов? // Российский экономический журнал. 2013. №4.

The average amount of non-equivalent foreign economic exchange between Russia and the world financial system through current investment returns is $50 billion per year. The amount of money transferred from the Russian economy to the world economy reached US $90–110 billion during the different eras of MP. The plan developed by D.A. Migaev illustrates the main process of non-equivalence exchange between the Russian financial system and the outside world (Figure 13-4).

Figure 13-4 Assessment of Russia's Transfer to the Global Financial System

Source: D. Migaev, Russian balance of payments data.

This non-equivalent exchange was predetermined by the offshoring of the Russian economy (a result of the shift of loan demand abroad), forcing the transfer of liquidated assets abroad. Monetary authorities did not stop the process but used another doctrine of the theory of monetarism—liberalization of foreign economic activities to prove that this process is reasonable, including the cancellation of foreign exchange control. Liberalization of foreign economic activities caused the outflow of capital to more than $1 trillion. Half of them became offshore assets, which are an important factor in economic reproduction (Figure 13-5). Most private sector investment in Russia is through offshore assets. At the same time, these outflows are placed under foreign jurisdiction, causing inevitable losses to the Russian economy. The other half returned to Russia in the guise of foreign investment, with tax breaks and legal rights to repatriate foreign earnings.

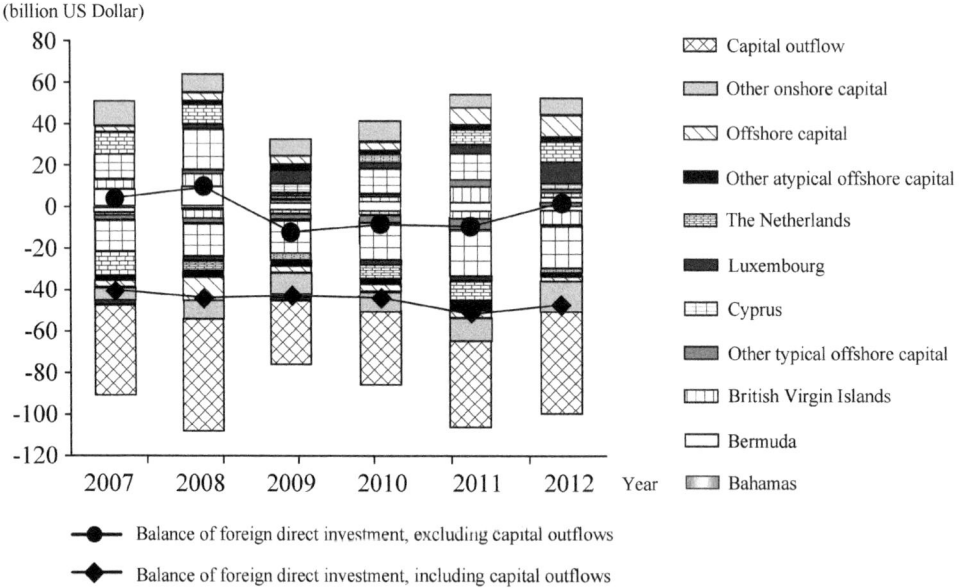

Figure 13-5 Russian Offshore Economy. Investment Funds Returning to Russia (+), Investment Funds Flowing Abroad (-) by Country and Jurisdiction Type (Offshore and Onshore), in US $billion
Source: Yu. K. Petrov, "The Formation of a New Economic Model: Limiting Budget Expenditures or Increasing taxes?" *Russian Economic Journal*, no. 4 (2013).

The lack of foreign exchange controls could lead to the transfer of assets pledged by Russian companies to foreign creditors, as the crisis has "eroded" the value of Russian securities. Half of the Russian industry is at risk, and much of it is already under the control of non-citizens.

The increasing monetization of the American debt pyramid, the sharp increase in currency issuance, and the outflow of Dollars from the US to acquire real economic assets have increased the damage to the Russian economy. In the absence of protective measures in the private financial system, the Russian economy has been "absorbed" by foreign capital and deprived of the ability to develop independently. In the context of the deepening of the global crisis, the Russian economy is bound to deteriorate.

The policies adopted by the IMF in previous financial crises led to these consequences. In the context of tying money issuance to access to foreign currencies, the inflow of foreign capital paralyzed the financial system. It led to the incorporation of corporate arrears into the budget, the uncontrolled depreciation of the domestic currency, the loss of liquidity of part of the foreign exchange reserves, declining production, and rising inflation. Cheap assets were repeatedly acquired by foreign capital, and the national economy lost its independence and was dominated by multinational companies linked to foreign distribution centers. In the cycle of artificially inflating and puncturing the "bubble" in financial markets, foreign speculators were privatized at bargain prices during the "loosening" of the financial pyramid. They acquired substantial assets after the collapse of the state financial system in 1998.[14]

The MP pursued by Russia objectively led to the "colonization" of the Russian economy by foreign capital. As A. Oderba and A. Kobyakov attest in an analysis, "For 25 years, the policy of Russian banks and the government was to create favorable conditions for foreign capital to control the Russian economy and the national wealth."[15] In this context, foreign capital associated with the global money issuing center gained an advantage.

The two authors rightly point out that modern credit capital and the capital created on top of it are the most effective instruments of economic expansion, enabling cheap access to other countries' resources and the exploitation of their populations. Victims of this policy, including Russia, have not prevented it from infiltrating the domestic economy and are even trying to attract this money, due to its low level of financial literacy. The Central Bank of Russia's policy making is based on the outdated concept of modern money, without considering the credit nature and function of money discussed above.

As a result, Russia's monetary authorities unthinkingly follow the lead of experts from the IMF and the US Department of the Treasury. They indoctrinate Russia with ideas that serve its own interests. The purpose of the IMF and US Department of the Treasury experts is to create money to acquire foreign exchange reserves (mainly dollars) and and limit foreign exchange reserves' growth. In this case, the local currency becomes a substitute for the Dollar, and the Russian economy is manipulated by the interests of American capital. The investment from American capital becomes Russia's main source of domestic credit. Industries that foreign investors are not interested in will be unable to obtain loans. These industries will decline in the future, and the economy will develop under the decisive influence of external demand.

If the national bank issues currency by obtaining foreign currency, it would not be beneficial for other countries to obtain income from insurance. In addition to production and administrative costs, the cost of money also includes the cost of products, which are paid for by the foreign exchange held by the Central Bank and may perform a safeguard function. In effect, these are high-cost "earning power"

14. Глазьев С. Уроки очередной российской революции: крах либеральной утопии и шанс на экономическое чудо. М.: Экономическая газета, 2011.

15. Отырба А., Кобяков А. Как побеждать в финансовых войнах. Альманах «Однако». Июнь-июль 2014 г. № 174.

currencies, making both the currency itself and the capital built on it uncompetitive. They fail to guarantee development and are also tools for foreign economic manipulators to carry out potential acts of looting against non-independent states. Foreign economic manipulators, who tightly control the two most important currency circulation processes in dependent countries, namely, injecting money into the market and collecting market funds. They can trigger financial crises and plunge the country into chaos by collecting funds and stopping further investment. This is happening now. Recently, the American monetary authorities cut off the external credit sources of the Russian economy. The Russian monetary authorities did not replace the external credit sources with domestic resources, but increased the domestic credit costs, resulting in economic lag.

Anti-crisis measures taken by the government could not stop the downward spiral because they did not reverse the decline in investment and business activity caused by the Central Bank policies. There is no doubt that macroeconomic policy is extending towards reduced government spending and a contraction in the money supply due to further declines in production and deepening economic deterioration. The reason for this is the continued strength of the two main components of inflation targeting.

The first component relates to the sharp rise in key interest rates. According to the objective situation of factors of production in 2014, GDP growth of 3%–5% was considered to be an economic rebound. Still, it was prevented by the Central Bank's key interest rate, which rose continuously to higher than the average profit level of the real economy. This practice aligns with the IMF's standard advice to reduce inflation by raising interest rates.

Taken together, this policy actually leads to stagflation. Over the past two decades, many studies have shown that raising interest rates and squeezing the money supply will lead to a decline in production and investment, banking crises, and bankruptcies.[16] In addition, the Russian economy is also facing an increase in inflation because it is monopolized and non-monetized.

The second component is a free float of the ruble exchange rate. The Central Bank's leaders see their own decision as necessary to move to inflation-targeting, but that view is no more than IMF speculation. Contrary to common sense, the IMF's advice is trusted by Russia's monetary authorities. There is no scientific evidence that a freely floating exchange rate is necessary to achieve an inflation target. On the contrary, the implementation of a free-floating exchange rate is incompatible with ensuring macroeconomic stability in the context that Russia's economy is excessively open, dependent on oil prices, and imports occupy a high share of the consumer market. Price fluctuations in global markets, an "attack" by financial speculators, or any other change in external economic conditions could overturn plans to hit the inflation target.

It should be noted that very few countries float their currencies freely. Norway, the only developed country with a freely floating currency, relies on hydrocarbon exports for much of its foreign exchange earnings. The Norwegian monetary

---

16. Обучение рынку / Под ред. С. Глазьева. М.: Экономика, 2004.

authorities attach importance to the removal of upward pressure on the exchange rate of the Norwegian currency through the "offset" mechanism, which in effect, ensures a balanced foreign exchange market. According to the current mainstream method, the free-floating exchange rate system and the inflation target system should be considered separately. In developed countries, neither is an element or condition for implementing the other.

In western economic literature, the current inflation targeting system is also generally regarded as independent of the free float system.[17] The vast majority of countries have more diversified and stable economies than Russia, so they do not need to risk switching to a free exchange rate, which is inconsistent with scientific management thinking. As mentioned above, the more complex the object under management, the more data and tools are needed to control the exchange rate at the desired level. For the Russian economy, giving up control of the ruble's exchange rate is like refusing to use the brakes on your car. However, as early as 2009 and 2010–2011, the "Basic Direction of the National Unified MP" proposed that there was a close relationship between the free-floating exchange rate, inflation targeting system, and strengthening the role of the Central Bank of Russia's interest rate. It proposed "a free-floating exchange rate system must be implemented to implement the inflation target system fully."[18]

At present, the Central Bank of Russia has established a free-floating exchange rate system based on the classification of the IMF. According to the IMF classification, the current floating exchange rate system should be called free-floating exchange rate system. Under this system, the Central Bank of Russia may not intervene more than three times every six months in exceptional circumstances, each intervention lasting no more than three days, and the IMF must be able to obtain information confirming Russia's compliance with the requirements, otherwise, the system will be classified as a floating exchange rate system. That sounds like a guarantee that speculators who manipulate national currencies will profit from it. If police are banned from trading floors for more than 18 days a year, and advance notice is required, fraudsters can plot during the remaining 347 days.

Thus, contrary to theory, national experience, and common sense in advanced market economies, the combination of these two errors led to the Central Bank of Russia announcing a shift to inflation targeting in the exact opposite direction of the target: a doubling of the inflation rate and a loss of trust in its currency and its managers. Though Russia's GDP and investment growth potential is 6%–8% a year, the economy is being dragged artificially into a stagflation trap.

Moreover, the refusal to use selective currency restraints is another component of the inflation targeting system, which leads to severe capital outflows and encourages corruption and offshoring of the economy, making it extremely vulnerable to external threats. Most countries, including the US, have selective currency regulation and restrictions on cross-border capital movements. At the system level, this restriction is carried out by BRICS partners who have been very successful in attracting foreign

---

17. G. Hammond, *State of the Art of Inflation Targeting* (Bank of England, 2012).
18. Вестник Банка России. 14. 11. 2008. С. 5.

direct investment. Facts prove that there is a strong need to control currencies to counter speculation and ensure macroeconomic, and the removal of exchange controls to legitimize capital outflows is threatening. To sum up, Russia has fallen into the "trap" of unequal foreign economic transactions of more than $100 billion yearly, and its financial system depends on foreign capital.

From a scientific point of view, these components of the inflation targeting system are typical errors made by monetary authorities, possibly the result of the Central Bank leadership ignoring academic and business advice. Under such circumstances, any anti-crisis measures are doomed to fail, especially loans allocated by the Central Bank to commercial banks for refinancing end up being used to acquire foreign assets (Figure 13-6).

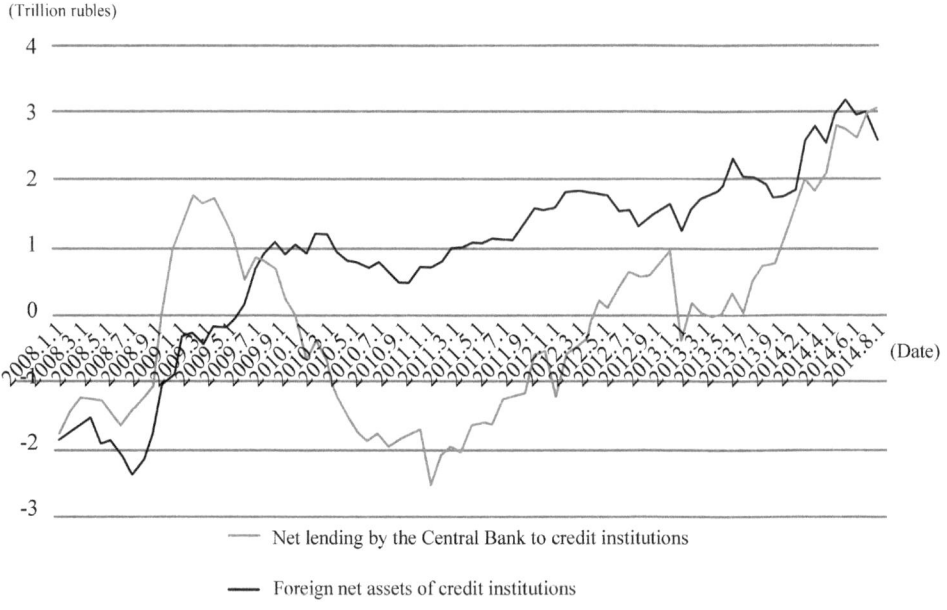

Figure 13-6 Foreign Net Assets and Net Debt Dynamics of Credit Organizations to the Central Bank of Russia

This is a natural consequence of the Central Bank's measures to raise interest rates, which are many times more profitable than manufacturing, and withdraw from foreign exchange markets. First, to shift cash flow from the reproduction channel to the speculative sector; second, it transfers control of the foreign exchange market to speculators who use it to manipulate the rubles to make excess profits from currency fluctuations. In turn, a sustained rise in interest rates leads to a reduction in credit and a tightening of the money supply, which usually leads to a decline in production and investment (Figure 13-7).

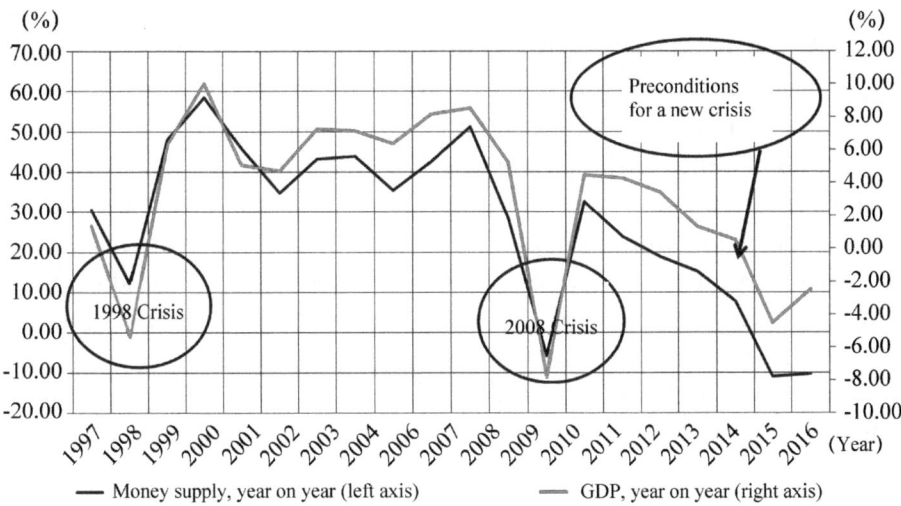

Figure 13-7 Dependence of GDP Growth (or Decline) on Money Supply Growth (or Decline)
Source: Блинов С. Ошибка доктора Кудрина // Эксперт. 2015. № 19. С. 30–38.

A "tidal wave" of inflation erupted immediately after the monetary authorities floated the rouble. The head of the Russian banks explained his actions with the ridiculous claim that "the floating rouble exchange rate remains a factor in mitigating the negative impact of external factors on the economy."[19] In fact, the free floating of the rouble exchange rates did not reduce the negative impact of external factors, but greatly enhanced it. The Central Bank believes that the free floating of exchange rate can cushion the negative impact of external factors on the economy. On the contrary, speculators manipulate the currency and financial market by taking advantage of the fluctuations in the external economic situation to obtain excess profits, thus destroying economic stability, and enhancing the impact of external factors. Actually, a controlled or periodically adjusted exchange rate regime can help mitigate the impact of external factors, safeguard against the threat of speculative activities and timely modify measures to respond to changes in underlying factors.

In changing external economic situations, countries and regions such as Japan, South Korea, Malaysia, Vietnam, China, India, and Western Europe have created economic miracles. The experience of these countries and regions shows that, quite contrary, their currencies remain stable despite floating exchange rates. Without this, it will not be possible to ensure accelerated investment in promising areas of economic development. These countries are currently continuing this policy to protect against external shocks through measures to stabilize their exchange rates, thus securing favorable conditions for investment growth in upgrading new technological paradigms.

The makers of the basic direction of the national unified monetary and credit policy did not consider the ratcheting effect of the floating exchange rate system.

---

19. См.: Основные направления единой государственной денежно-кредитной политики на 2017 г. и плановый период 2018–2019 гг. С.24.

This effect refers to the instantaneous decline in the exchange rate that triggers an increase in import prices, which in turn leads to an increase in inflation, and an instant increase in the exchange rate has little effect on import prices. In this sense, "economic entities adapt to exchange rate volatility moderately increases the risk of exchange rate dynamics to financial and price stability" is wrong.[20]

Russian monetary authorities have expressed and continue to emphasize that the implementation of an inflation targeting system should be based on the premise of free floating of the rouble exchange rate. There has never been any convincing evidence for this argument in monetary and credit policies, in the speeches of the leadership, or in the writings of the thinkers who formulated them. The authority of US financial institutions makes this view an incontrovertible conclusion, but it seems odd to anyone with a systems mind.

The monetary authorities announced an inflation targeting system, which in effect abandons the exchange rate, so that the prices of most consumer goods can be controlled. Anyone who adopts this approach looks crazy—like trying to heat a room without windows in winter, not realizing that the heat in the room depends not on the power of the heating equipment but on the temperature outside the window. This strange attitude to reality can be explained by dogmatic thinking based on blind faith.

In these circumstances, the monetary authorities see themselves, paradoxically, as a simple mechanism for manipulating the situation with interest rates. According to the inflation-targeting myth, the rouble should float freely if capital flows are not restricted, and there is only one tool for regulating monetary markets: interest rates. Indeed, if you were not the issuer of the world's reserve currency, Keeping the rouble at a level with the free flow of resources on the capital account would be impossible. But why limit yourself to just one management tool?

In other words, monetary authorities implement inflation targeting, which means that they retain only one lever of control: short-term manipulation of interest rates to balance the liquidity needs of financial markets. Their notion of inflation targeting runs counter to the systematic approach of rejecting all MP tools except the key interest rate. If they pursue an inflation-targeting policy, the first thing they should care about in the context of an open economy is managing the rouble exchange rate, which determines consumer prices to varying degrees. However, they gave up this control.

Based on the above, we will use the term "targeting system" to define Russian bank policy, since in practice the term is understood to refer to all objectives and instruments of MP except the key interest rate. We will argue that it is impossible to achieve the inflation target in this case because it is determined by factors beyond the control of the Central Bank. Worse, after the announcement of inflation targeting, the monetary authorities lost all control over inflation, subjecting the macroeconomic situation to external factors.

---

20. См.: Основные направления единой государственной денежно-кредитной политики на 2017 г. и плановый период 2018–2019 гг. С. 36.

The Real Meaning and Consequence of Inflation Targeting

Let's start with the monetarist logic, which exports the idea of inflation targeting to the Russian monetary authorities. Assuming that the control over cross-border capital flows in the capital account is given up, the monetary authorities can still control the ruble exchange rate and MP tools under the condition of free market pricing to control macroeconomic data, such as the discount rate and other instruments for obtaining liquidity, standards for mandatory reserves, capital adequacy ratios, the building of loan and securities reserves, trading of government bonds in the open market, and foreign exchange intervention, all of these jointly constituting the size of the monetary base. The scientific literature shows that it is impossible to guarantee open capital markets, fixed exchange rates, and an autonomous and independent MP without a "gold standard" of regulation. Obviously, based on this logic, the monetary authorities have chosen an independent MP and tended to manipulate interest rates at the expense of exchange rate control.

The theory (referring to the above discussed MP to ensure the capital market opening, fixed national currency exchange rate, and pursuing independent autonomy) was put forward by Olmstefeld, Shambaugh, and Taylor based on empirical research on MP between national banks in the period between World War I and World War II.[21] But a lot has changed since then: the rise of global financial markets with an international reserve currency, dollars issued by the Federal Reserve in the form of US Treasury bonds. Considering that the amount of US debt has multiplied and gone far beyond the stability limit of the American financial system, the theory should be enriched with the content of issuing international capital in the form of unsecured US debt. For the sake of accuracy, the theory of unsecured debt of EU countries (Greece, UK, etc.) should be added to the theory along with the additional issuance of euro, pound, and yen. The exponential growth in the issuance of major reserve currencies following the US dollar has resulted in a 3-5-fold increase in the monetary base of these currencies in global financial markets since the onset of the global financial crisis in 2008.

Thus, compared with the interwar period, modern capital markets are characterized by regular increases in inflation guaranteed by the unsecured issuance of international reserve currencies. That is why countries with open capital markets are inevitably under pressure to print money indefinitely in the form of speculative capital flows. This implies the emergence of monopolies in global financial markets that have enormous potential for manipulation, including the establishment of regulation of areas of the global financial system that are open to the free movement of capital in various countries. Unlike global commodity markets that comply with competition laws and are regulated by WTO rules, global financial markets are not strictly regulated, and the rules of the World Monetary Fund provide protection for this deregulation, which is beneficial to international financial speculators' benefits. These speculators have unlimited access to the global currency issuance field.

21. M. Obstfeld, J. Shambaugh, and A. Taylor, "Monetary Sovereignty, Exchange Rates, and Capital Controls: The Trilemma in the Interwar Period," *IMF Staff Papers*, no. 51 (2004).

To sum up, if the Central Bank cannot issue a global reserve currency, does not impose restrictions on cross-border capital flows, and its own currency is not backed by gold reserves, then it cannot control its own exchange rate and interest rate. Speculators have access to world currency issuance at the right time, raise interest rates, carry out speculative attacks at will, and extend any amount of credit to national borrowers at acceptable rates. In the case of Russia, they have proved this repeatedly. It should be noted that gold reserves provide 100% protection for the ruble, which theoretically enables the Russian bank to keep the ruble exchange rate at a reasonable level (in line with the basic conditions for the formation of supply and demand in the money market). Obviously, Russia gave up this advantage, with Russian banks withdrawing from the foreign exchange market, providing conditions for speculators to manipulate the foreign exchange market. Given the dominance of non-residents (who account for 3/4 of the Moscow Exchange's business), Russian banks floated the ruble. They left the foreign exchange market, handing control of Russia's financial markets to an international network of global financial speculators.

Therefore, to control the national monetary system, it is necessary to control the cross-border flow of capital in capital operations. Otherwise, our economic development will be decided abroad, adding to the chaos. Moreover, we are not talking about a single regulatory entity. In addition to multinational companies and foreign banks, these foreign oligarchic offshore business groups will also control Russia's financial markets. That, in effect, is the political consequence of moving to inflation targeting.

Politically, if a country loses control of its currency's exchange rate, it is at the mercy of currency speculators. Suppose the Central Bank provides loans to these speculators and transfers them to the management of the currency exchange. In that case, there will be currency fluctuations, the currency and financial markets will be in turmoil, and all external economic activities will be in chaos, as well as the reproduction of enterprises relying on external economic activities. The inflation targeting policy has led to these consequences for the Russian economy.

In addition to the failure to achieve the inflation target, the inflation targeting policy also negatively impacts the entire economic reproduction. The long-term negative consequences of this policy include the destruction of the stability of the rouble exchange rate and the transfer of money from the real economy to speculators.

Currency speculation became the most attractive activity in financial markets as the capital shortage worsened after the Bank of Russia announced it would abandon exchange rate supervision and raise interest rates. Since then, manufacturing margins have fallen to 5%–7%, and the solvency of real companies has fallen markedly. Companies' lending conditions had deteriorated as Russian banks raised key interest rates. After the Central Bank raised its key interest rate to 17%, most companies in the real economy could not obtain loans, and the remaining liquidity poured into the foreign exchange market. The subsequent corporate collapse was inevitable due to manipulation by speculators and misguided policies by monetary authorities.

From 2015 to 2017, Russia continued to implement the policy of stimulating currency speculation. To reduce the demand for foreign currency on the stock exchange, Russian banks implemented a foreign currency financing mechanism for foreign currency repurchase transactions, creating a new channel for speculators to make money. After obtaining a foreign currency loan at a 2% interest rate, the bank converted the foreign currency loan into rubles, bought Russian Federal loan bonds at a yield of more than 10%, then sold them and converted them again into foreign currency at the higher ruble rate. Given that the exchange rate increased by 1/3, the profitability of financial speculation in these currencies was the same as in 2014 when the ruble fell steadily, at 30%–40%. Undoubtedly, money from the real economy continued to flow into foreign exchange financial markets.

Excessive tightening of monetary and credit policies resulted in the devaluation of the ruble, and the manufacturing industry was unable to improve product competitiveness. Although national leaders had called for widespread import substitution and increased price competitiveness of local products after the devaluation of the ruble to expand competitive local production, this was not actually possible due to lack of credit. Unable to get credit for production, industrial firms tended to raise prices and reduce production. As a result, the inflation trend strengthened.

The credit resources issued by commercial banks in the process of refinancing amounted to 8 trillion rubles, which were mainly used for speculative financing recently. As shown in Figure 13-6, this is evidenced by the simultaneous growth of commercial banks' liabilities to the Central Bank and their foreign currency assets. Influenced by the monetary authorities' policies, foreign exchange became the main driving force for commercial activities in the Russian economy. In 2014, the volume of trading on the Moscow exchange was about $4 trillion, twice the country's GDP and ten times the volume of foreign trade. In 2015 it doubled again, to seven times GDP and 15 times foreign trade (Figure 13-8). Foreign currency business volume reached 100 trillion rubles, more than 95% of which was currency speculation. Profits at the Moscow exchange rose by RBS 600 trillion in 2015 in the context of falling production, revenues, and investment in the real economy.

The financial "bubble" could not have inflated on such a scale without speculators manipulating the rouble to make super-profits, who knew the regulations well and were convinced there was no risk. According to estimates by exchange brokers, speculators have made about $50bn in the past two years, artificially manipulating currency movements by depreciating the income and savings of citizens and companies that trust the state and accumulate money in rubles. Most of the excess profits from speculation were channeled out of the country through "fake" trading chains — non-Russian citizens accounted for 60%–90% of total foreign exchange financial transactions in the Russian market.

The ruble exchange rate finally broke away from the basic conditions of foreign economic exchange and became a tool for speculative games. Speculation caused by Russia's banking policies is sucking more and more money out of the banks and the real economy. Russian economy serves monetary and financial speculators, and the economy is facing imbalances and bankruptcy. When the ruble falls, speculators make excess profits by depreciating rouble-denominated savings and income. When the ruble exchange rate increases, cheap imports force real enterprises out of the market and their profits decline, while speculators take advantage of this opportunity to gain profits.

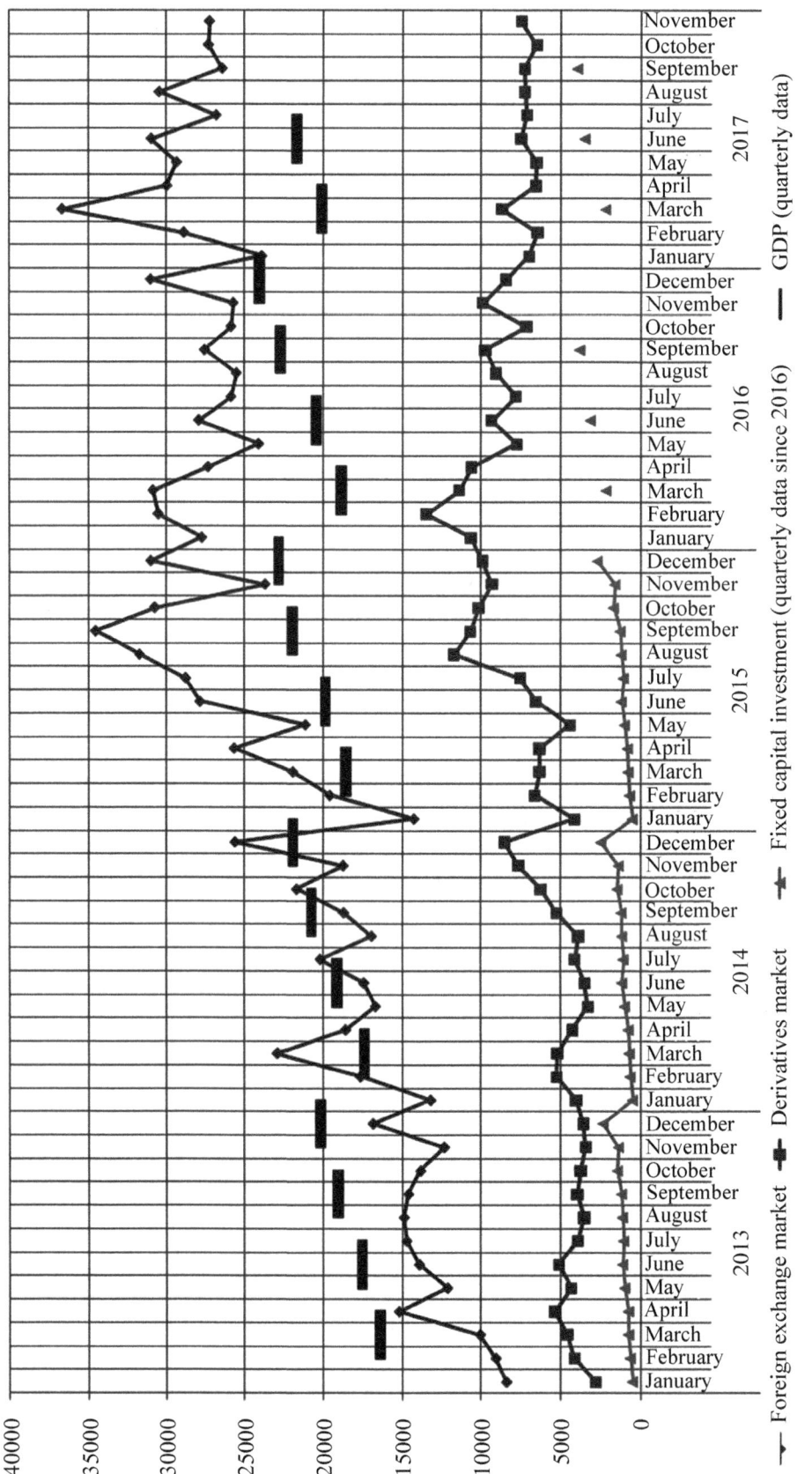

Figure 13-8 Moscow Stock Exchange Trade Volume, Fixed Capital Investment and GDP of Russia, January 2013–November 2017, Unit: billion rubles

Source: E. Matchenko, Central Bank of Russia and Federal Statistics Agency.

It is not hard to calculate that after a rise in interest rates, a 50% devaluation of the ruble and a jump in inflation to 16%, costs have risen by 20%–30% (depending on the proportion of imports). After the ruble appreciated by 1/3, the price competitiveness of export products decreased accordingly. Compared with last year, the currency depreciated by only 1/4, but the loan price doubled.

If the devaluation of the ruble must be forced for objective trade-balance reasons (falling export prices for oil and other raw goods, western sanctions, and capital outflows), it must be accompanied by "exchange rate stabilization to a new level" and not trigger a "wave" of speculation. For example, reducing the interest rate by 1/3 for a month to adjust the transaction to the change. At the same time, loans are provided to manufacturers to increase import substitution. In this way, there will be no "wave" of speculation, price competitiveness will be improved, and production will develop a 1.5 times increase after a sharp halving of the exchange rate. It is undoubtedly a "sure" way to destroy production and investment, mainly because of the great uncertainty and the unprofitability of productive activities from excess profits generated by currency speculation.

As early as 1992, people holding these ideas established the foreign exchange market in Russia. The ruble was then known as the "wooden ruble" because the official exchange rate meant nothing to the freedom of foreign economic activity for businesses and citizens. There was a huge gap between the official and the black-market exchange rates. The country had no foreign exchange reserves and seemed to be completely unable to bear foreign debt. In general, the country's financial situation at that time was not comparable to the current situation of having large foreign exchange reserves, a stable international balance of payments, and negligible external debt. Then, why were we able to quickly implement the market policy and guarantee the relative stability of the market, but at present enterprises cannot predict the direction of the rouble exchange rate to plan investment activities?

The answer is simple. At that time, the state controlled the currency market, but today it is manipulated by speculators. At that time, the country was in a state of weakness, but the ability and determination of the government and the Central Bank were outstanding. Nowadays, the country is powerful, but the government is caught in the illusion of a free market and cannot be determined to control it. The Central Bank relies on the recommendations of the IMF instead of its own decisive power.

We have noticed that the IMF does not like our measures to establish a modern foreign exchange market and transition to the ruble market exchange rate. These measures do not conform to the theory claimed by the US. These include:

- The exporting country compulsorily withdraws and sells foreign exchange earnings in the domestic market so that the importing country has sufficient foreign exchange supply, which is necessary for the transition to the market exchange rate.
- Carrying out currency control, prohibiting the export of capital, and only providing free currency convertibility for current income and expenditure.
- Export tariffs on raw materials guarantee up to 1/3 of federal budget revenues and limit rouble exchange rate growth and the outbreak of "Dutch disease."

- The sale of part of the foreign exchange earnings to build up the country's foreign exchange reserves at an exchange rate 1.5 times higher, thereby financing the purchase of key imports.

Relying on these measures, it is possible to quickly get rid of the desperate situation, establish a modern foreign exchange market, gradually shift to the ruble market exchange rate, ensure the stability of the ruble exchange rate, saturate the domestic demand for imported goods, start to increase the export of non-raw materials, and repay the foreign debt. Today, these measures have not been implemented, apart from the constant reduction of export tariffs required by the WTO.

The comprador oligarchy, monopolizing state power, was abolished immediately after the 1993 coup. The new oligarchs, having established control over the export of raw commodities, canceled the policy of selling foreign currency to the state because they were not interested in importing much-needed medicines and food. In a frenzy to accumulate wealth abroad, they legalized capital outflows, lifted exchange controls, and began to reduce the share of foreign exchange earnings they had to sell. Then they began to abolish export tariffs (transferring resource rents for exporting natural resources from the Treasury to the oligarchs' foreign accounts) and to make up for lost federal budget revenues, they started to issue Treasury bills at crazy rates.

The frenzied greed of the comprador oligarchy soon bankrupted the country. In August 1998, agents of the comprador oligarchic class could not pay their foreign debts under the supervision of the IMF and the US fiscal authorities. The Russian Federation Council established a temporary investigation committee to investigate the reasons, circumstances, and consequences of the resolution made by the Russian Federal Government and the Russian Central Bank on August 17, 1998. It included the restructuring of the short-term national debt, the devaluation of the ruble, the suspension of capital-based currency transactions, and those responsible for breaches often consulting with Washington's agents and concealing their plans from the President and Parliament. The committee found signs of treason in the actions of officials and some lapses in the activities of monetary authorities that had disastrous consequences for the country. Yeltsin dismissed the government and resigned from the leadership of the Central Bank. Primakov, Maslyukov, and Grashchenko immediately took the following remarkable measures to bring the country out of the disaster quickly:

1. Reinstating export tariffs in response to the budget crisis;
2. Reinstating mandatory sales of foreign exchange earnings to ensure the stable supply of foreign currency for domestic exchange rates and import financing in the domestic market;
3. Taking back the currency control power and determining the currency position of commercial banks to prevent capital outflow and keep the currency in the country, which is very important to stabilize the ruble exchange rate;
4. Tariff "freezes" on natural monopolies to prevent huge swings in inflation;
5. Instead of raising refinancing rates, the Central Bank began to refinance commercial banks according to export contracts with its customers, which led to increased turnover and expanded production of real enterprises.

These measures immediately stopped the crisis, stabilized the ruble, and boosted production. While commercial banks that had speculated in short-term treasury bills faced collapse, expanding credit to the real economy allowed companies to ramp up production at a rate of up to 2% a month (not "a year," as the government dreams of today). Inflation rate fell rapidly as the supply of goods grew and the exchange rate stabilized. Over the course of the year, the economy fully stabilized and embarked on a steady growth path that continued into 2008.

The ruble collapsed in 2008 when the global financial crisis hit. The financial crisis worsened the balance of payments but did not collapse the Russian economy. Still, compared with other G20 countries, Russia is the most affected. Medvedev invited investors to the St Petersburg Economic Forum six months before the crash to encourage investment in Russia, a "haven of financial crisis." But all the protection mechanisms established by Primakov and Grashenko were scrapped: foreign exchange restrictions on capital operations, forced sales of foreign exchange earnings, tariff "freezes" on natural monopolies, and debt refinancing by commercial banks to real companies. So, the global crisis immediately hit the "safe haven" of Russia, with capital flowing out of the country rather than foreign investment pouring in. Inappropriate actions by the monetary authorities to devalue the ruble smoothly will only exacerbate this process, stimulating the dollarization of the economy and the flow of money from the real economy to the currency exchange. Efforts to rescue the financial crisis by issuing money and spending budgets on commercial banks deepened the currency crisis, as banks converted loans from the central bank into foreign currency without currency restrictions, causing the ruble to fall further.

Russia has the highest reserves of resources among the G20 countries (gold reserves to ensure their currencies, the nominal exchange rate and the ratio of purchasing power parity (PPP), the stability of the trade surplus). Still, the Russian financial markets decline than the rest of the country, the cause of which is completely man-made. Russia's monetary authorities fail to take any measures to protect its financial markets, which makes it easy for international speculators to make excessive profits from manipulating the ruble exchange rate.

What is even more strange is that the monetary authorities firmly believe they can deal with inflation and ruble exchange rate fluctuations by controlling interest rates. Over the years of market reform, thousands of studies have shown no significant relationship between interest rates and the amount of money and the level of inflation, but a close relationship between interest rates and the amount of money and production and investment. Wherever and whenever the money supply shrinks and interest rates rise, production and investment decline, especially in the Russian economy.

The IMF's standardized advice is to raise interest rates to curb inflation and strengthen exchange rates. The standardization proposal is based on a mathematical model of market equilibrium, but the model does not conform to economic reality and can only demonstrate simple and superficially persuasive points. Monetarists argue that higher interest rates make bank deposits more attractive, the demand for money reduces, and prices lower. They also encourage the exchange rate to rise by concentrating idle funds and reducing their supply in foreign exchange markets. But this superficial judgment fails to consider that higher interest rates lead to higher costs for borrowers, which borrowers shift to production costs, leading to higher prices and putting downward pressure on their currencies. Similarly, due to the effects of economies of scale, the reduction in demand leads to a decrease in output and an increase in costs, which may not cause a price drop, but will instead cause a price increase. On the contrary, lowering interest rates and increasing the money supply can be translated into expanding production and investment, and accordingly, prices and costs will be lowered.

The real economy is as different from economic equilibrium models as biological organisms are from molds. Monetarists don't want to understand the obvious things about nonlinearity and imbalances in economic dynamics. In our case, where monetization is already very low, demonetization of the economy would be extremely damaging. So far, the expansion of the money supply in our economy has not led to an increase in inflation, which has declined due to better-than-expected production growth and lower costs in the context of higher capacity utilization in the real sector of the economy. At the same time, increased lending without control over the use of dedicated credit resources could result in credit flowing into financial markets, triggering a new wave of currency speculation, a renewed collapse of the rouble, and subsequent acceleration of inflation. It can be predicted that continued economic non-monetization will exacerbate the decline in production and investment.

Assessment Methods and Results of Economic Impact of Sanctions and Other Crisis Factors[22]

It is a prerequisite to solving a series of methodological problems in order to measure the impact of economic sanctions on Russian economy. First, it is necessary to distinguish the effects of the economic situation, including cyclical fluctuations in business and investment activity. Second, in addition to sanctions, Russia's economy is also affected by other external factors, such as economic conditions and systemic factors, which cannot be accurately assessed. Third, the consequences of sanctions are influenced by the economic policies[23] applied. Sifting through all the factors that affect the state of the economy to identify the impact of sanctions is entirely relative.[24]

Theoretically, the ideal trajectory of Russian economic development without

22. Данный подраздел подготовлен на основе сл. источника: Глазьев С. Ю., Архипова В. В. Оценка влияния санкций и других кризисных факторов на состояние российской экономики // Российский экономический журнал. 2018. №1.

23. Глазьев С. Ю. Экономика будущего. Есть ли у России шанс? М.: Книжный мир, 2017. С. 104–125; Ершов М. В. Какая экономическая политика нужна России в условиях санкций? // Вопросы экономики. 2014. №12. С. 37–53.

24. См., например: Широв А. А., Янтовский А. А., Потапенко В. В. Оценка потенциального влияния санкций на экономическое развитие России и ЕС // Проблемы прогнозирования. 2015. №4. С. 3–16; Гурвич Е., Прилепский И. Влияние финансовых санкций на российскую экономику // Вопросы экономики. 2016. №1. С. 5–35; Сухарев О. С. Экономические санкции: проблема оценки ущерба // Экономика и предпринимательство. 2017. № 8, ч. 4. С. 80–87; Crozet M., Hinz J. Collateral Damage: The Impact of the Russia Sanctions on Sanctioning Countries' Exports. Research and Expertise on the World Economy. CEPII Working Paper, № 2016 - 16 - June. P. 3–46; Russell M. Sanctions over Ukraine: Impact on Russia. Members' Research Service. European Parliamentary Research Service, March 2016. p. 1–12.

sanctions should be determined to assess the impact of sanctions on the Russian economy. If, as in our case, national policies exacerbate the negative effects of sanctions, the assessment of the consequences of their implementation needs to be compared with alternative policies, which may partially offset the negative effects of national policies and even benefit the development of the national economy. For example, in the implementation of counter-sanctions, if an embargo was imposed on food imports from countries that imposed anti-Russian sanctions, then import substitution in agricultural products would develop greatly. At the same time, the state has provided concessional loans (1.5 trillion rubles in 2016) and subsidies, and sanctions have boosted agricultural production. According to the Statistics Agency of the Russian Federation, the agricultural production index (calculated at comparable prices) of all types of farms reached 104.8% in 2016, 1.7% higher than the state planning target. The crop production index (at comparable prices) for all types of farms was 107.8%, 5.3% higher than the target, and the production of sugar beets (up 31.6%), sunflower seeds (up 18.6%) and cereals and pulses (up 15.2%) increased. Agricultural output in other sectors also increased significantly in 2016–2017.

Regrettably, except for the agricultural complex, the country's macroeconomic success in responding to sanctions has not been evident. These include machinery manufacturing, which serves the military-industrial and energy-power complexes. Foreign sanctions on these sectors are in the form of a ban on exporting equipment to Russia and individual Russian companies. To this end, under the direction of the Russian president, Russia has created new fields that can replace sophisticated technology imported from the west and Ukraine. Perhaps because of this, Russia has reduced its losses from the recent unwinding of economic ties, estimated at between $72–75 billion and $130–150 billion.[25] Measuring the effects of sanctions on various sectors requires research in the relevant areas, which is beyond the scope of this work. We try to separate the consequences of sanctions from the internal and external market situation and the impact of national macroeconomic policies, assessing only the macroeconomic impact.

For this study, we used the following dynamic indicators from 2010 to 2016: GDP, including household consumption expenditure and fixed asset investment; Foreign trade volume, including services; Indicators of retail trade, industrial and agricultural production. Static and dynamic methods were used to determine the relevant benchmarks for assessing the size of the crisis. In the first case, the pre-crisis averages of the corresponding indicators from 2010 to 2013 are used as a baseline. In the second case, the curve trend is constructed and extrapolated according to the average growth trajectory of Russian economy during 2010–2013 (Table 13-1). Therefore, our starting point is that the Russian monetary authorities have sufficient resources to ensure that the basic parameters of the macroeconomic situation are stable, which may offset the impact of internal crisis factors caused by changes in monetary and credit policies.

25. Косикова Л. Новейшие украинские шоки российской экономики (о воздействии «постмайданного» кризиса в РУ на воспроизводственные процессы в РФ) // Российский экономический журнал. 2017, №4. С. 69–82.

Table 13-1 Main Indicators of RussianEeconomic Development: Real Growth and Benchmark Growth (Year on Year)

Index	2010	2011	2012	2013	2014	2015	2016
GDP: real and benchmark growth	4.5	5	3.7	1.8	0.7 3.7	−2.8 4.01	−0.2 3.95
Household expenditure: real and benchmark growth	5.5	6.8	7.9	5.2	2.0 6.37	−98 6.58	−4.5 6.44
Actual retail volume indicator: real and benchmark growth	6.5	7.1	6.3	3.9	2.7 6.0	−10.0 6.2	−4.6 6.0
Gross fixed capital formation: real and benchmark growth	5.9	9.1	5.0	1.3	−1.8 5.3	−9.9 6.0	−1.8 5.8
Industrial production index: real and benchmark growth	7.3	5	3.4	0.4	1.7 4.0	−3.4 4.4	1.1 4.6
Total volume of foreign trade: real and benchmark growth	13.3	7.8	4.8	4.1	−2.9 7.5	−8.5 8.28	0.8 8.26
Agricultural production index: real and benchmark growth	−11.3	23	−4.8	5.8	3.5 3.2	2.6 3.1	4.8 3.2

Source: The census bureau data, the Russian federation, http://www.gks.ru/wps/wcm/connect/rosstat_main/rosstat/ru/statistics (use date: November 12, 2017).

Early in the study, we assessed the deviation of macroeconomic indicators of Russian economic reproduction from the benchmark trajectory. To obtain data for the assessment, we constructed an extrapolation of the expected trend for 2014–2016 and the curve for the next period based on the average pre-sanctions economic growth rate for 2010–2013.

It should be noted that most of the representative indicators (except for agricultural production) declined sharply from the baseline trajectory during 2014–2016. The dynamics of consumption indicators, which are usually relatively stable relative to the market, are worrying. The sharp decline in these indicators indicates that the country's economy declined during the study period. The dynamics of fixed asset investment expenditure are consistent with industrial production indicators. Foreign trade indicators are characterized by a relatively moderate decline. In 2016, according to the real growth rate, foreign trade, and industrial production indicators, entered the positive zone. During the sanctions period, the agricultural sector oriented towards import substitution showed its best economic status. In 2016, the real growth rate in this field exceeded the baseline trajectory.

It should be noted that the analysis of these indicators had begun to decline before the implementation of sanctions. The above indicators' rate of decline accelerated with the sharp increase of key interest rates after the increase of the refinancing rate of the Russian Central Bank.

Assessment of the impact of sanctions on the Russian economy is based on the following two methods: individual cases and common analysis. The calculation[26] of the impact of sanctions in this book will be described briefly, not in detail. The first method evaluates the impact of crisis factors on the domestic economy through the changing trend of activity indicators in various fields over a specified period. The second method measures the impact of crisis factors on the dynamic changes in GDP. Both methods assess the impact of sanctions based on the residual principle, which removes dynamic changes in representative target indicators from other influencing factors.

The first method includes:

1. Determining the overall economic losses of each sector in 2014–2016, the level of deviation between trade, investment, finance and budget sectors and representative targets during the sanctions period, and the level of deviation from similar average indicators that were relatively stable in 2011–2013;
2. Calculating the relationship between the Pearson correlation coefficient and representative indicators and factor indicators (foreign exchange and oil) during the sanctions period;
3. Taking the maximum correlation coefficient as the proportion of non-sanction factors' influence on Russian economy;
4. Assessing the impact of sanctions from 2014 to 2016, regardless of internal and external factors;
5. Detailed description of non-sanction factors, distinguishing two kinds of internal negative effects from the actions of the Central Bank of Russia: one is the fundamental impact, which is related to the changes in the policies of the Central Bank of Russia and the preparation work of the domestic economy to deal with the loss of sanctions. Second, the biggest negative impact of Central Bank policies;
6. Calculating the Pearson correlation coefficient when the overall non-sanction loss, during the sanction period, is eliminated from the influence of external non-sanction factors within the framework of the indicator factor group;
7. Assessing the net negative impact of sanctions.

The results of the above 1-6 points are listed in Table 13-2.

---

26. For a detailed description of the calculation, please refer to: Глазьев С. Ю., Архипова В. В. Указ. соч. 2018; Архипова В. В. Современный санкционный режим в отношении России: характеристика и глобальный аспект // Мир новой экономики. 2017. Т. 11, №2. С. 13–19.

Table 13-2 Assessment of the Overall Impact of Sanctions and Non-sanctions Factors from 2014 to 2016 (Including the Negative Impact of the Actions of the Russian Central Bank)[27]

Assessment Indicators	2014	2015	2016	Total: By Department
Commodity Trade Index (Total Foreign Trade)				
Deviation from 2011–2013 average (in billions of dollars)	51.9	317.7	376.7	746.3
Assessment of sanctions' Impact	**26%**	**37.7%**	**8.5%**	—
Losses due to Sanctions (in billions of dollars)	13.5	119.8	32	**165.3**
Non-sanctions factors that have the greatest impact	Foreign exchange	Foreign exchange	Foreign exchange	Foreign exchange
Influence of non-sanctions Fundamental influence of the Russian Central Bank	74% **0.7%**	62.3% **20.2%**	91.5% **95.5%**	— —
Influence of non-sanctions Fundamental influence of the Russian Central Bank	38.4 0.3	197.9 40	344.7 329.2	581 **369.5**
The biggest negative impact caused by central bank policies (in billions of dollars)	—	64.7	—	**64.7**
Service trade indicators (total foreign trade)				
Deviation from the 2011–2013 average (in billions of dollars)	7.1	32.8	48.2	88.1
Assessment of Sanctions' Impact	6%	62.7%	13.7%	—
Losses due to sanctions (in billions of dollars)	0.4	20.5	6.6	27.5

(Continued)

---

27. Источник сводной таблицы: Глазьев С. Ю., Архипова В. В. Указ. соч. 2018.

Non-sanctions factors that have the greatest impact	Foreign exchange	Foreign exchange	Foreign exchange	Foreign exchange
Influence of non-sanctions (in millions of dollars)	94%	37.3%	86.3%	—
Fundamental influence of the Russian Central Bank	0.7%	53.2%	5.2%	—
Influence of non-sanctions (in billions of dollars)	6.7	12.3	41.6	60.6
Fundamental influence of the Russian Central Bank	0.05	6.5	2.1	8.65
The biggest negative impact caused by central bank policies (in billions of dollars)	—	11.3	—	11.3
Indicators of net outflows of private capital				
Deviation from 2011–2013 average (in billions of dollars)	56	18.2	missing	74.2
Assessment of sanctions' impact	32.6%	26%	—	—
Losses due to sanctions (in billions of dollars)	18.3	4.7	missing	23
Non-sanctions factors that have the greatest impact	Foreign exchange	Foreign exchange	Comprehensive factors	Comprehensive factors
Influence of non-sanctions (in billions of dollars)	67.4%	74%	100%	—
Fundamental influence of the Russian Central Bank	42%	53.2%	96%	—
Influence of non-sanctions	37.7	13.4	missing	51.1
Fundamental influence of the Russian Central Bank	15.8	7.1	—	22.9
The biggest negative impact caused by central bank policies (in billions of dollars)	6.8	—	—	6.8

(Continued)

Indicators of inflows of foreign direct investment				
Deviation from 2011–2013 average (in billions of dollars)	36.4	53.7	27	117.1
Assessment of sanctions' impact	**41.9%**	**33.7%**	**28.7%**	
Losses due to sanctions (in billions of dollars)	15.3	18.1	7.7	41.1
Non-sanctions factors that have the greatest impact	Foreign exchange	Foreign exchange	Foreign exchange	Comprehensive factors
Influence of non-sanctions (in billions of dollars) **Fundamental influence of the Russian Central Bank**	**58.1%** 42%	**66.3%** 53.2%	**71.3%** 94.1%	— —
Influence of non-sanctions (in billions of dollars) Fundamental influence of the Russian Central Bank	21.1 8.9	35.6 18.9	19.3 18.1	76 **45.9**
The biggest negative impact caused by central bank policies (in billions of dollars)	6.1	4.4	—	**10.5**
Federal budget expenditure performance indicators				
Deviation from 2011–2013 average (in billions of dollars)	1513	3221	4026.8	8760.8
Assessment of sanctions' impact	0.5%	5.7%	6.2%	—
Losses due to sanctions (in billions of rubles)	7.5	183.6	249.6	440.7
Losses due to sanctions (in billions of dollars)[28]	0.2	2.9	3.8	6.9

(Continued)

---

28. To convert rubles into Dollars, we use the average nominal exchange rate of USD/ruble between the sanctions periods in each year: 43.5 rubles/USD in 2014, 62 rubles/USD in 2015, and 66.4 rubles/USD in 2016.

Non-sanctions factors that have the greatest impact	oil	oil	oil	Comprehensive factors
Influence of non-sanctions	99.5%	94.3%	93.8%	—
Fundamental influence of the Russian Central Bank	1.4%	53.2%	5.2%	—
Influence of non-sanctions in billions of dollars	1505.5	3037.4	3777.2	8320.1
Fundamental influence of the Russian Central Bank	21.1	1616	196.4	1833.5
The biggest negative impact caused by the Central Bank policies (in billions of rubles)	—	36.7	102.7	139.4
Impact caused by the Central Bank policies (in billions of dollars): including the fundamental and the biggest negative impact	0.5	26.7	4.5	31.7
	0.5	26.1	3	29.6
	—	0.6	1.5	2.1

The data results show that, in absolute terms, the trade sector has suffered the most from sanctions. On the one hand, this is because sanctions initially involved bilateral and multilateral trade restrictions. On the other hand, foreign trade has declined as a result of the direct ban on trade in goods and services in the areas subject to sanctions and the indirect secondary impact on trade in those goods and services in the context of deteriorating import and export conditions.

The financial investment sector is more sensitive to external shocks and responds accordingly to financial and economic sanctions in the first year of the sanctions period. The impact of sanctions in this area can generally be divided into direct effects (asset freezes and financial embargoes) and indirect effects, which are reflected in the negative attitude of economic actors towards domestic economic investment. It should be noted that, on average, capital exports from the banking sector accounted for 57% of total capital exports during the period under study, with commercial banks particularly intensive capital exports during the first two years of the sanctions period.

Losses resulting from the sanctions place an additional burden on the Federal budget, for which funds are allocated to reduce losses in the sectors affected by the sanctions and to compensate natural and legal persons. According to our calculations, the additional budgetary expenditure resulting from the sanctions (for these purposes) is about 440 billion rubles.

It should be noted that, in relative terms, the biggest negative impact of sanctions includes: the financial investment sector showed a shrinking trend in 2014; the trade sector showed a downward trend in 2015; in 2016, the budget department showed a shrinking trend; as expected, the sanctions initially hit the financial sector, leading to significant capital outflows. Since then, the foreign trade sector has suffered the most. Budget losses have increased throughout the sanctions period.

Relatively speaking, the Central Bank of Russia mainly continued to have a negative impact on the financial investment field. In 2015, the negative impact was mainly reflected in the increase of federal budget expenditure and changes in the volume of trade in services. In 2016, the loss of trade in goods also increased sharply due to similar reasons. In trade (services), the biggest negative impact caused by central bank policies is greater than the fundamental impact.

The upper and lower limits of the influence of sanctions and non-sanctions factors on the domestic currency exchange rate can be obtained according to the materials on the influence of the Central Bank of Russia on various sectors of the economy from 2014 to 2016 (Table 13-3). Identifying the scope of the impact of the sanctions on the ruble exchange rate in 2014–2016 and finding the maximum value in 2015 will help determine the overall impact of the sanctions on the trade sector in 2015.

Table 13-3 Scope of Impact of Sanctions on Ruble Exchange Rate during 2014–2016

Influencing factor index	2014	2015	2016
Non-sanctions factor: Central Bank of Russia (maximum and minimum ratios in Table 13-2)	1%–42%	20%–53%	5%–96%
Non-sanction factors: Excluding the Central Bank of Russia (maximum ratio/minimum ratio =100%-maximum ratio/minimum ratio of the influence of the Bank of Russia)	58%–99%	47%–80%	4%–95%
Sanctions (ratio =**100%**-maximum impact of non-sanctions factors)	<1%	<20%	<4%

Source: The Author's calculation based on data in Table 13-2.

In our definition, the net negative impact of sanctions refers to the difference between the loss caused by sanctions and by the maximum negative impact of the Central Bank of Russia. From 2014 to 2016, sanctions had the greatest negative impact on the financial investment sector, while the Central Bank of Russia had the greatest negative impact on trade (commodities) and financial investment sectors. (Table 13-4).

Table 13-4 Percentage of the Impact of Sanctions and Non-sanctions Factors on the Russian Economy from 2014 to 2016 (Considering the Maximum Negative Impact of Partial Sanctions Losses Transferred to the Central Bank of Russia)

Evaluation indicators used	2014–2016
Commodity trade indicators	
Deviation from the 2011–2013 average (in billions of dollars)	746.3
Assessment of sanctions' impact	13.9%

(Continued)

Russian Central Bank impact assessment	58.8%
Assessment of other non-sanction factors	27.3%
Service trade indicators	
Deviation from the 2011–2013 average (in billions of dollars)	88.1
Assessment of Sanctions' impact	18.4%
Russian Central Bank impact assessment	22.6%
Assessment of other non-sanction factors	59%
Indicators of net outflows of private capital	
Deviation from the 2011–2013 average (in billions of dollars)	74.2
Assessment of Sanctions' impact	21.8%
Russian Central Bank impact assessment	40%
Assessment of other non-sanction factors	38.2%
Indicators of inflows of foreign direct investment	
Deviation from the 2011–2013 average (in billions of dollars)	117.1
Assessment of sanctions' impact	26.1%
Russian Central Bank impact assessment	48.1%
Assessment of other non-sanction factors	25.8%
Federal budget expenditure performance indicators	
Deviation from the 2011–2013 average (in billions of rubles)	8760.8
Assessment of sanctions' impact	3.4%
Russian Central Bank impact assessment	22.5%
Assessment of other non-sanction factors	74.1%

Source: The Author's assessment based on data in Tables 13-2 and 13-3.

The assessment confirms previous conclusions based on causal analysis that the Central Bank of Russia's actions exacerbated the negative impact of sanctions.

Comparatively speaking, the second method to assess the impact of sanctions and non-sanctions factors on the Russian economy is called trend analysis. It analyzes the trend of GDP and its components before sanctions according to the expenditure method. The sanctions prevented real GDP growth from reaching the desired 4%, while the overall negative impact of the Central Bank's policies was about 58% (44% interest rate impact, 14% foreign exchange impact). The methods used to assess the impact of the Central Bank's exchange rate are similar to those used previously. GDP composition is the representative index, while ruble exchange rate and interest rate are the factor index.

Measuring the effect of sanctions on GDP at constant prices considered the deviation between actual GDP growth based on vertical estimates and the baseline trajectory, as well as comparisons with other estimates in Table 13-5. In absolute terms, our analysis of the total losses resulting from sanctions amounted to 696 billion rubles, a relative value close to the IMF experts' assessment of the impact of short-term sanctions. Meanwhile, the Central Bank lost 10.1 trillion rubles, or about 16% of GDP in 2013.

Table 13-5 Comparison of Evaluation Results of Sanctions' Impact on Russian Economy in Different Academic Works

Author and year of publication	Shroff, Jantowski, Potabenko (2015)	Experts at the IMF (2015)	Gurvitch, Prilipsky (2016)	Graziev, Arkhipova (2018)
Assessment of the negative impact of sanctions on Russia's **GDP**	In the medium term (to **2025**), **8%–10% of GDP**	**1.5%** of **GDP**(short term) and up to **9%** (medium term)	**2.4%** of pre-crisis **GDP** before **2017** (**0.4–0.6** percentage points per year)	From **2014 to 2016: 1.1%** of **GDP** calculated at constant prices in **2013** (average annual growth rate 0.3 percentage points), **2.5%** (maximum **3.9%**) of **GDP** calculated at current prices in 2013 (average annual loss of **1.2** percentage points)
Results of the comparison of existing difficulties	—	Unspecified short-term and medium-term deadlines for sanctions	Set conditions in the form of an oil price threshold	—
	The value characteristics of **GDP** are not indicated		—	—

Sources: Широв А. А., Янтовский А. А., Потапенко В. В. Указ. соч. С. 9, 16; Гурвич Е., Прилепский И. Указ. соч. с. 30, 33; Russian Federation: 2015 article IV consultation. IMF Staff Country Report. 2015. №15 / 211; авторские расчеты.

The deviation from the 2010–2013 average of GDP in current prices over the sanctions period is $1.4 trillion. In absolute terms, we estimate that the losses caused by the RBNC's exchange rate and interest rate policies are about $870 billion (or about 60% of the deviation): about $615 billion (42.4%) and $255 billion (17.6%), respectively. At the same time, sanctions accounted for about 4%–6% of GDP deviation from the pre-sanctions average in 2014–2016, or about $58 billion.[29] In relative terms, this value is close to the assessment of Gurvitch and Pllipsky (Table 13-5). It should be pointed out that during the analyzed time, the Central Bank policy has roughly the same impact on GDP calculated at current and constant prices. When analyzing the impact of the Central Bank policies on GDP calculated at current prices, the exchange rate factor in Central Bank policies plays a major role in analyzing the impact of Central Bank policies on GDP calculated at constant prices. The impact of interest rate manipulation in central bank policies is more significant.

We compared the result obtained with the evaluation conclusions of other domestic and foreign experts. As shown in Table 13-5, due to different research methods and preconditions formed by data and time interval characteristics, it is difficult to compare different research results on this issue (impact of sanctions on Russian economy). The significant characteristics of the method we proposed are that the statistical mathematical tools used are relatively simple and the initial premise and conclusion are clear, specific, and detailed. It can comprehensively study and evaluate the internal and external factors affecting the Russian economy and their interdependent and complementary relationship and can test the results and hypotheses.

It should be noted that our assessment of the impact factors of the crisis is measured by building a baseline trajectory by extrapolating the pre-sanctions trend. If the macroeconomic policies pursued during this period were not optimal and resulted in a decline in economic activity (in terms of potential output of goods and services), then an alternative assessment of the impact of the crisis could be obtained. If Russia implements an advanced economic development zone policy[30] and uses the methods of Expanding Credit[31] and Financial Boost (financial measures adopted to promote macroeconomic development) used by other countries,[32] then GDP is expected to increase by 7% and investment is expected to increase by 15%. In this case, the baseline trajectory would be different, with the deviation of real GDP growth from

29. The calculation method is similar to the previous method. The target index is GDP at current prices, and the factor indicators are Russian bank interest rates and the ruble exchange rate (quarterly data "3Q 2013–4Q 2016"). The correlation coefficients between the impact of sanctions and exchange rate of central banks are checked according to Table 13-2–13-4. Data sources: World Economic Outlook Database. International Monetary Fund. October 2017. http://www.imf.org/external/pubs/ft/weo/2017/02/weodata/weoselser.aspx? c=922&t=1 (use date on November 19, 2017).

30. Глазьев С. Стратегия опережающего развития России в условиях глобального кризиса. М.: Экономика, 2010.

31. Глазьев С. Очередной документ прокризисной стратегии «мегарегулятора» (о неприемлемости центробанковского проекта «Основных направлений единой государственной денежно-кредитной политики на 2017 год и на период 2018 и 2019 годов») // Российский экономический журнал. 2016. №5. С. 3–28.

32. Финансовые стратегии модернизации экономики: мировая практика / Под ред. Я. М. Миркина. М.: Магистр, 2014.

the benchmark average rising from 4.7% to 8.2% in 2014–2016. If we use the same method to calculate the potential growth in GDP during the sanctions period, the impact of the sanctions would not change in principle. It would be about 1% of GDP at constant 2013 prices (about 642–696 billion rubles), while the negative impact of the central bank's exchange rate and interest rate policies would rose from 16% to 29%–40%, reaching 18.6–25.7 trillion rubles.[33]

---

33. Source: Central Bank of Russia. The limits of the impact of sanctions and the upper limit of the influence of the Russian Central Bank are determined according to the following premises. As the target indicator increases at a ratio of about 1:2, it is reasonable to assume that the concentration of the analyzed indicator factor "stress" changes significantly. Thus, according to our assumptions, the share of external effects here should be halved: sanctions less than 2% and other factors less than 19% (however, the share of internal "shocks" in the monetary and credit sectors should increase to about 80% of GDP overall).

Chapter 14

Lessons and Experience for Economic Development

Economic Development Experience Russia can Learn from China

Compared with other countries, especially against Russia's recession, China's "economic miracle" is particularly convincing (Figure 14-1). During this period (1993–2016), China's economy has accelerated (its share of global GDP rose from 2% to almost 16%), while Russia's economy has been stuck in a "stagnation trap" for more than 25 years (Figure 14-2).

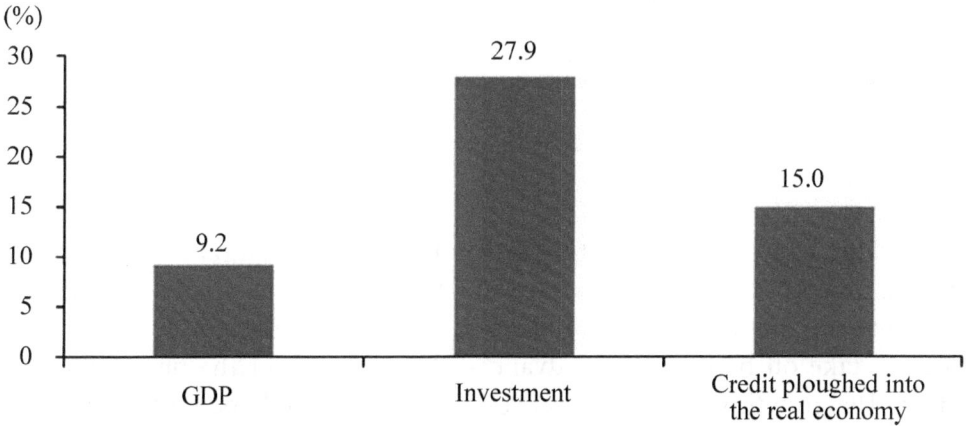

Figure 14-1 Growth of GDP, Investment, and Money Supply in China (1993–2016)
Source: M. Yershov, based on China's national statistics.

The reason for these differences is that Russia implements an IMF-recommended plan, integrating into the US-centered world economic paradigm, and deviating to the "periphery" of this system. At the same time, China follows a new model of progressive economic development management that forms the basis of the new world economic structure. As a result, Russia has fallen into the "trap" of unequal economic exchanges with foreign countries, with capital outflows of up to $100 billion a year. The unprecedented offshoring of Russia's economy has led to the loss of state control in most industrial sectors (Figure 14-3). The industry gradually declines due to the loss of high-tech industries. In fact, Russia is rapidly becoming a raw material client state of Europe and a contributor to the American economy, losing more than $1 trillion in capital outflows in 25 years.

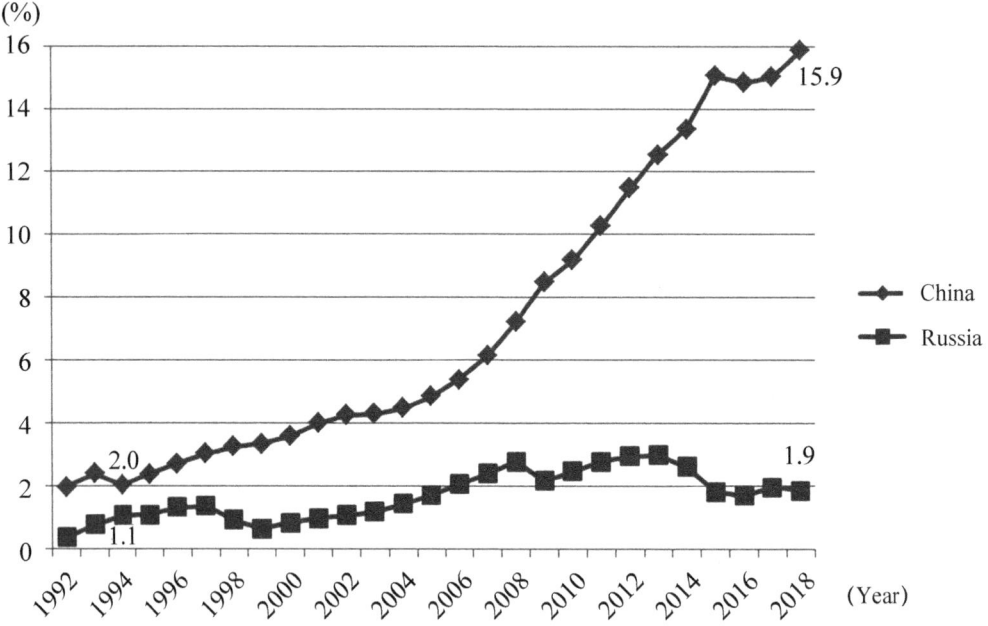

Figure 14-2 Russia and China's GDP as a Percentage of Global GDP
Note: Estimates are cited for 2018.
Source: The author calculated according to the GDP data calculated at current US dollar prices in the IMF World Economic Outlook database, October 2018.

At the same time, Russia's existing technological and natural resource potential could allow it to produce twice as many products as it does now. Under the background of deepening the implementation of the new economic paradigm, Russia's economy will seek to take off based on the advanced development of the new technological paradigm. The growth rate of Russia's economy will probably be no less than that of China. Its GDP can increase by 6%–8% every year, and its investment can increase by 10%–15%. To this end, Russia must draw on China's experience in economic development management and integrate it organically with Russia's management and cultural traditions.

To ensure expanded reproduction, the Russian economy needs to radically increase the level of monetization, the volume of credit, and the capacity of the banking system. Urgent measures are needed to stabilize the economy, which will require the Central Bank of Russia to increase the supply of liquidity and strengthen its role as a lender of last resort. Unlike reserve currency issuers, the Russian economy's main problems are not caused by excess money supply and the associated financial "bubble," but by low long-term monetization and long-term attrition due to a severe shortage of loans and investment.

Net losses to the Russian financial system through capital operations = $70 – $80 billion per year, including:

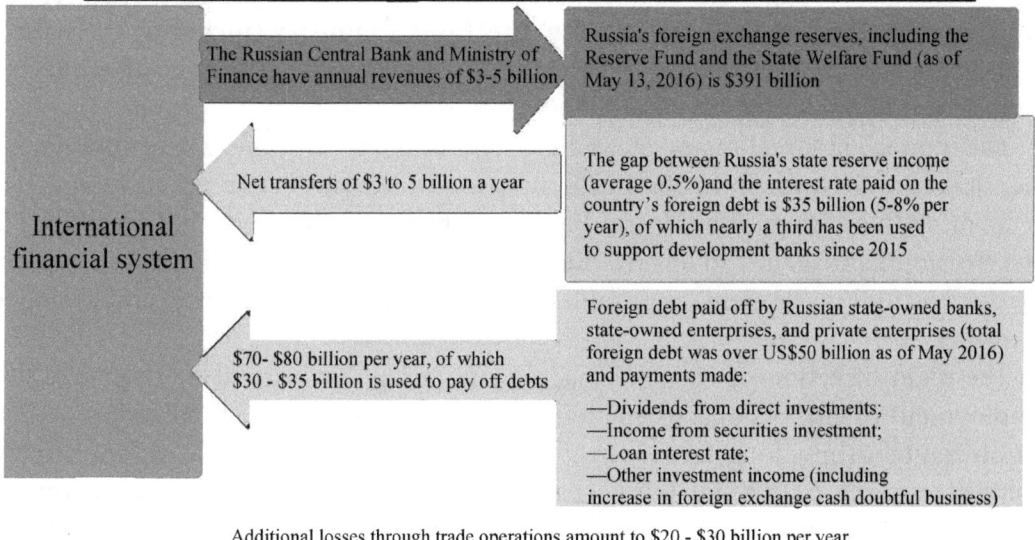

Additional losses through trade operations amount to $20 - $30 billion per year

Total loss ("contribution" to the outside world) = $90 - $110 billion per year or 6-8% of GDP

Figure 14-3 Assessment of Russia's Transition to the International Financial System
Source: Д. Митяев по данным платежного баланса России.

To achieve open and inclusive development opportunities in the growth "wave" of the new technological paradigm, it is necessary to vigorously promote the renewal of fixed assets and concentrate existing resources on the promising areas of modernization and economic development. Hence Russia needs to increase the investment rate to 35%–40% of GDP and focus investment on breakthrough areas of global growth. Special loans issued by the monetary authorities according to uniformly identified priorities are the source of funding for such investments, as demonstrated by the experience of China. It has successfully taken advantage of the window of opportunity provided by technological breakthroughs to increase financial support policies and credit to promising areas of economic growth. The People's Bank of China has become a development bank to issue the necessary funds to implement the unified plan of investment projects and programs.

Starting from the theory and practice of China's economic development, it is necessary to establish a money supply system by combining economic development goals and relying on a comprehensive method of internal currency issuance. The most important of these is the refinancing mechanism of credit institutions, which cannot provide loans for investments in the real economy and priority development areas. As shown in the previous section on currency evolution, we can learn from the indirect methods of currency issuance in developed countries (refinancing with state and solvent corporate guarantees) and direct methods (Co-financing national plans, providing state guarantees and financing development institutions).

It should be noted that developed economies will focus on special long-term and ultra-long-term treasury bonds (30–40 years in the US, Japan, and China), including treasury bonds related to long-term investment project financing, supplemented by medium-term refinancing instruments, which lays a strong foundation for the formation of long-term economic resources. Moreover, monetary and credit policies are consistent with the priority direction of industry (including the nature of industry, group, and region), so we can discuss the establishment of monetary industrial policy system.

The modern national financial credit system is in line with the task of stimulating the vitality of investment in the modernization of Russia's economic development. In forming this system, the Central Banks of China and Russia should play the role of a development agency to ensure the credit needs of private enterprises to expand production and investment, and implement national plans, strategies, and directive planning.

The main direction of national macroeconomic policy should be to ensure full employment of citizens and to create conditions for their self-actualization, which requires establishing long-term loan systems to provide long-term loan funds to the domestic market. To this end, it is necessary to extend special loans to manufacturers, whose sales are guaranteed by export contracts, state orders, contracts with domestic consumers, and trade networks, and to monitor the use of funds specifically for production needs strictly. These loans should be refinanced by the central bank in the form of corporate bonds issued by state-controlled banks and allocated to the ultimate borrower at an interest rate of no more than 4%.

The central bank raises funds through specialized development agencies at the federal and regional levels at an annual interest rate of no more than 2% (including mortgage loans). It doubles the preferential credit line to support small businesses, housing construction, and agriculture. In addition, private companies should perform state responsibilities, that is, produce a certain number of certain products (or provide services) at a fixed price as required by the state to guarantee access to state loans. Failure to fulfill the responsibility will result in national debt equivalent to non-production costs.

To maintain a stable macroeconomic environment, Russia must regulate cross-border capital flows and foreign exchange transactions to prevent speculation, loan abuse, and fraud in financial markets. This reduces costs and expands productive credit without the risk of spillover of credit funds into money and financial markets for speculative purposes. The exchange rate of ruble must also be controlled according to objective conditions to ensure the competitiveness of domestic commodity producers. Selective approaches to monetary regulation are well known and, as China's experience shows, can be very effective if monetary authorities implement coherent policies.

The creation of a fair, responsible national management system conducive to the development of production activities provides the necessary conditions for the formation of a social system for the ideological unity of all people. This social system is a new global harmonious social relationship based on the principles of traditional moral values, social justice, and partnership. It understands the need for sustainable human development while maintaining social diversity and order and respects for human rights and freedom, international law, fair competition, and reciprocal international economic exchange mechanism.

Learning from Mistakes

According to the Forecast of the Main Indicators of the Currency Plan (Table 14-1), the Central Bank of Russia plans not to provide funds before 2021, but to withdraw 3.5–4.4 trillion rubles of credit funds from the banking sector. With the addition of budgetary revenue from reserves, the total amount of credit funds drawn by the monetary authority from the economy will be 8–12 trillion rubles (page 106). In this case, the interest-bearing liabilities of the Central Bank of Russia will be repaid by the credit funds drawn by the monetary authorities, which obviously rely on the issuance of currency to make up for losses. This will be the only example of the Central Bank losing money in economic history.

In fact, the Central Bank of Russia is restoring the "Monetary Board" used by the IMF, which was once a currency system designed for the British colonies. The currency system only allows the issuance of the national currency under the condition that the currency of the sovereign country is purchased to increase the foreign exchange reserves of the national central bank. The Central Bank of Russia used the above system before the global financial crisis in 2008, and its negative effects were already apparent at that time. The difference between the current situation and the beginning of the 21st century is that since oil prices have stabilized at a moderate level, the increase in foreign exchange inflows has been much smaller. If during that period the excessive appreciation of the ruble was suppressed through the continuous increase in foreign exchange income and the Central Bank's acquisition of foreign exchange, the base currency would also increase by 30%–40% every year. Still, today the base currency has not increased in this way. At that time, the monetary authority invested part of the petrodollars in the federal budget received through the Stability Fund into foreign exchange reserves, eliminating the excessive growth of the money supply. The money supply has not increased, and the "liquidity surplus" formed by the increase in interest rates can be supplemented by banks withdrawing funds from the real economy. In other words, if this MP was adopted before, we refused to use the additional economic income obtained from abroad, then what is rejected today is not only the additional economic income, but also the working capital in the private economy. This is comparable to using bloodletting therapy to treat people who are malnourished (unwilling to chew and digest food) caused by man-made reasons. Not only does it fail to save their lives, but they also lose their final strength. The MP model currently in use is shown in Figure 14-4.

Table 14-1 Forecast of Main Indicators of Currency Plan (Unit of Measurement: trillion rubles)

	January 1, 2017 (actual)	January 1, 2018		January 1, 2019		January 1, 2020		January 1, 2021	
		Basic index	Selectivity index	Basic index	Selectivity index	Basic index	Selectivity index	Basic index	Selectivity index
1. Base Currency (narrow definition)	9.1	9.5	9.6	9.8	10.0	10.1	10.4	10.4	10.8

1.1 Cash in circulation (other than the Central Bank of Russia)	8.8	9.2	9.3	9.5	9.7	9.8	10.1	10.1	10.5
1.2 Mandatory reserves**	0.3	0.3	0.3	0.3	0.3	0.3	0.3	0.3	0.3
2. Deposit reserve	22.4	24.5	24.5	25.3	26.7	25.5	29.3	25.8	32.0
1 billion***	370	403	404	417	440	421	483	425	527
3. Domestic net assets	−13.3	−15.0	−14.9	−15.5	−16.7	−15.5	−18.9	−15.4	−21.2
3.1 Net lending of general government	−6.3	−5.4	−5.4	−4.9	−6.2	−4.9	−8.6	−4.9	−11.1
3.2 Net bank loans	−0.3	−3.7	−3.6	−4.9	−4.7	−5.0	−4.7	−5.2	−4.7
3.2.1 Total Bank Credit	2.3	1.0	1.0	1.0	1.0	1.0	1.0	1.0	1.0
3.2.1.1 Refinancing business require-ments ****	1.6	0.3	0.3	0.3	0.3	0.3	0.3	0.3	0.3
3.2.2 Current accounts of credit institutions with the Central Bank of Russia	−1.8	−2.2	−2.2	−2.3	−2.3	−2.4	−2.4	−2.5	−2.5

(Continued)

3.2.3 Deposits of credit institutions in Russian banks and coupon bonds of Russian banks *****	−0.8	−2.5	−2.4	−3.6	−3.5	−3.7	−3.4	−3.7	−3.2
3.3 Other unclassified net assets ******	−6.8	−5.9	−5.9	−5.7	−5.8	−5.5	−5.6	−5.3	−5.5

Notes:
* The currency plan indicators calculated at a fixed exchange rate are determined based on the official ruble exchange rate at the beginning of 2017.
** The deposit reserves transferred from the currency account of the Russian Federation of the credit organization to the account of the Central Bank of Russia (excluding the funds in the account between the credit institution and the Central Bank of Russia, these funds are part of the average law deposit reserve mechanism).
*** This includes the use of the combined funds of the Russian State Corporation Deposit Insurance Agency and the banking sector, the net interest expense of the Russian Central Bank, and the revaluation of monetary assets.
**** This includes requests to refinance rubles, involving guaranteed loans, repo transactions, and currency swaps in which the Russian Central Bank buys dollars and Euros in rubles.
***** This includes currency swaps in which the Russian Central Bank sells dollars and Euros for rubles.
****** This includes the use of the combined funds of the Russian State Corporation Deposit Insurance Agency and the banking sector, the net interest expense of the Russian Central Bank, and the revaluation of monetary assets.
Source: Central Bank of Russia.

Incorporating "absorption of liquidity surplus" (3.3–4.4 trillion rubles from the financial sector within three years) into the monetary plan means that the systemic banking crisis triggered by the monetary and credit policy implemented by the Central Bank of Russia in the past five years has deepened. At the same time, speculators continue to take advantage of the profitability difference between the Russian and foreign financial markets and the appreciation of the ruble to seek excess profits. In countries around the world, this "arbitrage trading" game is regarded as a threat to macroeconomic stability and is suppressed by the monetary authorities. On the contrary, the Russian monetary authorities support this behavior, artificially supporting this behavior of seeking excess profits by squeezing funds from the production and budget areas. The more monetary authorities allow speculators to do this, the more money will flow from investment to speculation. In the end, speculators will buy assets at low prices after the collapse of the national currency and leave the market after obtaining more excess profits.

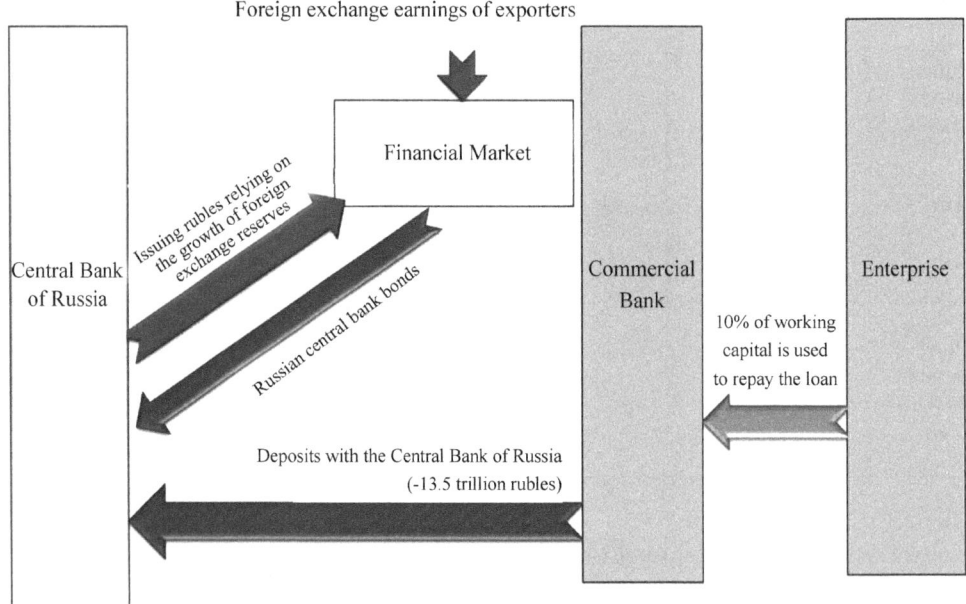

Figure 14-4 MP Model Predicted Based on the Main Indicators of the Monetary Plan of the Russian Central Bank from 2018 to 2021
Source: E. Matchenko, data from the Central Bank of Russia.

In the context of the economic crisis, the monetary authorities of other countries have implemented loose monetary policies for ten years, increasing credit allocation, raising funds for investment, and breaking the structural constraints based on the growth of the new technological paradigm. Compared with the monetary authorities of other countries, the Central Bank of Russia uses the completely opposite method. Russia artificially reduces credit funds, intensifying the decline in investment activities and hindering economic modernization and development. This counterproductive policy can be explained as a shift in the banking sector from a deficit to a liquid surplus. As stated in the draft document, this situation is affected by the long-term massive consumption of reserve funds (funds accumulated in the past) in the previous two years. For some reason, the drafters of the main direction of the national unified monetary and credit policy did not notice that maintaining the key interest rate above the industry's actual profitability by the Central Bank of Russia is the main reason for the formation of a liquidity surplus. This is similar to the famous logic of Queen Maria Antoinette of France. When she saw farmers too poor to eat bread, she said, "If there is no bread, wouldn't it be better to eat cake?" Similarly, seeing the destruction of damaged items in high-end stores, they affirm that production must be reduced when a large number of poor people are malnourished. Once the Bank of Russia lowers the key interest rate to the profitability level of the processing industry, the liquidity surplus will lead to a shortage of loan funds for production companies.

Our monetary authorities have long shocked the academic community. They make arbitrary judgments, are blindly and stubbornly reluctant to admit obvious mistakes, disregard international experience, and are unwilling to participate in discussions. The exaggerated claim to possess "secret knowledge" hides warlike ignorance. This reminds me of the speech of Cavallo, a well-known lecturer of the IMF, who visited Moscow in September 1998 as a prophet of anti-crisis measures. At that time, as a supporter of the "Washington Consensus," he proposed simple and direct anti-crisis measures, which were extremely consistent with the current measures: abolishing currency controls, deregulating the ruble exchange rate, and repeatedly raising refinancing rates, nothing done in terms of economic stability. Thankfully, I wisely and politely rejected these suggestions from Washington. I happened to talk in my parliamentary speech that these measures would lead to catastrophic consequences in many countries (including Argentina, where the policies of the country's Finance Minister Cavallo led to a serious crisis).

Today, the Russian economy is operating at half capacity due to the lack of credit funds for working capital financing and fixed asset investment. In the past three years, the Central Bank of Russia withdrew about 8 trillion rubles from the economy to supplement the US$200 billion in western loans that were recalled. The reduction in inflation is at the expense of restraining the final needs of the poor and suspending investment in enterprises. The bank savings-investment conversion mechanism has been suspended. On the contrary, the working capital of production enterprises is exported to the financial speculation field and abroad.

The saddest thing is that our monetary authorities do not know how to learn from their mistakes (whether it is the mistakes of others or their own). This makes us doomed to experience another round of "instability" and economic recession. This is the fourth time that the money supply has been tightened to combat inflation, which has reduced investment. Since then, economic and technological backwardness has intensified, competitiveness has declined, and the trade balance has deteriorated, which will cause another devaluation of the ruble and a surge in inflation. The monetary authorities repeated the same mistakes and caused domestic economic turmoil. 3/4 of the design bureaus and scientific research and design institutions have closed down, the output of technology-intensive industries has fallen sharply, and due to insufficient demand, more than one million high-quality experts have left the country.

The consequences of the dogmatic policy of the Russian Central Bank have been described above. All in all, the consequence is that the Russian banking system has become disordered, failing to realize the traditional function of converting savings into investments. The share of credit investment is approximately 5% of commercial bank assets. Commercial banks export a certain proportion of their assets abroad as their basic business. The implementation of monetary and credit policies has worsened the real economy's financial conditions and has repeatedly increased the losses caused by anti-Russian sanctions. At the same time, the monetary and credit policies implemented encourage the construction of a financial pyramid structure and the expansion of financial assets in the financial market.

The "cooperation" model between regulatory agencies and financial groups clarifies the essence of modern Russian monetarism, safeguarding the interests of currency holders. To increase the value of their purchases, these currency holders even do not hesitate to undermine the stability of the entire country's financial and economic system. This theory (the monetary credit policy proposed by the Russian monetary authority mentioned above) serves only the interests of currency holders. It imposes restrictions on the state in managing currency issuance to cause currency deficits. It uses seemingly scientific terms, but its method is close to quasi-religious dogma, because it does not accept doubts, ignores facts, and does not recognize experiments. This is why many thinkers regard monetarism as a modern version of the Old Testament Israel's gold-worshiping calf, a religion that deified money. To this end, the actual effects of the MP implemented since 1992 should be correctly evaluated: During this period, the Russian economy was mainly concentrated in the oil and gas sector, and the beneficiaries of this policy redistributed income by raising interest rates, extracting hundreds of billions of dollars from the real sector and sending them abroad.

During this period, China and other former socialist countries were not bound by the theory of monetarism and chose pragmatic economic development policies to increase their economic potential repeatedly. Under the guidance of monetarism, Russia and other post-socialist countries have fallen into the ranks of backward countries in terms of economic development, economic structure, and foreign trade structure. However, this does not prevent Russia from taking a leading position in the growth of billionaires and investment in the acquisition of high-end properties in London (London is considered an international oligarchic center). Domestic experts estimate that the amount of capital flight from Russia in the post-Soviet period is about US$1–3 trillion. Russia is the world's largest contributor to the US-centric financial system. It supports the US "debt pyramid" through natural resource exports, household income, and fixed asset depreciation.

Economic policies should combine the economic interests of different social groups, among which the interests of the ruling elite occupy a larger proportion, and their interests may not be consistent with the interests of the people, or even completely contradictory. The elites need to establish policies that are beneficial to themselves as the only correct policy and need to find agents in the scientific community for this. Most of these executors interpret the economic policies implemented from their own interests. Unlike physics, economics will inevitably become a vassal of the ruling elite's pursuit of self-interested economic policies. In the articles, reports, and plans published in most prestigious publications, experts seem to scientifically demonstrate the correctness of the ruling elite's policies based on abstract dogmatic ideas. We take the growth of social welfare (measured by the growth of GDP) as the criterion of economic policy, and conduct an objective scientific analysis of economics. Next, we will discuss the optimal macroeconomic policy based on this standard and with the help of relevant scientific knowledge of the laws of modern economic development.

PART V

RUSSIA GOING OUT OF THE PERIPHERY AND ENTERING THE WORLD ECONOMIC CENTER

Based on the analysis of the law and trend of global economic development and the evaluation of Russia's economic situation and the effect of the current macroeconomic policy, this part demonstrates the opinions of Russia's economic policy transition to the advanced development zone. The opinions include different levels of development planning systems, the most urgent part of which is to eliminate the risks of shrinking Russian economic reproduction, mainly relevant to financial markets and the monetary and credit policy situation, with an emphasis on eliminating threats to national security. In the medium term, it is necessary to create conditions for the growth of investment activities, while for investment financing, a fundamental change in monetary and credit policies is required. In the long term, there is a need to achieve the priorities for scientific and technological progress, including the deployment of strategic planning processes and the formation of a comprehensive system of development institutions. Nevertheless, it is urgent to protect national security from threats. Only in this way can all the above-mentioned possibilities be realized. Among the most serious risks are the freezing of foreign exchange funds, the separation of Russian banks from international payment systems and information systems, the prohibition of the supply of high-tech products to Russia, and the deterioration of Russian export conditions.

Chapter 15

Restoration of Sovereign MP

As shown above, the Central Bank of Russia's policies repeatedly exacerbated the negative impact of Western sanctions, as it compensated for the lack of foreign credit resources by reducing domestic credit and implementing stricter commercial bank supervision. The introduction of *Basel III* standards, which were used by Russian banks earlier than in other countries with more developed banking systems, intensified the deterioration in refinancing conditions. At almost the same time as sanctions, the Central Bank of Russia destabilized Russia by raising key interest rates and worsening credit conditions, tightening regulations, floating the Ruble, and privatizing the Moscow stock exchange (MOSE). It plunged it into chaos, leading to the current crisis.

The sharp rise in the price of hydrocarbons provided Russia with an opportunity to defend its sovereignty. Russian President Putin used this to have restored the country's status in the administrative and political fields. However, in macroeconomic policy, Russia is still a country that relies on the issuing country of the world currency, and its monetary and credit policy strictly safeguards the interests of the issuing countries of the world currency.

In the context of the US launching a war[1] against Russia, the decolonization of MP has become a necessary condition for survival. Modern countries can develop independently only when they have sufficient funds. The increase in the money supply will expand financial assets, and at the same time will promote competition among modern countries and reduce the cost of the money supply. However, the policy implemented by the Central Bank of Russia is not aimed at creating a high-quality currency needed to maintain the economy's normal development, but at limiting its quantity and replacing the dollar alternative formed on the basis of external financing. The increase in interest rates by the Central Bank of Russia has led to an increase in the cost of domestic credit and replaced internal credit with external credit provided by the monetary authority of the US and the European Union (providing preferential prices and loan terms). In the context of cutting off foreign credit due to sanctions, this policy has led the economy into a "trap" of stagflation. In the context of a shortage of long-term loans (the ratio of total Russian credit to GDP is lower than half of large developing countries and 1/3 of developed countries), this naturally leads to a reduction in business and investment activities, a decline in production and industrial degradation.

To achieve the goal set by the President, the annual growth rate of GDP should be at least 8%, which requires an increase in investment[2] of at least 15%. This demands leaps and bounds in credit growth, which means remonetizing the economy. The successful world experience of countries moving from economic backwater to advanced status

---

1. Глазьев С. Как не проиграть в войне / Аналитический доклад, июль 2014.

2. Россия на пути к современной динамичной и эффективной экономике / Аналитический доклад / Под ред. А. Д. Некипелова, В. В. Ивантера, С. Ю. Глазьева. М.: Российская академия наук, 2013.

demonstrates the importance of raising investment rates to 35%–40% of GDP, usually by increasing credit to 100% or more. Russia is likely to achieve this leap by relying on the existing scientific and technological potential, the excess profits (natural resources rents) obtained from raw material exports, and the sovereign currency and credit policy to finance innovation and investment projects in areas with economic development prospects.

The US and the European Union sanctions provide a unique opportunity to adopt this policy based on expanding domestic credit. Nevertheless, Russia is a donor, not the host country of the international financial system, refusing to become a donor country will fundamentally increase domestic investment. Mr. Maniewicz and Mr. Bukina[3] argue convincingly that if a country runs a trade surplus, it does not need foreign credit. As much external credit as a country attracts, its financial system is forced to reduce domestic credit and bear the excess costs of servicing foreign credit. Under the current circumstances, replacing foreign credit with domestic credit can clear up to 3 trillion Rubles of abnormal losses, and correspondingly increase the amount of credit in the national economy, providing production companies with cheaper and affordable credit.

So far, the world war waged by the US against Russia is mainly economic. The US ensures its dominance in war by issuing dollars without restrictions. This provides funds for unimaginable huge military and foreign policy expenditures and ensures its economic competitive advantage—unlimited free loans. Under the conditions of WTO's strict restrictions on tariff protection measures, such loan conditions have become a decisive means of international competition. In addition, countries that issue large amounts of cheap currency to provide loans to repay foreign debt have an advantage. Therefore, it is necessary to fundamentally change the currency issuance mechanism and transition from relying on currency issuance to protect foreign exchange reserves to relying on currency issuance to protect national debt and corporate debt.

Although the key interest rate of the Central Bank of Russia at present is the main control tool for the money supply, the Central Bank states that it would continue to comply with quantitative restrictions when determining the amount of currency issuance. It would arbitrarily set the maximum amount of funds in the auction of foreign exchange repurchase agreements (A week's credit resources are allocated according to the repurchase business, which constitutes the main part of the currency issued by the Central Bank of Russia).[4] These funds are designed to balance the current demand and supply of liquidity in the banking sector and cannot be used as a source of loans to the industrial sector. For this reason, before the sanctions were imposed, most credit resources flowed into foreign countries, causing the Russian financial system to assume an increasing amount of debt.

Let's again review the basic conclusions of the Nobel Prize winner Tobin,[5] a classic figure in monetary theory. He proved that the key goal of Central Bank's MP should be to create optimal conditions conducive to investment. Of course, macroeconomic

3. Макроэкономическая ситуация и денежно-финансовая политика в России / Доклад / Под ред. В. Е. Маневича и И. С. Букиной. М.: Институт экономики РАН, 2013.

4. Годовой отчет Банка России за 2013 г. URL: http://www.cbr.ru/publ/God/ar_2013.pdf.

5. Tobin J. Op. cit. 1958.

policies must be guided by ensuring economic growth. All the successful international experiences of the national economy demonstrate that under balanced development, it is necessary to curb inflation by increasing output and efficiency, rather than restricting the money supply and reducing productivity.

If the regulatory agencies for currency circulation and capital reproduction cannot ensure that the issued currency is converted into credit for the expansion of production and investment projects (which can promote the development of S&T and reduce the cost of S&D), then the issuance of currency will naturally lead to inflation. In other words, if the amount of money in the economy is saturated, then too much money will lead to a financial pyramid. However, as pointed out by M. Yersov, if the scale of economic monetization in Russia (M2/GDP ratio) is still relatively low (compared to the level of 100% of the main competitor, about 40%) Under the circumstances, it is still feasible to absorb financial resources[6] on a non-inflationary basis. Based on current experience (during 2000–2016, prices grew steadily and repeatedly lagged behind the annual growth rate of the money supply), we have concluded that from the perspective of ensuring economic growth, the advantages of monetization outweigh the risks of inflation caused by monetization and inflation should be minimized through banking regulatory agencies and antitrust policies.

In general, due to the current monetary and credit policies and foreign exchange policies, as well as the lack of a mechanism to ensure that savings are converted into investments, the Russian economy lost more than half of its investment capital sources in the post-Soviet period. Making full use of the sources can ensure that the capital investment in production and development will triple, and the fixed asset accumulation rate will be maintained at more than 30% without attracting foreign investment. In fact, the Russian economy has been relying on consuming scientific production potential accumulated during the Soviet era to export capital.

Russia can still implement a sovereign economic policy. The existing scientific production potential enables Russia to implement the advanced development zone policy based on the growth of the new technological structure. However, this cannot just stay within the framework of monetarist dogma. The policy of the advanced development zone requires strategic planning, scientific selection of priority directions, formulation of long-term modernization plans, relying on new technologies and large-scale application and commercialization of new technologies. To this end, we need internal long-term credit sources and innovative financing mechanisms. This requires the supervision of capital flows, including the supervision of foreign exchange. The funds are allocated through the institutional refinancing system of commercial banks and the Central Bank of Russia.[7] This refinancing system has a multi-channel nature and is based on the development of the real economy. This will be discussed below.

Under the background of changes in the structure of the world economy, the transition to the sovereign economic policy of the advanced development zone should be made in the context of the adjustment of relevant international economic relations.

---

6. Ершов М. О механизмах оживления экономики и поддержания равенства условий финансовой конкуренции после вступления России в ВТО / Аналитическая записка. 2014.

7. Глазьев С. Стратегия опережающего развития России в условиях глобального кризиса. М.: Экономика, 2010.

As the center of world economic activity shifts from the US to China, a new system of international cooperation systems is being formed (based on mutual respect for national sovereignty, coordination of interests, and responsibility for achieving common goals). The liberal globalization model centered on the US forces other countries to open up their economies for the free management of American capital. In contrast, Asia's capital reproduction model is guided by development cooperation while maintaining the diversity of integrated countries. Russia can form a new center with China and other countries to expand the reproduction core of the new world economic structure.[8]

We are moving in this direction. Currently, the EAEU has been established, the Shanghai Cooperation Organization is being developed, and the BRICS Union is strengthening its joint efforts. Russia has the opportunity to become a full member of the new center of world economic development, not as a "periphery" but as a part of the "core" of the new global financial and economic system. But for this, we must abandon monetarism, which is a false theory and has no practical value at all.

---

8. Глазьев С. Между Вашингтоном и Пекином // Экономические стратегии. 2015. Т. 1, №2 (128). С. 6–17.

Chapter 16

Safeguarding Financial Security

The US and its allies have an overwhelming advantage in the financial field. Now the US has taken the financial field as a key direction of attack in the hybrid war against Russia. Using their advantages in the world's monetary and financial systems, the US and its allies are manipulating the Russian financial market, destroying Russia's macroeconomic imbalances, reproduction, and economic development mechanisms. They attack the Russian monetary and financial system through finance blockades and speculative attacks.

On the one hand, the US authorities block medium and long-term loans and Western capital investment in Russia. On the other hand, the US and its allies led by it do not restrict short-term transactions, creating conditions for speculative financing of various scales in the Russian market. Due to long-term capital outflows and short-term speculative capital inflows, the Russian monetary and financial system has lost stability and fallen into turmoil.

Nothing can stop the US from launching a new round of attacks on the Russian monetary and financial system. After the Central Bank of Russia abandoned the regulation of the ruble exchange rate, speculators began to manipulate the exchange rate. More than half of Russia's monetary and financial markets have been occupied by non-residents, among which US funds dominate. Therefore, it is US funds, not the Central Bank of Russia, that determine the dynamics of the ruble exchange rate, and the benchmark of it is determined on the Chicago Stock Exchange.

If after the US and Europe announced sanctions on Russia, the Central Bank of Russia had adopted banking and foreign exchange control measures to protect Russia's financial system from external attacks, then Russia could have been protected from this financial aggression. Russia has been a donor to the world financial system for the past ten years. Russia can objectively be protected from external threats on the condition that the monetary and financial markets are fully protected. On a global scale, Russia has the best debt indicators, and its foreign exchange reserves are quite sufficient, enabling the ruble to stabilize at a reasonable level, thereby maintaining Russia's economic competitiveness. Russia's foreign exchange reserves are twice that of the base currency, which allows the Central Bank of Russia to resist any speculative attacks on the ruble. Objectively, the ruble is one of the safest reserve currencies in the world. Because of this, the ruble can resist any sanctions. In response to the financial blockade of the European Union and the US, Russia can take appropriate countermeasures to defuse the adverse effects.

The large foreign currency assets held by Russian residents can balance Russia's excessive foreign debt. And Russia has a large surplus in foreign trade, including with countries that have imposed sanctions on it. Therefore, Russia can easily respond to sanctions by establishing selective foreign exchange controls.

However, by announcing in advance its refusal to maintain the Ruble at its target level, the Central Bank of Russia effectively acted as a tool for outside forces. The

Central Bank of Russia is at the "periphery" of the global financial market. Under the conditions of a completely open foreign exchange financial market, the Central Bank of Russia has no way to control the exchange rate of its currency and market interest rates. Financial credit institutions that can issue the world's reserve currency could carry out speculative attacks on any unprotected country's financial market at any time, causing the exchange rate to collapse, while lending unlimited loans to borrowers in that country at an acceptable interest rate.

To manage the national currency system, controlling the cross-border flow of currency in capital operations is necessary. Otherwise, Russia's macroeconomic conditions and economic development will be manipulated by foreign countries. At the same time, managing the monetary and financial markets is impossible by reducing random factors in the traditional sense. The state cannot control the operating parameters of the foreign exchange financial market, making it dependent on the super speculators in the world currency issuance center.

To prevent this development trend, the Bank of Russia must fulfill its constitutional obligation to "protect and ensure the stability of the Ruble" and should take necessary measures. These include:

- Announcing that the fluctuation range between the Ruble exchange rate and the target exchange rate is 1%;
- Restoring the supervision of the Moscow Exchange by the Central Bank of Russia and eliminating the possibility of financial speculators using inside information;
- Adopting methods generally accepted in international practices to curb attempts to manipulate currency and financial markets, including the establishment of an advance declaration mechanism for cross-border capital transactions, credit leverage restrictions, currency intervention, and other means;
- To levy a Tobin tax (to reduce purely speculative transactions);
- If necessary, fixing the foreign exchange positions of Commercial Banks and selling foreign exchange proceeds in whole or part to resist speculation.

Equally important is the transition from implementing foreign exchange rates in the currency of the sovereign state in the colonial exchanges to the generally recognized foreign exchange rates in the national currency. For example, as of February 22, 2018, 100 Rubles were quoted at US$1.77 and 1.43 Euros.

The Bank of Russia neither takes measures to prevent capital outflows nor uses domestic credit to replace the dwindling foreign credit resources. As a result, a reduction in the monetary base leads to a reduction in credit, a decline in investment and production, and an increase in borrower defaults. This may trigger an economic "avalanche" and plunge the economy into the dilemma of reduced supply and demand, lower income, and reduced investment. Russia is trying to maintain budget revenue by increasing taxes, which has exacerbated the capital flight and reduced business activities. The decrease in the population's real income plunged Russian society into poverty in 2003, offsetting the social impact of economic growth in the past decade. In addition, the decline in production and investment stems from under-capacity production (30%–80% of the production load in the industrial sector), underemployment, savings over investment, and excess raw materials. At present, Russia's economic operation potential does not exceed 2/3 of its potential capacity, but Russia is still a donor to the world's financial system.

If emergency measures are not taken to fundamentally change the MP, establish a long-term domestic credit source, and ensure the stability of the Russian financial system, then Western sanctions will seriously undermine the reproduction model in key areas of the Russian economy. By manipulating the policies of Russia's financial market and monetary authorities, the US attempts to destroy Russia's economic development, affect the activities of the business community, and then affect social life. Under such circumstances, Russia cannot win in this hybrid war waged by the US. Therefore, Russia's independent foreign policy must be strengthened by restoring national sovereignty and strengthening control over economic reproduction and development. For this reason, it is necessary to ensure that the foreign exchange financial market is protected from external threats.

It can be seen from the above that it is necessary to protect Russia's economic from external factors to ensure its security and sustainable development. The first thing to prevent is attacks from foreign speculators associated with the Federal Reserve and other world currency issuing countries, which means selective control of the cross-border flow of speculative funds. Therefore, direct (licensing, retention) and indirect (capital export taxes, restrictions on foreign exchange positions of commercial banks) restrictive methods can be adopted. The rules and regulations related to the activities of credit organizations should be revised to stimulate Ruble business and reduce the profits of foreign currency businesses, especially in credit institutions creating reserves, assessing risks, and capital adequacy ratios.

It is also necessary to restore the national supervision of the Moscow Exchange and make it controlled by the Central Bank of Russia. The Moscow Exchange should return the controlling rights or establish a strict and comprehensive foreign exchange transaction supervision mechanism. In any case, the exchange should not have a commercial purpose nor establish any partnership with speculators. The function of the Moscow Exchange is to take timely measures to prevent speculative attacks, thereby providing services for trading and ensuring market stability. The Central Bank of Russia also needs to supervise the activities of the Moscow Exchange and resolutely crack down on all attempts to manipulate and destabilize the market.

In view of the ongoing movement of the US and other Western countries led by it to seize Russian assets (the Yukos incident, etc.), Russia urgently needs to sell the foreign currency assets of the US, Britain, France, Germany, and other countries participating in sanctions against Russia, and then to invest in gold and other precious metals and establish commodity reserves with high liquidity, including key imports (referring to raw materials and commodities that the country does not produce or produce in small quantities), investment in the EAEU, the Shanghai Cooperation Organization, and the BRICS countries' securities, and investment in the capital markets of international organizations in which Russia participates (including Eurasian Development Bank, CIS Transnational Bank, International Investment Bank, BRICS Development Bank, etc.), expanding their infrastructure to support Russian exports. Among them, the creation of an international securities trading platform, the use of Rubles for trade in Russian commodities within the jurisdiction of Russia, the establishment of an international distribution network, and the provision of high-value-added Russian commodities are of great significance.

Regarding the emerging trend that the monetary authority of Western countries has begun to obstruct the transfer of assets of Russian legal and natural persons back to Russia and "freeze" the private assets of legal entities and individuals, Russia can in turn suspend the handling of cross-border financial transactions, such as prohibiting loans and investments to countries that seize Russian assets.

It is necessary to implement the instructions of the Russian President to de-offshore the Russian economy. The current reproduction model of the Russian economy is overly dependent on the Anglo-Saxon model (minimizing the role of the state and maximizing the role of the market) and financial institutions, causing the Russian financial system to suffer US$60 billion in systematic losses every year (this is simply a loss in terms of the difference in the profitability of borrowed and allocated capital). In addition, the loss caused by the "loss" of illegal offshore capital is about US$50 billion.

With the loss of financial resources and reduced budgetary income, in the face of the current increasingly unstable situation in the world, the property registration of most large Russian non-state companies and their assets in offshore areas (companies' main business is carried out in this area) is becoming more and more complicated, which is harmful to national security. The 85% of Russia's foreign direct investment is concentrated in offshore areas, and these capitals include those that flow from Russia and those that flow into Russia. The issuance of unsecured world currencies is increasing, and the devaluation of the Ruble (less than 2/3 of purchasing power parity) has created favorable conditions for foreign capital to absorb Russian assets transferred to offshore jurisdictions, which poses a threat to Russian economic sovereignty.

The following is a list of measures to address these and other issues to protect the nation's monetary and financial systems from excessive losses and the threat of instability. Implementing these measures will likely activate the existing scientific productivity and human and resource potential to ensure that the Russian economy will be on track with sustainable growth—annual growth of GDP up to 8%, annual growth of production investment up to 15%, annual growth of production scale of new technology structure up to 25%.

1. Stabilizing the Ruble exchange rate and foreign exchange market, and stopping capital outflows
1.1 Currency speculation is expected to reduce several times by reducing "leverage," taxing speculative profits, reducing trading days, and using other World Bank stabilization mechanisms, such as restoring the state control of the MOSE and changing the exchange's staff.
1.2 Enterprises are prohibited from engaging in speculative activities through preferential refinancing channels and other state-supported funds, including purchasing foreign exchange without an import contract.
1.3 For loans provided to countries that have imposed economic sanctions on

Russia, the borrower shall apply force majeure clauses. In the case of escalation of sanctions against Russia, the implementation of loan repayment and investment services to sanctioning countries will be suspended. During the period of sanctions imposed on Russia, bank intermediaries of subsidiaries of American and European banks in Russia are prohibited from absorbing new funds from Russian individuals and legal persons.

1.4 Russian banks stop providing foreign currency loans to non-financial organizations. Passing legislation to prohibit the provision of foreign currency loans to non-financial organizations.

2. De-offshoring and prohibiting illegal capital outflow

2.1 The ultimate owner of shares in a Russian strategic enterprise is obliged to register its ownership in Russia, thereby putting the "shadow" offshore.

2.2 Signing tax information exchange agreements with offshore companies and reaching existing agreements with them to avoid double taxation, including offshore companies located in "tax havens"—Cyprus and Luxembourg. Determining a unified list of offshore companies, including those with onshore companies.

2.3 According to the Tax Transparency Initiative proposed by the Organization for Economic Cooperation and Development, it is legally prohibited to transfer assets to offshore jurisdictions that have not signed a tax information exchange agreement.

2.4 According to Russian law, offshore companies owned by Russian residents need to provide relevant information about company members (shareholders, investors, beneficiaries) and disclose tax information. All the company's income in Russia is subject to a 30% tax fee.

2.5 The perpetrators of illegal capital outflow will be severely investigated for their administrative and criminal responsibilities, including paying excessive interest in fake trade, credit operations, and loans to foreign countries.

2.6 Taxing on speculative currency transactions (the Tobin tax planned in the European Union) and capital outflows.

2.7 Improving the information statistics database for combating offshore economy, capital "loss," and tax minimization, including obtaining data on the balance of payments and international investment positions from all offshore companies at the national "level."

3. Improving the potential and security of the Russian monetary system, enhancing its position in the global economy, enabling the Ruble to function as an international reserve currency, and establishing the Moscow financial center

3.1 Encouraging the use of Rubles for settlement between the EAEU and the Commonwealth of Independent States, Rubles and Euros for settlement with the European Union, and Rubles and RMB for settlements with China. It is recommended that economic entities use Rubles to pay for imported and exported goods and services. In addition, to provide Ruble loans to importing countries of Russian products to maintain trade, it is necessary to use currency swaps (also known as currency swaps).

3.2 Through the Bank of the Commonwealth of Independent States, we will vigorously expand the service system of settlement in national currency between the EAEU and enterprises of the Commonwealth of Independent States, and use international financial institutions controlled by Russia (the Bank for International Economic Cooperation, International Investment Bank, Eurasian Development Bank, etc.).

3.3 The Central Bank of Russia will carry out special refinancing of Commercial Banks for a long time at an acceptable interest rate, and provide loans denominated in Rubles for import and export trade. Due to the expansion of foreign trade in domestic foreign exchange and the establishment of foreign exchange reserves of Rubles abroad by other countries and banks, it is necessary to consider the demand for additional Rubles in monetary and credit policies.

3.4 Organizing oil, petroleum products, timber, mineral fertilizers, metals, and other raw materials to be traded in Rubles in the exchange. To ensure market pricing and prevent transfer pricing for tax evasion, commodity traders must sell at least half of their products on exchanges registered by the Russian government, including exported products.

3.5 Restricting foreign loans of state-owned holding companies. Since the Central Bank of Russia has provided special refinancing to state commercial banks at appropriate interest rates, Rouble-denominated loans to state holding companies can gradually be provided through state commercial banks, replacing foreign currency loans.

3.6 Within the framework of the deposit insurance system, deposit guarantees are only provided for citizens' Ruble deposits, simultaneously increasing the legal reserve for foreign currency deposits.

3.7 On the basis of multinational banks in the Commonwealth of Independent States, a payment system with the functions of bank information exchange, risk credit assessment, and exchange rate quotation will be created for settlement in the national currencies of the member countries of the EAEU. Creating a dedicated independent international settlement system between the EAEU, the Shanghai Cooperation Organization, and the BRICS countries can eliminate the heavy reliance on the US-controlled SWIFT system.

To create an independent international settlement system, it is necessary to create a national bank card payment system and an international system for the exchange of information between banks to protect the Russian financial system from sanctions of the Western payment settlement systems VISA, MasterCard, and SWIFT. Establishing such an international settlement system must organize the BRICS member states to discuss together to ensure that Russian payment instruments can be applied at home and abroad.

3.8 In order to ensure Russia's national security under the conditions of a world hybrid war launched by the US and its NATO allies, it is necessary for the monetary authority of various countries to agree on their rules of action to protect the national currency system from speculative attacks and threats of turbulence. Contrary to the positions of the US and the IMF, it is recommended to reach a consensus on the establishment of a national protection system against the risks of global financial turbulence, including: (1) establishing a foreign exchange business capital transaction reserve system; (2) levying income from the sale of assets by non-residents, tax rate depending on the ownership period of the asset; (3) imposing restrictions on the cross-border movement of capital on businesses that may pose a threat.

Shifting from external credit to internal credit is the most important condition for ensuring the safety of the monetary system and eliminating the impact of Western sanctions.

Chapter 17

Transition to Economic Development Management

Building a Sovereign Loan System to Increase Production and Investment

To ensure the expansion of reproduction, it is necessary to fundamentally raise the level of monetization of the Russian economy, increase the scale of credit, and improve the capacity of the banking system. Russia should take urgent measures to stabilize the economy, which requires the Central Bank of Russia to increase the supply of liquidity and strengthen its role as the lender of last resort. Unlike the economy of the reserve currency issuing country, the main problem of the Russian economy is not caused by the excess money supply and the related financial "bubble," but by the long-term low degree of economic monetization and the severe shortage of loans and investment.

When the refinancing interest rate is adjusted to increase the enthusiasm for investment and innovation activities, the required level of the money supply should be determined by the demand for money by economic entities and national development agencies. If the other goals of macroeconomic policy are not achieved, including ensuring the stability of the ruble exchange rate and the growth of investment, production, and employment, it will be impossible to achieve a true inflation-targeting system. These goals can be achieved by prioritizing, setting restrictions, and flexibly using the country's regulatory tools in currency, credit, and foreign exchange. In this case, priority should be given to production and investment growth within the established inflation and the Ruble exchange rate restrictions. In addition, a complete system of pricing, price policies, currency and banking supervision, and competition development measures are needed to keep inflation within the prescribed range.

To seek open and inclusive development opportunities in the "wave" of growth in the new technological structure, it is necessary to vigorously promote the renewal of fixed assets and concentrate existing resources on modernization and economic development with development prospects. Therefore, it is necessary to increase the investment rate to 35–40% of GDP and focus investment in breakthrough areas of global economic growth. The source of funds for this type of investment is a special loan issued by the monetary authority in accordance with unified priorities. The experience of many countries has proved that all countries that have successfully used the "window" opportunities to achieve "technological breakthroughs" have increased their financial support policies and loan volume to areas with economic growth prospects. The central banks of these countries became development banks, issuing the necessary funds to implement the unified planned investment projects and plans.

Based on the new technological structure, the shift to an advanced development track requires stimulus, which requires investment activity to be raised to twice the level of investment activity in the current Russian financial and investment system. Under Russia's current economic situation, the only support source to achieve this goal is the state issuance of loans. Therefore, it is necessary to objectively assess the loan demand in each field of economic activity and consider the national priorities for long-term economic development.

Starting from the economic development theory and practice of developed countries, it is necessary to combine economic development goals with internal money supply to establish a money supply system. The most important of these is the refinancing mechanism of lending institutions, which currently cannot lend to the real economy and investment in priority development areas. As mentioned in the previous part of currency evolution, this can be achieved through indirect (refinancing by state and solvent corporate guarantees) and direct (co-financing of national planning and provision of state guarantees, provision of funding for development agencies) currency issuance methods, which are well-known and effective in the practice of developed countries. The possibility of creating money to meet national needs cannot be ruled out, as in the US, Japan, and the European Union, where central banks buy government debt.

In the context of currency expansion and the continuous adoption of measures to reduce the cost of financial resources by countries issuing currencies in the world, it is necessary to make Russian companies equal to foreign competitors in terms of the cost of financial resources, the time to obtain financial resources, and the level of risk. This requires reducing the refinancing interest rates set by the central banks of many developed countries to a level below inflation for a long time and extending the period for issuing credit resources to reduce the cost risk for borrowers. In addition, it should be noted that developed countries use national debt to form "long-term" and "ultra-long-term" special resources (including the US, Japan, etc., up to 30 to 40 years), including national debt related to long-term investment project financing. These investment projects are supplemented by medium-term refinancing tools, which have laid a strong foundation for forming "long-term" economic resources. In addition, the monetary and credit policy is consistent with the priority of the industry (including the nature of the industry, the nature of the group, and the regional nature), which allows us to discuss the establishment of a monetary industry policy system.

In view of the need to double investment in Russia's economic modernization, the Central Bank of Russia and the government of the Russian Federation need to link MP with the task of solving credit modernization and promoting Russia's economic development. At the same time, to prevent foreign financial resources from negatively impacting the Russian economy, it is important to ensure that internal monetization channels play a priority role, including expanding commercial banks' mid- and long-term refinancing of debts of manufacturing companies and government agencies. In addition, it is recommended to use internal credit to gradually replace the credit provided by foreign state-owned banks and enterprises.

While establishing a modern national credit financial system, investment enthusiasm should be given full play to realize the task of Russian economic modernization and development. The Central Bank of Russia should play its role as a development agency fully and provide loans to private enterprises to meet their needs for expansion and development of production. At the same time, there is a need to invest in the realization of national plans, national strategic plans, and indicative plans at the same time (Figure 17-1).

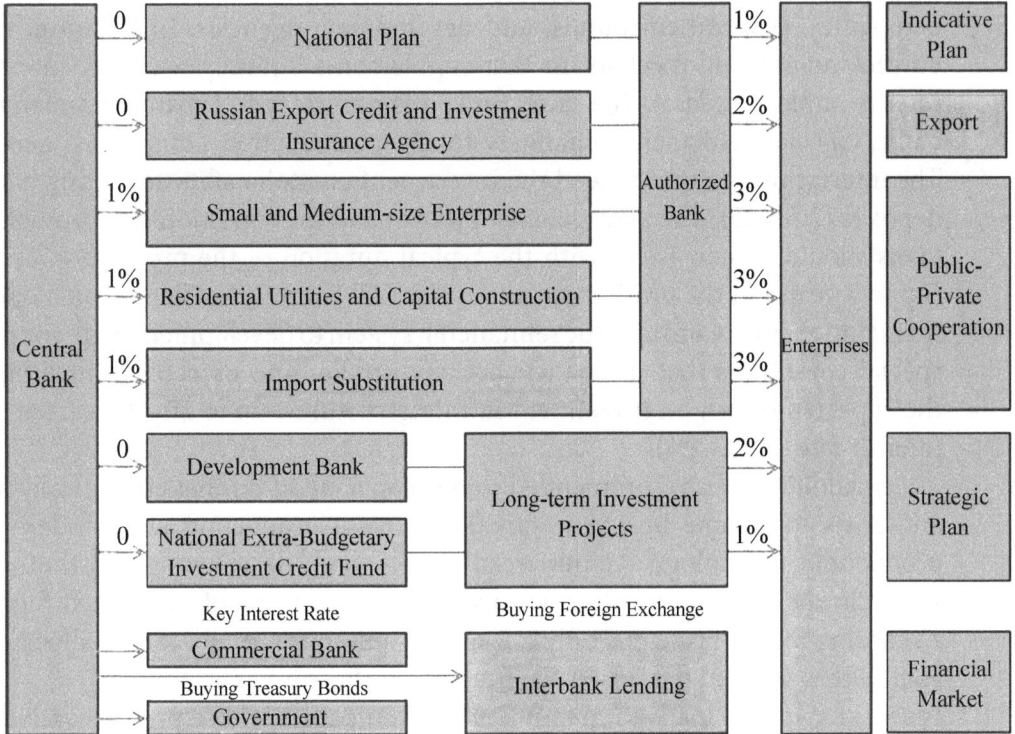

Figure 17-1 Proposed Currency Issuance Plan
Source: Глазьев С. Ю. О неотложных мерах по укреплению экономической безопасности России и выводу российской экономики на траекторию опережающего развития: доклад. М.: Институт экономических стратегий, Русский биографический институт, 2015. 60 с.

Given the above, the following measures are recommended in monetary and credit policies:

1. Adjusting the monetary and credit system to promote the development and expand lending opportunities in the real sector

1.1 To create conditions for economic growth, investment and employment expansion through legislation to include national monetary and credit policies and activities of Russian banks in the target list. For example, the Federal Reserve Act states that the goal of US MP is to "increase the amount of money consistent with the long-term potential of the economy, promote maximum employment, maintain price stability, and ensure reasonable long-term interest rates."[1] The transition to a multi-target MP can obtain benefits related to economic growth, inflation, and increased investment. At the same time, it can systematically manage interest rates, exchange rates, banks' foreign exchange

---

1. "Federal Reserve Act," URL: http://www.federalreserve.gov/aboutthefed/fract. htm.

positions, money issuance through various channels, and other factors related to money circulation.

1.2 Issuing currency while transitioning to a multi-channel bank refinancing system. This is mainly for commercial banks to refinance the debts of manufacturing companies, government bonds, and development agencies. In addition, the current refinancing mechanism that supplements liquidity with key interest rates is implemented. At the same time, it is necessary to expand commercial banks' special refinancing channels to meet production companies' needs. The interest rate cannot exceed the investment portfolio after deducting bank deposits (2%–3%). The average rate of return and the conditions for providing loans should be consistent with the typical duration of the production cycle (up to 7 years) in the production enterprise. All commercial banks must open financing channels and also the refinancing system to development banks under special conditions that meet their activity profiles and objectives (including the expected return on investment in infrastructure—up to 20–30 years at an interest rate of 1%–2%).

In addition, it is recommended to develop a credit business specifically for anti-crisis to resume business activities, expand production and modernize production technology. Commercial banks and development institutions shall allocate such loans in accordance with the principle of earmarked funds. According to this principle, only a specified amount of funds can be allocated, and there is no need to transfer the funds to the borrower's account.

1.3 Increasing special loans to manufacturing companies whose products rely on export contracts, government orders, and contracts with domestic consumers and chain retail stores to guarantee product sales. The Central Bank of Russia should provide loans at an interest rate of 2% through state-controlled banks to refinance corporate debt and provide them to final borrowers at an interest rate of 4% for 1–5 years, while strictly controlling the use of currency dedicated to production needs.

1.4 The prerequisite for the state to support private enterprises is that the private enterprise fulfills its obligations to the state. The enterprise should produce a given quantity of a specific type of product (or provide a service) at a fixed price within a certain time frame. An enterprise that fails to fulfill its obligations is deemed to have formed a liability to the country. The value of the unfinished product is the amount of liability to the country.

1.5 Significantly increasing the capital of development institutions through the issuance of long-term bonds of development institutions. These bonds are repurchased by the Central Bank of Russia and included in the list of mortgages of the Central Bank of Russia.

1.6 Creating a national extra-budgetary investment credit fund based on the model of KFW Bank, refinancing through the government reserve fund, and purchasing bonds by the Central Bank of Russia in accordance with the national investment plan.

1.7 Setting up a special credit line in the Central Bank through the Russian Foreign Economic Bank and refinancing banks and companies that use foreign loans because they cannot obtain external credit due to sanctions.

1.8 Increasing the financing of domestic technology equipment leasing institutions multiple times through the refinancing funds provided by the Central Bank with an annual interest rate of 0.5%, and the deposits of these institutions shall not exceed 1%.

2. Stabilizing the banking system. The bankruptcy "chain" created by the revoked Commercial Bank's license will lead to the instability of the banking system. To eliminate this threat, the following measures should be taken.

2.1 Providing Commercial Banks with the possibility of obtaining loans quickly to meet the urgent requirements of lenders, the amount of which can be up to 25% of citizens' deposits.

2.2 The Central Bank of Russia resumes its unsecured loan auctions for banks with insufficient liquidity.

2.3 The implementation of *Basel III* standards in Russia will be postponed for 2–3 years until the credit lines of economic entities return to their pre-crisis levels in the first half of 2008. Adjusting the standards of *Basel III* to eliminate artificial investment restrictions. In *Basel II*, credit risk calculation is based on banks' internal ratings instead of the ratings of international institutions. During the 2007–2008 financial crisis, such institutions experienced bankruptcy and a lack of professionalism.

3. Creating the necessary conditions to strengthen the capabilities of the Russian financial system

3.1 Gradually using the rubles in the international settlement of commercial transactions of state-owned companies and continuing to replace their foreign currency loans with ruble loans from state-owned Commercial Banks when the Central Bank of Russia provides corresponding funds.

3.2 The relevant exchange rate quotation is currently quoted in rubles instead of US dollars and euros. Determining the previously announced fluctuation range of the ruble exchange rate. If the ruble exchange rate faces the threat of exceeding the prescribed range, the limits of the range will be reset. This will catch speculators off guard and is aimed at avoiding large-scale capital outflows of the ruble and currency speculation and ensuring the rapid stability of the ruble exchange rate.

3.3 To prevent the refinancing of production activities and the "spillover" of funds for investment in the financial and foreign exchange markets, it is necessary to use corresponding banking regulatory rules to create conditions for the special use of such loans. Restricting the foreign exchange positions of commercial banks that request refinancing from the Central Bank of Russia.

3.4 To narrow the scope of financial speculation, expanding the financial leverage supervision system, including non-bank companies is recommended.

3.5 Switching to using the rubles to pay for foreign trade business expenses in stages.

Introducing Digital Management Technology for Currency Circulation

When formulating its MP, the Russian Federation should evaluate the macroeconomic impact of issuing rubles through multiple channels. Domestic credit resources are used to replace foreign credit resources to meet commercial banks' financing in corporate debt, national debt, and development agency debt. The external demand for the Ruble guarantees foreign exchange reserves, including foreign trade loans, capital operations, and the establishment of foreign countries and banks' ruble reserves. This can be done by using modern technology to digitize the currency, thereby marking each "factor" of currency issuance. This can achieve centralized control over the use of funds, which greatly simplifies the management of the above-mentioned special credit issues. Any attempt to misuse funds will be immediately recorded by the computer control system and automatically blocked. For the first time, it is possible to measure the velocity of money flowing through various channels and assess the change in its quantity with inflation. This can calculate the demand for additional credit resources for the main production processes of the Russian economy.

The digital management technology of currency circulation should start with issuing special loans and government expenditures. To this end, the monetary authority needs to create a digital ruble issuing operator to monitor all transactions by deploying a distributed registration network (created by the Russian Fintech Association like the blockchain main chain). The National Investment Credit Fund mentioned above can serve as such an operator. The issuance of the digital ruble must be carried out by the operator under the unified allocation of the Bank of Russia, and this part of the funds will always be stored in the account of the Bank of Russia. When funds get out of the bank's control, digital currency operators must ensure that digital rubles are exchanged for ordinary rubles. Operators will see all transactions in the network controlled by them and manage them according to the specific purpose of the issued funds. It is best to introduce this technology through specialized instruments for refinancing by Commercial Banks that intend to provide preferential loans for investment projects, loans for development agencies, subsidized loans for agricultural development, and loans for small and medium enterprises and public procurement systems. At the same time, the information system will automatically control the use of special funds and prevent unauthorized withdrawals. Funds issued for financing cannot be used for speculative activities, cannot be used to purchase goods and services not included in the approved special investment contract, and cannot be used for suspicious transactions. When paying salaries, import purchases, tax payments, and other permitted consumption behaviors, the system automatically converts the electronic currency in the Central Bank account into ordinary rubles. With the accumulation of experience, the number of digital currencies and their share in credit issuance will increase with the development of economic monetization. Credit organizations use this system to monitor loans and the intended use of funds invested.

Long-term special loans should be provided to the real economy in accordance with the national plan, which has pointed out the direction for economic growth and modernization. In particular, it is necessary to establish long-term cheap credit channels through state-owned banks in accordance with the indicative plan for the growth of investment and production in the military, agriculture, and construction industries, import substitution, and infrastructure development plans, export contracts, and the loan needs of small and medium-sized enterprises.

Generally speaking, the indicative production and investment growth plan are linked to the loan scale and price and can be realized in the form of a Public-Private Partnership within the framework of the established strategic planning system. The national structure should be the basis for constructing this system and simultaneously transmit the growth momentum to the market environment. Only the head of state can integrate all tasks into a unified system. To this end, it is necessary to establish a strategic planning committee, an S&T development committee, and an anti-monopoly supervision committee.

Promoting the Progress and Development of S&T

As we all know, apart from the leadership of the Russian monetary authority, scientific and technological progress[2] is a major factor in modern economic growth. The proportion of new knowledge reflected in technology, equipment, training, and production organizations in developed countries accounts for 70% to 90% of GDP growth. The introduction of innovation has become a key factor in market competition, which allows leading companies to use special technologies to obtain excess profits.

The development of scientific research and experimental design work and human potential largely determine the competitive potential of today's national economy. Those countries that provide favorable conditions for the advancement of S&T have won the global economic competition. The great importance of the state's incentives for STP to ensure modern economic growth depends on the objective characteristics of the innovation process, which creates insurmountable obstacles for private enterprises: high risk, dependence on the development of the general scientific environment and information infrastructure, huge investment in scientific research and uncertainty in the commercial application of its results, requirements for personnel's scientific and engineering qualifications, and the necessity of legal protection of intellectual property rights. Various companies have succeeded in global competitions because their national S&T policies are guided by strong scientific research.

Continuous management innovation is an important feature of modern economic growth. R&D accounts for an increasing proportion of investment, exceeding the cost of equipment and construction in high-tech industries. At the same time, the importance of national S&T, innovation, and education policies that define the overall conditions for STP is increasing. R&D expenses in developed countries have increased, reaching 4% of GDP, of which more than 1/3 of the input costs are provided by the state.

The ability of the national economy to continuously update its technological foundation and improve the technological level of enterprises is becoming a key factor in enhancing its competitive potential. Countries at the "frontier" of STP have realized

2. Глазьев С. Какая политика обеспечит опережающее развитие российской экономики // Завтра. 20 марта 2018. № 10.

their technological advantages when establishing price ratios, standards, and other international economic cooperation norms that are beneficial to them, which provides a guarantee for them to obtain knowledge and capacity rents on a global scale.

Narrowing the technological gap that has always existed between the "core" and "periphery" of the global economic system requires developing countries to implement active science, technology, and innovation policies.

The characteristic of technological change is that there is a nonlinear relationship between cost and innovation results. The development of any technology needs to overcome the threshold of the same cost period before realizing the return on investment. Moreover, R&D investment will increase due to technological lag, and R&D results will only appear after reaching the advanced technology level.

Investing in the development of breakthrough scientific and technological advancements in the early stages will have nonlinear effects, and it will be possible to obtain excess profits through the exclusive use of new technologies. With the promotion and improvement of new technologies, the continuous expansion and strengthening of production scale and capital intensity, cooperative relations will be gradually established, staff training will be conducted, and a market will be formed. The cost of acquiring this new technology is getting higher and higher. Therefore, the delay in mastering the new technology will lead to a nonlinear increase in reproduction costs, which sets up an insurmountable obstacle for backward countries.

To cite a typical example, since the development of nanotechnology, the scale of investment producing nanocircuits has increased by order of magnitude. At the same time, product efficiency will suddenly increase when transitioning to a new technology level. With the passage of time, the cost of R&D has increased nonlinearly, and the cost of overcoming technological lag has risen accordingly. Therefore, to stay ahead of competitors, it is necessary to provide strong support for acquiring new technologies in the early stages of the new technology life cycle. If it turns out that the investment is insufficient or delayed, the increase in technological lag will lead to a decline in competitiveness.

To join the ranks of developed countries, it is necessary to concentrate resources on promising scientific and technological fields. This should be guided by the country's economic policy, including its structural, fiscal, monetary, and credit components. The law of technological and economic development, imbalances, and the high degree of uncertainty in opening up new technological fields should be considered.

It is particularly important to determine the priority of national economic development policies. If the sequence of economic development is wrong, government investment will depreciate. Correctly determining the priority of the national economic development policy will have a positive effect and increase the competitiveness of products. As shown in Chapter 1, the cyclical and continuous replacement of related industries' overall structure (technical structure) has led to an imbalance in modern economic growth. Every time the world economy has a structural crisis, it brings new opportunities for economic growth.

Possessing the necessary scientific and technological potential and correctly choosing implementation priority areas can greatly improve economic competitiveness and complete the "leap" from technological backwardness to the forefront of economic development.

As mentioned above, a new technical structure is now being established. This technological model is entering a growth phase, and the economy is emerging from the global crisis. The crisis phase is ending, during which outdated technology "chains" take a toll on profits and competitiveness, resulting in impairments and "capital flight." At the same time, the cost of new technology structure production and its large-scale development and application is increasing at a rate of 20%-35% per year. A new technological route is currently being formed, a "chain" of industrial and technological cooperation is being established, investment in expanding production is increasing, and new management mechanisms and methods are also being formed.

The faster financial, economic, and political institutions are rebuilt according to the requirements of new technological structures, the sooner a new "long wave" of economic growth emerges. In addition, not only will the economic and technological structure change, but the economic system structure will also change, and the composition of leading companies, countries, and regions will also change accordingly. The more competitive companies between them will be able to quickly enter the growth trajectory of new technology orders and invest in their production components in the early stages of development. On the contrary, due to the nonlinearity of the dissemination process of new technologies, the entry barriers for lagging ones will become more expensive every year, and the entry barriers will be closed when the technology structure reaches the mature stage.

At this time, as mentioned above, countries with lagging technological development can catch up with developed countries and become "technology leaders" in another way by imitating the achievements of advanced countries to save costs, while focusing investment on promising growth areas in new technology structures. Growth areas of development prospects.

Promoting economic recovery based on new technologies requires economic stimulus policies. In the US, the European Union, and Japan, the crisis will end with the collapse of the dollar financial pyramid and the capital and financial "bubble" created by developing new technological structures, which will harm economic development. To eliminate this impact and accelerate the modernization of their economic potential, these countries have adopted many long-term cheap credit resources to fund increasing government expenditures, including funding for S&D, stimulating investment and innovation activities, and purchasing new equipment.

As mentioned above, the Central Bank of Russia adopts an opposite MP, which reduces the money supply instead of increasing it. Therefore, it has artificially restricted Russia's economic modernization and dragged the Russian economy into a "trap" of stagflation, making Russia doomed to lag behind other countries in the rapid expansion of the new technological structure. In the absence of long-term loans, Russian companies cannot even control their own development, and can only "stand by" and give up new product markets with development prospects. Because Russia has adopted this macroeconomic policy, it is doomed to fail in the competition to master key technologies in the long wave of the new economy, which is currently in its infancy. As other countries master the new technological structure, Russia's competitive potential will rapidly decline.

Russia's scientific and technological potential is declining, while that of other countries is growing rapidly. Russia is the only G20 member country where the number of scientists and engineers, scientific research organizations, and design organizations has decreased in absolute terms. Although Russia's funding for science has increased since the 21st century, it is still far below the Soviet Union's level. Regarding R&D expenditure as a percentage of GDP and investment per scientist, Russia is clearly lagging behind other industrialized countries. All countries in the world are increasing scientific research investment, and the share of scientific research expenditure in GDP is close to 4%, which is twice that of Russia's knowledge-intensive economy (Figure 17-2).

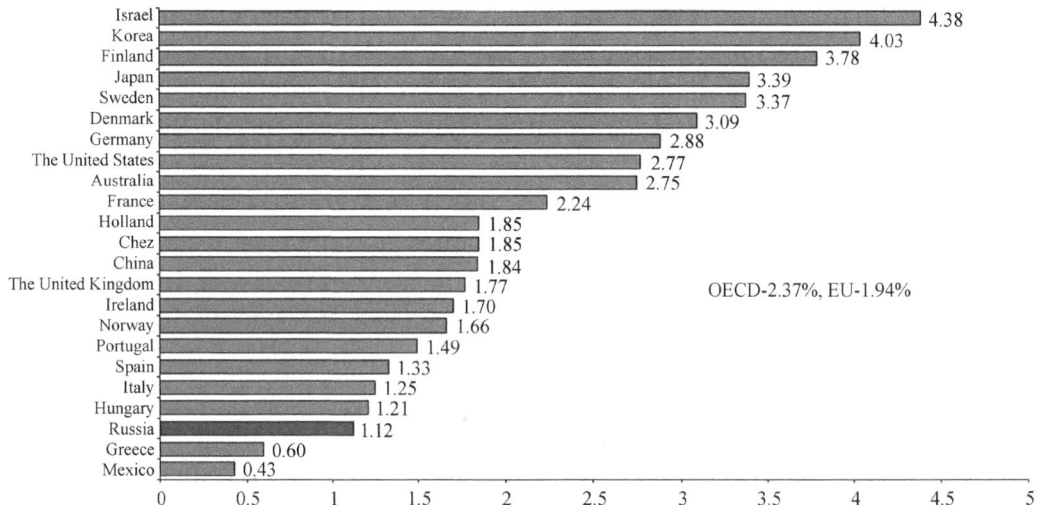

Figure 17-2 The Percentage of Domestic Research Expenditures in Russia and OECD Countries in GDP
Note: Russia's data comes from the 2014 evaluation report of the Institute of Scientific Development Issues; foreign countries' data are the latest. Russia ranks 21st.
Source: Миндели Л., Черных С. Расходы на науку: мифы и реальность / Общество и экономика. 2016 (№2); Данные по России приведены по Росстату; зарубежные страны: OECD (2015), Main Science and Technology Indicators, № 1 Paris.

The enthusiasm for innovation of enterprises is still very low. The number of patent applications in Russia is generally decreasing, and that of foreigners applying for patents is increasing. As a result, Russia's scientific and technological potential is threatened on a global scale, making Russia lag behind the US and the European Union in the field of S&T, and even behind China (Figure 17-3).

In the absence of excessive demand for scientific research by state and private companies, the "outflow" of Russian scientists and experts continues. According to statistics from countries that have absorbed these experts and scientists, the "brain drain" has caused huge losses to Russia. The number of highly educated brain drains has reached millions, of which more than 250,000 are scientists in advanced scientific fields.

At present, Russia is facing severe problems in the development of scientific research, the modernization of production technology, and the transition to a new technological structure. The reasons for this unfavorable situation are the long-term lack of funds for scientific development, the destruction of scientific research and production coordination mechanisms, the aging of scientific personnel, and the "brain drain." In summary, privatization has led to the collapse of the applied science industry.

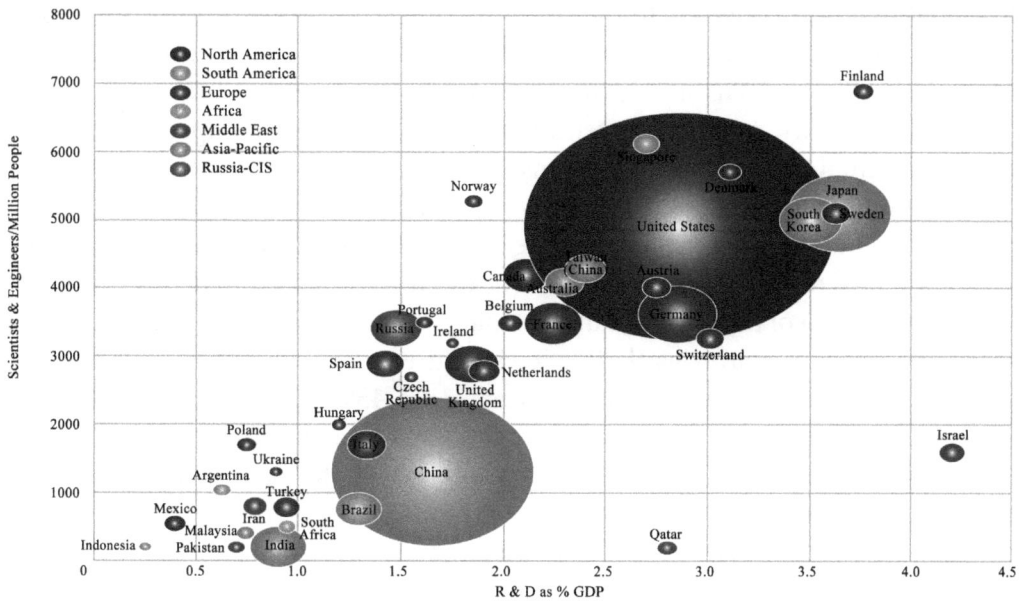

Figure 17-3 The Scientific and Technological Potential of Countries around the World
Source: Rogov S., "Russ's Position in a Multipolar World," Report submitted to the Russian Security Council Science Council meeting, December 20, 2012; using data from "World of R&D," 2012.

The import of high-tech products has partially alleviated Russia's lagging situation. These high-tech products reflect the results of foreign S&D, and their imports have exceeded the number of Russian high-tech products. However, the introduction of foreign technology has deprived Russia of its independent economic creativity, which is destined to be unable to carry out equal economic exchanges with foreign countries and poses a threat to national security. Russia's economic competitiveness is declining, and its trend of de-industrialization and degradation continues.

The integrity of Russia's economic reproduction is being lost, and unequal foreign economic exchanges with developed countries are like a "trap" for Russia, causing the economy to "slide" to the "edge" of the world economy.

The main threat of economic sanctions to Russia is to prevent Russia from acquiring new technologies. If this problem is not resolved, then in a few years, Russia's economy will be in an irreversible lagging state in developing new technological structure production. The new technological structure production will ensure the equipment level of industry and the military get a qualitative improvement in the "long wave" of economic growth. To prevent such a lag, it is necessary, on the one hand, to increase the allocation to scientific research in the basic direction of the growth of the structure of new technologies. On the other hand, it is important to strengthen the accountability of development agency heads for the effective use of allocated funds. For this reason, it is necessary to establish a modern system to manage the country's scientific and technological development. The system needs to cover the various stages of scientific research and the scientific production cycle, and emphasize economic modernization within the framework of the new technological structure.

To prevent the stagnation of S&T, Russia's S&D costs should be doubled. To solve this task, we must do a good job in two aspects. One is that the state must implement corresponding S&T policies to increase funding; the other is to stimulate the innovation of private enterprises through tax incentives, infrastructure development, and credit expansion. We should focus on advancing existing S&T, and earnestly promote the network activities of venture funds, engineering companies, innovative enterprises, and development institutions.

According to international experience, for the economy to enter the "wave" of growth in the new technological structure, a strong motivation is needed to promote the renewal of fixed assets. For this reason, the level of investment and innovation should be twice that of the current Russian financial and investment system. According to the experience of countries that have created economic miracles, it is necessary to force an increase in investment to reach 35%–45% of GDP. As shown above, increasing credit is the main source of funds to increase investment enthusiasm; the state issues national and corporate bonds through multiple channels to provide funds for upgrading, developing, and expanding a promising production technology system. Therefore, we can see the importance of repositioning the monetary and credit policy for development purposes. The measures to be taken to this end shall ensure:

1. Reducing interest rates and establishing refinancing mechanisms for investment and innovation activities through targeted issuance of government bonds, national development agency bonds, corporate bonds, corporate bonds designated under federal and regional investment plans, corporate bonds designated under development agency projects, and professional investment contracts within the framework of the strategic and indicative planning system;
2. Exempting taxes and fees on the income of enterprises that invest in the development of production, scientific research, and new technology development, and adopting an accelerated depreciation mechanism for fixed assets, while controlling the expected use of depreciation expenses;
3. Doubling the level of scientific research budget funds, establishing a targeted S&T planning system, and providing state support for innovative activities in the field of economic development with development prospects;
4. Increasing the amount of refinancing multiple times and improving the efficiency of development agencies. At the same time, the Central Bank of Russia needs to introduce investment activity plans in accordance with the required modernization and development priorities;
5. Constructing modern information infrastructure for scientific research and commercial activities;
6. Ensuring the effective protection of intellectual property rights, supporting the import of new technologies, and protecting Russian intellectual property rights abroad.

The construction of a modern technology development management system includes:

1. Establishing and promoting a mechanism through which a targeted plan for advanced economic development can be implemented based on new technological structures, which provides for increased investment measures for the development of production and technology complex, the creation of a favorable macroeconomic environment, and the formation of related mechanisms and management patterns;
2. Establishing a system of strategic planning, including the identification of priorities for economic, scientific, and technological development and the formulation of indicative plans and programs for their implementation;
3. Swiftly implementing the *Federal Law of the National Strategic Plan* and formulating relevant procedures to select priority areas for scientific and technological progress, formulate implementation plans for priority areas, and set target indicators for development agencies;
4. The activities of all macroeconomic regulatory agencies, including the Central Bank, the Ministry of Finance, and state-owned enterprises, should be consistent with the mandate of economic modernization and technological development and fully unleash their scientific and technological potential. This requires indicative plans for joint activities between the state and the enterprise under the investment contract with clear responsibility for achieving the objectives.

The rapid growth of innovation initiatives plays a key role in economic modernization and development based on new technological structures. Given the key value of scientific research results and uncertainty, the state assumes the function of an intelligence information center. It needs to supervise economic development and formulate strategic planning, while providing corresponding scientific and technological conditions, including establishing the basic knowledge of advanced and retrieval research foundation, supporting the development of applied research and experimental design organization, and encouraging the development and promotion of new technology systems.

The national economic management agency is subject to the task of economic development, which will allow Russia to enter the "core" of the new center of world economic development, thereby ensuring that Russia's economic competitive potential can be enhanced and fully released. Efficient use of the scientific and technological potential of the EAEU to promote cooperation between business entities will help establish regional and global value chains. Nowadays, this potential is relatively small in terms of absolute and relative indicators, and the main part of this potential is concentrated in Russia. It is necessary to introduce S&T policies into the functional departments of the EAEU, resume the formulation of inter-state target plans, and carry out joint S&D based on the jointly determined priority areas of scientific and technological progress.

The technical field of the EAEU faces the task of establishing advanced production and technical systems. To this end, it is necessary to solve the problem of enhancing the scientific, and industrial growth potential of the joint ventures of the alliance member countries with international competitiveness, as well as the problem of promoting the rapid spread of breakthrough technologies. It is recommended that the Eurasian Economic Commission (ECC) perform the functions of planning and organizing joint S&D, developing innovative infrastructure, and establishing an intellectual property protection system.

Establishing an Economic Development Strategy Management System

The current state of the Russian economy and its prospects are closely related to the global economic situation, which is transitioning to new technologies and the structure of the world economy. Russia needs to overcome the global economic crisis associated with the "storm" of the new order, which paves the way for developing new technologies.

The previous section outlines the special loan organization system for investment and production growth. Based on the advanced development of the new technological structure, the system should become a working mechanism for implementing strategic and indicative plans for developing economic modernization.

The development strategy necessary for the successful realization of modernization includes two aspects. The first is to accelerate the development of basic production of the new technological structure, and the second is to bring the Russian economy into the "long wave" of new economic growth with the new technological structure as soon as possible. For this reason, it is necessary to integrate resources to establish the "core" of the new technological structure and realize the synergy formed by establishing new industrial clusters. This means that macroeconomic policies should be coordinated with the long-term priorities of technological development.

The implementation of this policy requires establishing a strategic management system that can identify promising areas of economic growth and guide the activities of national development agencies and the implementation of economic regulation measures. The management system includes: predicting scientific and technological progress, strategic planning, selecting priority areas to enhance the potential of S&T, using institutions and mechanisms to achieve the above goals (conceptions, planning, and indicative plans), and introducing regulatory methods and accountability mechanisms for achieving necessary results. Considering the critical importance of state-owned banks, companies, and development agencies, it is necessary to implement mid-term annual plans for the activities of state-owned enterprises to strike a balance between production, investment, and the economy. Socioeconomic departments and regional strategic planning documents should be formulated based on the principle of commonality, which is a unified whole.

The implementation of the import substitution policy should be part of the advanced economic development strategy, starting with the deployment of a strategic planning system, ensuring that the country's resources available for modernization and new industrialization are systematically utilized based on the new technological structure.

The strategic planning methodology provides a medium and long-term and short-term forecasting system. It determines the priorities of economic development, the tools, and mechanisms for achieving economic development, including the medium and long-term vision system, planning and planning system, as well as institutions to organize related activities and controls and responsibilities for achieving established goals.

The *National Strategic Planning Bill* only stipulates certain elements of the creation of the system, mainly the procedures for the administrative department to formulate some related documents.

Interactive rules and mechanisms should be established to formulate long-term forecasts, ideas, mid-term planning, and indicative plans, and then negotiate and approve development goals. Based on Public-Private Partnerships, it is necessary to establish a monitoring mechanism and accountability mechanism for strategic planning participants through legislation to implement the agreed measures and tasks. It is particularly important to integrate development agencies, large companies, state-owned stock companies and banks, and large private financial and industrial groups into the national strategic planning system. To combine their production, financial and management potential, this integration reflected not only in the strategy formulation process but also in the strategy implementation.

Goals should be set for the work of state-owned banks, companies, and development agencies in their fields of activity. These goals aim to establish a new production technology model that is competitive in the world market and introduce real accountability mechanisms for the timely realization of these goals. Considering the importance of the strategic planning system and the important task of the Russian Federation government as the central executive agency, and given that the current strategic goals cannot be achieved and cannot be monitored, it is necessary to establish a national strategic planning committee under the leadership of the President of the Russian Federation and give its related powers.

1. Determining the internal and external conditions, development trends, restrictions, imbalances, and fiscal factors of the social and economic development of the Russian Federation.
2. Determining the priority directions of implementing social and economic policies and the methods for the goals and tasks of the Russian Federation's social and economic development, according to the order of the President of the Russian Federation.
3. Coordinating the work of the main body of strategic planning in selecting ways to achieve the goals and tasks of the Russian Federation's social and economic policies and coordinating and strengthening the national security of the Russian Federation to ensure the most effective use of available resources.
4. Developing a set of measures in accordance with the strategic plan document approved by the President of the Russian Federation to ensure that the tasks of the social and economic development of the Russian Federation are solved, the goals are achieved, and the national security of the Russian Federation is strengthened.

5. Coordinating the activities of the participants specified in the strategic plan and strategic plan documents to ensure the social and economic development and national security of the Russian Federation, including the direction of the budget policy, implementation period, expected results and resource guarantee parameters.

6. Organizing to supervise and control the implementation of strategic planning documents, ensuring the implementation of strategic plans for technology, information, resources, and talents.

The prediction and planning system for the socioeconomic development of the country and its regions should be based on the national legal framework, which should include a unified legal mechanism for interaction between federal and regional governments, regional self-government agencies, development agencies, scientific organizations, and companies. This mechanism is designed to ensure that the interests and resources of all parties are integrated when formulating and implementing federal, regional, municipal, administrative, and corporate strategic plans and programs. The subjects of the Russian Federation and municipal authorities should be able to participate in formulating, financing, and implementing special federal plans within their jurisdictions.

In many regions and the entire Russian economy, the direct manifestation of the slowdown in economic growth is the deterioration of social and economic development indicators. The degree of differentiation in the Russian region is still very high. The difference in per capita GDP of the various entities of the Federation is more than 20 times, and the difference in per capita currency income is more than five times. The accumulation of regional differences and the increasing differentiation between regions have exacerbated regional social conflicts.

In implementing national economic policies, regional issues have yet to be fully considered, including the development of productivity and the spatial differences of inter-regional linkage systems. The underestimation of spatial factors makes it difficult to coordinate the implementation of regional policy measures and plans by various federal agencies, federal entities, and municipal governments. Social and economic development strategies between regions do not agree on objectives, priorities, and forecast parameters. They are not aligned with higher-level strategy papers and do not consider interregional and intersectoral constraints, which have led to the increased loss of finances, labor, and natural resources, as well as regional imbalances.

A clear analysis of territorial differences (from the national economy to the administrative regions) should be carried out in all the main parts of the unified system of national forecasts, strategic and indicative planning, national plans, and national budgets for socioeconomic development. In view of this, it is necessary to finalize and adopt the Russian Federation's concept of spatial development, which aims to form a system of spatial priorities and determine the status of regional development strategies and plans in the strategic management system.

As a mechanism to integrate regional and sectoral aspects within the framework of a unified management system, it should be based on new methods to reformulate an overall development plan that is coordinated with social and economic development strategies, as well as a 10 to 15-year period of productivity placement and Relocation Plan (the *Spatial Development Plan of the Russian Federation*). The plan should determine regional specialization and regional economic proportions, and at the same time integrate the development resource base with the needs of companies and residents, demonstrate the location of infrastructure systems and capital construction projects, and form a unified list of such projects. The *Spatial Development Plan of the Russian Federation* shall coordinate the development of production and social infrastructure, energy and transportation, special federal plans, and industry strategies and plans.

Russia's investment in infrastructure is the most important factor in the country's investment needs, and it is also a mechanism to improve the economic development of individual regions. The inadequate development of Russia's transportation infrastructure has become an important factor inhibiting social and economic development, especially in the areas east of the Urals. At present, it is impossible to reasonably predict the transportation volume of all existing and potential participants in the unified transportation network (the transportation network is compatible with the regional social and economic development industry strategy and plan). In addition, Russia still lacks a practical analysis of the balanced development of transportation and economy. Based on this analysis, the actual demand for the development of transportation volume and transportation network can be determined. Therefore, the actual and forecasted tasks of balanced development of transportation and economy each year should be solved within the framework of the strategic planning system.

To achieve the sustainable development of the problem area, it is necessary to formulate a regional planning system that considers the level, regional and industry balance, and coordination, which is inseparable from federal policy. The key to this system is the formation of competitive regional production clusters and other promising forms of economic spatial organization. The priority is to establish this form of organization in economic innovation. To carry out this work, it is demanded to restore the Productivity Research Committee, established a century ago but cleared by the notorious former Minister of Economic Development Alexei Ulyukayev.

The positioning of strategic planning should be to accelerate the development of new technological paradigms. According to the strategic plan, a five-year economic modernization plan should be formulated. In the plan, measures should be formulated to accelerate the development of production and technological complexes, create a favorable macroeconomic environment, and form corresponding institutions and management systems. The Central Bank of Russia should expand the refinancing of development agencies, and at the same time, based on accelerating the development of the new technological paradigm, and in accordance with the priorities of economic modernization, formulate the development agency's activity plan.

In addition, it should be considered that in the transition from modern society to a knowledge economy, STP is a key factor in improving the efficiency of the knowledge economy. According to the experience of rapid and sustainable economic development, if the knowledge economy wants to embark on innovative development, it needs to fundamentally improve the role of science in the economy and the national management system.

For the management of scientific innovation activities, it is necessary to consider that scientific innovation activities run through all areas of the economy, and it is obviously ineffective to manage science as an independent sector in the form of a ministry. To implement the progress of S&T of the system management method and "interdisciplinary" and fully arouse the enthusiasm for innovation activities, there needs to reasonably create a federal agency responsible for formulating national S&T and innovation policies and coordinating the activities of sectoral ministries and departments in policy implementation. This federal agency is the Russian Federation's State Council for S&T Development under the leadership of the President of the Russian Federation. It is a committee-based organization composed of heads of relevant ministries, departments, the RAS, federal financing institutions, and scientific research and experimental design support agencies. Such S&T progress management systems should help all entities identify promising areas for development to maximize the use of available resources.

The most important task of the State Commission for Scientific and Technological Development of the Russian Federation is to create conditions for the rapid restoration of applied sciences, the main structural elements of which have been destroyed during large-scale privatization. The massive destruction of design institutions and design bureaus doomed Russian industries to import foreign industrial bases. To reverse this trend, states and the S&T community need to undertake systematic work on establishing a wide network of engineering companies, design, and engineering organizations. The "knowledge conveyor belt" from basic science to application development and then to enterprise innovation must be adjusted. It is therefore recommended that the Commission be given the following powers:

1. Determining the internal and external conditions, trends, restrictions, imbalances, and various potentials, including fiscal and socioeconomic development of the Russian Federation;
2. Choosing the roads and methods prescribed by the President of the Russian Federation to implement the priorities of the Russian Federation's social and economic policies and the goals and tasks of social and economic development;
3. Coordinating the work of the main body of strategic planning in solving task 2, and strengthening the national security of the Russian Federation to ensure the most effective use of existing resources;
4. Formulating a series of measures to help achieve objectives 2 and 3, according to the strategic planning document approved by the President of the Russian Federation;
5. Coordinating the actions of the participants in the strategic planning document and the activities stipulated in the strategic planning document in the field of social and economic development and safeguarding the national security of the Russian Federation. The activities include the direction of the budget policy, the time for the implementation of the budget policy, expected results, and resource guarantee parameters;

6. Organizing, monitoring, and managing the implementation of strategic planning documents to ensure the scientific and technological, information, resources, and talents of strategic planning.

The third element of the formation of a strategic management system is the National Anti-Monopoly Policy and Competition Protection Commission, which should be separated from the administration of the Russian Federal Government. In addition to anti-monopoly policies, competition protection, tariffs, and prices, the Commission should also mediate. Administrative disputes between state agencies and enterprises, including guidance, supervision, and law enforcement practices. While establishing a strategic planning system and credit mechanism to promote the growth of production and investment, it is also necessary to create conditions for improving the competitiveness of enterprises.

In addition, the destruction of the economic reproduction process and the distortion of market competition mechanisms have caused a systematic lack of price policies. This hurts economic development, undermining residents' ability to pay, and triggering inflation. The use of monetary means to resist inflation failed, resulting in the demonetization of the economy, leading to a decline in production and investment activities.

National Price Policy

Creating conditions for expanding the reproduction of high-value-added commodities, ensuring fair competition, protecting consumer rights, and curbing inflation are the country's pricing policy goals. For this reason, it is necessary to assess whether price fluctuations are consistent with the task of proportional economic development and increasing economic competitiveness, and to study a method to maintain price balance. It is necessary to systematize laws and regulations that regulate pricing, ensure fair competition, and at the same time strengthen the responsibility to comply with these regulations. It is necessary to ensure the transparency of the pricing process, the reasonableness of cost control, and analyze the consistency of the price with the objectively determined cost. The following measures are recommended to solve the task:

1. Formulating and approving the 2013–2020 national price policy concept of the Russian Federation (the project is compiled by scholars of the RAS), which should include the main objectives, tasks, and principles of the national price policy, as well as the methods for implementing the policy;
2. To rectify the current scattered legal basis in this field, it is recommended to pass the *Russian Federation Law on Price Setting and Price Policy* (a draft has been done) and a series of regulations to implement balanced national pricing and tariff policy legal measures;
3. Establishing a national price information system, which should be based on the exchange of price information between market entities, state agencies, and municipal agencies;

4. Introducing responsibility standards for the target cost of product prices (depreciation, labor remuneration, scientific research, experimental design work, etc.);
5. The legislation gives consumers the right to participate in the supervision and setting of prices and tariffs;
6. Establishing a management system to implement the national price policy. The system should be incorporated into the above-mentioned national price information system, the coordination committee composed of producers and business associations, consumer protection associations, and interest Related ministries and departments;
7. To systematically formulate and implement the national price policy, combine the price policy with the anti-monopoly policy and coordinate with the country's economic development strategy, it is recommended to establish a national anti-monopoly supervision and pricing committee under the leadership of the president of the Russian Federation, and grant its related administrative and quasi-judicial powers.

Improving the Competitiveness of Russian Companies

Our proposal for ensuring Russia's economic security and creating conditions for Russia's advanced economic development in the face of a mixed world war is mainly aimed at improving the efficiency of state institutions. At the same time, it also provides good conditions for improving the initiative of entrepreneurs and the enthusiasm of private enterprises. In addition to creating domestic sources of cheap long-term loans, tax measures should also be created to shift the tax burden from production to consumption.

To change the tax system, lower tax management costs, reduce tax evasion, and stimulate business activities and innovation, it is recommended to replace the value-added tax with a more manageable sales tax (PST), and only collect sales tax at the final consumption stage. The "loss" of budget revenue from the abolition of value-added tax can be compensated by imposing a 14% sales tax. The abolition of value-added tax will also save more than US$1 trillion in government procurement, prompting nearly one million accountants to shift to the field of production activities, and at the same time free up corporate liquidity to increase production and investment.

Progressive income tax can be used to make up for the loss of entrepreneurial tax reduction, which has become an inherent part of life in most developed countries. Most of the tax on the progressive income tax falls on individuals, mainly wealthy citizens. On the contrary, in Russia, more than 70% of taxes and fees are borne by legal persons, which inhibits business and investment activities. In addition, the main net income of individuals today has nothing to do with wages, but with property. The "non-wage" income of Russia's wealthiest citizens (20% of the population) accounted for 65% of their total income, while it was 90% in Moscow.

The high taxes and fees imposed on high-income groups have little impact on consumer demand. The reduction in taxation of investment activities is mainly due to depreciation fees, corporate profits, and loans. Although entrepreneurs pay part of their income to the state, they will benefit from investment and asset growth.

Therefore, based on the calculations in 2012, imposing a maximum progressive tax rate of 40% on personal income tax will increase budget revenue by US$5 trillion (only a 40% tax on 130 billionaires in Russia will increase budget revenue by 1.1 trillion rubles). By increasing the depreciation fee to the level of developed countries (accounting for 60%-70% of investment), part of the taxes and fees on the profits made by enterprises engaged in investment activities can be exempted.

At the same time, it is necessary to legislate to supervise depreciation deductions. Half of the depreciation expenses (4 trillion rubles) in 2012 were not used for development, but for financial investment-buying securities, providing loans, and other businesses. As a result, the investment amount was reduced by 13.7% from the estimate. In addition, the national income tax budget target of 400 billion rubles has not been achieved.

The depreciation markup is not estimated based on the mixed price of fixed cost, but the replacement cost, which will increase the fixed capital investment. According to calculations in 2012, it is also 5 trillion rubles, and the amount of compensation offset by the progressive income tax collection will not be 12.6 trillion rubles, but 17.8 trillion rubles. The share of compensation in GDP will increase from 20.1%–28.7%, and the growth rate will increase to 5%–6%. In addition to the above measures, if the time for the renewal of fixed assets is shortened (the last time it was carried out in 2002), the effect of increasing investment in fixed assets and accelerating GDP growth will be more obvious.

The key to improving domestic producers' competitiveness is strengthening the state's supervision of natural monopolies and reducing structural costs. For example, adjusting electricity prices in the power industry plays a special role, greatly affecting economic costs and inflation.

According to a 2013 study by V.Kudriavi, there are important methods that can be used to reduce excess expenditures in the power industry. Eliminating these expenditures can save nearly US $1 trillion and reduce electricity prices by 20%.[3]

The current legal environment cannot create sufficient incentives for most employees to realize themselves in production activities. The existing civil law is based on the superficial concepts introduced by the ancient Roman Empire at that time, and regards ownership as a combination of possession, use, and disposal. Since then, the diversity of legal relations has expanded many times and has complex characteristics. Especially, to overcome the alienation of labor and private property and create conditions for the employment of production workers to realize their own value, regardless of the form of ownership of the enterprise, labor participation in enterprise management has become common in developed countries. This practice will become important to the new (integrated) world economic structure system. Based on this, Academician Kleiner proposed a method system to improve the legal environment of business operations systematically:

---

3. Кудрявый В. Риски и угрозы российской электроэнергетики. Пути преодоления. 2015.

1. Legislation gives labor collectives, experts, and managers the right to create their committees (workers' committees, scientific engineering committees, and management committees), and elect their representatives to participate in the highest strategic management body (council) to ensure that the interests of all participants of the company's activities and the development interests of the enterprise as an economic entity;

2. If the bankruptcy of the enterprise leads to the liquidation of the enterprise and the disappearance of jobs, the labor collective should have the right to supervise it, including reorganizing it into a state-owned enterprise;

3. Providing a clear basis for the accountability of managers who make decisions in the event of conflicts of interest, consequently leading to negative consequences, experts who violate technical standards and regulations, and employees who violate production disciplines. The investigation of civil, administrative, and criminal liabilities should refer to the degree of damage caused to the enterprise and the guilty employee's authority level. If the owner directly intervenes in the operation of the enterprise or damages the interests of the enterprise when disposing of property (transfer of profits and assets, forced false operations, malicious bankruptcy, attacks, etc.), the owner shall also be liable;

4. Corporate strategy and social distribution: As far as strategic distribution is concerned, it is not allowed to transfer foreign capital control or close down companies similar to military-industrial complexes. In terms of social distribution, it is not allowed to close companies that are similar to urban construction companies and established banks. In the case of enterprise bankruptcy, provide the labor collective with the opportunity to become a state-owned enterprise through debt restructuring;

5. Conducting a corporate census, helps to better understand the situation of business owners, managers, and employees and is beneficial to restoring the coordinated relationship between economic entities and legal entities. Companies are required to provide so-called comprehensive reports, which can not only comprehensively evaluate the current situation of the company, but also evaluate the company's business prospects in the ever-changing environment based on the company's extensive activity indicators;

6. Establishing a corporate activity monitoring center, which aims to collect, accumulate, analyze, and summarize data and other information on the status of domestic enterprises.

Looking for Development Ideas

The year 2017 (before writing this book) coincides with the 100th anniversary of the October Socialist Revolution, which is very suitable for reviewing the concept of competition that dominates the world.[4] If the world is all mankind, then the criterion for success in the ideological competition should be the speed of socioeconomic development measured by the GDP index and the Human Development Index (HDI).

---

4. Глазьев С. Какая идеология поднимет Россию / Завтра. 9 января 2018 г.

China has been an absolute leader in these two indicators in the past three decades, and Ukraine is an absolute outsider. Thirty years ago, the standard of living in Ukraine was much higher than in China, but now it is 2/3 lower.

Russia has been standing still for years, with life expectancy, population size, health, and production of low-value-added goods hardly returning to Soviet-era levels. Over the years, other countries continued to develop, and most of them surpassed Russia. Russia fell below the average and entered the ranks of third world countries.

After the disintegration of the Soviet Union, although the number of socialist countries in the second world declined in terms of geographic area, apart from India, and some countries in the Indochina Peninsula (such as Myanmar, Laos, and Cambodia) are all countries with socialism as the direction of development. Whether in terms of human development or GDP, the second world has become absolute and relatively large. The second world will be 2–3 times faster than the social and economic development of the first world countries and are likely to rule the world within ten years.

The first world countries have been stagnant for two decades, failing to resolve the growing imbalance. Although the first world countries have annexed the territory of the Soviet Union, Soviet political economists have not stopped describing the general crisis of capitalism. The former socialist countries exported US$2–5 trillion and millions of new laborers to Western companies, which only delayed the intensification of this crisis, and this crisis now has enlightening significance.

Critics of market reforms are correct. They warned that Russia's transition from socialism to capitalism would cause it to be "marginalized" in Latin American and African countries. However, the arguments of the convergence supporters are pertinent. They propose to combine the advantages of capitalism and the socialist system and abandon the disadvantages. Half a century ago, Sorokin called the socialist market economy an "integrated system" and predicted the end of Soviet socialism and American capitalism.

As shown above, the integrated system combines overall planning with market competition, state-owned infrastructure and basic sectors with private enterprises, socialist ideology, and the possibility of personal enrichment. While supporting the activities of entrepreneurs, the state adjusts the activities of private enterprises to develop on a track that is conducive to social interests. The comprehensive system integrates the activities of various social groups and professional associations, thereby increasing social welfare.

If profit is the main criterion of economic activity in the capitalist system, then increasing production is the main criterion in the Soviet system, and improving people's living standards in China is the main criterion. For 30 years, China has maintained a leading position in the world in terms of the speed of social and economic development. This is due to an effective management system in which all institutions can operate in a coordinated manner thanks to the ideology supported by the vast majority of the people and the steady growth of public welfare. Although some basic theories contradict the system, they are all rejected.

Deng Xiaoping rejected the doctrines of scientific communism that prohibited wage labor and the accumulation of private capital. The number of private entrepreneurs in the agricultural population increased, and agricultural production began to grow rapidly, so China solved the food problem that the Soviet Union could not do. Unlike the leadership of the Soviet Union, the Communist Party of China did not listen to the opposing dogmas of liberal and democratic ideas. The limited liability system took most of the property from Russia and plundered US$2 trillion. After the Chinese business ethics system established a code of ethics for behavioral responsibility, the limited liability system emerged in China. China does not distribute property for free, does not allow financial speculation, and regulates cross-border operations. Entrepreneurs increase their wealth by producing products that are useful to society.

Unlike Russia, China does not comply with the "plan" of the "Washington Consensus." China does not intend to abolish foreign exchange controls and restrictions on cross-border capital flows, nor will it abandon state investment loans. At the same time, it will retain the state-owned nature of basic sectors and supervise the pricing of bulk commodities. The Chinese do not allow the West to instill the idea of economic system transformation. On the contrary, they established a socialist market economic system with Chinese characteristics. The Chinese use the latest definition to emphasize the diversity of socialist system models and demonstrate innovative methods for managing social and economic development. They build international economic ties in the same spirit. The Belt and Road Initiative strategy proposed by Xi Jinping is based on joint investment in promising economic and trade cooperation areas, focusing on the mutually beneficial combination of competitive advantages. Unlike the US financial system, which interferes with the internal affairs of other countries and imposes political conditions, China's development system aims to provide joint investment in projects with common interests and does not attach any political conditions.

Reference Materials: Development Characteristics of China's National Financial System

This column[5] is dedicated to analyzing the role of China in the international monetary and financial system in the new stage of the evolution of the international monetary and financial system. The task of this research is to evaluate the development level of China's financial industry and the reform achievements of RMB liberalization and internationalization, reveal the characteristics and dynamics of the above process and the operation of related institutions, determine China's position in the International Monetary and Financial Organization (МВФО) in the current and long-term stages based on cross-country comparisons (mainly taking Russia, the US, Japan, the United Kingdom and the United Kingdom, and eurozone countries as examples), and make recommendations for quantitative and qualitative growth and improvement.

China's financial industry is characterized by an absolute advantage in bank assets, a high degree of bank concentration, and low financial depth. All these facts show that China shares common characteristics with the "peripheral" countries of the US dollar-

---

5. Доклад В.Архиповой «Роль Китая в формировании новой системы международных валютно-финансовых отношений». – М.: 2019 г.

centric international monetary and financial organization (MBΦO), including Russia. Compared with the operating mode of the Russian banking system, one of the advantages of the Chinese banking system is that it provides high loans to the entities of the national economy (this is an indicator of the high efficiency of banks).

When analyzing the currency field, we should pay attention to some key indicators. One of the indicators is the dynamic change of the real effective exchange rate. As shown in Figure 17-4, in the past 25 years, Russia has experienced rapid "surges" and "collapses" in the 1990s and 2010s. Japan has five clearly traceable periods of severe "waves." Compared with these countries, China's real effective exchange rate has the most stable dynamic changes, and its development is relatively stable and harmonious. Interestingly, after experiencing the severe period of the global financial crisis, the analysis indicators for all countries were close to each other in 2010–2011, which set the benchmark for the new stage of the development of the International Monetary and Financial Organization (MBΦO). However, the analysis indicators are scattered again due to the different operating modes of the national economic system and the status of the international monetary and financial system.

In addition, the share of the currency of the analyzed country in financial market transactions is an important indicator for analyzing the currency field.

The total share of the currencies of the "core" countries (including the US dollar, the euro, the Japanese yen, and the British pound) in the US-centric IMF is still very high (about 90%).

To understand the reason why the RMB has not yet dominated the contemporary world monetary system when the RMB exchange rate is relatively stable, it is necessary to understand the history of RMB liberalization and RMB internationalization.

It must be emphasized that China's monetary and liberalizing reforms follow the country's overall reform policy step by step, adopting a gradualist strategy, especially when creating institutional experiments and establishing transitional institutional "chains" (e.g., the dual exchange rate in the period of 1980–1990), while taking advantage of the "low starting point." The gradual process of currency liberalization has increased the experience of foreign exchange supervision, while avoiding the free floating of exchange rates. The balanced combination of "freedom" and "management" on the one hand brings constraints to China's monetary, financial, and economic development; on the other hand, it also prevents damage from external "shocks" and protects the stability of the internal "environment."

China's foreign exchange control and supervision aim to guarantee the "healthy" and balanced development of overall economic policies, and institutions that implement foreign exchange supervision (including adjustments to the foreign exchange market) are responsible for performing control functions and assuming corresponding responsibilities. In addition, the actions of China's foreign exchange regulatory authorities align with the implementation of monetary and credit policies. In emergencies, the regulatory authorities need to respond to certain changes in a timely manner.

What needs to be emphasized is that China has formulated regulations regulating foreign exchange market access, maintaining the balance of the foreign exchange market, types of customer transactions, and the operation of the inter-bank foreign exchange market.

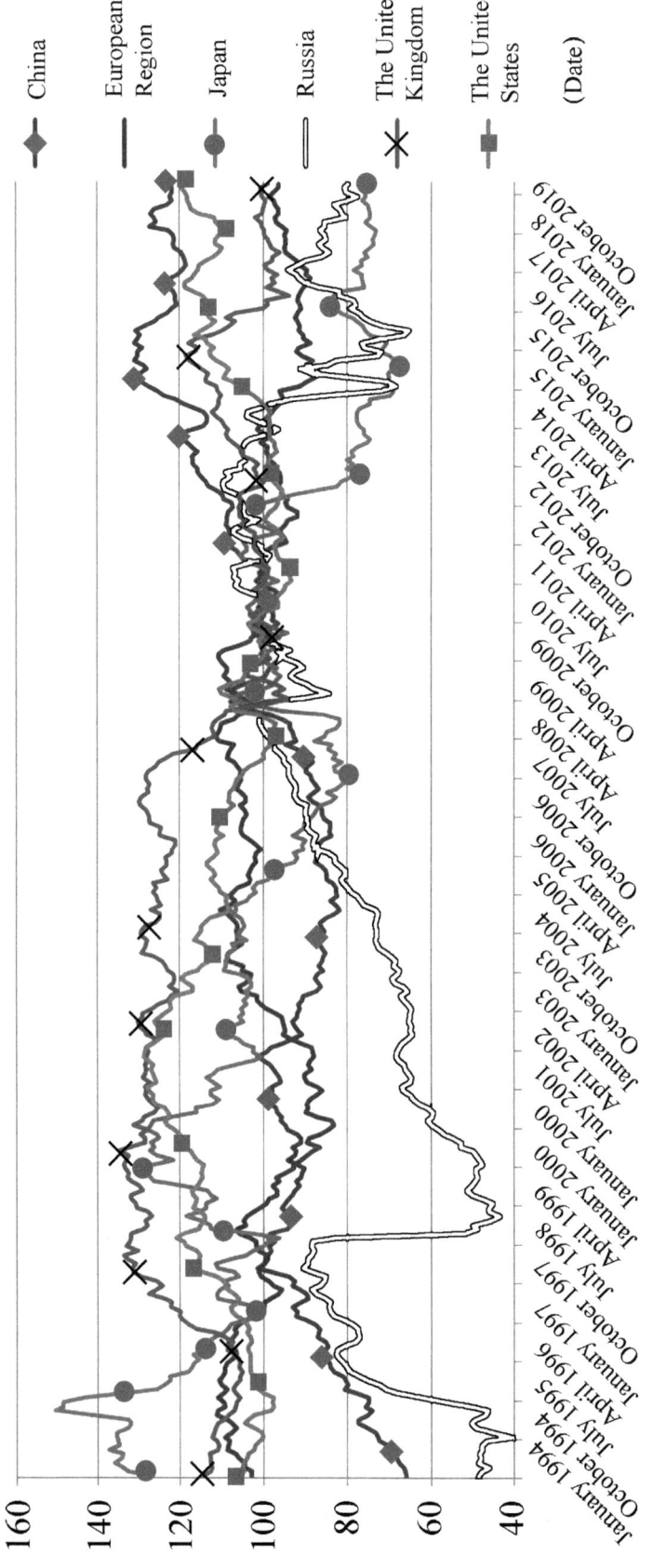

Figure 17-4 Real Effective Exchange Rate, Expanded Index, Monthly Average Data, 2010 = 100
Source: Bank for International Settlements.

Supervising foreign exchange settlement accounts is an important part of currency law, especially capital trading accounts. For example, the maximum foreign currency cash amount is determined according to the currency law. These foreign currency cash must undergo the necessary declaration procedures when entering China. The currency law also stipulates that direct investors (legal persons and individuals) who use basic and derivative financial instruments to conduct transactions within and outside China must be registered.[6]

The national system for submitting, collecting, verifying, and processing statistical information is the most important tool for foreign exchange supervision, especially in obtaining foreign exchange supervision licenses. In China, non-bank financial intermediaries and other financial credit institutions that provide commercial loans abroad are subject to special comprehensive inspections. China encourages the reporting of violations of foreign exchange regulations and has formulated a relevant fine system.[7]

In addition, G. Petrova believes that since 2012, the Bank of China has started to carry out ruble cross-border settlement business in the trade field and is willing to provide appropriate financial services for companies participating in the transaction of the two countries, and start individual ruble cross-border settlement business (2015),[8] which is an important step for China to develop the business to Russia. In 2017, the China Foreign Exchange Trading Center started the "simultaneous settlement" business of RMB against the ruble, greatly accelerating the transaction time.

The open reform of China's MP is still advancing. For example, China has recently canceled the initial permission to enter the financial intermediary market, expanded the volatility limit of the inter-bank spot exchange rate of renminbi against the US dollar, canceled the volatility limit of the over-the-counter market, and adopted some measures to promote RMB trading.

In 2016, the RMB was incorporated into the world's reserve currency, which became the "peak" of the internationalization of the renminbi during the period between 2000 to 2010. It can be considered that this is a special recognition and high appreciation of the renminbi by the IMF. However, the fact that the renminbi is not yet freely convertible is an important distinguishing feature of its new reserve currency. This fact, combined with the maintenance and development of currency supervision experience and the restriction of cross-border capital flows, retains the potential for further liberalization of the renminbi.

A question arises here: How can China quickly make a breakthrough in the internationalization of the renminbi, making it one of the reserve currencies, and circumventing the requirements and standards of currency exchange in Article 8 of the IMF Agreement or the IMF Charter?[9] At present, the expert community has no unified answer to this question, but the following arguments demonstrate the current status of the renminbi:

6. Приведено на основе: Петрова Г. В. Указ. соч. С. 103–111.

7. Приведено на основе: Сюйянь Ц. Указ. соч. С. 152–155; Петрова Г. В. Указ. соч. С. 103–111.

8. Петрова Г. В. Указ. соч. С. 104.

9. СМ., "Articles of Agreement of the International Monetary Fund," Washington, DC: International Monetary Fund, 2016.

1. Joining the primary standards of the "periphery" of the International Monetary and Financial Organization (МВФО) and the requirements of the IMF. According to recent data, if there is no so-called "free convertibility," the renminbi is the most influential currency in the world. In addition, the pure US dollar is considered the standard for a fully convertible currency, but this is not the case. This also makes the "accommodation" standard of the SDR currency basket hollow;[10]

2. Principles of political games. Some experts believe that China has received reliable support from many countries, which are affected by IMF standards, mainly Germany and Australia;[11]

3. Theories and methods of macro-prudential policy analysis. According to this scientific research direction, currency internationalization is driven by the market and requires the country to take decisive action, especially at the "critical moment of restoring institutional balance." Against the background of the cyclical development of the national and world economic system, China has used its "super-large" economic advantages to establish a decentralized and coherent system project and formulated an intermediate system (or "System Bridge"). Therefore, it is wrong to interpret the process of RMB internationalization as some kind of "international project." First, RMB internationalization is related to internal strategy and mobilization. Incorporating the renminbi into the special drawing rights basket requires China to re-adjust its current monetary and financial development strategies and improve national policies based on macro-prudential methods;[12]

4. The criterion of interest combination: the possibility of improving the attributes of SDR. According to calculations by Chinese experts, including the renminbi into the world's reserve currency can reduce the covariance between SDR and gold, oil, and natural gas prices by 44%, 61%, and 65%, respectively. In addition, the addition of the renminbi has increased the correlation between the SDR and the real effective exchange rate of major currencies, thereby increasing the "shock" of the SDR on the stability of IMF. In view of this, it is possible to "moderate" price fluctuations in the world's raw material markets and the dynamic development of exchange rates and cross-border settlements. The "impact"[13] of payment rights on the stability of international monetary and financial organizations. In view of this, it is possible to "moderate" the price fluctuations in the world's raw material markets and the dynamic development

10. Катасонов В. Юань против доллара, фунта стерлингов и евро / Русское экономическое общество им. С. Ф. Шарапова. Март 2018, http://reosh.ru/valentin-kata-sonov-yuan-protiv-dollara-funta-sterlingov-i-evro.html.

11. Linling W., "China Rallies Around Yuan as IMF Mulls Reserve-Currency Inclusion," June 15, https://defence.pk/pdf/threads/china-rallies-around-yuan-as-imf-mulls-reserve-currency-inclusion.381196/.

12. Weitseng C., "Lost in Internationalization: Rise of the Renminbi, Macroprudential Policy, and Global Impacts," *Journal of International Economic Law* 21, no. 1 (2018): 31–66.

13. Jianping D., Jian X., and Lizhu Y. "Volatility of the Exchange Rate After Renminbi Inclusion into the SDR: Test of Stability and Representation," *China Economist* 11, no, 3 (2016): 77–91.

of exchange rates and cross-border settlements. Regardless of why the RMB was included in the IMF's world reserve currency, it is undeniable that at the current "peak period" of RMB internationalization, China has completely completed reforms in the International Monetary and financial organizations and the international financial legal system. This requires the international community to consider the rationality of the proposed evaluation standards and the quality of their implementation, as well as to reconsider the role of countries in market development, formation, and transition in the context of the ever-changing IMF.

As shown above, according to its own key development indicators (such as low financial depth, etc.), China is not among the leaders of the global monetary and financial system centered on the US. But at the same time, since the mid-2000s, especially during the transition phase of the international monetary and financial system in the 2010s, China can no longer be clearly positioned as the "core" or "peripheral" country of the international monetary and financial system and should be in the middle of "near the core."

First, this aspect is manifested in China's breakthrough achievements in combining internationalization and transnationalization in the monetary and financial fields. On the other hand, it has combined restrictions on liberalization. Here are some specific examples.

Let us review the dynamic changes in the number of foreign banks in China and Russia from the year 1995 to the year 2009 (for comparison). This stage is just before the beginning of changes in the international monetary and financial system and the strengthening of the liberalization process of emerging market countries in the world. It can be said that China has adopted prudent policies and strict supervision for the "startup" of foreign financial intermediaries. Only since 2006, the dynamics of this indicator have changed. The share of foreign bank assets in the total assets of the national financial system in 2009 was only 1%, 12% in Russia, 50% in Chile and Colombia, 85% in Romania, 87% in the Czech Republic, 91% in Hungary, 99% in Slovakia, 95%–98% in Argentina and Hong Kong, China.[14]

In addition, China's cross-border capital circulation indicators in 2018 reflect that compared with the enthusiasm and openness of financial expansion in the US and the United Kingdom, the activity of overseas Chinese financial intermediaries and foreign financial institutions in China is relatively low.

However, as of 2018, the "health" of the global systematically important banks determines the level of well-being of the international monetary and financial system in the future. Among them, four Chinese Institutions-Bank of China, Industrial and Commercial Bank of China, Agricultural Bank of China, and China Construction Bank play an important role.[15] In the 2016–2017 global systemically important insurance

---

14. "World Development Indicators Database," World Bank, 2013; Архипова В. В. Указ. соч. С. 206–208.

15. "2018 List of Global Systemically Important Banks (G-SIBs)," Financial Stability Board, November 16, 2018.

institution rating, the only representative in Asia is Ping'an Insurance (Group) Co., Ltd. of China.[16]

In addition, some scholars state that China and Russia have joined the "advanced competition" platform initiated by the Global Mutual Fund. This platform aims at establishing and implementing emergency buying and selling of financial assets for countries in economic development and transition, especially during the period of "tortuous progress" of these countries affected by the Mexican financial crisis (1994), Asian financial crisis (1997) and Russian debt crisis (1998).[17]

At the current stage of development, China has become one of the major countries that accept foreign direct investment. However, the process of foreign direct investment has distinctive features in China. It is worth noting that China, as an inflow country of foreign direct investment, has achieved considerable results in attracting capital: if the inflow of funds into the country in 1983 was less than US$1 billion, then by 1993, it was already US$26 billion. In 2006, it was US$69.5 billion; in 2017, it was US$136 billion. This has ensured China's solid position among the top ten inflow countries of foreign direct investment. To supervise this type of business, the National Development and Reform Commission of China has formulated a management plan for foreign investment, which includes relevant regulations in the area of financial capital and has issued procedural rules for foreign companies' mergers and acquisitions of Chinese companies.[18]

Thus, in sustaining and developing China's 2000–2010 "capital cycle" process, the practical significance of direct investment is exaggerated and complicated. We have also noticed that China's direct investment in other countries reached US$125 billion in 2017, almost 1.6 times less than the same indicator in 2016. China took a self-critical approach to explain the decline and linked it to the reduction of "irrational investment," despite which it remained the leading investor among the top ten.[19]

Let us refer to the indicators for integrating the analyzed country into the global financial system. According to the level of financial interconnection (Table 17-1), China has risen to eighth place in just ten years.

The above table reflects that China, together with the "core" countries of the global monetary and financial organization system, such as the US, the United Kingdom, Germany, and Japan, firmly ranks among the top ten countries with the highest levels of cross-border and international cooperation. Russia occupies a negligible position in the top 30 of the McKinsey Global Institute and has dropped one place since 2005.

In our view, the coefficient of economic closeness (from English, meaning economic cooperation with foreign countries and regions) can be regarded as part of measuring

16. "2016 List of Global Systemically Important Insurers (G-SIIs)," Financial Stability Board, November 21, 2016; "Review of the List of Global Systemically Important Insurers (G-SIIs)," Financial Stability Board, November 21, 2017.

17. Kaminsky G. L., Lyons R. K., and Schmukler S. L., "Mutual Funds Investment in Emerging Markets: An Overview," *The World Bank Economic Review* 15, no. 2 (2005); Kaminsky G. L., Reinhart C. M., and Vegh C. A., "The Unholy Trinity of Financial Contagion," *Journal of Economic Perspectives* 17, no. 4 (2003).

18. Абзац подготовлен на основе данных и аргументации: Конотопов М. В., Сметанин С. И. Указ. соч. С. 551–553; "World Investment Report," UNCTAD, 2018; Eichengreen B., and Lombardi D., "RMBI or RMBR: Is the Renminbi Destined to Become a Global or Regional Currency?" NBER Working Paper, no. 21716 (November 2015), 5–7.

19. "World Investment Report," UNCTAD, 2018, 6, 48.

the level of economic conjugation. The coefficient of the closeness of economic relations shows another interesting trend, and it shows in detail the distribution of countries and regions with the closest cooperation with China. In 2017, we added and compared the fund circulation indicators (turnovers) of projects and contracts between China and other countries and regions and found that China has the highest connection with Asian and African countries (52% and 30%, respectively). Pakistan ranks first among Asian countries, with a coefficient of economic closeness with China of 6.7% (accounting for 13% of the total coefficient in Asia). Algeria ranks first among African countries, with a coefficient of the closeness of economic relations of 4.7% (accounting for 15% of the total coefficient in Africa). Overall, the coefficient of the closeness of economic relations between European countries and China is 5.5% (of which Russia is the highest at 1.2%, accounting for 21% of the total coefficient in Europe). Latin American countries are 7.7% (Venezuela ranks first with 1.9%, approximately 26% of the total coefficient in Latin America), 1.3% in the US (94% in North America), 2% in Australia, and only 0.2% in Japan. The coefficient in 2016 is close to that in 2017.[20]

Table 17-1 Financial Interconnection Level Table (Latest Update: August 2017)

Grade (Changed since 2005)	Countries	Foreign Capital, Percentage of GDP					Foreign Liabilities, Percentage of GDP			
		Foreign Direct Investment	Equity	Debt Securities	Loans and Others	Foreign Reserve Assets	Foreign Direct Investment	Net Value	Debt Securities	Loans and Other Assets
1	The USA (Net capital recipient)	40	38	152	21	2	39	35	59	28
3(-1)	The UK (Net capital provider)	71	64	71	191	5	59	58	99	183
5(-2)	Germany (Net capital provider)	57	29	57	84	5	42	20	61	68
6(+1)	Japan (Net capital provider)	29	29	50	35	25	5	30	28	48
8(+8)	China (Net capital provider)	12	2	1	15	29	26	5	2	9
21(-1)	Russia (Net capital provider)	33	<1	5	28	29	32	11	4	25

20. The author calculated the data based on the 2018 China Statistical Yearbook, http://www.stats.gov.cn/tjsj/ndsj/2018/indexeh.htm.

Therefore, the monetary financing and general economic links between China and the world are reflected in its central position in the new world economic structure, which is close to the indicators of the integration of the core countries in the US-centric financial system (formed after the collapse of the Soviet Union). China is forming its monetary financing space in accordance with the new world economic structure system.

The prerequisites for China to become a core country in the new international monetary and financial system:

According to the previous data analysis results obtained in the above three paragraphs, China's goal is to develop financial and general economic cooperation, to a greater extent, with the "peripheral" countries in the IMF system centered on the US (total indicators conjugated with Asian and African economies exceed 80%), rather than with the "core" countries. At the same time, China and the developed countries led by the US have launched a competition for their influence on "peripheral" countries (in fact, China's capital reserves are used to develop the domestic economy).[21]

At present, two very outstanding giants—China and the US—have appeared in the world economy. As a result, the professional term Chimerica (a combination of "China" and "America") has emerged to describe the state of the global economy. This phenomenon shows special direct and indirect links between the two opposing economies: hardworking and consuming, thrifty and overspending, and regulation and hyper freedom. This shows the dialectics of the interaction between the new and old world economic structure centers. At present, the centers of the new world economic structure, dependent on the imports of technology from the centers of the old world economic structure, are forced to pay the rents of knowledge, including lower wages and natural resources rents, through the export of labor-intensive products and raw materials. As the reproduction model of the new world economic structure takes shape, its centers will become self-sufficient, and the old center of the world economic structure, which plunders supplies from the periphery, will decline.

As shown above, China's financial system and economy generally have significant advantages. The first is the relative stability of development when sustained reforms are implemented effectively. As mentioned above, the stability level of the banking system is one of the main indicators of the successful operation of the financial sector, which in turn depends on the number of "non-performing" loans. The number of those in China has decreased sharply since 2000 (even during the global financial and economic crisis) and was the lowest since 2010 (Figure 17-5). In addition, the experience in the supervision of monetary finance and economic procedures enables China to resist the risks of financial "collapse" and "bubble," as well as the risk of "sudden cessation" of cross-border capital flows, which is mainly related to the risks of uncontrolled events and destabilizing factors worldwide.[22]

21. Оценки масштабов финансово-экономической транснационализации и экспансии на постсоветском пространстве см.: Глинкина С. П., Куликова Н. В., Тураева М. О., Голубкин А. В., Яковлев А. А. Китайский фактор в развитии стран российского пояса соседства: уроки для России. Научный доклад. М.: Институт экономики РАН, 2018.

22. См.: Архипова В. В. Указ. соч. С. 78–223.

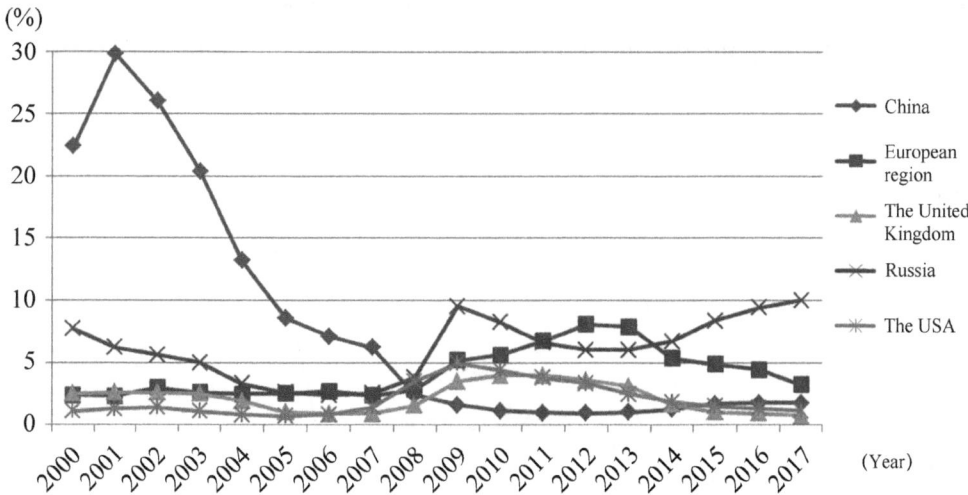

Figure 17-5 Non-performing Bank Loans as a Percentage of Total Loans
Source: World Bank's 2019 World Development Indicators Data Collection.

In addition, some researchers stated that the effectiveness and economic security of China's 2009–2010 anti-crisis plan are much higher than similar indicators in the US.[23]

Based on the dialectics of financial interaction between the new and old world economic structure centers, the following measures can be proposed to eliminate the pressure caused by this.

1. To occupy a leading position in international monetary finance, China needs to develop international monetary financing relations and the real economic sectors they serve so as to achieve "breakthroughs" in them and establish a foothold in new "areas," for example,"[24]

   - The evolution of the digital economy: In terms of total e-commerce retail sales, China's share has increased from 0.6% in 2005 to 42.4% from 2016 to early 2017 and has surpassed the US's 24.1% in the final stage of the study.
   - Mobile payment: From 2016 to early 2017, China's total mobile payment was valued at US$790 billion, compared to US$74 billion (China surpassed the US nearly 11 times).
   - Global private startups (also known as unicorns) with a valuation of more than US$1 billion are in the "growth" stage: As of 2016, China accounted for about 34% of the global total, compared with 47% for the US and 19% for other countries.

23. См.: Гордиенко Д. В. Указ. соч. С. 244–279.
24. Orr G., "What Can We Expect in China in 2018?" December 2017, https://www.mckinsey.com/featured-insights/china/what-can-we-expect-in-china-in-2018.

In addition, China should continue to improve its banking system and national financial markets, because China may also become a leader in these areas (Figure 17-6), thereby eliminating the so-called "failures" of reforms in the monetary and financial sectors.

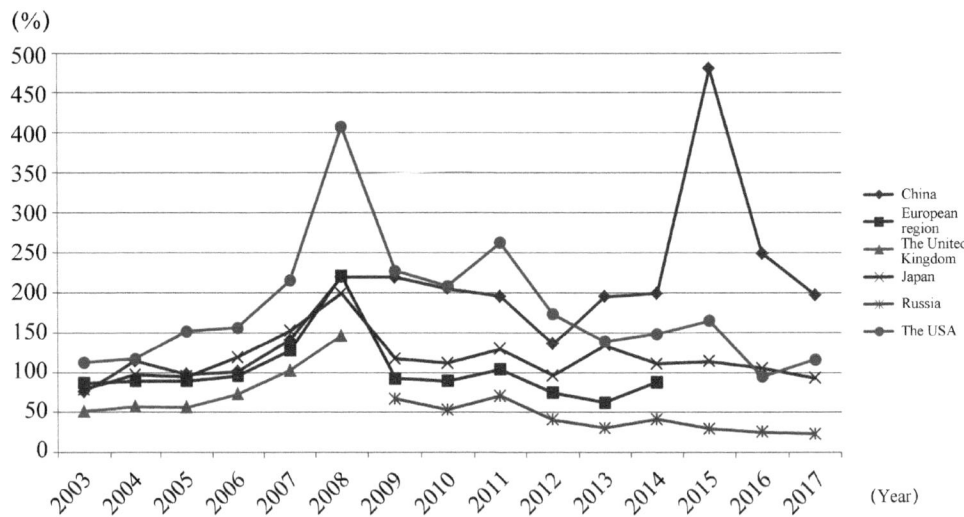

Figure 17-6 Domestic Stock Turnover Rate
Source: World Bank's 2019 World Development Indicators Data Collection.

2. In view of many similar characteristics of the Chinese and Russian financial sectors, it is recommended to develop a financial strategy that links the banking systems of the two countries. According to A.V. Kuznetsov's assessment, from 1913 to the present, the US dollar has lost more than 95% of its original value or purchasing power, which is reflected in the reduced confidence in the US dollar.[25] Therefore, considering the evaluation and analysis results within the framework of this research, it can be predicted that the international status of the RMB will increase in the future.

3. We believe that China should not rush to speed up the internationalization of the RMB to achieve a level of free convertibility. At this stage, China can start by consolidating monetary and financial relations between regions and countries and strengthening its global position. For example, according to the China-Russia vector proposal, the following specific resolutions are adopted: (1) establishing government instructions on switching to domestic currency settlements in the two countries, (2) establishing specialized banks to develop domestic currency settlements, or (3) temporarily abandoning currency partnerships and the docking of the two countries' banking systems. The last of the above options is the worst because it will weaken the position of the Yuan and the Ruble and strengthen the position of the Dollar on a regional and global scale.

---

25. Кузнецов А. В. Указ. соч. С. 193.

The main conclusions of statistical analysis and comparison of a series of indicators between China and Russia show that:

- The dynamic changes of exchange rate indicators with real effectiveness have two "close" periods: 1995–1998 and 2005–2013;
- China's MP reform shows a basic stable trend. The reform policy is coordinated with the development goals of the national economy and foreign policy and evolves in stages, while the main trend in Russia is the cycle of instability and relative stability;
- Russia has at least two possible MP approaches: maintaining dollarization when changing the base currency (USD→RMB) or stimulating the development and internationalization of the Ruble through the initial promotion of regional monetary and financial cooperation under the sanctions regime.

4. It is recommended to develop a strategy to realize the connection between the national payment systems of China and Russia (especially during 2013–2017, the total number of Russian households using the international payment system SWIFT decreased by 31%).[26]

The Communist Party of China has abandoned dogmatism and established an integrated ideological system. This system combines the realization of socialist goals with self-fulfilling creative freedom and patriotism. After suffering from the 'Cultural Revolution," the idea of integration got rid of the radicalism inherent in the main ideological trends of the 20th century: communism, liberalism, and Nazism.

India combines Gandhi's socialist ideas, democratic values, and national interests to move towards an integrated system in another way. On this road, India, like China, has accelerated its social and economic development, and its GDP growth in 2016 ranked first in the world. Some countries in the Indochina Peninsula (such as Vietnam and Laos) have embarked on the path of socialism with their own cultural characteristics and have also shown high economic growth rates. Even African countries have introduced the management system established by China, and the economies of these countries have also accelerated. One example is Ethiopia. The country has gotten rid of poverty, and its GDP growth rate has reached double digits.

In the past thirty years, examples of replacing socialist ideology with liberal ideology have existed. The "Japanese shareholding system" model is well-known, emphasizing the consistency of Japan's socioeconomic structure. If Japan did not implement liberal economic policies under the pressure of the US in the 1980s, Japan might maintain a relatively high economic growth rate. It can be said that under the pressure of the IMF in the 1990s, similar economic liberalization hindered South Korea's economic miracle. Finally, let's talk about the miracle of the Soviet Union's socioeconomic development.

---

26. Источник данных: Банк международных расчетов (год обновления данных: 2018). URL: https://stats.bis.org/statx/toc/CPMI.html; идеи и модели интеграции платежных систем сМ.: Гладышев Д. А. Интеграция платежных систем на мировом финансовом рынке. Диссертация на соискание ученой степени кандидата экономических наук. М., 2014.

After the disintegration of the Soviet Union, most of the republics abandoned their socialist ideology and instead supported the Washington Consensus, which brought catastrophic socioeconomic consequences to the Soviet Union. It is also worth reviewing the miraculous recovery and rise of Germany, France, and Austria after the war, and the successful development of Scandinavian countries guided by democratic socialist ideology.

As we all know, practice is the only criterion for testing truth. The correctness of the theory must be verified through practice. Not long ago, the basic theories of social sciences passed the test of practice. Two basic dogmatic theories that claimed to be the ultimate truth collapsed: Soviet-style dogmatic communism and its opposite liberalism (including the modern manifestation of the Washington Consensus). This means that Russia's approach to its socioeconomic policies is wrong. After the disintegration of the Soviet Union, one dogmatic ideology was replaced by another, which brought Russia into a historical impasse. Russia is in a "quagmire," and all attempts by the Russian president to resolve the national crisis have been submerged in the "quagmire."

There is no doubt that Russia's economic policies led it from being the richest country into the miserable situation of a third world country. Although India and China previously lacked oil and natural gas resources and were far behind the Soviet Union in S&T, India, and China are now five times higher than Russia in terms of GDP and other scientific and technological development indicators. In recent years, China's average wage has been higher than that of Russia, and Russia's labor productivity level is increasingly lagging behind that of developed countries. Russia's socioeconomic development level is continuously declining in global rankings, and Russia is in a leading position in terms of social problems such as disease, suicide, abortion, and the growth rate of offshore oligarchs. The reason for these results is not the lack of new technologies to improve efficiency and output, but the misappropriation of elements of national wealth, such as the privatization of state-owned property, rents from natural resources, or rents from administrative agencies.

Russia's national wealth is taken as its own by some small groups who use the national wealth to accumulate personal wealth. In the four years of this privatization and the continuous four-year reduction of residents' real income, the increase in the number of billionaires clearly shows the goal positioning of the existing social and economic development management system. State leaders have been trying to make the social and economic development management system in line with the people's interests. Still, the result is only to speed up the self-interested officials' "rich money" activities. In the absence of national ideology, the position of the social and economic development management system is occupied by the desire for benefits.

As noted by Danial Lanin, a prominent St. Petersburg scholar, the absence of ideology manifests liberal ideology, which is the ruling elite's program of action. If people's social value is reflected by the amount of money they have, then money will become a measure of success (including government leaders). The high salaries of the heads of state banks and state-owned companies are outstanding examples of this ideology. Their salaries do not depend on the objective results of their work. If the goal of realizing human value is to obtain personal income, then it shouldn't be surprising that the company's leaders who are at a loss receive huge rewards.

In the existing management system, officials typically perform their duties in a false manner and cover up the abuse of power to obtain personal wealth. The basic structural element of the existing management system is the "team." As mentioned above, it is established based on mutual shielding. Those in power are systematically profiting from criminal groups. Corresponding fractals can be seen at all levels of management—from village committees to federal ministries and commissions.[27] Therefore, there is no need to doubt the "highest achievements" of this management model, such as the privatization of the world's largest real estate company at a loss; the Treasury bill pyramid ended in bankruptcy; the central bank with hundreds of billions of Rubles became a "bubble"; one trillion US dollars flowed into foreign countries.

Attempts to curb the "disintegration" of the management system by increasing the number of regulatory and law enforcement agencies will only exacerbate its disintegration, because the regulatory and law enforcement agencies also succumb to the power of money. This is why regulatory and law enforcement agencies coexist with business groups under the protection of entrepreneurs from mutual protection. The result is a vicious circle: corruption dominates the economy, and the increase of powerful regulatory agencies is to suppress free entrepreneurs, incorporate them into these business groups, or force them to cease business activities. At the top of the pyramid that has the power to deal with economic problems are those bankers who take state-owned assets as their own and care about the value of high assets. After pushing up interest rates to three times the profit rate of the processing industry, they became economic stewards and decided the fate of bankrupt companies. High-interest rates and tax pressure have squeezed all the income of the real economy sector, and the income of the real economy sector has been declining due to reduced investment.

The world center of liberal ideology coincides with the gathering place of currency wealth. Therefore, the proponents of this ideology have a strong desire for wealth. They are eager to travel to New York and London and hide their income in the Anglo-Saxon jurisdiction in advance. The offshorization campaign ordered by the President led many large Russian businessmen to move there. They regard money as the highest value and follow it to a place where they worship money. Undoubtedly, when choosing to block accounts or betray the country, most Russian businessmen subject to the latest American sanctions will choose the latter.

If a clear and understandable ideology is not promoted among all citizens, achieving the national socioeconomic development goals set by the Russian president will be impossible. In Russia, this ideology can only be a socialist ideology.

First, without ideology, it is impossible to make the social and economic development management system consistent with the urgent requirements expressed by the state leaders. This is the same as letting the Red Army command the White Army. Through suppression and obstruction, it is possible to force the subordinates of the opposition to execute orders temporarily. Still, without this suppression, it is impossible to properly develop the modern knowledge economy.

Second, if no standard matches decision-making with the improvement of social welfare, the management system will lose its "core." Officials and heads of state-owned

---

27. Макаров В. Л. Социальный кластеризм. Российский вызов. -М.: Бизнес Атлас, 2010. 272 с.

enterprises are responsible for the results of their work. Otherwise, the management system will remain corrupt and incompetent.

Third, social justice is the dominant value in social consciousness. The public will not recognize its legitimacy if the management system does not conform to this value. The people will pretend to obey the management system, and the officials will falsely behave in management. This system of universal pretending to follow can create the appearance of national unity, but it will collapse when it is tested for the first time. Therefore, the Russian Empire collapsed a century ago, and the Soviet Union collapsed 25 years ago.

Fourth, the choice of socialism is progressive, opening up prospects for Russia to be included in the "core" of the new world economic structure. Without the "asylum" of official ideology, preserving liberalism means becoming a "money cow" for "peripheral" countries and American oligarchs.

Fifth, if no ideology unites society and subordinates individual interests (including the interests of the ruling elite) to those of the whole people, we will not be able to survive the mixed world war waged by the US to maintain its global hegemony. If the Soviet National Bank works under the orderly guidance of the German Reichsbank, the state plan is subject to Eastern Fascism, Goebbels supervises the publication of Soviet newspapers, and Martin Bauman leads the party building, it is almost impossible for us to win the last world war.

Of course, the socialist ideology must be in a modern form. The first is humanity, with respect for human rights and freedoms as the starting point. Second, it should be full of patriotism, giving priority to national interests and formulating foreign policy accordingly. The modern socialist ideology must be guided by the new technological structure, advancing social and economic development, and making this ideology more focused on S&T, pragmatism, and progress.

PART VI

DEVELOPMENT OF THE EURASIAN ECONOMIC INTEGRATION STRATEGY

Under the formation of the new world economic order, the implementation of the advanced development strategy not only involves macroeconomic, technological, and regional factors, but also depends on the role of external economies, of which the integration of Eurasian economics is the key. The Eurasian economic integration in the post-Soviet space refers to the customs union (CU) and unified economic space (UEC) formed by some post-Soviet countries. Now it has developed into the EAEU composed of Russia, Belarus, Kazakhstan, Kyrgyzstan, and Armenia. Although the alliance has always adopted an open-minded attitude and established economic and trade preferential systems with other countries, including distant countries, from a practical point of view, the geographical distribution of Eurasian integration is limited to the post-Soviet space. Moreover, the heterogeneity of the post-Soviet space has been recognized by the core countries of the EAEU who are most willing to reintegrate. Other CIS member states connected by the unified free trade area have also more or less participated in this process.

From a land perspective, the scope of Eurasian inte-gration is broader, including the Shanghai Cooperation Organization, China's Belt and Road Initiative, ASEAN+, the EAEU's free trade zone with Vietnam, and projects with India. This chapter aims to interpret many aspects of the Eurasian Project in a broad sense, with the focus on the EAEU. The EAEU is a regional group connected through supranational management institutions, and it is the most complete and important form of Russia's economic development. This is not to say that the organization is fully established—we still remember the "eternal" agreements that Russia signed with Ukraine, Georgia, and the Baltic states centuries ago. The EAEU is authorized to implement all member states' foreign trade policies and implement unified tariffs and technical supervision. The current Russian economic development strategy should include the EAEU in overall consideration.

Chapter 18

Prerequisites for Eurasian Economic Integration

Judging from historical, economic, and political reasons, Russia has played a key role in organizing the process of Eurasian integration. The research of the integration "scale"[1] on public opinion proves that the recognition that Russia is the center of unity is firmly retained in all the CIS countries. People look forward to the emergence of innovative breakthroughs and innovative signals to implement systemic reforms in Russia. This reform is regarded as the national interest of the countries participating in the Eurasian integration process. Most republics in the post-Soviet space are oriented towards Russia on the issue of political friendship and military assistance. Interviewees from 9 CIS countries[2] have the above thoughts.

The formation of the recognition of Russia as the gravitational center of Eurasia depends not only on Russia's vast territory and abundant resource potential. Eurasianism is an ideological, political, historical, and cultural concept. The earliest origin of Eurasianism can be traced back to the end of the 15th century and the beginning of the 16th century. It originated from the letter of the elder Philofey, the monk of the Pskov Yelizarov Monastery, who regarded the Russian nation as the inheritor of Byzantium tradition. The works of Homiakov, Kiryevsky, Aksakov, and Trubetskoy appeared before Eurasianism, and the book *Europe and Mankind*, published in Sofia in 1920, played a prominent role. This work started the Eurasian "cultural-historical philosophy" movement of Russian intellectuals, which became popular in Europe after 1917. Like Trubetskoy, the geographer Savitsky and the historian Vernatsky are also outstanding representatives of this movement. As the Soviet regime inaugurated proletarian internationalism, these great thinkers thought deeply about how the Soviet regime would subsequently develop and perish, and what ideological foundations would allow the historical commonality of a nation united for centuries to be preserved within the framework of the Soviet Union and the Russian Empire.

One of the connotations of Eurasianism theory is the "multilinear concept of world history," which makes "the originality and uniqueness of culture" its inherent traits and characteristics. This theory denies the exclusivity and absoluteness of European culture. Participants in this movement interpreted the concept of "Eurasia" from different perspectives. The first is that they regarded it as a pure geographical space and took it for granted that the West and the East were divided into Europe (Western Europe), Asia (South and East Asia: India and China), and Eurasia (the plain areas of Asia and the European continent). The second is that from the perspective of race, Eurasia had formed a special "Turan mentality," "Russian is neither European nor Asian, but Eurasian." The third is that from a purely economic point of view, Russia,

---

1. Интеграционный барометр. М.: Центр интеграционных исследований Евразийского банка развития, 2013, 2014.
2. В Казахстане сопоставимо значимо российское направление.

which straddles Europe and Asia, is a continental country. It not only needs to develop global maritime economic ties, but also develop ties within the continent.[3]

Trubetskoy's predictive talent is worthy of recognition. He foresaw in 1927 that the collapse of the communist empire and the unification of the new nation on this land were based on an understanding of the common destiny of history. Later, Gumilev contributed greatly to the formation of modern Eurasian theory. After the disintegration of the Soviet Union, he pointed out in an interview before his death in 1992: "I know one thing, and I can tell you as a secret that Russia can and can only survive as a major Eurasian country and can only survive with Eurasianism."[4] This can be regarded as a guide for practical action, which complements the modern Eurasian expression. Modern Eurasianists admit that the prerequisite for safeguarding the welfare of Eastern Europe, the Caucasus, and Central Asia is not to use individual country preferences to attract investment when cooperating with the West or the East, but to establish a transcontinental integration system from the Atlantic to the Pacific. Russia in the old world is the only country "from this sea to the sea." It can communicate with the three world economic and technological development belts of Western Europe, East Asia, and North America.

Russian scholar Pod Beretskin pointed out that Russia's unique geographical location and its importance to the process of Eurasian integration are determined by the following aspects:[5]

1. Russia is not only a country, but also a civilized country. Except for China and Russia, there is no other example in the world. This is true both from a sociocultural and a historical perspective. Therefore, affected by globalization, Some Internationalists tried to "liberalize" it and change its traditional appearance, but the national identity remains;

2. Russia has a unique geographical location. From a geographical point of view, Russia is the center of Europe and Asia, connecting the three sides of East, West, and South;

3. Russia's reserves of minerals and biological resources and the area of adjacent seas occupy a unique position in the world;

4. Based on the cultural spirit of openness and non-discrimination, Russia unites the world's mainstream religions and religious groups headed by Orthodox Church to form a world-shocked and unique spiritual universe that opposes agnosticism and secularism;

5. Russia is a unique information exchange and transportation hub in the world, and its role is rapidly increasing.

Over the decades, the member states of the EAEU developed into a single country with a common economic complex. The economies of the constituent republics of

3. Трубецкой Н. С. История. Культура. Язык / Вступ. ст. Н. И. Толстого и Л. Н. Гумилева. М.: ПРОГРЕСС; УНИВЕРС, 1995.

4. Опубликовано в ежемесячном дайджесте социального соразмышления «Социум». 1992. №5.

5. Подберезкин А., Боришполец К., Подберезкина О. Евразия и Россия. М.: 2013.

the Soviet Union complement each other, and thousands of cooperative links form a complete production cycle-from raw materials to finished products, from basic science to mass production technology. In addition, the economy of the Soviet Union was not inferior to the level of developed countries, which includes the manufacturing industry's share index, such as machine manufacturing and high value-added production. Of course, it cannot be said that the economic space at that time was homogeneous. The space was uniform, whether it was legal norms and economic organization forms, or all other economic systems: prices, standards, qualification requirements, planning procedures, and decision-making rules. Relying on the specialization and cooperation of production to maintain unity, no consortium of republics, including the Soviet Federal Socialist Republic of Russia at that time, could be self-sufficient; that is, products produced were made using raw materials and components supplied by other republics.

Due to the different levels of economic development in various countries, doubts about the process of economic integration in post-Soviet space often arise. Still, the integrity and unity of the post-Soviet space overturn those doubts. Of course, in the twenty years after the disintegration of the Soviet Union, the economies of the former republics of the Soviet Union countries were very depressed, but the degree of degeneration was proportional to the complexity of existing production. The Russian Federation has suffered the most in high-tech production. It has the same export share as the Central Asian raw material economies in exporting raw materials, metals, and energy carriers. For this reason, if the theory that the economies of integrated countries are homogeneous and at the same level has certain economic significance, then it should be realized that compared with the Soviet period, the level of the former republics of the Soviet Union countries in this category is similar. From this logic, the former republics of the Soviet Union countries have a higher degree of integration.

The integration process of post-Soviet space is unique. Until recently, a unified national economic space was still part of a country with a unified national economic complex. On the one hand, the common history and the complex cooperative relations formed over the decades have determined the natural characteristics of the integration process. Its essence is that the integration process has been revived after hundreds of years. Under the new legal foundation and economic conditions, UES has emerged. On the other hand, the separatist syndrome abruptly breeds due to excessive fear of losing the national sovereignty that has just been acquired. Independent countries must build their own trade and economic cooperation strategies from the ground up, and fundamentally establish a new coordination mechanism consistent with modern geopolitical realities.

The disintegration of the Soviet Union was caused by subjective rather than objective factors. Objective factors required the Soviet Union to retain a unified economic space as a necessary condition for the country's stable development. Experts pointed out that the post-Soviet space has experienced two production declines, partly because the emergence of national borders has led to the disconnection of existing production technologies. Critics of Eurasian integration did not take this into account when criticizing the unbalanced level of economic development of the Soviet space states. Experts try to apply the non-historical view established in the theory of regional economic integration to a region that has always been a unified economic organization for hundreds of years. The integration process in the region should be seen as a reintegration of existing reproduction, not just a newly created integration process. This is why in this case, the old theories related to the previous union of independent countries (whether it is the European Union or the North American Free Trade Area) do not work here. Explaining the process of Eurasian integration is much more complicated than explaining the traditional view that the current economic space and economic development level are similar. Highly developed areas are usually in a symbiotic state with the sources of raw materials, energy, and labor. The highly developed areas and underdeveloped areas are unified into the same reproduction cycle through flow. The UES of any country is composed of spaces with different levels of economic development and complementary to the needs of production specialization and cooperation at the time. Whether it is between cities or countries in the world, the economic system of any region is the same.

On the contrary, countries with similar levels of economic development usually have a single product type production competition, expelling similar products through tariff barriers, and adopting various protectionist measures. Trade frictions often break out in these countries, but they have never happened in finished product manufacturing and raw material supply.

The above is not to say that the similar level of development among countries will become an obstacle to integration, but that it may be the opposite. Modern economic growth is characterized by a global supply chain of professional globalization, production cooperation, and the production of complex product accessories. Under the trend of globalization, increasing competition forces developed countries to integrate to reduce costs, increase production scale, and expand their scientific and technological base.

The above argument only proves that trying to explain the process of economic integration by the level of economic development is too superficial and does not conform to the complex process that drives its development. The same applies to the "gravity model" of economic cooperation between countries. The factor determining the degree of integration is not the scale and level of national economic development, but the production specialization and cooperative relationship formed in the history of the universal reproduction framework.

The resolution to establish the Eurasian Economic Community in 2000 was fully in line with the idea of reintegrating the economies of the former Soviet Union countries at a time when there were differences in speed and level of development. The then President of Kazakhstan, Nazarbayev, played a special role in Eurasian integration. As early as 1994, when Nazarbayev gave a speech at Moscow State University, "God personally commanded US—the countries of the former Soviet Union—to trust each other, cherish and strengthen our unity. We have seen that some forces want to divide us, weaken us and sow the seeds of mistrust and hatred. In this situation, all people can feel is sadness. Our people have lived together for hundreds of years. It is in the fundamental interests of millions of people to strengthen good-neighborly relations, which is not restricted by any current situation…"[6] Mansurov, who served as the Secretary-General of the Eurasian Economic Community for a long time, designed and developed Eurasian integration based on the practical experience of integration and coalition in the research and propaganda work of the leaders of Kazakhstan.[7]

In the mid-1990s, the then leader of the Russian Federation ignored the Eurasian Economic Community and was eager to use the achievements of the 1993 national reform to occupy state assets and national wealth privately. The newly emerging offshore oligarchs also have no time to consider Eurasian integration. Only after Putin was elected President of Russia did the draft of Eurasian integration begin to be implemented. The Eurasian Economic Community was established in 2000, and in 2003, Russia, Belarus, Kazakhstan, and Ukraine started building a UES.

At the same time, the motivation for integration from "zero" is largely influenced by the pro-American forces of the Russian power class. They claimed that all methods of post-Soviet spatial integration are degraded and immature from an economic point of view. Putin's idea of reintegrating the economic potential of the Commonwealth of Independent States based on the market and filling the integration potential with actual content has incurred non-public opposition at home, and public opposition comes from abroad. The false claims that post-Soviet countries cannot prioritize accession to the WTO while establishing a CU have delayed the integration process for several years. Those responsible for advancing integration are either passively sabotaged or tried to make national leaders think that the initiative is obviously unrealistic, and the purpose is to discredit the idea of Eurasian unification.

To some extent, the global crisis has diverted the attention of geopolitical opponents and their party members in Russia, distracting them from the integration process of the post-Soviet space for the time being. They believe that Russian leaders will stick to the doctrine of the priority of accession to the WTO, which will block the integration process for a long time. The heads of government of the three member states of the CU issued a resolution on June 9, 2009, suspending individual talks on accession to the WTO, and setting up a unified delegation to discuss the accession of Belarus, Kazakhstan, and Russia to the WTO on the same terms. Only then did Brussels and Washington understand the seriousness of the above-mentioned plan.

The EurAsEC was established in accordance with the classic model of regional integration, which is divided into three stages: CU (2008-2011), UES (2011–2012), and Economic Union (2012–present). In the first three years of the project's launch at the end of 2008, the first supranational institution in the post-Soviet space—the CU Commission—based on the direct implementation of the "Customs Law" on health, veterinary, phytosanitary, part of the traffic control functions and technical management system Uniform Transit Tariff (UTT) control. While the establishment of the CU was completed, in 2011, a basic agreement on constructing a UES was prepared

---

6. Выдержки выступления Президента Казахстана Н. А. Назарбаева взяты с портала «История Казахстана». URL: http://e-history.kz/ru/publications/view/567.

7. Мансуров Т. Евразийский проект Нурсултана Назарбаева, воплощенный в жизнь. М.: Реал-пресс, 2014; Мансуров Т. Евразийская экономическая интеграция: опыт и перспективы. М.: Русский раритет, 2014.

and signed.[8] These agreements laid the foundation for the transition to the EAEU.

Two major factors enabled the EAEU to be built in a short period. The first factor is choosing the right integration model, calling on member states to help them realize their economic potential and the prospects of regional economic relations, and ensuring the improvement of global competitiveness. The second factor is the high degree of consistency of national interests of its members. The above-mentioned countries have coexisted as a big country for hundreds of years. They have formed close economic relations and in-depth production technology cooperation in the national economic complex that the Soviet Union has implemented for decades. The establishment of the EAEU has formed a common market with a population of 180 million, a total of US$2.2 trillion in the gross national product, and a corresponding increase in the scale of production and categories, which will help to enhance the economic benefits and economic potential of the member states. The medium-term prospects can improve economic efficiency, and the economic growth rate can be increased by 1.5–2 times by restoring cooperative relations and common economic space.

The foreign trade and mutual trade statistics for the first year of implementing the unified customs zone have confirmed the benefits of eliminating tariff barriers. Compared with 2010, the joint trade volume of Russia, Belarus, and Kazakhstan in 2011 increased by more than 1/3 year-on-year. The volume of mutual trade within the CU exploded, especially in the border areas (more than 40%). The most sensitive product categories (agriculture, food) benefited the most due to the elimination of border crossing barriers.

Russia is the foundation of the Eurasian integration process. After Russian leaders gave priority to the joint process, the Eurasian integration process developed very smoothly. Once the Russian leadership ceases to give due attention, the process will stall. Russia's key role in Eurasian integration is determined by historical and objectively indisputable economic and political advantages. Russia occupies 87.6% of the economic potential of the EAEU, 78.4% of the population, and 83.9% of the land. This not only creates Russia's advantages, but also determines the difficulty of establishing the Eurasian economic integration structure.

When Russian leader Putin mentioned the integration of Europe and Asia, he pointed out: "We propose a powerful supranational consortium model, which can become a pole of the multipolarity of the contemporary world and play the role of an effective 'link' between Europe and the Asia-Pacific region." Putin's article "A New Integration Project for Eurasia: A Future which is Being Born Today"[9] also goes beyond the economic significance of pure Eurasian economic integration.

Putin has repeatedly mentioned the prospect of establishing a Eurasian cooperation zone from Lisbon to Vladivostok on the basis of free trade relations and mutually beneficial cooperation. The Russian leader's understanding of Eurasian integration is far more profound than the establishment of the EAEU. Integration requires the

---

8. Мансуров Т. Евразийская экономическая интеграция: опыт и перспективы. М.: Русский раритет, 2014.

9. Путин В. Новый интеграционный проект для Евразии-будущее, которое рождается сегодня // Известия. 2011. 3 октября.

EAEU to connect with China, India, the SCO, and "Greater Europe."[10]

The President of Kazakhstan also pointed out the strategic priority of Eurasian integration in an article in November 2011: "The Eurasian Union should become a link connecting European-Atlantic and Asian development areas. It can become a link between the European Union, East Asia, and Southeast Asia, a bridge to the active economy of South Asia."[11]

The President of Belarus agreed to the above remarks. He pointed out: "I see the Eurasian Union as an integral part of pan-European integration, and our union has the potential to be a key regional player that can build relationships with the world's major economic organizations. For these reasons, the three participating countries have proposed cooperation with the European Union, which will eventually lead to the creation of a common economic space from Lisbon to Vladivostok, and we will provide integration work."[12]

Eurasian thought and Eurasian policy are not only the traditional "geopolitical concept that has an advantage in the region," but also a struggle to establish a common value system. The essence of this system is to safeguard sovereignty and protect national interests in Eurasia. Putin's speech at the Valday Club in 2013 was not accidental. He said: "Here we are discussing more than just an analysis of Russian history, country, and cultural experience. First of all, I refer to a general discussion about the future, the strategy, and the value base of our country's development. How globalization affects our national identity, what kind of world we want to see in the 21st century, and what our country, Russia and our partners, will bring to the world."[13]

With the transition to a new world economic order, the limitations of free globalization have emerged. The independent new world economic centers that run counter to the dominance of the US, namely China, ASEAN countries, India, and the EAEU, have been formed. The above-mentioned countries and regions have unique characteristics of cultures and civilizations, their own distinctive value system, historical and cultural spirit, and unique national and regional characteristics. Obviously, despite the multi-faceted significance of mutual integration and penetration in globalization, no power center will abandon its particularity and ideological and cultural identity. Under the framework of the gradual formation of world economic integration, countries will develop their characteristics and ideological and cultural values and enhance their competitive advantages as much as possible.

Obviously, Russia is faced with a choice: either become a powerful ideological and civilized center (this is the characteristic that Russia has always maintained in the last thousand years) and an economic and social center, or abandon the national identity and stay on the edge of the new world economy. To choose self-sufficiency and self-

---

10. Запесоцкий А. Россия между Востоком и Западом: новый контекст старой дискуссии (к вопросу о современной теории и практике евразийства). СПб: Санкт-Петербургский гуманитарный университет профсоюзов, 2013.

11. Назарбаев Н. Евразийский союз: от идеи к истории будущего. - Известия. – 25 октября 2011 г. (URL: https:/ iz.ru/news/504908)

12. Лукашенко А. О судьбах нашей интеграции // Известия. 2011. 17 октября.

13. Putin's speech at the plenary meeting of the Valday Club, September 21, 2013.

reliance based on understanding their own ideological and cultural mission requires restoring the relatively high weight of Russia and the EAEU in world economic, trade, and technological cooperation. To this end, the Russian economic leap-forward development strategy demonstrated in this book should be implemented.

As stated above, Eurasian integration in a broad sense, including Europe, China, and India, can become a powerful stability maintenance and anti-war factor like the Middle East and the Near East, helping to fight the global economic crisis and create new development opportunities. The most thoughtful and responsible regions and countries of the international community recognize that to avoid another wave of self-harming confrontation and to ensure stable development, it is necessary to adopt global supervision and the fairness of mutually beneficial cooperation and transition to a new model of world outlook based on mutual respect for sovereignty. Russia has a unique historical opportunity to return to its role as a world united center. A completely different balance of power and a new framework for monetary, financial, and trade economic relations will be formed around this center based on the interests of all nations in Europe and Asia.[14]

---

14. Глазьев С. Евразийская интеграция как ключевое направление современной политики России // Журнал «Изборский клуб». - 2014. - №1.

Chapter 19

The Historical Basis of Eurasian Integration

The history of both China and Russia are deeply related to the reproduction of superpowers. Russia changed its form three times during the historical periods that we all know, retaining control of the Eurasian region, and placing most of the region in a common social state system.

After the entire life cycle of the Roman-Byzantine dynasty ended, the Eurasian space united into a new empire, covering almost all the land of Eurasia and entering the Russian chronicles in the form of Mongolian-Tatar rule. Although the official version stated that the Mongol-Tatar rule was ended by Dmitrii Ivanovich in the Battle of Kurikovo, Moscow and the Khanate still maintained complex bilateral relations for a long time. From the perspective of the continuity of Russian history, it should be said that the "major chaos" is the end of the era. During the chaos, the Rurik dynasty ended and temporarily lost its status as a state system. After that, the Russian Empire appeared in the northern part of the region and was destroyed by the February Revolution a century ago. Six months after that, the Soviet Union was born from the October Revolution and swept across the same geographic space. After the Second World War, the Soviet Union became the first of all empires to reincorporate most of its territory by uniting the member countries of the Council for Mutual Economic Assistance, China and Mongolia, established with Soviet assistance, and India and Indochina, freed from Anglo-Saxon occupation and had established a socialist system.

For centuries, the above-mentioned empires allowed most of the common territories and ethnicities to be preserved despite vast differences. The lands and peoples distributed in the modern EAEU remained within the scope of these empires. To further analyze and evaluate the prospect of Eurasian integration, we collectively refer to these empires as empires, considering that the historical continuity would be lost every time the socialist state system was changed. Every time an empire collapsed and was rebuilt, new powers, new ideas, and another social and national system would exist. Facts have proved that there is still "soil" for the next "seedling" among the people.

Has the national consciousness of Eurasian civilization been completely preserved in the "soil," or has it been disintegrated in the raging "virus" of globalization? Has the era of the Eurasian Empire come to an end with the disintegration of the Soviet Union, or is there a new system that awaits us? What role does Russia play in the Eurasian space and the world in different situations? What lessons should we learn from the mistakes of the past? This chapter will give some thoughts on these questions. This chapter only deals with the historical experience of Russia that the author thinks is more familiar, and uses examples of historical experience to study the reproduction mechanism, collapse, and institutional reconstruction mechanism of the imperial state system. The first problem we have encountered is the lack of a unified understanding of the history of our social state system.

Using Destruction of Historical Experience as the Basis of Modern Theory

Although the cognition that social constitutions and regulations lack a dominant ideology[1] is constantly imposed on us, there is no doubt that the dominant ideology still exists and runs counter to our unique history. Completely erasing historical memory will force Assadov's poem "Ivan who forgets his relatives" to accept various myths that favor the power elite. If the power elite believes in a foreign thought that is different from the masses of the people, its essence would be a buyer ideology, which uses its superior position to exploit its own people in order to seek benefits for other countries.

The slander and adaptation of the past that occurred before our eyes aim at detracting from the historical significance of the state system and distorting historical events, degrading the role of the country's state system in the development of civilization, and fabricating stories about Russia and the Soviet Union oppressing various nations. This is nothing new. This systematic act of erasing historical memory and rebuilding common consciousness has occurred three times. The first time began in the "Great Chaos" period. At that time, the pro-Western thoughts formed by power elites that despised the enslaved people and imitated Western powers ended in Yekaterina's golden age. The country's great history was rewritten by the "Norman Theory"[2] created by specially invited German scholars who did not even know Russian. The creators of the "Norman theory" are generally believed to be Bayer, Miller, and Schleitzer. To prove the superiority of Western Europe, the three scholars distorted the basic situation of the Russian state system in the colonization of Prussia and the origin of the Russian state system. "Norman theory" denied the possibility of the Russian people's independent construction of the state system, which caused the Russian intellectuals to feel inferior for centuries. Obviously, the thinking of German scientists in creating historical myths is to eliminate the historical memory of local residents, replace them with the vile attitude of Western agents, and impose historical myths fabricated by foreign writers on public consciousness.

In the century after the Great Chaos, the Russian Khanate Empire's state system was ruthlessly eradicated and represented by the infamous Mongolian-Tatar rule in the writings of German Russian historians to represent. At that time, Moscow was already the largest city in Europe. There were far more immigrants living in the western European German suburbs of Moscow than in the German capital. They plundered state property and destroyed all cultural relics: military medals, works of art, chronicles and documents, and even celebrity cemeteries.[3] They eliminated ancient customs, rituals, etiquette, behaviors, dress habits, palaces, and public places' interior decoration. All traces of the past, even hairstyles and beard styles, were mocked and replaced by

---

1. In point 2 in chapter 13, the Russian Basic Law states that no ideology can be established as the state's or subject to ideology.

2. *Norman's theory* pointed out that historical data tended to be that the Varans and Scandinavians (i.e., Normans) established Kievan Rus, the first Russian country.

3. Носовский Г. В., Фоменко А. Т. Татаро-монгольское иго: Кто кого завоевывал. М.: АСТ: Астрель, 2008; Носовский Г. В., Фоменко А. Т. Русь. Подлинная история Великой Русско-Ордынской Средневековой Империи. М.: АСТ: Астрель, 2009; Носовский Г. В., Фоменко А. Т. Старые карты Великой Русской Империи. М.: АСТ: Астрель, 2009.

European etiquette. Only the Orthodox faith was not successfully eliminated. Despite the confiscation of land and wealth, the Orthodox Church, which was divided and succumbed to bureaucracy, was eventually retained. These immigrants even tried to damage the people's memories of the country's various eras through fairy tales, songs, hymns, and idioms.

Although pro-Western power elites continued to destroy historical memory, the national spirit was sufficient to rejuvenate a great empire. One hundred years after the fall of the Rurik Dynasty, the great empire was revived as the Russian Empire, which inherited the Orthodox faith, national symbols, and parts of its territory, as well as a self-sacrificing people. Although the power elites themselves retained the inherent defect of Western worship, despising ordinary people and talking with "a mixture of French and Nizhny Novgorod,"[4] they still harbored imperial ideology and national interests. If Russia were not a victim of the new turmoil a century ago, there is no doubt that Russia today would become the hegemon that governs the Eurasian region.

After the Bolsheviks seized power, they immediately set out to eliminate the ideology, symbols, architectural monuments, and cultural relics left by the Russian Empire known as the "People's Prison." History was fabricated and rewritten once again. The Russian Empire was slandered, and its destroyers were called heroes. Many historical testimonies were destroyed or kept secretly. The sub-ideological carrier was eliminated, and churches were bombed or used as warehouses. However, unlike the last century, historical memory was preserved, and many written materials aided the revival of the empire.

Since the beginning of the global revolutionary thinking and the country's demise, the Bolsheviks completed their conception by establishing socialism based on a strong state power system. The imperial state system was reborn in another form and with a new ideology, and the country once again became a superpower. The communist power elite won a head-on confrontation with the West in World War II, but they failed to refute their ideological aggression or offset political subversion.

The three catastrophic downfalls of the empire were all caused by external factors and the interference of the new Western "allies" in internal affairs. The large-scale external intervention took place during the chaos. Although adventurers from all over Europe organized a miscellaneous army to invade Moscow, it is generally believed that the mastermind of the intervention was the Poles. This team arranged in advance the "Western partisans" ideological subversion activities in the court of Ivan IV, and then divided the power elite, and almost wiped out all the notorious Tsar cavalry in the elite group.

The fall of the Russian Empire began with the spread of new ideological and political technologies in Western Europe and ended with the intervention of the western Allies. Unlike the Great Chaos, when the dominant role of external powers was hidden behind historical fiction and nonsense, the fall of the Russian Empire this time was chronicled by the two revolutions of 1917. Russia was involved in a pointless world war; killing scores of opponents in the war against Germany; intensifying the war by murdering

---

4. Quoted from Griboyedov's comedy Woe from Wit (1824) used by Chatsky to satirize the Russian nobility's worship of French, often referring to a lack of knowledge of French.

the Austrian crown prince; overthrowing the Masonic conspiracy of the Petersburg elite, spreading fear of starvation in the capital, fomenting mass panic, and eventually launching a military coup that forced the Czar and his brother to abdicate—British agents had a hand in every step of their deadly game.[5]

This of course does not mean that there are no internal reasons. Just as the human body became weaker and more susceptible to the virus after long-term labor, the empire was gradually declining due to wars and internal struggles. It was persecuted by external enemies hidden under the identity of allies. London regarded the overthrow of the Tsar as a victory: British Prime Minister Lloyd George said publicly that "one of the most important goals of the World War has been achieved" after learning of this. Freemasonry members under external control[6] formed an interim government and accomplished the task of defeating the Russian Empire by splitting the army and creating chaos. The survivors of the Russian Supreme Command turned to the Western manipulators for help, who were more than willing to intervene to disintegrate and occupy Russian land.

It is no longer a secret that Western agents fostered alternative political forces, overthrew the interim government, and had a hand in seizing power in the civil war. The civil war was entirely a plan implemented by the Western European powers to capture the Russian Empire. According to their thinking, the Russian empire should have been greatly weakened, thus losing its national status and then collapsing. At that time, the nation would collapse in a fratricidal war and then succumb to foreign rule. However, even if the power holders and most capable elites were eliminated, the goal would not be achieved. The Bolsheviks took control of the national spirit and restored the empire. After losing millions of people and most of its production capacity, Soviet Russia not only survived, but also regained its status as a world power after only 25 years.

But the Soviet Union did not even reach its 75th anniversary. Only those innocent people would think that the Soviet Union collapsed on its own. Reading through the memoirs of the leaders[7] of the US Secret Service or visiting the museums[8] of major US political institutions is enough to prove that the above-mentioned departments are destroying the Soviet state system, fostering separatist forces, maliciously discrediting the Soviet leadership, and embroiling them in the meaningless war in Afghanistan. To overthrow the regime by cultivating influence agents in the Soviet leadership. Just as the British extolled Nicholas II as a great leader, the Americans celebrated Gorbachev as the savior of civilization, to build trust and "stick a knife" in the empire's back. On

---

5. Курлов П. Г. Гибель императорской России: Воспоминания. М.: «Захаров», 2001; Родзянко М. В. Государственная дума и февральская 1917 года революция. Берлин, 1922; Суханов Н. Н. Записки о революции, 1991; Шацилло В. Первая мировая война 1914 1918. Факты и документы. М.: Олма-Пресс, 2003.

6. См.: Катков Г. Россия в 1917 г. Февральская революция; Аронсон Г. Россия накануне революции: Исторические этюды. Монархисты, либералы, масоны, социалисты.

7. Швейцер П. Победа. Роль тайной стратегии администрации США в распаде Советского Союза и социалистического лагеря. Минск, 1995.

8. The non-profit organization International Republican Institute (IRI) and the US International Institute for Democracy (NDI) were established by the US government in 1983 to promote and support the democratic process in the world, especially in developing countries. The above-mentioned institutions implement plans in the political and democratic fields and provide donations.

both occasions, it was a case of using agents of influence previously cultivated at the very top of the local elite to test the "knife."

In addition to the above-mentioned external coincidences, we can see a general mechanism for destroying and restoring empires that once ruled Eurasia in different periods. Fact data can trace the above-mentioned mechanism in detail in the life cycle of the birth and disintegration of the Soviet Union and its role in the fall of the Russian Empire. There are still many "blank spots" regarding the development of the latter and the destroyed Russian-Khanate Empire before it. However, the general mechanism involved in the following can be observed in the Russian Empire.

The Regularity of System Reconstruction in Eurasian Countries

The reconstruction of all Eurasian countries will follow the following systems. These cycles can establish social connections and maintain stability.

1. An ideological system that unifies the people based on a consistent understanding of the meaning and correctness of social and national systems. For example, the Soviet empire had a communist ideology. The ideology of the Russian Empire was embodied in a concise formula: authoritarian system, Orthodox Church, and nationality. The ideology of the Russian-khanate empire was also religion, although the beliefs of the power elite of the empire were not the same. The Christian ideology formed during the Byzantine Empire in Europe was preserved, and there was no spiritual unity in Asia. In addition, Islam, Buddhism, Hinduism, Shamanism, and other doctrines were dominant in different periods and regions. When we put aside the disputes over the origin of religions above, we will find that all ideologies that existed in the imperial social consciousness in history required social justice in conformity with the social state system. Breaking this condition will destroy ideology and chaotic social consciousness.

2. The political system that unifies the people through the state power system. Whether it was the Soviet Union or the Russian Empire, the political system was established in a hierarchical manner, led by the Central Committee of the CPSU and the Tsar, respectively. A similar hierarchical system existed in the Russian-Khanate Empire, which stipulated that the supreme ruler transferred power through edicts. This reproduction system is based on the corresponding ideology that guarantees its legalization of social ideology. Destroying the ideological system will lead to illegal state power in the public consciousness and shake the reproduction system.

3. A normative system that unifies the people based on rules of conduct and sanctions against rule-breakers. The normative system is made up of a political system that approves laws, orders, resolutions, and other enforcement standards. Shaking the political system will weaken the legitimacy of the normative system and create conditions for the large-scale destruction of laws and violations of power institutions. Therefore, overthrowing the Tsar led to the rapid destruction of social organizations and the situation of illegality

and civil war. Similar examples include: the Soviet Communist Party's self-destructive behavior triggered the rapid illegalization of the Soviet legal system, the growth of national separatism, the disintegration of the country, and the emergence of criminal behavior in society. In the first historical cycle, before the fall of the empire, there were wars among several people who tried to gain supreme power. With the economic development of the empire's components, the war became a struggle for the independence of primitive state entities. The internal division of the ruling elite was a direct sign of the empire, which led to the suppression of the municipality and chaos during the Great Chaos period.

4. The economic system unifies the economic activities of the people. This system is composed of laws and regulations governing different types of economic activities. The illegalization of the regulatory system will destroy complex economic activities and degrade the economy. The direct economic consequences of disasters in ideological, political, and normative systems and the collapse of the unified state system are economic depression, the flight or disappearance of most of the accumulated capital, the destruction of productivity, and the decline in people's welfare. It will take a long time to restore the above phenomenon under the new economic reproduction system formulated by other laws, politics, and ideological systems.

5. Family-clan system to ensure population reproduction. The family system and blood relationship are deeply affected by the above reproduction system. Still, they retain the autonomy to protect historical memory from destruction and the ability to transform social consciousness into another social structure regeneration and transformation. The collapse of the family-clan system is often accompanied by a surge in uncontrollable social abilities, the latter being characterized by extreme intrusion and loss of the inertial thinking of people's lives and connections. This phenomenon will lead to social fragmentation and the barbarization of most groups in society, the decomposition of the family-clan system into self-organizing hostile groups, encouraging violent behavior, and the appearance of outdated social structures. To prevent this chaos, anti-social behaviors should be violently suppressed through the powerful organization of the new imperial reproduction system mentioned above.

These three disasters that led to the collapse of the empire were caused by the continuous destruction of reproduction activities. The initial collapse of the ideological system will undermine the stability of the political system. Once the political system is weakened, it will trigger the illegality of the normative system and the subsequent degradation of the economic system. Under similar conditions, the family-clan system cannot retain people who have lost the norms of daily life, and most people will radicalize and participate in the revolution. The common manifestation of these disasters is that the majority of the population will get out of control at an alarming rate. With the collapse of the five reproduction systems of the social state system, the group will return to the most primitive form of anti-social behavior, while the remainder of the social-state system is also destroyed. The essence of the subsequent social self-organization is the violent image carrier of the new social organization, another ideology that determines the framework of other reproduction systems.

The powerful external forces in the above three stages lead to the new social state system. These forces will first destroy ideology, and then destroy the political reproduction system. In addition, the main target of influence is the power elite, and a class of influence agents who advocate for the superiority of the new ideology has formed in this group.

Because the ruling elite did not firmly break away from the political reproduction system, it was gradually disintegrated by the "new ideology." Then its ideological reproduction system was eroded, and the political reproduction system was also destroyed. Immediately afterwards, the regulatory system was devastated, and the economic system also declined. The family-clan system is relatively stable, can guarantee future population reproduction, and is gradually included in the new social rights relationship system and the corresponding reproduction system.

Before the gradual decline of the autocratic system, most of the elite's faith was lost with the long process of vilifying the Orthodox Church. They believed that the social-state system at that time was stale, inefficient, and disgraceful for the country. The influence agents cultivated by external forces would be guided by Western values, models, and policies to overthrow the autocratic system. Then the reproduction system of all other social-state systems would soon die out. The elimination of the CPSU and the subsequent fall of the Soviet Union went through a similar process.

It should be noted that after the fall of the Byzantine Empire, Western European societies experienced substantial changes in production structure. The earlier ideological and political reproduction systems, bound together in a strict theocratic state hierarchy and led by emperors with both secular and spiritual powers, collapsed and could only be partially rebuilt in fragile forms. Under the above conditions, the family-clan reproduction system was of greater significance, reflected in the feudal system of primitive European countries. The small size of the original European states and the insufficiently dense distribution of potential elites prevented the centralization of power that was necessary to revive the imperial reproduction structure. So was the separation of ideology, which always separated the Papacy in the Vatican from the system of political production banned in Western Europe. Although everyone tried their best to rebuild the empire, no one could rebuild it to its former appearance. The Russian emperor accomplished this achievement within a short time after defeating Napoleon's Western European Union Army. However, the erosion caused by the national ideology and political system in Western European Society was too deep, and the Eastern Orthodox Pope could not replace the influence of the Roman Pope. The morphological system was still open. The Holy Alliance built by Alexander I was fragile because its reproduction activities were too costly.

The erosion of ideology and the restriction of the political reproduction system in Western Europe provided the possibility for the reproduction of the relatively autonomous family-clan system and economic system. The intertwined development of the two contributed to the accumulation of capital. The economic system's pursuit of self-improvement intensified the contradiction between trade-loan sharking and the aristocratic class that ensured the reproduction of the economic and political system. The above contradictions were solved by the formation of a powerful economy organization. The organization's form evolved over time, from the Crusades to state monopolies. It has been used to expand abroad and eliminate internal conflicts of interest by looting other countries for excess profits. This could also be achieved by colonizing underdeveloped societies outside of Eurasia, demolishing the reproduction systems of Eurasian countries, destroying their social-state systems, and disrupting their economic space. These three Great Chaos were caused in this way, inducing the catastrophic collapse of the empire and forming the Eurasian space in a famous historical period.

Since the first major chaos, the political and economic organization of Western European society had undergone actual changes. Capital reproduction, which we call the "world economic order,"[9] went through a transformation from an organizational system under the development of productive forces.[10] Holland used a trade monopoly world economic order to protect the concentration of capital, which was enough to organize the world trading system. This economic order was replaced by the colonial world economic order dominated by Britain. The British East India Company and the Dutch West India Company were established under the aegis of the British royal family, which made it possible to mine and further concentrate capital on various continents. The development of the Industrial Revolution ushered in an era of modern economic growth based on machine production. The direct economic order dominated by the United Kingdom was replaced by the imperial (or monopolistic) world economic order. In this order, the Federal Reserve finally occupied the dominant position by issuing world currency and funding American multinational corporations.

It should be noted here that there are differences in the systems of the three successive world economic orders, which have ensured the reproduction of capital in European countries in different historical periods. The above-mentioned economic and political systems did not change the power-economic institutions created by the power elite. These institutions were always oriented towards external expansion, and their purpose was to rely on non-equivalent economic exchanges with the subject countries to obtain high profits. The limits of this expansion were determined by the national boundaries of the Eurasian Empire. Western capital always tried to expand its national boundaries by destroying its reproduction system. Although the form of this destruction technology was different, its logic and consequences remained unchanged.

The first is the collapse of the ideological system, which is the core component of the reproduction of the imperial society-state system. Because ideology is based on the primacy of social justice and unity, to destroy it, values that oppose individual freedom and individual rights should be used. The opposing values of individual freedom and power artificially oppose social and collective values. The state is discredited, and the principles based on the social system are ridiculed as corrupt and absurd.

---

9. Глазьев С. Мирохозяйственные уклады в глобальном экономическом развитии // Экономика и математические методы. 2016. Т. 52, № 2; Глазьев С. Прикладные результаты теории мирохозяйственных укладов // Экономика и математические методы. 2016. Т. 52, №3; the author of this material has registered *Hypothesis about the periodic changes in the world economic order* (the author registered for Certificate No. 41-N in 2016 under the guidance of the Russian Academy of Natural Science.)

10. Arrighi G., *The Long Twentieth Century: Money, Power and the Origins of Our Times* (London: Verso Press, 1994).

Thus, enlightenment thought was used to dismantle the ideology of the Russian Empire, based on the main principles identified in Uvalov's famous formula: Orthodoxy, autocracy, and nationality.[11] These elements opposed the scientific worldview, democratic rights, and individual freedoms. They led to a split in the ruling elite, much of which rejected traditional values, essentially creating an environment hostile to the empire. Subsequently, further cultivating a network of external influence agents in this environment became a political technique.

The same was used to destroy the Soviet Empire. Undermining its communist ideology was achieved by pushing democratic power and personal freedom to the power elite. It is based on the consumption ideology that can embody the material and technological advantages of capitalism. They smeared socialist countries that emphasized their own material and technological advantages under the principle of "from each according to his ability, to each according to his work."[12] Some power elites were initially bewitched by these ideas, first undermining the ideological system and then beginning to eliminate the political system. The CPSU built by the above-mentioned system destroyed itself, and the influence agents who were subsequently manipulated by the outside used the same political and technological means to further destroy the empire.

The Causes of the Periodic Crisis in the Institutions of Eurasian Countries

If the power elite had historical memory, when the reproduction cycle of the social-state system was completed, disasters like 1917 and 1991 would have been prevented. Once there are internal divisions involving all systems, external forces will also play a role in promoting and destroying. The complacency, dogmatism, and ignorance of the power elite made it possible for the enemy's external influence agents to erode and shake the reproductive system of the empire's social-state system.

We try to prove the power elite's main shortcomings, and these shortcomings have led to the destruction of ideology and political systems.

First, dogmatism prevents ideology from adapting to changes promptly. As a result, ideology loses not only its ability to defend the social-state system but also its ability to explain changes. Therefore, the Soviet propaganda department continued to assert that capitalism would inevitably die out quickly due to class antagonism, contrary to the remarkable achievements of all advanced capitalist countries with a higher

---

11. "Orthodox Church, Authoritarian system, Nationality," the Minister of National Education Sergey Uvalov successfully introduced the power and social relations in the empire into the ideology with the help of three words. The construction of ideology is the first attempt (the monk Philofis built Moscow into the Third Rome in the 16th century) to promote the concept of national regulations and national goals systematically and widely. According to the concept, the trinity of the empire should maintain a long-term connection with the empire and strengthen its meaning.

12. On June 11, 1936, the Soviet Central Election Commission agreed to the proposal for a new Soviet constitution. The first section (Social Stability) pointed out that the Soviet Union has the principle of socialism, that is, "everyone does his best and distributes according to work" ((от каждого по его способности, каждому— по его труду). But the terms of the Soviet Constitution of 1936 changed insignificantly in 1977 (От каждого— по способностям, каждому— по труду).

standard of living than the Soviet socialist countries. The power elite of the Russian Empire completely lacked an understanding of the importance of ideology and only resorted to the same old "God Blessing the Tsar." As a result, there was a serious split in ideology. From the perspective of citizens, the collapse of the power system did not show any serious resistance.

Second, the arrogance of the power elite who planned to remain in power forever. The imperial reproduction ideological system was destroyed, and even the power elite's opposition did not expect its power-economic status would inevitably be lost due to its destruction. Almost all people who overthrew the ideological system's foundation could not retain their power and wealth status after the regime's collapse. Many of them even lost their families, freedom, and lives.

Third, the naivety and irresponsibility of the national leadership. On the one hand, the leadership underestimated the level of treacherous Western "allies," and on the other hand, they handed power over to the conspirators too easily. It is already obvious today that the Allied Powers during World War I were a "trap" for Nicholas II, and the friendship with Western leaders was a trap for Gorbachev. Both former leaders could continue to govern, but they did not use political oppression to restrain themselves. Obviously, they underestimated the consequences of their compromise.

The above three shortcomings all have subjective characteristics, although there is also an objective basis for the lack of competition in the reproduction of long-term power relations. The most common consequences are corruption, favoritism, incompetence, complacency, and irresponsibility. The bad selection mechanism of cadres based on personal contributions and material benefits-this is a conventional feature of hierarchical bureaucracy, which is well known in modern management theories.

The following measures have also been determined to counteract: stipulating the time and age limits for the replacement of official positions; rotation of positions; regular assessment; principled struggle combating against corruption and favoritism; officials objectively assessing the performance of their leading institutions; the executive power agency evaluated by the results of the social and economic policies it has implemented; and the cadre recruitment and examination system.

The quality of the power elite is the main weakness of the state system of the imperial society. To avoid reproduction decline, the power elite should at least conduct self-criticism. Let us take a closer look at the errors that were typical of the power elite in the Soviet era that led to the collapse of the social-state system ideology and subsequent political reproduction cycle. The main failure in the ideological field was the unrealistic task of building communism[13] quickly, which caused the people to have too high hopes for this task and disappointment in failing to achieve their hopes. It was

---

13. In 1961, the 22nd meeting of the CPSU adopted the (third) CPSU program. Among them, it is stipulated within 20 years, by 1980, the Soviet Union should build the material and technological foundation of communism, guaranteeing the abundant material and cultural wealth of Soviet citizens. Within 10 years, by 1970, the Soviet Union should rank first in the world in terms of per capita output. The party program established a unified form of public ownership, improved the "public ownership" of collective farms, and finally combined collective farm ownership with ownership by the whole people. The task of overcoming the differences between urban and rural areas, as well as the differences between mental and physical labor, was also on the agenda. The above-mentioned measures were aimed at creating a classless society in Soviet society.

also wrong to ignore many facts in the theory of scientific communism, which damaged the trust in the theory and cast doubts on its scientificity. Denying all mistakes was another point of vigilance. One was that it would cause irresponsibility of the power class, and the other was that it would make the power elite bear all the responsibility for all the mistakes committed before and even the crimes that caused millions of innocent victims. The latter included the exploitation of rich peasants and their forced relocation to uninhabitable places as a result of a false ideological narrative about the intensification of the class struggle after the establishment of the Soviet regime; the forced Ukrainianization, imposition of the Ukrainian language and artificially created state power on lands that had been inhabited by Russians since ancient times in order to suppress the imagined threat of Great Russian chauvinism; the total dismantling of churches, the killing and suppression of clergy for the purpose of social consciousness The total dismantling of churches, the killing, and repression of clergy for the purpose of atheistic "cleansing" of the social consciousness. These crimes of ideological collapse were not understood and overcome in the social consciousness, which allowed national separatists to use them for anti-Soviet propaganda.

There are more mistakes in the political realm. The national leadership verbally claimed that it would be loyal to ideological principles, but then took actions that were inconsistent with the words. This caused panic among the power elite, discredited power at the level of social consciousness, and cast doubt on its authority and ability to govern. The self-destructive behavior of the CPSU was the top mistake that undermined the legitimacy of all state systems, caused the country to lose control, and aggravated the level of chaos. The mistake lies in disclosing the information space by pretending to be transparent to discredit the country. Another fault was the adoption of regional economic accounting, which led to the intensification of national separatism. This error exacerbated the collapse of the older system, which laid the foundation for the regional system of the Union of Republics established by human factors. The above-mentioned problems were not corrected timely, and it was doomed to the demise of the primitive state system with a unique primitive national identity established by the Soviet power class. In the early stage of the empire's development, the similar primitive state system soon took on the characteristics of a real country. In the early stage, it was a single nation split into several new nations based on opposing the unified motherland.

Ideological errors extended to the field of foreign affairs. First, this is related to the funding of the Communist Party and the rebel movements in Western countries and their controlled areas, which led to frequent political tensions and arms races. The latter took up a lot of resources and harmed the welfare of the Soviet people. The Soviet army's invasion of Afghanistan culminated in this doomed policy. After the policy was withdrawn, another similar error occurred: the failure to control the internal affairs of the member states of the Warsaw Pact. As a result, this initiative was intercepted by geopolitical opponents. In the absence of resistance, the espionage organizations of NATO member states quickly suppressed the activities of communist and socialist parties in Eastern Europe. The collapse of the state-political system of the central Eastern European countries caused a chain reaction of the collapse of the world socialist system.

The same serious mistakes occurred in the economic field. According to the ideological principle that private property cannot be used as the basis for the revival of capitalism, nationalization of the economy was fully implemented, which resulted in a significant decline in economic activity, a drop in the quality of daily necessities, insufficient development of the service industry, and low innovation enthusiasm. On the one hand, the opposite basic principle of ideology, that is, compared with market competition, the dominant planned economy led to the underestimation of the degree of complexity of production technology linkages and the growing variety of goods; on the other hand, the options of the planning department are limited. In the end, it could only routinely expand the reproduction of the mastered technology, resulting in a technological multilayer of the national economy that linked together the limited resources of obsolete productive activities.[14]

Ideological principles dominated Soviet leadership until the collapse of the Soviet Union. The attempt to develop market relations without private property participation by expanding the autonomy of state-owned enterprises and improving the electoral system for state-owned enterprise leaders, cooperatives, and youth S&T creation centers did not take into account the main issues (the driving force of the market economy is competition) and exaggerated the secondary issues (strictly restrict the free disposal of private property and the income derived from the exploitation of hired workers). Not only did the leadership of the CPSU fail to perfect the ideology based on reality, but it also tried to use reforms to adapt to the principles of unrealism, shake the existing reproduction system of the national economic system, and exacerbate the growing imbalances.

It should be noted that the systematic mistake of the Soviet leadership is that despite the serious deviation of ideology from the facts, it was still unwilling to improve it, which eventually led to the country's management system being kidnapped by unrealistic dogma, and finally became increasingly inefficient, resulting in socioeconomic stagnation and increased chaos.

Regrettably, the Russian reforms have inherited the dogmatism of thinking, merely replacing the scientific communism hypothesis with an antithetical one contrary to reality. Market self-organization has replaced the central position of the plan; universal privatization replaced full nationalization; the memorandum of the IMF has replaced the classic works of Marx-Leninism. The controllability of the economy has been completely lost, and its reproduction is subject to external factors' influence. Contrary to the current disastrous economic policies, the private economic system has lasted for thirty years. The leadership of the country is swayed by market fundamentalism and does not care about the results of its failures, international experiences, trade union requirements, and the recommendations of the country's scientific and industrial associations.

We have to admit that for us, history has taught us nothing. It is very necessary to find an explanation for the mysterious phenomenon of the ineducability of the power elite.

The first reason is that all the power elites were replaced with the fall of each empire. Those in power in these three disasters were the overthrower of the former ideology,

14. Глазьев С. Теория долгосрочного технико-экономического развития. М.: ВлаДар, 1993.

which was characterized by dogmatism. These three disasters have opposing ideas, which are regarded as beliefs by the dogmatic public consciousness. The previous dogma was replaced by the opposite one and was promoted in the form of coercion. Since these dogmas were established by the empire's external hostile power centers, their purpose was to overthrow the empire, with no expectation that these dogmas would be successfully implemented. For example, it is well known that no Bolshevik Western patron would believe that these dogmas would be successfully implemented. Similarly, the Western patrons of the "advocates of Soviet reform" simply condoned the country's destruction.

The second reason is premised on the revolutionaries' hatred towards their own country and nation. The Bolsheviks saw the fire of the world revolution in Russia, and the Russian people were treated as "cannon fodder" in the war against the petty bourgeoisie in Europe. Russian market reformers were concerned about the liquidation of the Soviet Union, not caring about the local people, most of whom were "not suitable for the market."[15] The task they were faced with was to liquidate the empire by overthrowing the state system, even breaking up the country at the expense of the people. As for the criteria of successful socioeconomic development, they did not even consider them.

The third reason, which seems to be the most mysterious, is the empire's amazing regenerating ability. The empire was reborn with a new social-state system in a new reproduction system. These systems were built on the family-clan production system preserved during the transition period, and provided social support for the new elites in power. So far, the latter has not been able to resist the temptation of the imperial power class. After the first and second disasters, the power elite who overthrew the previous empire at that time disregarded the original plan and established a new empire. Therefore, the Bolsheviks destroyed the Russian Empire, overthrew the regime, established socialism, and finally built the world socialist system. After the fall of the Rurik dynasty, Romanovs ruled the Moscow Empire. It clashed with European allies and established the Russian Empire. Now, thanks to Putin's policy of rebuilding the national system, the market fundamentalist system is transforming into a great new country.

Facts have proved that regardless of the actors' wishes, as the ideology, politics, and economic system undergo radical changes, the empire will be reborn. And the historical memory will be formatted every time. The new ruling elite will rewrite history according to their own ideology and deny the continuity of everything. Then the empire will be once again interfered with by external forces holding another ideology. Then the ideology and political structure will be split and collapsed, and the empire will be destroyed. As a result, individual rights replace social justice, individual freedom replaces unity, and the division of society into hostile groups of class, ethnic, or religious nature replaces national unity.

Of course, this process is constantly moving forward. Philosophers have pointed

---

15. "What are you worrying about those people? Thirty million people have died, not even registered in the market. If you don't consider this issue, new worries will breed." According to Breva, former chairman of the State Property Management Committee Nov's statement, this was mentioned by his predecessor Chubais in a private conversation with him.

out repeatedly that history is moving forward in a spiral. With the development of productivity, the social management system and the social state system have become increasingly complex. This spiral development is discussed in the theory of technological changes and the world economic order.[16] The life cycle of technology and the world economic order determines the pace of modern social and economic development. This is particularly obvious in Western countries but has been erased in empires. In the Western world, crises and wars trigger technological changes and the world economic order. In the empire, only when resources are scarce can the two influence each other. The reproduction system under the imperial social state system regards the technological and institutional changes in the external environment as challenges. Therefore, assimilation must be accepted to maintain stability. However, when the imbalance situation exceeds the assimilation capacity in the socioeconomic environment, the change has a revolutionary character. At the same time, the entire social state system changes and collapses.

In this complex process, just as the regime of the ruling elite of the empire cannot be continued, the memory of history will be wiped out. Perhaps, when a new historical period arrives, everything will be completely new.

Eurasian Integrated Reproduction System Interaction

The history of human civilization as we know it begins with a social state system that can accumulate knowledge and experience. Before this, tribal society had a flexible structure, which was divided according to status, led by an economic department dominated by a big figure or a powerful department dominated by a tribal chief. Therefore, the reproduction of the social structure is guaranteed by the religious department led by the shaman, and the shaman sanctifies all important changes, including personnel changes.

It should be emphasized that individual and social principles were combined in the reproduction of primitive society. If under stable reproduction conditions, the old rules are followed to create and accumulate material wealth, and the material wealth between families is divided according to certain clan rules. Then under unstable conditions, the existing rules will be integrated into the universally unified rules. Levi-Strauss called it "Communitas,"[17] replacing the existing social rules to build a new public order, corresponding to the new reproduction conditions. Interestingly, whenever the social structure collapses during the revolution, this mechanism of spontaneous communism emerges.

The social structure of primitive society is flexible, so retaining new information and accumulated experience is difficult. Only when tribal organizations have successfully developed to a huge scale, and can govern surrounding tribes and achieve

16. Глазьев С. Мирохозяйственные уклады в глобальном экономическом развитии // Экономика и математические методы. 2016. Т. 52, № 2; Глазьев С. Прикладные результаты теории мирохозяйственных укладов // Экономика и математические методы. 2016. Т. 52, №3; Глазьев С. Последняя мировая война. США начинают и проигрывают. М.: Книжный мир, 2016; Глазьев С. Экономика будущего. Есть ли у России шанс? М.: Книжный мир, 2016.

17. Леви-Стросс К. Структурная антропология. М.: Изд-во ЭКСМО-Пресс, 2001.

stable reproduction conditions, will the social structure be sufficiently stable for the emergence of the first batch of countries. They were established based on the above-mentioned reproduction system, where they have accumulated information, practical experience, and material wealth, which are also retained in the hierarchical structure of religion, military, and economic power. These hierarchies are led by a sacred ruler, who also serves as the highest priest, leader of the primitive country, and economic leader.

With the formation of a stable hierarchical structure, the expanded reproduction of primitive countries is expansive. With the ability to accumulate information, experience, and material wealth, they became the first group of countries ahead of other weakly organized tribes, governing all surrounding social spaces until it was difficult to expand their geographic boundaries.

The first empires had a totalitarian theocracy system in which all reproduction systems were centered on divine rulers. The ruler created conditions for a stable ideology and political system reproduction system. Family farm activities created most of the material wealth, and the economic system regulated family farm activities and redistributed this wealth according to the entire society's needs. The reproduction of the family system was produced under a hierarchical structure, which could guarantee the continuity of generations and divide the profession of personnel according to the type of activity. This resulted in a hierarchical society typical of the early empire.

The reproduction system maintains the integrity and stability of the social state system in terms of ideology and politics and adjusts the distribution of material wealth. This wealth is created by family farms through the economic system, and family farms have relative autonomy, which brings certain difficulties to the control of the family reproduction system, because private property is accumulated under the framework of the system. The use of private property is restricted by other reproduction systems, to suppress social contradictions arising from increasing social imbalances.

Then the ideological and political reproduction system was destroyed, forcing the family system to lose control, which created opportunities for the accumulation of private property and the birth of capitalist relations of production. The development of capitalist production relations affects the economic system, making its reproduction subject to the benefits of capital accumulation, leading to the political system's corruption and further erosion of the ideological system. With the erosion of ideology, the reproduction system of the social state system will also be destroyed, eventually leading to the empire's collapse. Since then, the reproduction of the social state system has been subject to the benefits of capital accumulation to exert maximum influence on family organizations.

The ruling elite controls the reproduction system of the empire, and they will also die with the empire's collapse. The difference is that family organizations can increase their capital and strength indefinitely. The expanded reproduction of family organizations is limited only by countries that compete and retain the monarchy. Faced with countries that retain the monarchy, capitalist family organizations strive to eliminate them and place them under their own influence to expand their living space. We have seen this phenomenon during the demise of the Soviet Union, the Russian Empire, the Golden Horde, the Byzantine Empire, and the Ottoman Empire.

With the destruction of the ideology and political system, the family capitalist system formed during the imperial period created its own living space based on the interests of individual expansion of reproduction. The family capitalist system turns the economic system into its own jurisdiction, controls the political system, and eliminates the ideological system generated by society and the state in reproduction. The cause of this imbalance is the inertia of social relations, which are determined by ideological hypotheses, cultural stereotypes, production relations, and capital reproduction mechanisms. They construct a stable reproduction process, and the established stable institutions will incorporate them into a unified world economic order.

The world economic order will change according to its own rhythm outside the ideology and political system of the empire, and will also induce corresponding changes in its own structure. Since ideology and political reproduction systems are rarely hindered by economic changes, changes in the economy themselves will affect each other. The social and economic structure of the empire will acquire multilayered characteristics, leading to increasing economic imbalances and causing the old and the new world economic and technological order to reappear in the economy simultaneously.

The modernization of the empire requires the efforts of generations. Only with the development of productive forces can the important part of the reproduction of the social state system be changed. However, the development of productive forces will be restricted by existing systems, inherent cultural concepts, ideological hypotheses, and production relations. This change is always revolutionary and violent, because in the process all links of the social reproduction system will be destroyed, and the remaining relevant social team members will also be suppressed. In addition, the ideology, politics, and economic system of the old social state system will be destroyed, and new systems will appear as the carrier changes. At the same time, the family system will also be affected by these changes to a lesser extent. Therefore, when the world economic order changes, the process of capital accumulation in family organizations will continue, and its influence will increase daily.

The family system was copied during the Empire era to adapt to its social and national structure. Therefore, the family system would retain relative autonomy to prevent it from being affected by the ideology and political system. As the ideology and political system split, the family system would exert a reactionary force on the social political system's ideology and structure. Ideology and political structure would eliminate the empire's control and gain freedom. At the same time, it would exist in the form of changes in the world economic order under the framework of the family system, and would be subject to the laws of capital reproduction. In countries free from imperial control, there would be a continuity of the world economic and technological order and its own rhythm of social and economic development.

Every new world economic order can provide opportunities to increase capital accumulation, and its living space has been continuously expanded due to market competition promoting technological progress. The empire would have to resist the corrupting influence of capitalist relations and master the new technologies necessary to develop the economy and improve the well-being of its residents. The hierarchical structure guaranteed the operation of the ideological, political, and normative reproduction system. Still, because the hierarchical structure inhibited competition, the empire would not reach the level of innovative activities unique to the capitalist economy. The empire kept catching up with the capitalist countries, introducing or imitating new technologies.

According to available information, although Russia's empires and the Soviet Union ruled Eurasia at various times, they did not lead in terms of technological and economic development, but this does not imply that they didn't achieve comparable results. On the contrary, they achieved a slew of technical and economic successes. It is only that for a long time, the public perception of these achievements lagged far behind the level of the leading Western countries, giving the ruling elite the illusion of backward development of the country. The empire frequently attempted to catch up with the West, but did not achieve that goal (except for military and prestigious projects) because of the relative lag in competition.[18]

In fact, the Empire imitated the achievements of Western technology and achieved different results. This involved the methods of organizing production, the reproduction of capital and the system of economic regulation. The results achieved in the West also brought about corresponding changes in the empire, usually weakening it. Thus, the empire tried to prevent the technological and economic expansion of the West, while at the same time trying to benefit from it for its own sake.

The West achieved socioeconomic and technological progress, whereas the empire expressed concerns about retaining the country's expanded reproduction. The economic capacity of scientific research, experimental design, and production scale couldn't prevent domestic enterprises from imitating imported technology at a lower cost and smoothly gaining a competitive advantage in the global market. Moreover, the empire didn't intend to seize the market, but rather to solve various tasks to meet the needs of the domestic market.

An empire with abundant resources could prevent the expansion of private capital, using national interests to restrict private capital at home and resist wanton external aggression. The most dangerous behavior for mankind was the world hegemony that Napoleon, Hitler, and Truman tried to build, and the empire prevented this attempt. In fact, the empire was indeed a force (Katehon) to contain the world's evil. At present, the essential role of the empire in metaphysics has been erased by Russia. Not only is it no longer an empire, but it is also unwilling to become an empire. According to the Constitution, "No ideology can be established as a national ideology or a compulsory ideology." (Article 2, Article 13) For Russia, this clause is similar to the prohibition on possessing armed forces in the Japanese Constitution.[19]

Two questions now arise: How will humanity develop if there is no power to restrict Western capital? Can the empire return to Eurasian space and play a role in modern

---

18. Эволюция технико-экономических систем: возможности и границы централизованного регулирования / под ред. Д. Львова, С. Глазьева, Г. Фетисова. М.: Наука, 1992.

19. In 1947, two years after the end of the Second World War, Japan passed its constitution. The constitution prohibits the possession of troops and the use of armed forces as a means of resolving international disputes. This provision has not been cancelled yet till now. Over the years, Japan has become an economic power, but due to its lack of military and political influence, it has been dubbed the nickname "economic giant, political dwarf."

conditions?

As we all know, after the disintegration of the Soviet Union, the US government set a major goal for the post-Soviet space, that is, "Our first objective is to prevent the re-emergence of a new rival, either on the territory of the former Soviet Union or elsewhere, that poses a threat to us."[20] Therefore, when the heads of Russia, Belarus, and Kazakhstan proposed the establishment of the "Eurasian Economic Community" and later the "CU" and "EAEU" initiatives, the US government was over sensitive and radical in this regard. Although the EAEU was only a unified market established in accordance with WTO rules and lacked a unified supranational political institution, the American political elite immediately saw the shadow of the Soviet Union's revival.[21]

At the same time, China poses a real threat to the US. Chinese leaders uphold the socialist ideology with Chinese characteristics, creatively learn from the experience of Soviet socialist construction and analyze their own shortcomings. Then, based on the combination of planned economy and market regulation, they established an effective social and economic development management system under the control of socialist countries. The Chinese Communists retained the ideology and political system of Soviet reproduction, changed the economic system based on the market mechanism, released the social energy of the family system, and used it to solve the task of developing the economy and improving the welfare of the people.

The social state system that combines the imperial reproduction system with capitalism is a unique system of the Russian Empire. However, during the historical period when the empire and the capitalist world coexisted, the new world economic order first appeared inside the empire and expanded to the peripheral capitalist countries. Perhaps this is the prerequisite for the replacement of a longer civilization cycle. Some experts believe that the era of capitalism is coming to an end,[22] and another believes that it is transitioning to a post-industrial society.[23] Some experts believe that it will transition to an intellectual civilization that has a paradigm of sustainable development and world harmony.[24]

An integrated world economic order is being established in China and neighboring Asian countries, which stipulates that capitalist activities are completely restricted to a framework acceptable to society. And different from the practice of the Russian Empire, the practice of the above-mentioned countries is completely based on rational ideology. It is rigidly stipulated in the political and economic reproduction system in the form of law. The above-mentioned reproduction system selects the criteria for various regulations not to conform to ideology, but to enhance the economic benefits of commodities in terms of output and quality, thereby improving residents' living

---

20. Report prepared by the US Department of Defense, Fiscal Year 1994–1998, National Defense Directive.

21. Former US Secretary of State Hillary Clinton stated publicly in a Press conference on December 6, 2012, "There are efforts being made to re-sovietize the region. It will be called the Customs Union, the Eurasian Union and so on. But we will not be deceived. We know what their goals are, and we're trying to figure out effective ways to slow or impede their achievement."

22. Яковец Ю. Политическая экономия цивилизаций. М.: Экономика, 2016.

23. Тоффлер Э. Третья волна. М.: АСТ, 2010.

24. Акаев А. А. Экономика xxi века - это нооэкономика, экономика справедливости и разума // Проблемы теории и практики управления. 2014. № 11. С. 8 - 12.

standards and quality. The economic growth achieved under the framework of this world economic order can ensure its rapid development and expansion into larger world space.

The world economic order, led by the US, had previously monopolized the financial sector, and its reproduction had become imbalanced internally. This problem could not be solved under the framework of its institutional system.[25] Due to the index-based issuance of credit currency and the existence of unsecured debt, capital accumulation appears to be an illusion. Due to the pooling of capital and commercial activities in the financial pyramid, the expansion of reproduction in the real economy has been terminated. In this core country of the world economic order, the residents' living standards have declined, and social imbalances have increased.

Modern Eurasian Integration System

The further development of productivity requires transitioning to a new integrated world economic order. The new world economic order will be formed in China, India, and Indochina. Its foundation combines planned economy and market regulation, infrastructure, and private enterprise ownership by the whole people. Under the coordination of the state, the interests of the whole people are required to be higher than that of enterprises. Compared with the current financial monopoly-type world economic order, the new world economic order shows a major advantage in this regard.

The transition to the new world economic order for the first time in history has nothing to do with the expansion of capitalist development capacity, but with the restriction of its development capacity. As mathematicians said, this major difference means that the derivative function of socioeconomic development is also changing simultaneously. The capitalist world ceases to develop rapidly, and it should return to the control of the ideology and political reproduction system of the imperialist social state system. Once this system acquires global characteristics, it also becomes a sign of changes in the civilization cycle, from a local conflict civilization to a global diversified cooperative civilization, whose goal is to promote the harmonious development of mankind.

The reason for forming an empire under modern conditions is not that one country occupies another country or imposes power on another country. It can only be established in the form of alliances of states in accordance with international law. The countries in these alliances intend to join the integrated world economic order and resist the aggressive penetration of transnational capital. Unless the Anti-war Alliance is established, this change will not happen on its own. To gain empire-like influence, this type of alliance must be a complete social state organization with its reproduced ideology and political system. To this end, it is necessary to restore the historical memory of the common development of the Eurasian peoples under the framework of the three world empires, so that we can recognize the significance of building a modern Greater Eurasian Partnership, which has all the reproduction system required for sustainable development.

---

25. Кобяков А., Хазин М. Закат империи доллара и конец «Pax Americana». М.: Вече, 2003.

The overall ideological system should conform to the modern paradigm of sustainable development and the principles of integrated modern economic order. It has the following requirements for the reproduction system.

The political reproduction system should be established based on international law, respect the sovereignty of all member states of the alliance, and uphold the principle of mutual benefit and voluntary cooperation based on common interests, so as to achieve harmonious and sustainable development.

The economic system needs to be flexible enough to integrate the diversified economic systems of the member states and give countries the freedom to exercise any external economic restrictions to ensure their own sustainable development. The economic system aims to protect the member states' economies from external forces, from falling into unequal financial transactions, and from restricting technological development. At the same time, it must provide member countries with the necessary resources for economic development. The prerequisite is to have a unified strategic planning, development mechanism, and a UES.

The family system in the state system of the alliance society should obtain favorable conditions for harmonious development, which means giving priority to the development of education, health, culture, and science and establishing a unified labor market and education space.

The opposite needs to be considered to prove the necessity of the transition to the new world economic order and the new civilization cycle. If this transition is not completed, the world will face the following catastrophic events, which are also widely discussed in modern movies:

- The mixed war in the world has further escalated, entering a stage of out of control, and possible use of weapons of mass destruction;
- Using the results of the new technological paradigm for non-humanitarian purposes (human cloning, manufacturing biochemical cyborgs, S&D, and use of biological weapons);
- The irrational development of the production of the new technological paradigm has caused man-made global disasters.

Existing scientific and technological predictions indicate that the above-mentioned threats are realistic. This also proves that there is no choice but to transition to an integrated international economic order and to establish an imperial Anti-war Alliance that protects mankind. On the contrary, human civilization will self-destruct because of world wars or entering a new field of biotechnology. The origin and continuation of human civilization will depend on the process of Eurasian integration. To meet the current challenges, a solid ideological foundation must be established based on the historical memory of the people of Eurasia.

Chapter 20

Development Prospects of Eurasian Integration

The development of the Eurasian integration process in post-Soviet space follows two routes. The first is the internal route to promote new countries to join the EAEU. The second is the external route to establishing free trade zones and signing relevant agreements with other countries on preferential economic and trade cooperation systems. Currently, the first route is limited to post-Soviet space. Tajikistan was once one of the founding countries of the Eurasian Economic Community and is expected to become a member of the EAEU. There is also Uzbekistan, which once participated in the National Defense Political Union-CSTO.

The US invaded and occupied Ukraine, forced Ukraine to join the European Union, and deprived it of its sovereignty. The US is currently preventing Ukraine from returning to the process of Eurasian integration. Similar situations also occurred in Moldova and Georgia. They handed over their national sovereignty to the European Union and formed an alliance with the European Union as unauthorized primary partners. Putin once proposed the establishment of a UES from Lisbon to Vladivostok or the later formation of a greater Eurasian partnership. If the proposal can be successfully implemented, these countries and the Baltic countries which have become EU members will theoretically still have the opportunity to participate in the second route of Eurasian integration. There are also two independent countries in the post-Soviet space-Azerbaijan and Turkmenistan, which participate in Eurasian integration in the form of free trade under the framework of the second route. These countries have abundant oil and gas resources, and they have developed by exporting these resources, but have fallen into dependence on importers (Turkey and China, respectively). The next role they play in Eurasian integration depends on the relationship between the EAEU and these regional superpowers.

Therefore, under the current geopolitical conditions, the development of the internal structure of Eurasian integration has reached a critical level. The participation of Tajikistan and Uzbekistan in the EAEU is still of political significance. This will bring more competitive advantages and development opportunities to the EAEU, although this will not fundamentally change the status of the EAEU's international division of labor.

At present, the GDP of the EAEU accounts for 3.5% of the global GDP, and its foreign trade accounts for 2.8% of the total global trade. Obviously, this is not enough for it to achieve self-sufficiency and sustainable development.[1] Only by establishing a preferential system for economic and trade cooperation with fast-growing Eurasian countries (China, India, Indochina countries, Near East and Middle East countries) under the framework of the second route of Eurasian integration, can it be possible to enhance the EAEU's proportion in the global economy.

---

1. C. Rogov's data, USCA, Russian Academy of Sciences.

The first agreement related to this is the free trade area agreement signed between the EAEU and Vietnam. Currently, free trade zone agreements between the EAEU and Egypt, India, and Israel are being formulated. Other potential partners include South Korea, Chile, South Africa, Iran, Syria, and Indonesia. The signed and effective agreement is the "China-EAEU Economic and Trade Cooperation Agreement," and the work being done is docking the Eurasian integration process with China's "Belt and Road" initiative.

Both the EAEU and the "Silk Road Economic Belt" initiative are integrated initiatives spanning multiple continents. The implementation of the joint initiative proposed by the heads of China and Russia can create conditions for the sustainable development of Europe and Asia and open up and expand prospects for mutually beneficial cooperation. The two initiatives can be organically combined and have complementary advantages.[2] Each integrated program has its own set of implementation mechanisms, including two development institutions, the Eurasian Development Bank and the Asian Infrastructure Investment Bank (authorized capital of US$100 billion).

The docking between the EAEU and the "Silk Road Economic Belt" initiative can expand development opportunities. The process can start from both parties. For the EAEU, it is recommended to implement the projects that have been formulated but not yet started, that is, the development of trans-Eurasian transportation infrastructure investment projects, including railways, highways, and aviation corridors.

It is reasonable to establish a preferential trade system between the EAEU and ASEAN. The ASEAN member states are part of the UES, with a total market population of 615 million. The economies of the member states of the alliance are complementary to those of the member states of the EAEU. Their cooperation will create broad prospects for cooperation without affecting domestic producers. ASEAN has established a free trade area with India, while the EAEU has established a free trade area with Vietnam. If ASEAN and the EAEU can build special economic and trade relations, it will take a substantial step towards advancing the UES from Lisbon to Vladivostok. In any case, it can create opportunities for the establishment of a UES from St. Petersburg to Jakarta, which will include the EAEU, India, and ASEAN, with a total market population of 2 billion and a GDP of US$6.6 trillion (according to purchasing power in parity terms, GDP is US$16.5 trillion).

Harmonious and complementary economic and trade relations, coupled with the broad prospects of attracting capital investment from existing international regional development institutions to transportation, logistics, and infrastructure, the organic combination of the two can bring opportunities to create a unified development space, including the construction of reliable transportation and logistics corridors and technological chains of industrial cooperation, in order to connect the EAEU with the rest of the Eurasian continent. Joint use of the mechanisms in the EAEU and other Eurasian integration organizations can provide facilities for realizing the potential of each initiative. For example, close cooperation can be carried out under the framework of cooperation among Russia, China, India, and Iran to establish unified airspace, open

---

2. "How Russia Took Advantage of China's Economic Miracle," S. Glazyev's report at the club seat in Izborsk, September 2015.

new aviation corridors, and then transition to independent S&D and manufacturing of aircraft; or open domestic waterways to build and use self-produced ships; or build a transportation corridor across Europe and Asia, and develop its own railway and highway machinery manufacturing base. Similar methods can be applied to the construction of a unified energy space, while at the same time, a unified machinery manufacturing base should be built. For example, the prerequisite for exploiting natural resources is the S&D, production, and use of domestic machinery and equipment. The prerequisite for operating the pipeline system is to invest funds for upgrading the pipeline system and improving efficiency.

The Russian President proposed to build a UES from Lisbon to Vladivostok, and the development of Eurasian transportation infrastructure is an important part of the implementation of this initiative. It will combine the "Belt and Road" initiative proposed by Chinese leaders to develop high-tech transportation corridors with neighboring countries in the East. At present, nearly 60% of global production value comes from the Asia-Pacific region, and the total global transportation cost is about 3-5 trillion US dollars, most of which is generated by shipping. Therefore, 80% of the most economical international corridor from East Asia to the Atlantic Ocean is the Russian transportation network. According to forecasts, the volume of land transport between the EU and neighboring countries has doubled since the end of the 20th century. Objectively speaking, the EU intends to coordinate with the EAEU and the Asia-Pacific region to formulate clear rules for long-term cooperation. This first involves joint investment in transportation infrastructure and communications, which can build a solid economic foundation and avoid the threat of political situations.

Russia has the potential to transship most of the goods from Europe and Asia. 50% of the revenue of the transportation industry comes from Russia, reaching US$1.5–2.5 trillion, which is more than Russia's GDP. At present, Russia's potential share in the Eurasian transport logistics service market is only 5%–7%. If Russia is identified as an important transportation hub for unifying Eurasian infrastructure, it can realize the connection of raw materials and industrial areas, and promote the development of industrial complexes and socioeconomic fields in the vast eastern region. It will also promote the development of railways, metallurgy, mining, inland waterway shipbuilding and shipping, energy-saving technology, aerospace navigation equipment, natural gas industry, forestry, telecommunications, and other technologies.

The process of developing Eurasian integration according to the two routes is carried out in accordance with WTO rules, and its goal is not to separate from the international market. Instead, it is open to all countries that intend to cooperate, based on equality and mutually beneficial cooperation, and through the complementary combination of comparative advantages to increase development opportunities and improve national economic competitiveness.

Recently, the US and its allies have tried to propose a new version of the world order to replace the Eurasian integration process. On the one hand, they plan to maintain their hegemony by disrupting the economic periphery that is not under their control, and on the other hand, to strengthen their dominance in the areas under their control. For this reason, the US and its allies have launched a mixed war against Russia for the economic periphery. For the areas under their control, they have wooed them to join the US-led *Trans-Pacific Partnership (TPP)* and *Transatlantic Trade and Investment Partnership (T-TIP)*.[3] The focus is to strengthen the control of American capital in peripheral areas of its capital accumulation system by weakening the state power, including the US itself. Issues related to transoceanic economics and trade agreements deserve separate analyses.

The two trans-oceanic economic and trade agreements that have been signed, including the already signed *Trans-Pacific Partnership* and the *Trans-Atlantic Trade and Investment Partnership* that are under preparation, are regarded by public opinion to enhance the economies of member countries, introducing a new stage of the liberalization of mutual trade between large-scale regional markets with the goal of competitiveness. According to the traditional view of market fundamentalists, the elimination of trade barriers should have expanded international trade and deepened economic cooperation, promoting economic activity, investment, and the growth of common market participants' welfare. Therefore, US and EU experts who support the signing of the T-TIP claim that the agreement is expected to bring economic benefits of US$120 billion and US$90 billion to the EU and the US, and create value for third countries by US$1,000 billion in additional output. As a result, they estimate that mutual trade and total exports will increase by 17%–18%.

Since the calculation method has not been published, we cannot confirm and refute these assessments. The economic mathematical models usually used for these purposes are very stylized, but their prerequisites are divorced from reality. Historical experience confirms that trade liberalization can bring advantages to countries with more developed economies and enhance their ability to control the markets of less developed countries. Underdeveloped countries can take measures to protect their own markets, artificially intervene and maintain the competitiveness of their own producers. These kinds of protection measures have different effects. They can cause the country to fall behind and promote the country to become a national leader, depending on the operational capacity of the development agency and the strength of the country's control.

According to this logic, once the relevant agreements of the transoceanic partnership come into effect, the US, the world's most technologically developed country, will surely win. However, the US is gradually losing its advantages in production competition, including in high-tech fields, with China, India, and Indochina countries. The US has a huge trade deficit with the new global economic center. Although the partnership agreement that the US plans to sign excludes China and India, problems in the US economy and trade forced most of the American society that has established links with economic entities to turn to support Trump. Trump became the first leader who included a protective tariff policy in foreign trade policy after World War II.

But the core of transoceanic partnerships is not foreign trade liberalization. At present, the European, North American, and Pacific markets are highly integrated. The

---

3. The regions where the countries involved in the negotiations for the establishment of the Trans-Pacific Super Group are located account for an important proportion of global imports (about 85%). North America accounts for about 18% of the world's imports, Europe accounts for nearly 36%, and Asia accounts for 32%. Most of Russia's exports go to these regions. 53% of the EU's domestic supply depends on imports, while APEC countries are more than 17%.

implementation of these agreements only benefits the existing development situation; that is, manufacturers in developed countries can obtain additional advantages, while the competitiveness of enterprises in underdeveloped countries will be weakened. However, considering that the trade barriers between the US and the European Union are relatively low (the weighted average tax rate for most imported goods is 2%–4%, with an average reduction of 3%, almost reduced to zero), and free trade is mainly carried out in the Pacific region. The above situation may not necessarily occur in the industry.

It is not so much a trade policy issue as it is that the investment partnership guidelines of these agreements are novel. The agreement has added content about protecting the interests of foreign investors, but this part of the content has undermined the foundation of the current legal system for protecting the country's economic interests. They give foreign capitalists priority over their own entrepreneurs, undermine the established economic regulation legal system, harm citizens' interests, and put the country in a subordinate position. This involves the process of mediating disputes between foreign investors and the state. Under the framework of this procedure, investors can have the opportunity to conduct special international arbitration against the interests of national legislation.

Therefore, one hundred well-known European lawyers pointed out in their petition against T-TIP that the chapter on investment protection in the agreement provides foreign investors with important procedural privileges at the expense of society as a whole.[4] To protect the rights of foreign investors, it is necessary to establish a special international arbitration court composed of three judges, whose function is to examine investors' appeals against political, administrative, and legal resolutions that harm their interests. Even if laws and regulations passed by the state are not discriminatory to foreign investors, foreign investors have the right to require the state to compensate them directly and indirectly for their loss and the protection of the environment, citizens' health, workers' rights, and social interests such as the rationalization of transportation and engineering. Therefore, foreign investors do not bear any responsibilities, but the country must fulfill these responsibilities.

As the lawyer stated in the petition, if the T-TIP passes regulations on the protection of investment and the court ruling process for foreign investors to sue the country, it will strengthen the rights of foreign companies by restricting citizens' democratic rights, harming national interests, and suppressing the country's potential. After every legal amendment, the country will receive various complaints from foreign companies and spend billions of funds from its budget for compensation. In disputes with foreign investors, the country also lost the political will to protect the interests of the whole people. On the other hand, foreign investors get additional opportunities to interfere in the internal affairs of where they are located and impose their own interests on other countries.

According to European lawyers, reviewing litigation by three international arbitrators cannot avoid corruption by itself, because the judges' salaries are linked to the review of

---

4. Глазьев С. Последний виток либеральной глобализации // Информационно-аналитический портал «Катехон», http://katehon.com/ru/article/posledniy-vitok-liberal-noy-globalizacii.

litigation submitted by investors. The judges will generate material benefits when they consider cases according to procedures. Compared with the current procedure system, this procedure can give them more rights and opportunities. And most importantly, once the various disputes are fully resolved in the national judicial system, the procedures mentioned in the T-TIP will destroy the current system, including international arbitration.

One point should be added to the lawyer's conclusion that the T-TIP stipulates that companies are included in the legislative process. Companies have the right to submit their substantive recommendations on the work schedule to the European Commission and the US. In other words, before the legislature discusses and approves the resolution, the enterprise can obtain legislative motions from the early stage of legislation and become an active participant in the legislative process.

T-TIP has political characteristics, which means that the European Commission and the ECB will further cooperate with relevant American agencies. The above-mentioned agencies have the right to ask each other questions on the draft laws of the regulatory agencies and to completely veto the bill before the legislators deliberate the bill. The US and the European Union are establishing a forum for regulatory agencies to assess the regulatory impact of draft legislation on all aspects of business activities. The Federal Reserve and the ECB established a form of direct cooperation to control the unified capital market comprehensively. At the same time, the powers of the European Union's monetary institutions have been continuously expanded; that is, the ECB has no obligation to negotiate with countries on its resolutions.

In view of the trust nature of currency, the principles outlined in these agreements will lead to the privatization of the international monetary system by the financial oligarchs in the USA. The US financial oligarchs have virtually dominated the international financial system. They have controlled the Federal Reserve, manipulated the ECB and the Bank of Japan through European officials and the Japanese political elites under the control of the US State Department, and managed the MP of Russia and other post-Soviet space countries through the IMF. The implicit contents of TPP and T-TIP include the abolition of the legal use of the national economic regulation system and the merger of the Federal Reserve, the ECB, and the Bank of Japan. It will allow the American oligarchy to control the global financial system, thus controlling the global economy, and pave the way for its domination of the world and establishing a global oligarchy dictatorship. Oligarchic groups are not bound by any obligations or legal rules. Perhaps this is the outcome foreseen by Atali and Fukuyama. Trump's election as the US president has politically killed these agreements, and economically enabled China and other Southeast Asian countries to rise in the wave of establishing new technologies and the world economic order.

Therefore, TPP, T-TIP, and similar unreviewed EU and Canadian comprehensive economic and trade agreements essentially mean that member states will eventually give up their economic sovereignty. The two agreements have deviated from WTO rules, restricting the country's regulation of foreign trade and the entire country's economy. This unified Pacific-American-European market was established at the expense of the people's interests, and these countries were deprived of the ability to independently control the economy, thereby bringing benefits to multinational companies. By further weakening the country's lost sovereignty in economic and trade activities, multinational corporations gain important legal rights to exert influence on the supervision of their own activities.

It should be pointed out that none of the aforementioned agreements under review allows China, India, and other BRICS countries to participate. This isolates the US and the European Union from the fastest-growing countries in the world, which account for 28% of global trade, 28% of GDP, and 49% of the population. This is not accidental. Recall that the United Kingdom, which occupied a leading position in world trade, tried to draw a clear line from the US during the Great Depression. Its method was to restrict the export of American goods to the United Kingdom. But this did not help Britain maintain its leading position in the world, but it eliminated all doubts about whether the US would retain the British Empire. Therefore, after World War II, Roosevelt and Stalin agreed that they should be given the independent status of the countries belonging to them. The US used the European Union, the Commonwealth, and Japan to establish a unified market to push out the BRICS countries, but this did not allow the US to maintain its global leadership. The WTO rules do not provide much protection to this market, and the BRICS countries may not necessarily formulate rules for resolving economic disputes through supranational arbitration.

Therefore, once the Trans-Pacific Partnership under consideration enters into force, the world economy will be split into two parts of different regulatory models. The core country and its peripheral countries in the imperialist world economic order will eventually fall into the "swamp" of free globalization and lose the legal ability to protect their own interests while cooperating with multinational companies. The core countries in the integrated world economic order retain the national judicial power to control foreign economic activities under the framework of WTO rules, which may bring certain competitive advantages to their multinational companies. Countries within the New World Economic Center scope will retain the legal mechanisms to protect the domestic market. On the contrary, countries within the scope of the Old World Economic Center will abolish these mechanisms, and their status will also be weakened.

Perhaps Trump understands that once the TPP and T-TIP take effect, the US will fall into a certain danger zone. At the same time, his implementation of the protective tariff policy also shows that American society has no confidence in maintaining its global dominance. In fact, the US government is restricting the recklessness of large-scale capital (mainly from the US) and defending the country's judicial power. The abolition of the TPP and the refusal to sign the T-TIP means tightening the space for large-scale capital reproduction in America and tightening the financial "noose" around the US' neck. The US and its peripheral economic countries are attempting to isolate half of the world's countries, proving that their economies are entering a recession stage.

The core countries in the new world economic paradigm have seen through these initiatives of the US, just as the American business community has seen through the United Kingdom's attempt to sever ties with the US during the last world economic crisis. They all use this as an excuse to break the existing world economic order and transition to the new world economic order. If the US tries to improve its own competitive environment by sacrificing corporate interests, it will also lose the basis for further maintaining the American debt pyramid, which is the core of the US capital accumulation system. China's resolution to stop accumulating US dollar reserves also indicates the limits of peacefully resolving the contradiction between the expanded reproduction of US dollar debt and global investment opportunities.

The world economic system has begun to split. Together with China, Russia and India began to shake off the influence of the US. The "peripheral zone" of American capitalism began to shrink. The process of creditors withdrawing from the American financial pyramid may present an avalanche characteristic, destroying the American financial system and the current world economic order established on this basis.

Compared with transoceanic economic and trade agreements, Eurasian integration has more development prospects in building a super-large region with economic and trade preferential systems. This conclusion can be drawn according to the law of the long-term global economic development described above. According to this law, the world economic center is shifting to Southeast Asia. The two largest developing countries, China and India, constitute the core of the new world economic paradigm. Since the two countries are not included in the transoceanic economic and trade agreement, their development prospects are relatively slim. At the same time, the integration plan can weaken Russia's position, reduce the opportunity for Russian products to enter the European Union, the largest market in Europe and Asia, and hinder the expansion of Eurasian integration in the Far East and ASEAN. Therefore, it is necessary to speed up the development of the second line within the framework of the Eurasian integration process.

To efficiently realize the potential of Eurasian integration, Russia needs to master the strategic planning method based on national interests and guarantee equal cooperation with China. Under the framework of this method, it is necessary to study, approve, and implement a series of measures to combine the advanced development zone in eastern Russia with the all-round development of Eurasian integration to establish a stable and sound international economic and political network.

Although Eurasian economic integration is fully in line with the recognized standards for global regional economic integration (including WTO rules), the US still tries to undermine the rules and deliberately hinders the development of the EAEU.[5] Eliminating the cautious attitude towards Eurasian integration should help increase the economic attractiveness of the EAEU to potential member states and the efficiency of the integration management institutions.

While promoting economic prosperity and developing advanced technologies, the EAEU can also become an alliance of nations and nations that safeguard national traditions, spiritual values, and cultural characteristics. With its historical experience, spiritual tradition, and geopolitical significance, Russia is naturally the center of Eurasian integration. In fact, the Eurasian integration covers the area west to east from Lisbon to Cape Dezhnev, and north to south from Novaya Zemlya to Indonesia. The Eurasian integration program has the potential to become the most

---

5. On December 6, 2012, US Secretary of State Hillary Clinton warned: "The US is trying to prevent Russia from recreating a new version of the Soviet Union under the ruse of economic integration."

important part of building a new world economic order. Only after the Russian state system exhibits the characteristics of fairness, efficiency, and people-oriented, can this plan be successfully implemented. Without fundamentally changing Russia's economic policy and establishing an attractive development and expansion model for the EAEU, Eurasian integration will still not be successfully implemented. In other words, to realize the potential of Eurasian integration, Russia must rationalize natural resources, geographical advantages, and management capabilities, learn from history, use technology to promote economic modernization, and implement advanced development strategies on the basis of new technological paradigms.[6]

---

6. Глазьев С. Уроки очередной российской революции: крах либеральной утопии и шанс на экономическое чудо. М.: ИД «Экономическая газета», 2011.

PART VII

BUILDING A GREATER EURASIAN PARTNERSHIP

Chapter 21

Effective Implementation of the Conceptual Proposals for the Greater Eurasian Partnership

"...I believe that by adding together the potential of all the integration formats like the EAEU, the OBOR, the SCO, and the ASEAN, we can build the foundation for a larger Eurasian partnership.

Specifically, it means establishing bilateral and multilateral agreement systems to simplify the regulation of some areas, such as customs, epidemic prevention, phytosanitary monitoring, industrial cooperation, investment, and protection of intellectual property rights.

The formation of this partnership is undoubtedly a long and arduous process. This process involves different depths, speeds, and levels of integration, depending on the willingness of each participating country.

Ultimately, this will be able to form a UES from the Atlantic to the Pacific..."

The above point of view comes from Putin's speech at the "Belt and Road" International Cooperation Summit Forum (May 14, 2017, Beijing).

Goals and Conditions of the Greater Eurasian Partnership

The Greater Eurasian Partnership aims to turn the Eurasian region into a region of peace, cooperation, and prosperity. Its task is to establish a preferential system for economic and trade cooperation; develop land transportation, information, and energy infrastructure; connect with the development plans of various countries and coordinate international cooperation in production and technology; transition to a fair monetary and financial system; and eliminate existing and new armed conflicts.

It is necessary to consider the characteristics of Eurasian countries' socioeconomic and political systems when establishing methods to solve the above-mentioned tasks. The Greater Eurasian Partnership does not require unity, the starting point of which is to unconditionally respect the sovereignty of participating countries, maintain their economic, political, and cultural diversity, and not interfere in their internal affairs. This is a necessary condition for healthy competition and common development of national judicial power based on integrating the competitive advantages of various countries.

The foundation for building the Greater Eurasian Partnership is a flexible legal system, joint projects, and various systems that consider the diversification of the interests of member states and the voluntary nature of cooperation. Partnerships established through integration can only be diversified and multi-level, giving each participating country the freedom to choose its obligations.

Extensive Eurasian integration is regular and objective. It may not be possible to find a country that does not participate in any regional alliance in the Eurasian region. The foundation of Eurasian integration is the historical cooperation experience accumulated over the centuries and the common creative activities of the Eurasian people. The concept of a "community with a shared future for mankind" put forward by Chinese leaders confirms the idea of Eurasian integration proposed by Russian philosophers a hundred years ago based on the common experience of the Eurasian people.

The Russian philosopher Trubetskoy, who as early as 1927 proposed the prospects for Russia's development after the collapse of the Soviet Union, argued that the new people's union should be based on the recognition of common interests based on centuries of history and common life experience within the framework of a unified state. He therefore stressed the need for equality of all peoples in the new union and pointed out the threat of nationalism. The elimination of nationalism requires every effort to develop a correct understanding of history and actively interpret the common historical experience, which is the basis for creating a positive outlook on a common future and a future together.

The new scientific results of mathematical and DNA genealogical analysis of historical data prove the historical homogeneity of the peoples of all ethnic groups in Europe and Asia, who live in vast imperial countries and UESs for most of their time, and share common genetics, languages, cultures, and spiritual roots. They also proved Eurasia's importance in human development and the dominant position of Eurasian empires in the entire civilization construction process that continues to this day. On this historical basis, a contemporary Greater Eurasian partnership can also be built. The contractual legal structure and cooperation principles will form the basis of the new world economic order.

Prerequisites for Building a Greater Eurasian Partnership

At present, there are more than ten regional economic alliances with different levels of integration and control in the Eurasian region. However, only the European Union and the EAEU have supranational regulatory agencies, and other integrated organizations have only transnational regulatory agencies. Most regional alliances are designed to eliminate trade barriers, establish free trade zones, and unify technical, customs, tariff, and non-tariff regulatory regulations. Since almost all Eurasian countries are members of the WTO, the organization's rules have naturally become the basis of various regional economic alliances.

Standard regional alliances such as CUs and free trade areas are established to build a unified market for goods, services, labor, and capital. Like such alliances, there are currently many regional initiatives dedicated to promoting investment and implementing joint investment projects, including developing joint investment projects in large-scale transportation and energy infrastructure. International banks and development institutions play an important role in supporting regional integration initiatives under the framework of corresponding regional alliances and the entire Eurasian continent.

The EAEU is a classic regional alliance dedicated to building a true common market within its member states, while the "Belt and Road" aims to promote co-investment in large-scale infrastructure projects. The docking of the two can become a model for forming the Greater Eurasian Partnership. This model combines free trade principles and various comparative advantages based on joint investment to realize the synergy and mutual benefit of all integrated participating countries.

At present, the UES covers the European Union and the EAEU countries, which unify the economic activities of the countries. The two unified markets reached US$17 trillion and US$1.8 trillion, with populations of 512 million and 182 million. Free trade practices include countries in the Commonwealth of Independent States (CIS), ASEAN (ASEAN), Economic Cooperation Organization (ECO), South Asian Association for Regional Coorperation (SAARC), Gulf Cooperation Council (GCC), and European Free Trade Association (EFTA). Among them,[1] China, Japan, Vietnam, India, South Korea, Singapore, and Israel have all signed free trade agreements with other Eurasian countries. The European Union has established free trade relations with neighboring countries and a UES with the European Free Trade Association. The European Free Trade Association and many countries in Europe, Asia, and other continents and their economic alliances have built a close intersecting free trade network. The EAEU has established a free trade relationship with Vietnam, and the EAEU is currently negotiating with Egypt, India, Iran, Singapore, Syria, Serbia and Montenegro. More than 40 countries and international organizations have expressed their desire to establish a free trade zone with the EAEU.

The subcontinent free trade zone is gradually taking shape. The total GDP of ASEAN,[2] which unites 10 Southeast Asian countries, is US$2.6 trillion, and the total foreign trade has reached US$2.5 trillion. Currently, ASEAN is negotiating with China, Japan, and South Korea to establish a free trade area. After the negotiation, there will be a super region with preferential economic and trade cooperation in Southeast Asia. The total population of this region accounts for 30% of the global population, the total GDP accounts for 24% of the global GDP, the trade volume accounts for 25% of the international trade, and 47% of the global high-tech product exports. If India, Australia, and New Zealand also participate in forming the Regional Comprehensive Economic Partnership (RCEP) of the "ASEAN+6" model, then this super-region will cover 50% of the world's population and account for nearly 30% of the world's total trade and GDP.

The subcontinent free trade zone can also connect transoceanic integration organizations. The EU and Canada have signed the Comprehensive Economic and Trade Agreement (CETA), and the Southern Common Market (MERCOSUR) is negotiating the establishment of a free trade area. Britain and France established

---

1. ECO: Economic Cooperation Organization (Afghanistan, Azerbaijan, Iran, Kazakhstan, Kyrgyzstan, Pakistan, Tajikistan, Turkey, Turkmenistan, and Uzbekistan); SAARC: South Asian Association for Regional Cooperation, or SAARC for short (Afghanistan, Bangladesh, Bhutan, Maldives, Nepal, Pakistan, India, Sri Lanka); GCC: Gulf Arab States Cooperation Council, or GCC (Bahrain, Qatar, Kuwait, United Arab Emirates, Oman, Saudi Arabia); EFTA: European Free Trade Association (Iceland, Liechtenstein, Norway, Switzerland).

2. ASEAN: Indonesia, Malaysia, Singapore, Thailand, Philippines, Brunei, Vietnam, Laos, Myanmar, Cambodia.

preferential economic and trade relations with former colonies in other parts of the world. All 12 countries in the Asia-Pacific region have signed the Trans-Pacific Partnership (TPP).[3] The issue of establishing the world's largest free trade zone within the Asia-Pacific Economic Cooperation (APEC)[4] framework is still being discussed.

Like traditional regional alliances that implement preferential trade systems, many international economic cooperation agreements have emerged, including trade in goods and services, the elimination of non-tariff barriers, the liberalization of financial market access, the convergence of various norms and standards, the protection of Intellectual Property Rights, international transportation infrastructure (road and railway corridors) development agreements, mutual access for national procurement, the establishment of a unified electricity market, unified competition rules, mutual recognition of vocational education certificates, and formulation of common principles and mechanisms for the neutralization of regional and global conflicts.

A promising form of regional integration is China's "Belt and Road" initiative, which is committed to implementing large-scale joint investment projects, including upgrading and transforming existing and building new transportation corridors connecting the economic spaces of Eurasian countries, facilitating the development of economic and trade cooperation. The initiative has been supported by 100 countries and international organizations. If Europe and Central Asia have formed regional alliances of supranational management agencies in Brussels and Moscow, then the process of regional integration in other parts of Asia is far from complete. Regional superpowers are establishing their own centers of Eurasian integration.

Currently, several integrated systems are rapidly forming in the Eurasian region. As Putin said at the 2016 Eastern Economic Forum,

> "They are flexible and complementary to each other and can implement projects based on the principle of mutual benefit." "We can agree on cooperation projects in science, education, and high technology based on a series of bilateral and multilateral trade agreements with different depths, different rates of development, different levels of cooperation, and different levels of market opening, depending on the readiness of certain economies for cooperation. All such agreements should be future-oriented, laying the foundation for common and harmonious development based on efficient and equitable cooperation.[5] We believe this integrated network is a system of multilateral and bilateral agreements, including free trade zones, which

---

3. The Trans-Pacific Partnership (TPP) partners are Brunei, Chile, New Zealand, Singapore, Australia, Peru, Vietnam, Malaysia, Mexico, Canada, and Japan. The US was an advocate of the Trans-Pacific Partnership (TTP), which it signed with other countries to establish on February 4, 2016, and withdrew from the TTP on January 23, 2017.

4. Since the adoption of the Bogor Declaration in 1994, APEC members have been discussing the prospects and rules for the establishment of an FTA. Countries in the Asia-Pacific region currently account for 40% of the world's population, 57% of global GDP, and 48% of global trade. Trade tariffs in the region have fallen by nearly 70% in the last 25 years.

5. "Speech by Russian President Vladimir Putin at the General Assembly of the St. Petersburg Economic Forum," St. Petersburg, June 17, 2016.

can become the basis for building a greater Eurasian partnership."[6]

The existing preferential trade system, international development agencies, joint investment projects, multinational companies, and consortia form the framework of the Greater Eurasian Partnership, giving it harmony, transparency, and attractiveness.

Principles of Greater Eurasian Partnership

The principles of the Greater Eurasian Partnership are voluntariness, mutual benefit, equality, transparency, and strict compliance with international law and its obligations.

The principle of voluntariness refers to non-interference in the internal affairs of nation-states, while the European Union and the US did exactly the opposite. They planned a coup in Ukraine and forced Ukraine to establish unequal relations with the European Union. Each country should independently decide which alliance to join, and fulfill its obligations based on national interests and legal procedures. The leader of integration establishes a political system in line with their interests by planning national coups, revolutions, and external funding of political forces, and then forcibly promotes integration. This operation should be regarded as a crime against mankind, and the obligation imposed on the corresponding country is illegal. It cannot be recognized by the participating countries of the Greater Eurasian Partnership.

> "We believe that effective integration can only be established on the basis of equality, mutual respect, and consideration of mutual interests among all participating countries, and will not coerce participants politically and economically and force unilateral resolutions. We think of integration as a predictable, long-term rule that is open to other states and alliances, east and West."[7]

The principle of mutual benefit means that all participating countries in the integration process should obtain tangible economic benefits and provide additional opportunities for their social and economic development, including raising social production, consumption, and residents' living standards, expanding employment, and enhancing the competitiveness of the national economy. If the effect of integration is uneven, such as some countries in the European Union that use the advantages of a unified market to harm the interests of other countries, they should take measures to modify the integration agreement and establish a mechanism to balance the conditions of integration.

The principle of equality means that each integrated participating country has the right to choose a decision-making method that fully considers its national interests.

---

6. "Speech by Russian President Vladimir Putin at the plenary session of the Eastern Economic Forum," Vladivostok, September 3, 2016.

7. "Speech by Russian President Putin at the General Assembly of the Eastern Economic Forum," Vladivostok, September 3, 2016.

In this way, a series of important issues related to the transfer of sovereignty functions to supranational institutions can be reached through consensus and resolutions, which are stipulated in the legal basis of the EAEU treaty. The principle of equality involves decision-making procedures and economic equivalent exchanges between integrated participating countries. The integration mechanism should curb income inequality distribution, including the distribution process of knowledge, monopoly, and administrative dividends or seigniorage from the issuance of international reserve currencies. This is a common problem in trade exchanges between countries with different levels of development. The principle of transparency involves all supervisory functions handed over to supranational institutions that affect income distribution conditions and the efficiency of economic activities: customs supervision, currency, banking, technology, antitrust and tax supervision, and tariff distribution within a CU. Participating countries should see and understand how other state authorities implement common regulations and management functions. Transnational negotiation and transnational management procedures should be completely transparent. To ensure the implementation of the principle of transparency, a unified information system must be operated in the supervision process, including sub-systems and integrated departments of various countries.

Compliance with international law and each country's obligations in the integration process is clear conditions for the effective implementation of all the above integration principles. Evidently, this principle has not been universally observed in the actual activities of international organizations. Many countries uphold the principle that their national laws are superior to international obligations and believe that these obligations or even the general rules of international treaties can be disregarded. For example, the US and the European Union allow themselves not to comply with WTO rules and wantonly impose economic sanctions on other countries.

The Greater Eurasian Partnership Is a Super Civilized Project

On May 14, 2017, Russian President Vladimir Putin pointed out at the "Belt and Road" International Cooperation Summit Forum that the Greater Eurasian Partnership is a super civilized program:

> "Russia sees the future of the Greater Eurasian Partnership not only as building new links between nations and economies, but also as transforming Eurasia's political and economic landscape and creating peace, stability, prosperity and high quality of life for Eurasia… In this sense, the Greater Eurasian Partnership is not an abstract geopolitical framework but, quite literally, a civilizational solution for the future."

We regard the Greater Eurasian Partnership as a unique cross-civilization scheme, covering the areas where eight types of regional civilizations of the fifth generation exist and collaborate: three European civilizations (Western Europe, Eastern Europe, and Europe), five Asian and North African civilizations (China, India, Japan, Muslims,

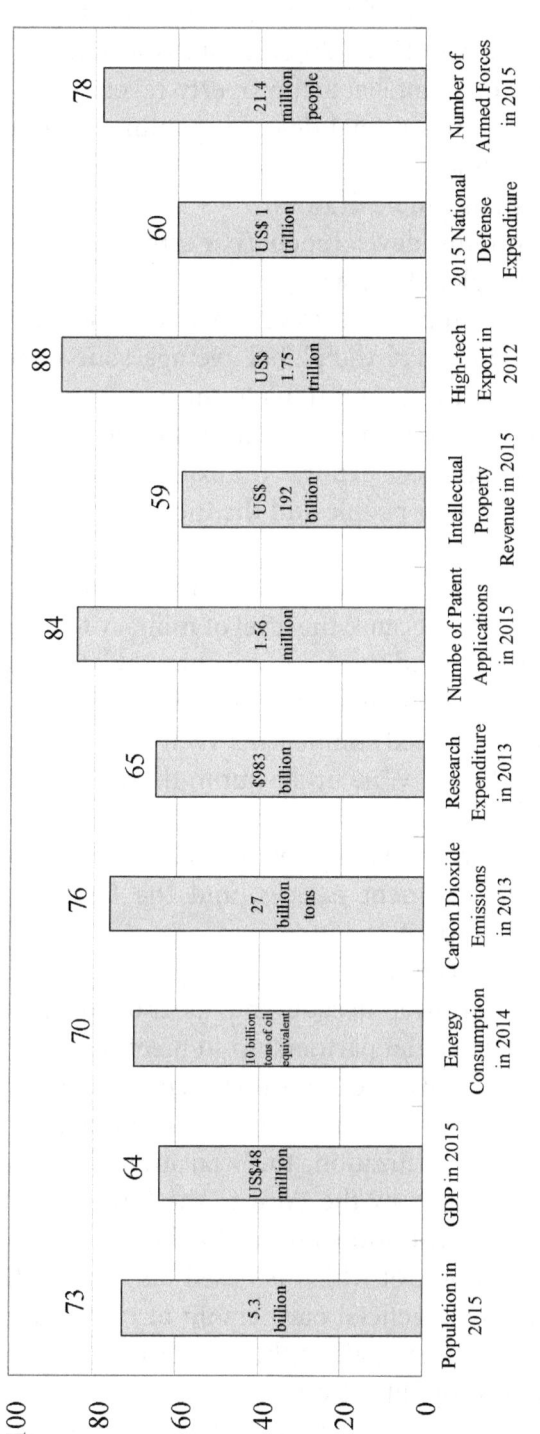

Figure 21-1 Major Macro-indices of Greater
Eurasia as a Percentage of the World

and Buddhism), while the Arctic civilization is also regarded as part of the civilizations of Europe, Western Europe, and North America.

Data from the World Bank shows Eurasian population accounts for 73% of the world's population, GDP accounts for 64%, energy consumption accounts for 70%, carbon dioxide emissions account for 76%, scientific research and experimental design expenditures account for 65%, intellectual property revenue accounts for 59%, high-tech exports account for 88%, national defense spending accounts for 60%, and the armed forces account for 78%.

The following conclusions can be drawn:

The overall level of economic development (per capita GDP) of the greater Eurasian countries is lower than the global average.

Per capita, energy consumption is lower than the global average, and carbon dioxide emissions are higher than the global average (due to the sharp increase in carbon dioxide emissions in China and India in the past 25 years).

Under the conditions of a high level of enthusiasm for invention and creation and an increase in the share of high-tech exports, the expenditure on scientific research and experimental design per million people and the income level of intellectual property rights is lower than the global average.

The proportion of people employed in the armed forces of large Eurasian countries is higher than the global average because the level of military technology and equipment (the proportion of defense expenditure) is lower than the global average.

Greater Eurasia is the main source of geopolitical conflicts, the proliferation of international terrorism, and armed conflicts between countries. The Napoleonic Wars and the First and Second World Wars broke out in the area, which is currently full of clashes between civilizations.

Thus, Greater Eurasia plays a leading role in the world economy, natural ecology, S&T, and geopolitical development indices, and the fate of global civilization is determined by the Eurasian space.

The beginning of the 21st century creates prerequisites for establishing the Greater Eurasian Partnership in the near decade and its transformation into an effective form of dialogue and civilizational partnership to meet the new century's challenges. First, mankind enters a new historical era that changes the ultra-long civilizational cycle, i.e., the decline of industrial capitalism, the formation of a unified, humanist intellectual sphere of world civilization, the transition from the fourth generation of a local civilization dominated by the West to the fifth generation of a civilization dominated by the East. The civilizational transition begins with a protracted and deep civilizational crisis, the solution of which is based on constructive dialogue and the establishment of a mutually beneficial partnership of civilizations and great powers, which should be carried out, first of all, in the greater Eurasian space.

Second, the escalating geopolitical crisis, the trade war, the economic sanctions imposed by the US on Russia, China, and the European Union, and the ever-increasing clash of civilizations have prompted all parties to actively respond to the above challenges and gather the strength of Eurasian civilizations and major powers. To this end, Russia has proposed initiatives to consolidate the multi-polar world order, integration and establish a Greater Eurasian partnership, which have received positive responses from leaders of many countries.

Third, we are currently creating conditions for integrating the two major projects of the Greater Eurasian Partnership and the "Belt and Road" Initiative. The overall goal is to make the Greater Eurasian region a space for peace, advanced development, and civilized partnership.

Based on the content of the above-mentioned strategic objectives of the Greater Eurasian Partnership, determine the strategic priority directions, implement the relevant plans and projects of the Greater Eurasian Partnership, and the EAEU and the "Belt and Road" initiative. The implementation period of this strategy is tentatively set to 2030 and will be extended in the future based on accumulated experience.

Achieving the above goal requires a long-term and huge effort. It is necessary to build trust and promote cooperation among different civilizations and countries in Greater Europe and Asia. At the same time, it may be necessary to determine the content of specific objectives in the table.

The following tasks need to be completed when formulating a strategy for the Greater Eurasian Partnership:

1. A reliable scientific basis must be established for formulating strategic priority directions and consolidating collaboration among large Eurasian countries, civilizations, and integration alliances to meet the severe challenges of the 21st century.
2. It is necessary to formulate an overall long-term "Strategy for Building a Greater Eurasian Partnership" based on established science.
3. For the Greater Eurasian institution responsible for approving and implementing the "Greater Eurasian Partnership Strategy," it is necessary to optimize its membership. The Eurasian Summit is the most effective governing body for the Greater Eurasian Partnership. The members of the meeting can include major countries in Western Europe (Germany, France, United Kingdom, Italy), Eastern Europe (Czech Republic), Eurasian (Russia, Kazakhstan), China, India, Japan, and Buddhist countries (South Korea, Vietnam), and Muslim civilized countries (Egypt, Turkey, Iran, Pakistan, Indonesia). To provide legal support for the Greater Eurasian Partnership, a Greater Eurasian Parliamentary Assembly composed of representatives of the legislative branches of the aforementioned countries should be established. To coordinate "integration within integration," it is necessary to establish a representative council of the Eurasian Integration Alliance, including the European Union, the Shanghai Cooperation Organization, ASEAN, the Organization of Islamic States, the League of Arab States, and the Black Sea Economic Cooperation Organization. It is also necessary to establish a coordination work organization to promote cooperation in science, economy, and humanities among large Eurasian countries. Due to conflicts of interest between Eurasian civilizations, the establishment of these institutions requires long-term efforts. Russia and China can initiate and organize this work.

Table 21-1 The Strategic Objectives of the Greater Eurasian Partnership

Objective for the First Phase	1. Eurasian Energy-Ecological Partnership	1.1. Evaluation and Conservation of Natural Resources
		1.2. Replacement of Natural Resources with Renewable Energy
		1.3. Comprehensive Management of the Environment
		1.4. Natural Disaster Monitoring and Early Warning
		1.5. Saving the Arctic
	2. Eurasian Innovation Technology Partnership	2.1. Protecting and Supporting Scientific Inventions, Primary Inventions, and Innovations
		2.2. Assessing and Supporting Basic Innovation
		2.3. Large-scale S&D of New Technology Paradigms
		2.4. Innovative Partnerships in the Fields of Science, Education, State, and Business
		2.5. Restraining the Excessive Polarization of Technology between Countries
	3. Economic Partnership	3.1. Eliminating the Bubble Economy
		3.2. Transformation of Economic Structure and Establishment of Transport Infrastructure in Europe and Asia
		3.3. Eurasian Antitrust Supervision
		3.4. Eliminating the Gap between Rich and Poor between Countries
		3.5. Establishing Eurasian Special Fund System
	4. Eurasian Social Demographic Partnership	4.1. Overcoming Population Decline
		4.2. Optimize Immigration Flow
		4.3. Effective Use of Labor Potential
		4.4. Improving Living Standards and Quality and Eliminating Poverty
		4.5. Leapfrog Development of Health Services

(Continued)

	5. Establishing an Integrated Social and Cultural System	5.1. Promoting the Development of Science by Leaps and Bounds and Initiating a New Scientific Revolution
		5.2. Improve Partnerships Related to the Foundation, Effectiveness, and Continuity of Education
		5.3. Protection of World and National Cultural Heritage and Cultural Diversity
		5.4. Promoting the Revival of Humanistic Ethics and Strengthening the Family System
		5.5. Protecting the Civilization Value System
Objective for the Second Phase	6. Partnership in the Social and Cultural Field	6.1. Leapfrog Development of Science
		6.2. Improving the Creativity, Foundation, and Continuity of Education
		6.3. Protection and Enrichment of Cultural Heritage and Cultural Diversity
		6.4. Consolidate the Spiritual Foundation of Society and Family
		6.5. Protecting the Civilization Value System
	7. Strengthening the Security of the Eurasian region	7.1. Elimination of Terrorism and Extremism
		7.2. Ending the Arms race and Ensuring weapons control
		7.3. Strengthening of Partnerships with Social Forces
		7.4. Ensuring Information Security
	8. Eurasian Partnership Agency	8.1. Eurasian Summit
		8.2. Assembly of the Greater Eurasian Parliament
		8.3. Integration in Eurasian Integration
		8.4. The Docking of Three Large-scale Projects

With the end of the process of times changes, in the next three decades, national and world leaders in the 2020s will make and implement strategic decisions. Relying on the widespread use of information technology, it is crucial to shaping the worldview of these leaders in the spirit of dialogue and partnership among civilizations. The International Program for the New Generation of Digital Civilization Education takes this as its purpose.

At the same time, it is necessary to make full use of the modern information network, enrich the humanitarian content, and popularize the concept of the Greater Eurasian Partnership and the strategy of establishing the Greater Eurasian Partnership on the information network. It will help the new generation to shape the worldview in the spirit of dialogue of civilizations and partnership, overcome the crisis of modern civilization, and build a humanist intellectual circle.

Greater Eurasian Partnership Integration Field

Almost all Eurasian countries are members of the WTO, the World Customs Organization, the International Organization for Standardization, the UN Conference on Trade and Development, and other UN departments and regional organizations. The guidelines, procedures, and recommendations of the above organizations are naturally Eurasian integration components. Most of the Eurasian countries are parties to international agreements establishing the Trans-Pacific Partnership and Free Trade Area, thus linking the countries of the Greater Eurasian Partnership with the rest of the world. Each country and regional organization in Eurasia has a network of treaties signed with other countries and regional organizations (including organizations located on other continents). Therefore, the Eurasian partnership must be a multilayered and complex alliance of states, each with specific relations with other countries and the resulting international obligations and limits of state sovereignty.

The Greater Eurasian Partnership involves economic cooperation issues, including trade, industry, investment, innovation, technology, and other fields, not involving issues of military, politics, religion, and ethnic integration. In each field involved, there are corresponding regional and international organizations operating, which will not hinder the establishment of the Greater Eurasian Partnership.

The establishment of the Greater Eurasian Partnership can firstly bring additional integration effects in some areas, "making the transportation of goods in Eurasia the fastest, the most convenient, and the easiest,"[8] areas including "customs affairs, sanitary and plant Quarantine supervision, industry cooperation and investment, protection of intellectual property rights..."[9] It can start from simplifying and unifying the supervision of industry cooperation and investment fields, as well as non-tariff measures in technology, plant quarantine supervision, customs management, intellectual property protection, etc., and gradually in the future reducing and removing tariff restrictions..."[10]

In customs supervision, it is recommended to coordinate customs clearance procedures and supervision guidelines based on the customs data automated processing system program. More than 90 member states of the UN Conference on Trade and Development have used the system to simplify the customs clearance procedures effectively. Introducing this system can enable legal participants in foreign economic activities that conduct business in the Eurasian space to transfer most of the goods

---

8. Excerpt from Russian President Putin's speech at the "Belt and Road" Forum for Cooperation, Beijing, May 14, 2017.

9. Excerpted from Russian President V.V. Putin's speech at the Leaders' Round table Summit of the "Belt and Road" Cooperation Summit Forum, Beijing, May 15, 2017.

10. Excerpt from Russian President V.V. Putin's speech at the plenary meeting of the St. Petersburg International Economic Forum, St. Petersburg, June 17, 2016.

through the "green channel."

In terms of sanitation, veterinary medicine, and plant quarantine, the EAEU has unified the standards based on modern science. These standards can be used as the basis for coordinating the work of various countries and regions in Europe and Asia.

Industry cooperation includes multiple components, the most integrated of which are transportation, telecommunications, fuel energy, and agro-industrial complexes. "The basis for effective integration is the comprehensive development of infrastructure, including transportation, telecommunications and energy complexes..."[11]

The development of the transportation sector and transportation infrastructure has always been a key part of the Eurasian integration plan, including the EAEU and the "Belt and Road" initiative. Work is currently underway to upgrade and further develop the main transport corridors (roads and railways) in Europe and Asia. When implementing large-scale joint investment projects in this field, the most promising way is to create multinational consortia, state-owned enterprises, private enterprises, banks, and other development institutions. National, regional, and local authorities can all become participants in the consortium. By combining capital, technology, land, and the above industries, such consortia with supranational management institutions can establish development corridors based on leases, linking Eurasian countries' production and technological potential.

Such measures will bring new opportunities for regional development, increasing the attractiveness of regional investment, strengthening inter-regional cooperation, and accelerating the development of various fields of the economy. At the same time, according to the national interests of the member states of the Greater Eurasian Partnership, the organization model for the distribution of benefits from the integrated operation of logistics and transportation infrastructure should be optimized.

It is reasonable to start work in this field under the framework of the docking work between the EAEU and the "Belt and Road" Initiative. One of the tasks is to establish a common electricity market and a market for intercontinental fiber optic communications. This work should include the coordination of technical and economic control, security norms, and investment guarantees.

Cooperation in the field of telecommunications also includes cybersecurity issues. Although modern information technology connects various countries and continents to form a unified information space, some criminal organizations and countries also use information technology for criminal purposes. To combat this phenomenon, an international cybersecurity treaty should be signed, stipulating that parties must not use information technology for illegal purposes, including the use of computer viruses that implant programs and electronic devices, and the use of secret tools to monitor, monitor data transmission, and interfere with electronic systems et al. In addition, this illegal act must be cracked down in accordance with national laws. International treaties can provide filters to protect the information systems of contracting states from external network attacks and cut off the source of viruses in the global information network. International treaties may also provide for collective sanctions against certain

---

11. Excerpt from an article by Russian President Vladimir Putin entitled "The 25th APEC Da Nang Summit: Together Towards Prosperity and Harmonious Development," November 8, 2017.

countries that are unwilling to join the treaty and abuse their own advantages in operating systems, social networks, and telecommunication service markets to carry out electronic espionage, hacking, and sabotage activities in the territories of the contracting states. Sanctions include prohibiting the supply of electronic equipment and remote communication services and forbidding the use of information systems, including social networks. In addition, the treaty can also provide for the creation of advantages for developing and using domestic information technology in the contracting states.

The important content of the international cybersecurity treaties should be to provide legal norms for the operation of the Internet and other global information systems in the Eurasian region, elevate Internet management from national jurisdiction to the field of international law, and formulate relevant rules to eliminate any discrimination against consumers at the national level. It should also provide for common certification and testing systems for equipment used by Contracting States.

Under the framework of the Greater Eurasian Partnership, other issues in the management and control of Eurasian cyberspace can also be resolved, including the identification of workers in the Eurasian information and communication network, combating tax evasion, illegal export of funds, and illegal commercial activities carried out on the internet, including e-commerce and financial services.

The fuel energy complex has always been an industry in which Russia has a competitive advantage. We have been proposing to create a Eurasian energy market, including natural gas, oil, and electricity markets, which will quickly play a role in the UES of the EAEU. The fuel energy field guidelines formulated by the EAEU can become the basis for establishing a unified energy market in Eurasia. The development of the Eurasian pipeline network is an important part of the work of establishing a unified Eurasian energy market. A multinational consortium can be created to modernize, upgrade, and develop the pipeline network.

In terms of agricultural complexes, the main task is to coordinate national and regional markets and effectively integrate the competitive advantages of Eurasian countries. Efforts need to be made to eliminate tariff and non-tariff barriers, unify national standards in the grain field, and establish grain exchanges in countries with advantages in producing grain products. There is a certain attraction to developing a Eurasian food security system that would guarantee a sustainable supply of food and provide food aid to all member countries of the Greater Eurasian Partnership when necessary.

Implementing Large-Scale Investment Projects

The key direction for developing the Greater Eurasian Partnership is to compile a database of priority investment projects. Russia is preparing to put forward its own initiatives in this area, including "building a 'super energy ring' connecting Russia, China, Japan, and South Korea, or establishing a transportation channel between Sakhalin Island and Hokkaido..."[12]

---

12. .Из статьи Владимира Путина «XXV саммит АТЭС в Дананге: вместе к процветанию и гармоничному развитию» (8 ноября 2017 г.).

Other investment projects proposed by Russia include:

- The construction of transcontinental high-speed railroads and freeways within the EAEU will be used to complement the discussions with the Chinese side on the interface between the EAEU and the "Belt and Road" initiative.
- Create a European-Asian aviation joint enterprise to produce various types of aviation equipment (make full use of the potential of the design bureaus of Ilyushin, Tupolev, and Antonov).
- Build a pipeline network to form the structure of the Eurasian hydrocarbon market.

The implementation of the long-term investor club's plan to create a "trans-Eurasian development belt" may become a key component of the priority investment project pool. The plan is to combine plans to create a new generation of integrated infrastructure, regional production planning, and long-term direct investment financing methods to create an efficient Eurasian integrated transportation framework. To implement the "Trans-Eurasian Development Belt" plan, it is proposed to create an international joint enterprise. The participants include relevant enterprises, investment institutions, and regional administrative agencies. Establishing such a joint enterprise requires the allocation of land and natural resource use rights by the national government and regional administrative agencies, in addition to the issuance of bonds and the establishment of special joint-stock funds. The participants will be the Eurasian National Development Agency, the Eurasian International Development Agency, regional administrative agencies, state-owned enterprises, and private enterprises of relevant countries. Relevant international agreements must be signed to approve the "Trans-Eurasian Development Belt" plan and create an international joint enterprise.

A public-private partnership mechanism should be adopted to create a library of investment projects through special investment contracts. A series of special investment contracts will be deployed as an indicative planning structure network for the Greater Eurasian Partnership. From the perspective of integration effects, major investment projects should be co-invested with international development institutions such as the Asian Infrastructure Investment Bank, the BRICS Development Bank, the Eurasian Development Bank, and the International Investment Bank. The largest of these projects is the creation of inter-state management institutions and granting them extraterritoriality, which requires the signing of relevant international agreements.

Currency regulation and the creation of a general currency circulation system, which is not yet included in the regional integration process, may become the most important area of control of the Greater Eurasia Partnership, which is of interest to all countries that may join it.

Eurasia has no world currency of its own. It uses the US dollar, euro, and yen as world currencies, which has triggered inequality in economic exchanges due to the unilateral raiding of minting taxes by world reserve currency issuers based on the use of world currencies by other countries. Another problem that is currently highlighted is that the arbitrary politics implemented by the governments of the world's reserve currency issuers threaten the stability of international economic relations. The economic sanctions imposed by the US, the European Union, Japan, and other countries on Iran, Russia, North Korea, and other Eurasian countries go beyond the norms of international law. They caused serious damage to Eurasian integration and to countries forced to use US, European, and Japanese currencies as reserve and settlement currencies. The world currency issuing countries abuse their dominant position in international monetary and financial relations, irresponsibly imposing financial embargoes, freezing accounts and assets, and paralyzing the settlement business of countries they dislike, including their leaders and enterprises.

The increasing global instability, the higher risks of lacking currency circulation standards in the world, and the use of currency for illegal purposes by currency issuing countries require the Greater Eurasian Partnership to take unified measures to eliminate the threat of destabilizing international economic relations. To this end, there is a need to create an automated digital currency environment, which will facilitate users and facilitate payment settlement, financial investments, and currency exchange operations in the member countries of the Greater Eurasia Partnership, which are necessary for mutual trade and international economic cooperation.

The digital currency environmental infrastructure of the Greater Eurasian Partnership should include:

The Greater Eurasian Partnership is a supranational digital settlement and reserve currency, which is linked to the currency basket of the member countries of the Greater Eurasian Partnership, and its proportion should be proportional to the circulation of the member countries' currencies in mutual trade.

A currency issuance and settlement center. The member states of the Greater Eurasian Partnership sign an international treaty on the digital currency environment, and the currency issuance and settlement center conduct work in accordance with the treaty, which provides guidelines for the issuance of supranational currencies, with member countries contributing to the supranational currency in their own currency, and they are obliged to guarantee the stability of the exchange rate between their own currency and the supranational currency.

Establishing currency exchange to carry out the currency exchange business of the Greater Eurasian Partnership, and stipulating control measures to ensure the stability of the currency exchange rate, including preventing the use of exchange rates to carry out speculation that has nothing to do with trade and direct investment.

In the international treaty providing for the issuance and circulation of supranational currencies of the Greater Eurasia Partnership, it is also necessary to provide for the mechanism of distribution of loans in the form of supranational currencies. It can be implemented by establishing funds by the international development agencies recognized by the Greater Eurasia Partnership and authorized national development agencies. The currency of any country willing to join the treaty will be included in the currency reserve pool and added to the Greater Eurasian Partnership supranational currency basket. When allocating credit resources in the form of supranational currency, the interests of the above-mentioned countries are considered, and funds are allocated according to the established algorithm. The previous tools, such as the Bank for International Economic Cooperation[13] and the Bank of the Commonwealth of Independent States, can be used when establishing an issuance center.

Using one currency for international settlement will greatly reduce the currency risk of exporters and importers, reduce the scope of currency speculation and limit exchange rate fluctuations.

Blockchain technology can be used to issue and guarantee the circulation of the supranational currency of the Great Eurasian Partnership. The blockchain contains a complete transaction record registry for each supranational currency. This technology can easily control the circulation of supranational currencies and bypass the politically-affected SWIFT system to exchange bank information for remittances, while ensuring the highest reliability and credibility in the entire transaction process. This is very important for anti-corruption, combating the legalization of criminal proceeds, preventing terrorist financing, and preventing financial market manipulation and speculation.

The advantage of using blockchain technology to issue and circulate supranational currency is that it can work in both the new and existing monetary and financial systems. The new financial platform, as a more technologically advanced, legal, transparent, and safer payment method, will gradually eliminate the existing opaque and unfair US dollar-centric system. It is difficult to improve the US dollar-centric system within the Greater Eurasian Partnership framework because it requires the issuing country to undertake a lot of international obligations.

Under the framework of the creation of a unified currency circulation system, the current mutual trade and joint investment business of the member states of the Greater Eurasian Partnership must switch to local currency settlement. It is recommended to fully encourage relevant work to replace the US dollar, euro, and pound sterling with the currencies of Eurasian countries willing to undertake the following international obligations in international currency settlement.

The issuing countries of the world reserve currency should ensure the stability of the world reserve currency by complying with the restrictions on national debts and trade balance deficits. In addition, they should also comply with relevant requirements to ensure the transparency of their currency issuance guarantee mechanism, all assets (including new technologies) traded on the territory of the issuing country can be exchanged without hindrance through the currency of the issuing country. Those foreign non-state banks that adhere to reliable and transparent guidelines provide national refinancing systems. They need to abide by the principle of fair competition and non-discriminatory access to their own financial markets, which are important

---

13. The Bank for International Economic Cooperation was created in 1963 (as an international organization registered with the United Nations) by the former socialist countries for the purpose of multilateral settlement using the international currency of the Council for Mutual Economic Assistance ("transfer rubles"). It is not subject to the threat of economic sanctions, and its assets and liabilities are protected by international law. The Bank has correspondent accounts in Russian banks, a tax-exempt status, a special system of banking supervision, and the support of government departments of member countries, including Bulgaria, Vietnam, Cuba, Mongolia, Slovakia, Slovenia, the Czech Republic, Poland and Romania. The unique capabilities of the Bank must be used to overcome the restrictions imposed by sanctions on Russia's access to global financial markets.

requirements for them.

To ensure macroeconomic stability, it is necessary to formulate a Eurasian financial regulatory standard system, including financial markets (including currency markets), to control systemic risks. Especially in the risk assessment of listed assets, to reduce the systemic bias that is beneficial to a country, it is necessary to formulate Eurasian rating standards and rating agency activity standards, and ensure that the rating agencies of the Greater Eurasian Partnership unified supervision.

An important task of the Greater Eurasian Partnership countries is to formulate and implement a system of methods related to creating fair and efficient international financial and economic relations. This can provide the conditions for sustainable economic development, employment, and residents' well-being. This task must be completed before the long-term reform of the international monetary and financial system. The system of methods related to the creation of regional monetary, financial systems, and international financial institutions can be implemented under the framework of the Greater Eurasian Partnership. It aims at ensuring stable, fair, and mutually beneficial currency circulation conditions, while promoting the development of new technological paradigm production and stimulating investment and long-term loan mechanisms for innovative activities.

Establishing the Legal Basis and Institutions of the Greater Eurasian Partnership

When establishing a Greater Eurasian partnership, a series of complex issues need to be resolved, involving issues such as relations between countries, the further improvement of the international legal system, and the coordination of the international legal system with the laws of the Greater Eurasian countries. An inter-parliamentary conference of major Eurasian countries should be established to solve the above problems. Participants include representatives of the legislative branch and representatives of countries participating in the Eurasian Summit. At the same time, we can learn from the rich experience of the CIS Inter-Parliamentary Conference, including developing a model law on important issues of common concern. The inter-parliamentary meeting of the major countries of the Greater Eurasian Partnership can be held in St. Petersburg, where small executive agencies and international scientific and legal centers can be used. The first inter-parliamentary conference can be held in St. Petersburg in 2021.

Planning to Establish a Greater Eurasian Partnership

To coordinate and give full play to the production potential of Eurasian S&T, and to stimulate the promotion of new technological paradigms of great social significance, it is necessary to implement the Eurasian social and economic development strategic plan. The plan includes:

- Drawing up long-term forecasts for the development of S&T.
- Clarifying the development prospects of the regional economy, regional economic organization, and large-scale national economy.

- Identifying and eliminating trade imbalances and bottlenecks that hinder the full utilization of existing resources.
- Determining whether it is possible to eliminate the existing imbalances, including the development level gap between the member states of the Greater Eurasian Partnership.
- Choosing the priority development direction.

To implement the priority development tasks, it is necessary to incorporate the indicative plan jointly developed by the experts and business circles of the member states and authorized international organizations into the planning system of the Greater Eurasian Partnership.

The establishment of a Greater Eurasian Partnership requires planning, clarifying the sources of funds, compiling a library of priority investment projects with financing mechanisms implemented in the form of public-private partnerships, and formulating a list of international treaties and joint venture projects and a roadmap.

The plan should determine the goals, tasks, resolution mechanisms, and implementation phase for establishing the Greater Eurasian Partnership. In the future, the plan will also include a strategic plan and indicative plan for developing the Greater Eurasian Partnership. It is recommended to draw on the successful experience accumulated by the Greater Eurasian Partnership countries in formulating long-term technological and socioeconomic development plans when working on this plan.

Eurasian powers and influential Eurasian countries have strong development institutions and extensively use economic planning and state regulation tools that serve the public interest. They can gather the strength of scientific analysis of the above-mentioned countries to forecast the development of Eurasian countries in the context of global structural changes. They can also gather strategic planning and indicative plans of Eurasian development, which helps to enhance the capacity of member countries to develop scientific, technical, and productive potential, enabling them to pool resources to solve the tasks of building partnerships.

To establish a strategic management system at the level of the Greater Eurasian Partnership, it is necessary for national and international specialized scientific institutions to carry out planning work jointly. It is recommended to organize this work based on the Moscow Institute of International Studies, which has corresponding status and work experience. It is necessary to convene an international conference of representatives of relevant countries and scholars when launching the mechanism for establishing the Greater Eurasian Partnership.

For the plan to establish a Greater Eurasian Partnership to be practical, the plan must specify the activities involved, and the sources of funding for the inter-state and supranational regulatory agencies created. For this reason, it is recommended to introduce scientific and reasonable taxation in the currency exchange business. The tax amount is 1‰ of the transaction volume, which is collected according to the laws of the member states of the Greater Eurasian Partnership and transferred to the authorized agency of the Greater Eurasian Partnership for control. This will also help reduce turbulence in the Eurasian financial markets. The funds collected through such taxes can be used to maintain the operation of the Greater Eurasian Partnership's agencies and implement the Eurasian social plan under the supervision of the international organizations authorized by the member states of the Greater Eurasian Partnership.

Especially in the conditions of structural changes in the world economy based on the new technological paradigm, relying on this source of funding to create an international educational network of leading Eurasian universities, to train citizens of developing and less developed countries, and to implement new skills retraining programs for the unemployed in developed countries, is of great importance for ensuring employment rates and realizing the potential of human resources in Eurasian countries. This will help to use humanistic cooperation (necessary for coordinated economic development) to strengthen the economic function of the Greater Eurasian Partnership and make the common cultural, historical, and spiritual heritage more relevant. Such scientific and educational activities will also contribute to creating an ideological platform for the harmonious coexistence of Eurasian peoples in the 21st century.

Chapter 22

Transportation Framework of Greater Eurasian Logistics

To ensure the smooth progress of the docking between the EAEU (EAEU) and the "Belt and Road" initiative, China and Russia have formulated a package of cooperation investment projects. For these projects, the need to take the lead in investing in the logistics and transport infrastructure of the Greater Eurasia Partnership, which currently has high transport costs and low efficiency in the region, has not been fully considered.

From the perspective of long-term development, to establish an efficient logistics transportation framework, it is necessary to formulate, approve and implement a series of large-scale investment projects in the field of logistics and transportation. As the center of the "East-West-East" transportation route in the 21st century, Russia must fully consider its own interests. The first projects carried out are as follows:

- Laying high-speed railways and intercontinental highways on the territories of the EAEU countries.
- Creating a European and Asian aviation joint enterprise that produces various types of aviation equipment (make full use of the potential of the design bureaus of Ilyushin, Tupolev, and Antonov).
- Establishing a pipeline network to build the structure of the Eurasian hydrocarbon market (please refer to the previous chapter).

A key component of the pool of priority investment projects may be implementing a plan to create a "trans-Eurasian development belt," which should be proposed by the long-term investor club and approved by the highest-level experts.[1]

The "Greater Eurasian Development Belt" plan should integrate a new generation of integrated infrastructure construction plans, regional production planning plans, and long-term direct investment financing methods to establish an efficient Eurasian Integrated Transportation Framework (ITF). When implementing the plan, it is necessary to establish an international joint enterprise, and the participating parties include relevant groups, investment institutions, and regional administrative agencies. The establishment of such an international joint enterprise requires the national government or regional administrative agency to allocate land and natural resource use rights. In addition, it also needs to issue bonds and create a special joint stock fund. The members will include the Eurasian National Development Agency, the Eurasian International Development Agency, the regional administrative agency, and state-

---

1. Реализация Транс-Евразийского транспортного мегапроекта как драйвер экономического роста ЕАЭС // Материалы Научно-методического семинара Аналитического управления Аппарата Совета Федерации 7 апреля 2016 г. - Аналитический Вестник Совета Федерации. -№ 19 (618), 2016.

owned and private enterprises in relevant Eurasian countries. Approval of the "Trans-Eurasian Development Belt" plan and the creation of an international joint enterprise require the signing of relevant international agreements.

In terms of technology and operation, it is recommended to implement this program according to the following directions:

1. Carrying out joint work on coordinating economic interests and formulating project tasks, including formulating and implementing joint innovation projects—paving the "Innovative Silk Road."[2]
2. Developing joint international infrastructure projects to realize the long-term economic benefits of participating countries. Russia proposes to lay a transportation and energy ring near the Sea of Japan. Modernizing by upgrading the Trans-Siberian Railway, connecting the railway with the main railways of China and Mongolia, and extending the "Western China–Western Europe" international highway from Xinjiang, China to St. Petersburg, Russia; jointing railways, highways, aviation infrastructure, and the northern waterway.
3. Simultaneously developing the area along the road infrastructure (including railway and highway trunk lines), which can effectively improve the economic benefits brought by establishing trans-Eurasian transportation trunk lines, and increase the investment attractiveness of trans-Eurasian transportation trunk lines to develop existing and new regional production complexes.

The implementation of this plan can start with the development of the Northeast Asia International Transportation Corridor, the establishment of a transportation and energy loop near the Sea of Japan, the connection of railway infrastructure and the northern waterway, and the creation of a new generation of logistics parks in the smart city space. The South Primorye Sea Territory and its cross-border area connect the Vladivostok Port Concentration Area and the logistics centers of China, North Korea, South Korea, Mongolia, Japan, and other countries. The area can be designed as a space for social and infrastructure development.

To implement the Trans-Eurasian Development Belt (TEDB) program, it is proposed to create a TEDB consortium with the participation of interested enterprises, investment institutions, and regional administrative bodies. The consortium must have a supranational strategic planning body.

The TEDB international conglomerate should be established as an international development group, authorized to enter the financial markets of member countries through the issuance of bond loans, and ensure the formation of a regional strategic base for a new technological paradigm. To achieve this goal, it is necessary to introduce

---

2. The "Innovation Silk Road" may become an important component of the "Greater Eurasian Development Belt," which provides for a complete cycle of innovation activities: from joint S&D in the field of high technologies to their introduction into competitive production ensuring high added value. The infrastructure of the Eurasian innovation system created in this way should be several scientific and high-tech centers, which are established based on national scientific centers, universities, industrial parks, innovation parks and other elements of innovation infrastructure dedicated to the development of innovation in the EAEU.

special legislation, formulate an institutionalized mechanism for corporate financial activities, and a strategic planning system, determine the standards for accomplishing the set goals, and whether the results achieved meet the predetermined goals.

Various large-scale investment projects need to be implemented to implement the TEDB program and establish a conglomerate for this purpose. The TEDB program must connect with the Eurasian region's cheap credit mechanism to provide funding sources for the above-mentioned investment projects. The above-mentioned credit mechanism includes the Great Eurasian Partnership Supranational Currency Issuing Institution (in the future, such institutions may be created in the form of traditional currencies or encrypted currencies), or development institutions funded and established by the Central Bank of relevant countries, Eurasian securities markets, national and international financial institutions. A tradable co-investment fund can be created to finance the program, and the participants of it will be Eurasian development agencies (inter-country or some countries' international cooperation development agencies, investment funds, and banks). In addition to land, Russia can also use geological information-based information assets, rights to prospect and exploit mineral resources, and rights to use forest, agricultural and marine biological resources as funding methods.

The proposed integrated platform in the form of TEDB and its corresponding international group and the pool of priority projects for the development of logistics transportation infrastructure in Greater Eurasia serve as a coordinator of numerous (sometimes multifaceted) Greater Eurasia development programs. Most importantly, the latest studies confirm the economic benefits of the main Trans-Eurasian arteries developed within the framework of the concept of the "Greater Eurasian Development Belt" and mentioned earlier, one of which was carried out by the Eurasian Development Bank's Center for Integration Studies.[3]

When analyzing the prospects of participation of the EAEU countries in the implementation of the "Belt and Road" initiative, the search for optimal transport routes on the axis of China–the EAEU–EU (based on the criteria of cost and time of transportation of goods, as well as the necessary amount of investments) is an important element of the analysis. To this end, we have studied the following four international corridors that could ensure intercontinental cargo flow:

1. The Nordic Asia Corridor (China–Russia–Europe, via the territories of the Far East and Eastern Siberia);
2. Central Eurasian Corridor (China–Kazakhstan–Russia–Europe, entering Russia's transportation infrastructure through the territory of Kazakhstan);
3. Trans–Asia Corridor (route south of Russian territory);
4. "North–South International Transportation Corridor."

Each corridor has differences in length, number of transit countries, transportation capacity, and development level of logistics and transportation infrastructure.

3. Транспортные коридоры Шелкового пути: потенциал роста грузопотоков через ЕАЭС / Доклад. – СПб: Центр интеграционных исследований. Евразийский банк развития. - 2018 (№49).

The most promising routes are filtered based on the sum of volume indicators. Cargo delivery time can be derived from the length of the route, but this cannot be used to compare routes with different origins and destinations. The main criterion for evaluating the route's effectiveness is the potential transport capacity of the route, but this is not the only important indicator. Routes with one to two modes of transport and a minimum number of border crossings are more advantageous because of lower transport prices and faster delivery. Transportation costs are an important criterion for assessing the current effectiveness of a route. Still, unlike most other indicators, they can change due to the development of logistics and transportation infrastructure and optimization of the logistics system. In addition, the number of necessary investments in the route was analyzed to fully utilize the full potential of the route and increase its competitiveness.

According to the route efficiency indicators and the comparative analysis of current and future cargo flow indicators, the land transportation corridors with the most development potential are:

- Central Eurasian Corridor
- Nordic Asia Corridor

The Central Eurasian Corridor connects the main lines passing through China, Kazakhstan, and Russia. It passes through Lianyungang, Zhengzhou, Lanzhou, Urumqi, Khorgos, Almaty, Kizilorda, Aktobe, Orenburg, Kas Mountain, Nizhny Novgorod, Moscow, then enters the Baltic Sea port via Brest or St. Petersburg, also passes Urumqi, Dostyk, Karaganda, Petropavlovsk, Yekaterinburg, Kazan, and finally arrives in Moscow. Among the land transportation from Europe to China, this route has the largest cargo volume. The total length of the line is 0.7–0.75 million kilometers (depending on the roads passing by).

The development investment of the basic route of the Central Eurasian Corridor (China–Kazakhstan–Russia–EU) may reach US$6 billion (laying and upgrading transportation routes in Russia and Kazakhstan, and establishing 4-6 large logistics centers). Taking the route Urumqi–Almaty–Orenburg–Moscow-EU as an example, the cost of transporting one container will be reduced by 38% after such investments (from $US1300 to US$800), and the maximum transport capacity will increase from 200,000 TEU/year to 500,000 TEU/year after modernization and upgrading.

The central link of the Nordic Asian Corridor is the line that passes through the Trans-Siberian Railway and the Bea Main Line (the utilization rate of the Trans-Siberian Railway is 100%). Important hubs on this route include Vladivostok, Irkutsk, Krasnoyarsk, Novosibirsk, Omsk, Tyumen, Yekaterinburg, Kazan, and Moscow. In addition to playing an important role in the development of eastern Russia, this route also has huge potential for cross-border transportation. In the transit transportation plan of goods between Europe and Asia, the corridor can greatly reduce the delivery period, shortening it by 10–15 days. However, due to the imperfect infrastructure, the expansion of transit transportation capacity will be greatly restricted. Therefore, the transit transportation capacity of the corridor may not be greatly improved in the short term. It is planned to improve the transit transportation capacity of the corridor in accordance with the implementation results of the Beakan Railway and the Trans-Siberian Railway Development Plan.

The development of the North-Eurasian Corridor project can be financed with up to US$2 billion, and the investment in the project can reduce the cost of shipping by 23%, from US$2,200 to US$1,700 per TEU (along the route Shanghai–Vladivostok–Great Siberian Railway–EU). The current priority is to use the financial budget to invest in the Trans-Siberian Railway development project, which usually affects the speed of project implementation. It is particularly important to attract private investment in developing logistics transportation infrastructure in the Nordic Asia Corridor.[4]

The following table shows a series of priority directions (projects) for the development of transportation routes in the EAEU countries.

---

4. См. указ Соч.

Table 22-1 Introduction to the Most Potential Routes.

Route	Length	Theoretically Calculated Transit Transport Capacity	Numbers of Shipping Methods	Number of Border Ports	The Transportation Cost/TEU	Necessary Investment	Current Maximum Transportation Capacity	Maximum Transportation Capacity after Modernization and Upgrade	Price after Modernization and Upgrade
1. Shanghai–Vladivostok–Novosibirsk–Moscow–Brest–EU*	12,000 km	250,000TEU	1 (railway)	2 (China–Russia, Russia/Belarus–EU)	The transportation cost from Shanghai to Brest is US$2200/TEU.	US$1.2–2.0 billion is used to improve the transportation capacity of the Trans-Siberian Railway.	900,000 TEU	1,500,000 TEU	The shipping price from Shanghai to Brest is US$1,700 per TEU.
2. Urumqi–Almaty–Orenburg–Moscow–Brest–EU	5,500 km	300,000TEU	2 (railway, highway)	2 (China–Kazakhstan, Russia/Belarus–EU)	The cost of rail transportation is US$1,300/TE, and the cost of road transportation is US$3,000/TEU.	US$6 billion for the construction and renovation of railways and logistics centers	200,000 TEU	500,000 TEU	The price of railway transportation is US$800/TEU, and the transportation price of Urumqi-Brest road section is US$2,000/TEU.
3. Urumqi–Almaty–Semipalatinsk–Novosibirsk–Moscow–Brest–EU	8,400 km	–	2 (railway, highway)	2 (Kazakhstan–China, Belarus/Russia–EU)	–	–	200,000 TEU	500,000 TEU	The price of railway transportation is US$800/TEU, and the transportation price of Urumqi-Brest road section is US$2,000/TEU.
4. Urumqi–Aktau–Makhachkala–Tbilisi–Poti–Constanta / Burgas–EU	5,900 km	100,000TEU	3 (railway, highway, sea transportation)	2 (Kazakhstan–China, Russia–EU)	The cost of rail transportation is US$3,200/TEU, the cost of road transportation is US$3,000/TEU, and the transportation cost to Constanta is US$4,000/TEU.	US$4 billion to upgrade port capacity and shipbuilding	30,000 TEU	300,000 TEU	The price of railway transportation is US$2,000/TEU, the price of road transportation is US$2,500/TEU, and the transportation price of Urumqi-Constancha section is US$4,000/TEU.

(Continued)

* Statistics for the Shanghai-Vladivostok-Novosibirsk-Moscow-Brest-EU route, which considers the transit cargo volume and the Russian domestic cargo volume.

Route	Distance	Capacity	Number of transport	Number of countries	Cost of transportation	Investment			Notes
5. Urumqi–Aktau–Makhachkala–Tbilisi–Poti–Constanta/Burgas–EU	5,700 km	50,000 TEU	3 (railway, highway, sea transportation)	3 (Kazakhstan–China, Russia–Georgia, Georgia–EU)	The cost of rail transportation is US$3,700/TEU, and the cost of transportation to Constanta is US$4,500/TEU.	US$4 billion is used to upgrade the port capacity and shipbuilding industry, and US$500 million is used to upgrade the Makhachkala–Tbilisi section.	20,000 TEU	250,000 TEU	The price of rail transportation is US$2500/TEU, and the price of transportation from Urumqi to Constanta is US$3,500/TEU.
6. Urumqi–Dostyk–Almaty–Beineu–Beleket–Incheburun–Tehran	6,500 km	300,000 TEU	2 (railway, highway)	3 (Kazakhstan–China, Kazakhstan–Turkmenistan, Turkmenistan–Iran)	The cost of rail transportation is US$1,700/TEU, and the cost of road transportation is US$2,700/TEU.	US$2 billion to halve transportation costs	50,000 TEU	500,000 TEU	The price of rail transportation is US$1,300/TEU, and the price of road transportation from Urumqi to Tehran is US$1,700/TEU.
7. Urumqi–Aktau–Baku–Poti–Constanta/Burgas–EU	5,800 km	50,000 TEU	3 (railway, highway, sea transportation)	4 (Kazakhstan–China, Kazakhstan–Azerbaijan, Azerbaijan–Georgia, Georgia–EU)	The cost of railway transportation is US$5,000/TEU, and the cost of road transportation is US$4,000/TEU.	US$8 billion to upgrade port capacity, road maintenance and tunnel construction	20,000 TEU	250,000 TEU	The transportation price from Urumqi to Constanta/Burgas is US$3,000/TEU.

Source: Eurasian Development Bank (Table 11).

Chapter 23

The Core of the Establishment of the Greater Eurasian Partnership for the Docking of EAEU and the "Belt and Road" Initiative

As mentioned in the previous chapters, in 2015, the heads of state of China and Russia put forward the concept of combining the EAEU and the "Belt and Road" initiative, which has become a form of the integrated regional integration project. As noted in the joint statement issued after the fifth dialogue between Chinese and Russian experts, initial progress has been made in the integration and docking of the integration initiative in the past three years.

At the same time, the ups and downs of Eurasian geopolitics and security policies have brought a series of challenges to Russia and China. China and Russia are the two pillars of the complementary projects of the integration initiative. The two countries will adhere to mutual trust and understanding, cherish the golden time for progress, take advantage of development opportunities, and contribute to maintaining economic and trade stability in Greater Europe and Asia.

The last Sino-Russia Dialogue Research Report analyzed the difficulties that hinder the integration of the "One Belt, One Alliance," and identified the following issue:

Small Amount of Trade and Investment with a Simple Structure

Mutual investments between Russia and China have increased significantly in recent years, but the overall scale of investments remains small, which constrains the development of bilateral trade. Frequent interruptions of investments, insufficient investments in promising areas of economic cooperation, and unbalanced regional distribution of investments are of particular concern.

Reference: Investment Cooperation between Russia and China

In 2008, Asian countries accounted for 17.1% of Russia's foreign trade, and the European Union accounted for 52%.[1] From 2013 to 2017, the proportion of Asian countries rose from 21.9% to 25.5%, while the proportion of the European Union dropped from 49.4% to 42%. Obviously, the sanctions against Russia have led to a sharp drop in Europe's share of foreign trade.

---

1. «Ośrodek Studiów Wschodnich (Польша): Россия совершает «разворот на Восток»? », Витольд Родкевич интернет-проект ИноСМИ. Ru, 21. 11. 2018https://inosmi.ru/politic/ 20181122/244067768. html.

The increase in trade between China and Russia is the main reason for the growth achieved in the share of Asian countries. China's share in Russia's foreign trade was 7.6% in 2008, growing to 10.5% in 2013 and 14.9% in 2017. The share of ASEAN member countries was 1.4% in 2008, 2.1% in 2013, and 3.2% in 2017. Japan's share was 3.9% in 2008, 3.9% in 2013, and 3.1% in 2017. The share of South Korea was 2.5% in 2008, 2.9% in 2013, and 3.3% in 2017. The share of India was 0.9% in 2008, 1.1% in 2013, and 1.6% in 2017.

Table 23-1 Sino-Russia Trade (Unit of Measurement: million US dollars)

Year	2013	2014	2015	2016	2017
Export	35,618	37,492	28,602	28, 011	38,918
Import	53,065	50,773	34,950	38,021	48,055

Source: Russian Federal Customs Service.

The structure of Sino-Russian trade has not changed substantially in recent years, with the share of trade in machinery, equipment, and transportation at 3.81% in 2013 and rising to 6.86% in 2017. The Russian side remains concerned about the low share of Chinese purchases of machinery products. At the same time, China has reacted in a mediocre manner, saying that it is not the fault of the Chinese side and that the structure of Russian exports to China is not significantly different from that of exports to the rest of the world.[2]

Table 23-2, "Accumulative Foreign Direct Investments in Russia," presents data on the major Russian investors' cumulative direct investment in Russia. To compare figures and obtain more real information, the following three data sources are mainly used: official data from the Central Bank of Russia, the report *EAEU and Eurasian Countries: Direct Investment Supervision and Analysis*[3] published by the Eurasian Development Bank Integration Research Center, and *China Statistical Yearbook* published by the National Bureau of Statistics of China.

---

2. «Россия – Китай: почему «горячо» в политике и «холодно» в экономике», Чжао Хуашэн, Международный дискуссионный клуб «Валдай», April 11, 2018, http://ru.valdaiclub.com/a/highlights/rossiya-kitay-goryacho-kholodno/.

3. Выпуски «ЕАЭС и страны Евразийского континента: мониторинг и анализ прямых инвестиций» за 2015, 2016, 2017 годы. Доклад за 2017 год содержит данные по итогам 2016 года. В 2018 году ЕАБР упразднил Центр Интеграционных Исследований. Соответственно, исследования по итогам на конец 2017 года не проводились.

Table 23-2 Accumulative Foreign Direct Investments in Russia (Unit of Measurement: million US dollars)

County	Source	Year			
		2013	2014	2015	2016
Holland	Central Bank of Russia	48,948	41,846	30,816	41,165
	EDB Center for Integration Studies	—	—	11,190	11,270
the UK	Central Bank of Russia	21,759	7,257	8,671	11,694
Germany	Central Bank of Russia	18,898	13,745	12,971	16,630
France	Central Bank of Russia	14,075	9,698	10,003	14,653
Switzerland	Central Bank of Russia	6,040	10,595	8,620	11,259
Austria	Central Bank of Russia	11,816	7,553	4,756	4,941
	EDB Center for Integration Studies			5,460	6,460
Ireland	Central Bank of Russia	5,210	4,648	8,253	6,583
Sweden	Central Bank of Russia	16,176	3,268	2,431	3,886
Italy	Central Bank of Russia	1,151	715	957	3,853
Finland	Central Bank of Russia	4,166	2,724	6,777	3,856

(Continued)

The USA	Central Bank of Russia	17,979	1,686	1,336	2,558
Japan	Central Bank of Russia	1,675	1,273	1,317	1,922
	EDB Center for Integration Studies	15,001	14,912	14,843	15,057
India	Central Bank of Russia	143	99	66	708
	EDB Center for Integration Studies	5,839	5,819	5,794	9,104
China*	Central Bank of Russia	4,684	3,051	1,908	3,462
	EDB Center for Integration Studies	4,056	4,340	5,221	8,225
	China Statistical Yearbook	7,581	8,694	14,019	12,979
Turkey	Central Bank of Russia	758	749	759	1,420
	EDB Center for Integration Studies	5,134	4,977	5,039	5,147
Korea	Central Bank of Russia	1,886	1,677	1,339	2,246
	EDB Center for Integration Studies	1,898	2,011	2,122	2,122
Singapore	Central Bank of Russia	164	499	493	14,564
	EDB Center for Integration Studies	601	626	685	786

* China and Hong Kong, China

Source: Central Bank of Russia, EDB Center for Integration Studies, and National Bureau of Statistics of China.

It should be noted that there are indeed significant discrepancies in some important data in the above tables, which are undoubtedly caused by differences in calculation methods, and we believe that the data from the EDB Center for Integration Studies are closer to the real situation. The research was carried out by the EDB Center for Integration Studies together with members of the expert group of the Institute of World Economy and International Relations of the RAS under the guidance of Kuznetsov, a corresponding member of the RAS.

The database of the EDB Center for Integration Studies is based on the "top-down" principle, i.e., it is compiled based on company statements and other first-hand information. It includes information on investments made through offshore companies and other institutions and on the reinvestment of earnings obtained abroad. The difference between the statistics of the database and the official statistics of the Central Bank of Russia is also due to this. The salient feature of the statistical methods of the EDB Center for Integration Studies is that the amount of investment is counted according to the actual location of localization of assets, rather than according to the first country into which foreign direct investment (usually offshore companies) formally flows. The EDB Center for Integration Studies methodology is now commonly used in the member countries of the Organization for Economic Cooperation and Development. Investment assessment is generally carried out mainly on the basis of the recommendations of international institutions. Still, it is also more popular to use indirect methods for FDI assessment (e.g., on the basis of information on companies' fixed assets or similar transactions of other companies).

The statistical method of the EDB Center for Integration Studies also considers all projects with a cumulative FDI amount exceeding US$3 million, as well as a slightly smaller group of projects (preferably in industries with a low capital consumption rate). Still, it excludes the real estate sector, where the geographical location of FDI is more important to consider.

The Central Bank of Russia's data is based on the balance of payments. As a result, the data of the Central Bank of Russia and that of the EDB Center for Integration Studies are subject to an error of 1 to 3 times. Therefore, the statistics of the EDB Center for Integration Studies can supplement that of the Central Bank of Russia, but cannot replace it.

It is not certain which method the *China Statistical Yearbook* uses to count foreign direct investment, but to a certain extent, it considers foreign direct investment by offshore companies.

According to the data from the Central Bank of Russia, the EDB Center for Integration Studies, and the National Bureau of Statistics of China, the following conclusions can be drawn from the data presented in the table "Accumulative Foreign Direct Investments in Russia": China is far from the leading country in accumulative direct investment in Russia and its cumulative direct investment in Russia is still less than that of major European countries and some Asian countries (Japan and India). Overall, the cumulative direct investment of Asian countries in Russia is indeed not as good as that in Europe. If we refer to the EDB Center for Integration Studies data, Holland is undoubtedly a major investor in the Russian economy.

Investment in Russia is only a very small part of China's overseas investment. If China-Russia trade is 2%[4] of China's foreign trade volume, then China's investment in Russia will account for less than 1% of China's overseas investment.

Table 23-3 China's Foreign Direct Investment (Unit of Measurement: million US dollars)

Year	2013	2014	2015	2016	2017
In Total	107843.71	123119.86	145667.15	196149.43	158288.3
Investment in Russia	1022.25	633.56	2960.86	1293.07	1548.42
Share of investment in Russia	0.95%	0.51%	2.03%	0.66%	0.98%

Source: National Bureau of Statistics of China.

At the same time, it can be determined that China is a large investor in Russia and has the potential to become the largest investor in the next few years.

Despite the increasing trade between China and Russia, the scale of it is still small: in 2017, the trade volume between China and Russia was about 13% of that between China and the US in the same period. China-Russia trade and investment cooperation needs further improvement and development. The trade structure between China and Russia has long been relatively homogeneous, dominated by energy, raw materials, and other low-value-added commodities. Raw material price fluctuations can substantially impact on Sino-Russian economic relations, affecting not only trade volumes but also overall economic development.

Practical Issues of Financial Cooperation

Many factors have now become obstacles to China-Russia financial cooperation. First, the uncoordinated economic and trade cooperation has severely restricted the development potential of financial cooperation between the two countries.

Second, the financial cooperation support mechanism is not perfect, and the package of tools for preventing and controlling the consequences of financial risks is insufficient and inefficient. For example, the lack of effective payment and settlement channels for Russia and China in the context of Western (mainly EU countries and the US) sanctions makes the national financial system more vulnerable and increases the risks of doing business in Russia. Unfortunately, all this can seriously affect the normal functioning of Chinese financial institutions. Many countries interested in cooperation with Russia are influenced by pessimism and abandon it. It is necessary to expand the exchange of information on bilateral financial cooperation between Russia and China and to strengthen various regulations.

---

4. The National Bureau of Statistics of China on China's foreign trade statistics in 2017.

Third, large state-owned enterprises and private companies are unwilling to settle in local currency. There are many reasons for this. The leaders of large Russian companies transfer foreign exchange income to offshore companies through freely convertible currencies. To accelerate the realization of the potential of cross-border transactions in the local currency, China only tends to realize the full convertibility of the renminbi. At present, China is restricted by administrative barriers when conducting cross-border capital transactions.

Finally, the sanctions imposed on Russia by the US and its allies have hurt Sino-Russian cooperation, with Chinese banks refusing to provide services to Russian natural and legal persons, dollar settlements being blocked, and Russian companies caught in the sanctions fiasco losing the opportunity to settle with their Chinese partners traditionally.

Limitations of Existing Cooperation Models

At present, China and Russia mainly carry out economic cooperation at the government level, mainly for large-scale infrastructure construction joint projects and national security cooperation projects (such as cooperation projects in the energy and aerospace fields). These cooperation projects only have an impact on the above-mentioned fields. Practice has proved that similar cooperation models have shortcomings and limitations, restricting the expansion of economic ties between China and Russia under the conditions of a market economy, especially cooperation in production, innovation, and services.

The low level of cooperation in the high-tech field is a shortcoming in expanding the diversified cooperation between the two countries. For many years, joint projects between the two countries in the aviation industry, oil and gas machinery manufacturing, electrical machinery industry, and other machinery manufacturing fields have long been stagnant.

Large joint infrastructure projects in Europe and Asia are stalled. The Russian side lacks sources of investment, and the Chinese side does not see a mechanism for the repayment of funds.

China and Russia should continue to develop bilateral economic and trade cooperation based on market economy principles. In view of the limited growth of production and consumption in the Russian Far East, the two countries should invest in areas with the greatest export potential.

The two countries have insufficient research and understanding of each other's markets, and trade barriers exist in various economic sectors.

There is no progress in Sino-Russian agro-industrial complex cooperation. Due to China's tariff and non-tariff restrictions, and the lack of credit sources for Russian exporters, bilateral cooperation cannot tap the huge potential.

One of the important reasons for the backwardness of Sino-Russian cooperation in agriculture and the agro-industrial complex is that Russian exporters cannot meet China's needs. For example, in 2017, China imported 95.42 million tons of soybeans, while Russia's soybean output was only 3.6 million tons. The main reason for the slow development of Sino-Russian cooperation in agriculture and the agro-industrial complex is that Russian companies have not done enough research on issues related to entering the Chinese market. To solve this problem, an entrepreneur forum aimed at expanding Sino-Russian agricultural cooperation should be launched.

Inadequate Understanding of the Actions of National Government Agencies

Many scholars, officials, and citizens strongly support Sino-Russian economic cooperation. However, the implementation of win-win projects still faces numerous obstacles, as China and Russia are not able to fully facilitate the implementation of certain projects in both countries even after the signing of the contract, or it leads to the postponement of the project. In the framework of certain projects, Russia often restricts Chinese investments in relevant areas through quotas, standards, quality control, etc. Chinese companies should pay as much attention to the lifestyle of local Russian residents when making investment decisions as they do to investment projects and reaching win-win situations.

Russia's strategic positioning for multi-field cooperation with China is reasonable, but the strategic objective system is not yet perfect. Various obstacles are still encountered in formulating the incentive standards for the best cooperation model. Before starting international trade, Chinese companies should conduct market research, make relevant preparations, and consider the needs of local people.

Developing Green Finance

China and Russia are countries with vast territories and rich natural resources. One of the main tasks facing China and Russia is to protect the diversity of natural areas and ecosystems. However, ecological, natural resource, and climate problems are worsening yearly, and the state has a very limited budget for investment in green projects; thus, taxpayers must bear an additional burden. For example, in 2015, China set the share of spending on green projects: 10%–15% from the state budget and 85%–90% from other financing sources.

The proverb "one tree does not make a forest" reminds us that international cooperation is necessary to implement green initiatives. It is recommended to jointly develop inter-country green financial instruments to solve ecological problems and help expand national financial markets and implement joint initiatives at the international level.

Despite the difficulties, the economic and trade cooperation between the member states of the EAEU and China has achieved overall success. In 2018, the bilateral trade volume between China and Russia exceeded the 100 billion mark (US$107 billion). Cooperation between China and other member states of the EAEU is also progressing rapidly.

Central Asia, especially Kazakhstan, is a key region for docking. China and Kazakhstan signed contracts for 55 projects in the construction sector with a total value of US$27 billion. It is important that cooperation in the field of construction is closely connected with the national plan of Kazakhstan, "Bright Road." In addition, Kazakhstan got its own cargo base in Lianyungang, China, and the "Double-West Highway" (Western Europe–Russia–Kazakhstan–Western China), which passes through Kazakhstan, has six transportation channels, which brings Kazakhstan more than US$1 trillion in transit revenues.

Another representative example of the implementation of the Great Eurasian Partnership is Belarus. On 11.25 hectares of land near the Belarusian International Airport, the "Boulder" Industrial Park of Belarus was established, where unprecedented preferential policies are available. Belarusian President Lukashenka said that Belarus is ready to become a bastion of Chinese interests in the Eurasian region.

Docking of "Belt and Road" and the EAEU Project

In 2015, the establishment of the EAEU (EAEU) was proposed, and its member states include Russia, Belarus, Kazakhstan, and Armenia. Initially, EAEU planned to establish a free trade zone with China. Still, after the decision of the EAEU and the Chinese leadership, in May 2015, China and Russia signed the "Joint Declaration of Docking Cooperation between the Construction of the Silk Road Economic Belt with the EAEU between the People's Republic of China and the Russian Federation," stating that the two sides will take coordinated actions to carry out collaborations throughout the construction of EAEU and the "Silk Road Economic Belt." The synergy of work is carried out on bilateral and multilateral platforms, first within the framework of the Shanghai Cooperation Organization.[5] EAEU, which covers about 200 million people, and the Silk Road Economic Belt initiative, which covers 3 billion people, are closely integrated with cultural norms.

It is expected that within the EAEU member states (Russia, Kazakhstan, and Belarus), the economy of the expansion zone of transport infrastructure (road and railroad) along the route Druzhba (Dostyk)–Almaty–Orenburg–Kazan–Moscow–Minsk will develop at a faster pace, just as that of the regions along the route developed rapidly after the laying of the Great Siberian Railway and the Middle East Railway in the late 19th and early 20th centuries. The long length of these two railroads and their access to the sea led to the rapid development of the areas adjacent to the lines, both in Russia (Eastern Siberia and the Far East) and in China (Heilongjiang, Jilin, and Liaoning) when the laying of the tracks began.

The two projects of the EAEU and the "Belt and Road" initiative will, on the one hand, enable Russia and other EAEU member states to build a large cross-border area for European goods to enter Asia and expand the market for the products of China and other Asian countries. On the other hand, it will expand the market for selling Chinese products and broaden the channels for importing raw materials into China. The two projects of the EAEU and the Belt and Road will largely strengthen the economic and trade cooperation between the SCO member states. They will ensure the development

---

5. "The Silk Road Economic Belt," Moscow: Institute of Russian Biography, Institute for Economic Strategy, 2015, 22–23.

of economic and trade ties between Russia and China. The northern route of the "Silk Road Economic Belt" passes through Russia, China, and Kazakhstan. As the project develops, it will reach Central and West Asia, up to the Gulf and the Mediterranean. This allows the Silk Road Economic Belt to absorb not only other SCO countries (Kyrgyzstan, Tajikistan, Uzbekistan), but also a group of neighboring countries and reap economic benefits from the cooperation.

In implementing the "Silk Road Economic Belt" initiative, the parties should work together on the economic development problems of the member countries of the Silk Road Economic Belt project, considering the economic, political, and legal realities of both sides to align their strategies. The "Silk Road Economic Belt" project plans to build and improve the cross-border infrastructure in the areas along the route. The main cross-border infrastructure project in Russia should be the construction of the Beijing-Moscow high-speed rail line.

It can be said that China and Russia currently have three main cooperation tasks in the "Silk Road Economic Belt" project:

- To implement the five major goals proposed by the Chinese leaders, it is necessary to ensure the docking of the "Silk Road Economic Belt" and the EAEU, and it is necessary to build a free trade zone between China and the EAEU.
- In the field of infrastructure development, China and Russia need to build Moscow-Beijing high-speed rail and Moscow-Kazan high-speed rail.
- It is necessary to rapidly develop infrastructure in the Russian Far East (construction of Heilongjiang and Ussuri bridges, cross-border passages, highways and airports, and expansion of ports) to strengthen ties with Northeast China.

China-Russia strategic cooperation is the main content of the Greater Eurasian Partnership. To ensure the connection between the EAEU and the "Silk Road Economic Belt" project, five major tasks should be determined.

1. Improving the policy of expanding China-Russia economic and trade ties. In May 2015, China and Russia issued a joint declaration, saying they would cooperate on the docking of the EAEU and the "Silk Road Economic Belt" project. After that, in May 2018, China and the EAEU signed the "Agreement on Economic and Trade Cooperation between the People's Republic of China and the EAEU," achieving bilateral trade and investment liberalization.
2. Another important task of the EAEU and the "Silk Road Economic Belt" initiative is to strengthen bilateral infrastructure links. The Skovorodino-Mohe section of the "Siberia-Pacific" oil pipeline has been completed. The Sino-Russian gas pipeline "Power of Siberia" is under rapid construction. After the project is put into operation, China will be able to obtain natural gas from Russia, and cooperation in other areas between the two countries can also be further developed. There are also two bridges under construction:

the highway bridge (Heihe-Blagoveshchensk) and the railway bridge (the following Ningskoye-Tongjiang). These two bridges can provide a bridge from northeast China to Vladivostok, Russia. A large transportation corridor was established between Stoke ("Marina 1") and Zarubino ("Marina 2"). In this way, the transport link between the EAEU and the "Silk Road Economic Belt" initiative can be raised to a new level.

3. There is another important aspect of the docking between the EAEU and the "Belt and Road" initiative; it greatly broadens the foreign trade relations between China and Russia. Statistics in 2018 show that the total amount of foreign trade between China and Russia exceeded the US$100 billion mark set in 2015 for the first time, reaching US$107 billion.

4. New achievements have been made in financial investment cooperation. The Central Bank of Russia opened a representative office in China, the Russian RMB clearing center was launched in Moscow, and the China Development Bank and the Export-Import Bank of China also opened representative offices in Moscow. In the field of Sino-Russian investment cooperation, China plans to establish a Sino-Russian regional cooperation development investment fund with a total scale of 100 billion yuan (1 billion rubles) in Russia. The first phase of the fund will raise 10 billion yuan to promote the development of small and medium-sized enterprises.

5. People-to-people and cultural exchanges between China and Russia play a vital role in developing bilateral relations. Every year, the number of people-to-people and cultural exchanges between China and Russia exceeds 3 million, of which 80,000 students are exchanged between the two countries.

Regarding the participation of the member states of the EAEU in the "Silk Road Economic Belt" initiative, it should be pointed out that Kazakhstan and Belarus are implementing joint infrastructure projects. The cross-border channel Chunja-Khorgos expands the volume of Aktau cargo on the shore of the Caspian Sea, which allows cargo to be transported to Baku to be ferried. In Belarus, the construction of the "Great Stone" Industrial Park between China and Belarus in Minsk is underway at full speed. Regrettably, there are no large-scale projects between China and Russia as between China and Kazakhstan and between China and Belarus.

Analyzing the possibility of docking between the EAEU and the "Silk Road Economic Belt" project, it should be recognized that the docking plan has three development results: no docking at all, complete docking, and partial docking. There are two methods for project docking, namely, through the Shanghai Cooperation Organization and through a free trade zone. The latter is more reasonable because the volume of foreign trade under the framework of the Shanghai Cooperation Organization is not large, and the organization is semi-closed. A few years ago, when the EAEU and the "Silk Road Economic Belt" project were connected through a free trade zone, it aroused strong doubts about the expansion of Chinese goods into the Russian market. However, after the ruble depreciated sharply against the US dollar, the euro, and the renminbi in December 2014, the situation changed, and the prices of Chinese goods on the Russian market rose sharply. The establishment of a free trade zone will enable the region to gradually get rid of the restrictions of trade and investment barriers, and trade and investment cooperation will become a powerful uniting factor. Obviously, although China faces some problems, such as a large population and a relatively small proportion of the labor force, insufficient energy sources such as oil and gas, and environmental pollution caused by the rapid development of manufacturing, the Chinese economy will continue to develop rapidly.

Table 23-4 2009–2018 China's Foreign Trade Volume (Unit of Measurement: billion US dollars*)

Countries and Regions	1995	2003	2010	2015	2016	2017	2018
China	280.9/100	851.0/100	2974/100	3957/100	3685/100	4105/100	4620/100
USA	40.8/14.5	126.4/14.9	385.4/12.9	558.3/14.1	516.5/14.1	583.7/14.2	632.3/13.7
EU	—	125.0/14.7	479.6/16.1	564.8/14.3	543.9/15.0	616.9/15.0	681.3/14.7
ASEAN	—	78.2/9.2	292.9/9.8	472.2/11.9	449.8/12.3	514.8/12.5	586.8/12.7
Russia	5.5/2.0	15.7/1.8	55.5/1.9	68.1/1.7	69.1/1.9	84.1/2.0	107.0/2.3
Hong Kong, China	44.6/15.9	87.4/10.3	230.6/7.8	343.6/8.7	303.0/8.3	286.7/7.0	311.0/6.7
Taiwan, China	17.9/6.4	58.4/6.9	145.4/4.9	188.2/4.8	178.7/4.9	199.4/4.9	225.8/4.9
Japan	57.5/20.5	133.5/15.7	297.8/10.0	278.7/7.0	273.4/7.5	303.0/7.4	327.0/7.1
Korea	17.0/6.0	63.2/7.4	207.1/7.0	275.8/7.0	251.1/6.9	280.3/6.8	312.7/6.8

The participants in the Sino-Russian Scholars Dialogue discussed the issues of cooperation between the two countries as follows:

- All businesses of enterprises and banks in China and Russia implement local currency settlement.
- Docking the payment system, requiring the central banks of China and Russia to directly join the electronic system for the exchange of information between the two countries' banks.
- The State Bank of Russia's payment system "Peace" and the Chinese payment system "UnionPay" jointly launch a dual-label debit card.

---

* National Bureau of Statistics of China, *2018 China Statistical Abstract, 102; Statistical Bulletin on National Economic and Social Development in 2018.*

- Using a payment system that can stably pay digital assets based on the blockchain.
- Setting up a specialized development bank to finance joint investment projects that only support local currency payments.
- Establishing an inter-country consortium involving enterprises from China and the EAEU member states to implement cross-border high-tech investment projects involving extensive production cooperation.

To deepen Sino-Russian cooperation as a whole and remove the shortcomings in the relationship between the economic agencies of the two countries, the following measures should be implemented:

Further Deepen and Consolidate Political Cooperation and Mutual Trust through Joint Action

To improve the efficiency of Sino-Russian economic cooperation, it is necessary to fully implement the principle of "selecting the best solution for the specific situation."

The Chinese and Russian personnel who participated in preparing this report suggested that the two sides should establish a standing committee on economic cooperation issues at the head of the state level. The two countries' first vice ministers participate in related work, and the heads of state personally appoint personnel to lead. We are willing to formulate a strategic action plan for economic cooperation development. The decision made by the committee under this plan must be binding within the established authority and be reflected in the corresponding national documents. In the near future, China and Russia should establish a special institution for investment and economic cooperation between the two countries in due course. The institution should simplify investment procedures and deepen cooperation between the two countries' enterprises.

The aggressive behavior of the US is intensifying, breaking the international trade and legal system, and dismantling the current financial and economic order in the world. In this regard, China and Russia should jointly solve the above-mentioned problems and continue to promote the reform of the global financial system with the support of the BRICS and the Shanghai Cooperation Organization.

Improving the Level of Cooperation in Trade, Finance, and Investment

In the sphere of mutual trade and financial cooperation, the following measures should be taken: ordering the central bank to start using local currency for mutual trade credit and investment operations between the two countries; using the ruble/yuan exchange currency credit mechanism for mutual trade credit and investment; finding ways to ensure the interconnection of national systems of information exchange between banks, Previously established agreements and existing agreements may retain the requirements of the agreement in the same way as before, but the new agreement should be based on the local currency (unless the two countries do not want to pay the penalty for unexpected changes), and special incentives for companies and banks (such as tax incentives, investment standards, interest rate incentives, etc.) should be used rationally to encourage the use of local currency settlement.

Bilateral mechanisms for buffering risks (currency and financial risks) need to be established for the markets of the two countries. These mechanisms are based on the joint participation of the large state-owned banks of the two countries. Special funds may be established to achieve the set goals. These mechanisms should include organizing transaction insurance, simplifying the hedging mechanism, and using RMB and rubles to price oil futures contracts reasonably.

In the field of green finance, it is recommended to coordinate national legislation by introducing "green" finance. To exchange experience, a Sino-Russian green finance development working group should be established at an appropriate time. The working group should be composed of authorized personnel who make decisions and implement supervision in green finance.

In investment cooperation, it is proposed to increase the share of mutual investments and establish investment funds and banking systems to guarantee direct investments and investment credits in local currency. A similar system and the existing joint funds for direct investments may include joint funds for regional development, venture capital, and industrial development.

Relevant procedures need to be simplified to stimulate companies and banks of the two countries (including organizations on the sanctions list) to issue stocks and bonds in each other's financial markets, including the transfer and withdrawal of funds obtained from RMB bonds.

In addition to starting to use local currency to calculate and establish specialized financial institutions, digital currency tools should also be used rationally to create an inter-country digital currency called "Eurasian," including Russia, China, and other participants in the EAEU and the "Silk Road Economic Belt." Economies connected with the economic belt can use this currency for cross-border settlement. A special international clearing house should be established for the issuance of the currency, ensuring that the digital currency can be exchanged in local currency at the exchange rate standard pegged to the gold price on the Shanghai Exchange. The digital currency "Eurasia" will be made available to all participants through a distributed registration system to a blockchain-like system (for example, in the "master chain" system developed in Russia). The pilot operation of the mechanism should be started in the Vladivostok Free Port jurisdiction. It is recommended to pre-define the mechanism of efficient synergy between newly created and existing digital currencies; to develop a buffer mechanism for external risks/shocks that are likely to be caused by cyber threats and existing financial technologies; to enhance the effectiveness of monetary and credit policy mechanisms and to achieve their harmonious coexistence with the new digital environment.

In addition, it is also recommended that Chinese and Russian companies use the opportunity of participating in the first International Import Expo to be held in China in November 2018 to attract the best companies in various industries and promote the development of Russian technology, services, and products.

Other Efforts for the Docking Cooperation between the EAEU and the "Silk Road Economic Belt"

In recent years, the projects aimed at effectively realizing the docking between the EAEU and the "Silk Road Economic Belt" has been relatively coordinated. However, the number and results of these projects are still limited, especially the implementation of cooperation projects in infrastructure construction in the Eurasian region. Russia's foreign investment quota is relatively large. Nonetheless, the overall proportion of total investment in China and the investment in implementing the "Silk Road Economic Belt" initiative are still low, and there are still opportunities to expand the proportion of these investments.

It is necessary to ensure the smooth progress of the convergence of the EAEU and "Silk Road Economic Belt" through timely development and implementation of joint strategic plans and national strategic plans. To this end, it is necessary to analyze these plans jointly and include in them the content of large-scale infrastructure projects for attracting investments, and attract investment for the projects with the assistance of investment funds and development agencies. The construction of infrastructure ports along the "Ice Silk Road" is a promising direction for investment cooperation.

To develop cooperation in the field of infrastructure, it is recommended to establish inter-state consortia, which lease transportation corridors for paving roads and developing adjacent areas. At the same time, it is recommended to rely on the issuance of bonds in the financial markets of China and the EAEU to achieve financing, and attract loans from the Asian Infrastructure Investment Bank, the Silk Road Fund, the BRICS New Development Bank, and the Eurasian Development Bank.

Deepen Cooperation in the Field of S&T

It is proposed to expand cooperation in the research and application of high technologies, including the processing of raw materials, while developing traditional forms of cooperation in the energy sphere. It is necessary to form a network of joint ventures with scientific manufacturing potential, including the construction of an aviation manufacturing joint venture, and to identify sources of investment. It is proposed to transfer rights and production equipment to united airlines to produce civil aircraft and transport aircraft developed by Antonov, Tupolev, and Ilyushin; to oblige the national airline to plan the operation of these aircraft; to establish a joint investment fund for aviation construction to ensure credit for the production and purchase of these aircraft; to provide leasing services to airlines.

Machinery manufacturing industries in the fields of oil and gas, chemical, forestry, food, shipbuilding, power, and electronics industries have a large potential for development. They can achieve import substitution of products from hostile countries in case of a hybrid war with Russia and China, and similar systems of joint production, production and investment should be established in these areas.

It is also proposed to establish a Strategic Center for Scientific Cooperation, which would be able to implement the preparation of scientific projects in economic and high-tech applications and prepare common materials and project documents required for the G20 Summit, BRICS Leaders Summit, SCO Leaders Summit, and APEC Leaders Summit. At the same time, this center can organize cooperation between Russian and Chinese scholars, engineers, and specialists, ensure collaboration of national research institutions and enterprises, and develop collaboration between Russian and Chinese scientific communities.

New Opportunities for Cooperation in the Field of E-commerce Great Potential for Growth

In the past few years, the cooperation between China and Russia in e-commerce has made great progress, becoming the second largest cooperation direction after energy. More and more Russian companies relying on e-commerce platforms can gain new opportunities to open up the Chinese market. In addition to e-commerce, the two countries have also made great progress in telecommunications technology (including inter-city telecommunications technology). Cooperation in the above-mentioned fields needs further development, including expanding the scale of cooperation in agriculture and agro-industrial complexes.

There is a need to fully use the relatively competitive assets of both countries, namely China's demographic advantages and Russia's fertile land. Expanding agricultural cooperation between the two countries along the Russian coastal border and in northeastern China should be a priority direction of cooperation, which requires a high level of mutual political trust between Russia and China.

It is recommended to accelerate regional and inter-city cooperation between the two countries, improve and consolidate Sino-Russian regional cooperation and the results of the 2018 and 2019 local cooperation and exchange years, and develop collaborative links.

Expanding and Strengthening the Exchange of Experts under the Framework of Cooperation between the Analysis Center and Other Centers

Considering that many Russians see themselves as Europeans and adhere to the Western way of life, many Chinese, including the elite, do not always understand the behavior of the Russian state and its people. The proposed exchange of experts in various fields and dialogue based on the topics covered in the report could greatly facilitate cooperation between Russian and Chinese analytical centers, and such initiatives have already received a positive response.

Interaction and communication between the peoples of the two countries are of great importance, and friendship between people depends on mutual understanding. Although Russia and China have achieved a high level of mutual trust at the level of state leaders, the general public still does not understand each other on certain issues. Some people in Russia and China still promote such ideas as the "China threat theory" and "Russia is unreliable." Therefore, it is necessary to strengthen people-to-people exchanges further and carry out a series of activities to deepen mutual trust and understanding, including the "Year of China," "Year of Russia," "Year of Tourism," "Year of Languages," "Year of Youth," "Year of Language," and "Year of Youth Friendship," etc.

Conclusion

Introduction to the New Model of Economic Science

The new world economic and technological order has been formed and is transitioning to orderly economic development, which requires forming a new scientific model. If we regard economic science as the objective knowledge of subject research, rather than the defense of the ruling elite, this model should be able to reveal the laws of economic development and be the basis of relevant economic policies.

Based on the research, the following analyzes the basic issues of the crisis in economic science and the development of a new scientific model. The new scientific model helps to explain many anomalies that do not correspond to mainstream economic thought, reveals the reasons why mainstream economic thought cannot explain the crisis that is currently occurring, and shows the modern process of economic development that contradicts the starting point of non-classical economic theory. The neoclassical economic theory focuses on the state of market equilibrium, but this equilibrium cannot be achieved in the real economy, which leads to the fact that the explanations proposed for the process of distribution of social goods do not correspond to reality and are reduced to a defense of the current order of economic control.

This work proposes a new method for studying economic development issues. The change in the economic system is the main analysis object. Usually, the change in the economic system is nonlinear, unbalanced, and uncertain. The law of economic change has been explained above. The law of economic change is restricted by the characteristics of scientific and technological achievements, the life cycle of technology and the international economic structure, the technological trajectory, and the formation mechanism of the scientific production cycle. Therefore, it can be concluded that the development process of the modern economic system is a movement process from one attractor to another. Still, new methods of creating new attractors will continue to appear, so this development process will never be realized. Finally, a new method of studying economic development issues can explain the reasons for periodic economic crises in the process of economic growth, and provide effective suggestions for formulating correct economic development policies.

The Relationship between Economic Thoughts and Interests

Mainstream economic thought, including the representatives of mainstream economic thought in government, is unable to predict the global economic crisis, provide a rational explanation for the economic rise of China and India, analyze the reasons for the decline of old industrial areas in the United States, or understand why countries that replicate the successful experience of American reforms trigger social and economic disasters in their own countries.[1]

It should also be remembered that neither contemporary economists nor economists in the Soviet era could predict that the most advanced and promising socialist system they agreed on would collapse. To make matters worse, the suggestions of these economists have caused great damage to the socialist system, created chaos, and shaken its foundation.

But these facts alone do not make it possible to say that economists have misled national governments and public opinion. These facts simply convey the principles of a basic economic doctrine that defines the current ruling elite as having a sense of defending economic policies and practices, an economic doctrine that does not itself need to react to true knowledge. It is only important for the ruling elite to approve policies that are favorable to them, and this is the essential reason for the differences between the dominant schools of economic thought in a given society at a given time.

Any economic policy reflects the material interests of different social groups, a claim that no experienced business executive can necessarily dispute. For example, the above has been able to demonstrate who are the ongoing beneficiaries of Russia's current macroeconomic policies, which have deeply undermined productivity and led to the poverty of the people. It can be concluded from this that the theories defending the rationality of the state's macroeconomic policies are nothing more than self-interest under the banner of science, and that those scholars working on vague theories cannot even identify which interest group they are representing. But the reputation and recognition of these scholars depend on the mass media, the titles and awards they are awarded, the prestigious forums they attend, the extent to which they are needed by the state authorities, the leadership of government agencies, universities, and other institutions controlled by the ruling elite, the interests of them being the criteria of the selection of "scientific" proposals and their related theories. If this theory questions the dominance of the ruling elite in society and the right to truth, it will eventually be considered wrong by both government agencies and the social consciousness, as well as by the popular education system. These theories hover on the fringes of mainstream economic thought, and the ruling elites do not need them for the time being and will use dogmatic theories to replace them.

After the victory of the socialist revolution, Marxism won, and the capitalist economic theory that had previously been in a dominant position was defined as a biased theory because it only represented the interests of capitalists. However, Marxism itself quickly degenerated into a dogmatic theory defending the practice of socialist construction in the Soviet Union. With the disintegration of the Soviet Union, it quickly disappeared from the corridor of power and the hall of honor. The opponents of Marxism declared themselves the ultimate victors and rushed to claim that the "history of Marxism is over."[2]

In fact, the history of Marxism has not come to an end, but it has been clearly studied from the point of view of economic theory. Today, Marxism has become a

---

1. В книге «Зомби-экономика: как мертвые идеи продолжают блуждать среди нас» Джон Куиггин (М.: Издательский дом Высшей школы экономики, 2016) очень подробно описал этот процесс, который как раз и привел к последнему кризису.

2. Фукуяма Ф. Конец истории и последний человек. М.: АСТ, 2010.

formalized set of concepts in "economics,"[3] codified in "economics" on an impractical theoretical basis. Although Western mainstream economic thought has been criticized for the past half century, the foundations of Western mainstream economic thought have remained unchanged for a century since the emergence of the marginal concept of market equilibrium, on which increasingly complex false structures have been built that have gradually drifted away from economic reality.

It is long past time to hope for pertinent evaluations or useful advice from mainstream economic science. Everyone has become accustomed to the fact that economic forecasts are less accurate than weather forecasts, and that officials and businessmen need to rely on "clear heads" rather than so-called "scientific advice" in order to do their jobs successfully. And in countries where the ruling class is less educated, the uneducated ruling elites have plunged their countries into socioeconomic disaster by relying on pseudo-scientific advice received from the IMF.

It can be seen from the above that the neoclassical model surrounding the theory of market equilibrium is essentially a religion in the cloak of science in economic science. It defends the sacred right of private property, rejects government intervention in the economy, and believes that government intervention is clearly destroying the economy and hindering the "invisible hand" of the market from optimizing the allocation of resources. This theory safeguards the right of the owners of the means of production to arrange the means of production arbitrarily. It stipulates that the state should guarantee to follow this theory. In its crude monetarist version, this theory expresses the interests of currency owners, and is essentially a modern pseudo-scientific expression of the pedantic belief in money worship.

Economic Science Crisis

It goes without saying that within the neoclassical theoretical framework, one has come to many interesting conclusions that explain the different cases in which the economy deviates from the market equilibrium. These marginalist doctrines look very elegant, playing with the concept of marginal utility and applying it to a diverse and infinitely variable combination of factors of production, reducing the concept of factors of production to a single equivalent exchange at the point of market equilibrium. The mathematical tools introduced from traditional mechanics are intended to convince the reader of the significance of their explanations based on the distribution of social goods according to the marginal productivity of labor and capital. The presentation of these explanations provides scientific proof of the fairness and perfection of the free market economy.

However, the problem is that all these formal discussions are related to economic reality, just like using the second law of thermodynamics to explain the natural evolution of biology. The theory of market equilibrium is essentially a reproduction of economic methods. The only thing that needs to be explained in advance is this equilibrium state, which physicists associate with maximum entropy, and economists

---

3. The term in this article refers to the typical argumentation system based on market equilibrium theory used in most modern economics textbooks.

interpret it as the maximum use efficiency of limited resources. The basis of this explanation is to formally prove that any behavior that deviates from the equilibrium point is accompanied by a decrease in the total results of economic activities and the differentiation of the conditions of economic entities (the conditions of some economic entities continue to deteriorate, and the conditions of other economic entities continue to improve). According to the best code of conduct, the results of economic activity at the point of market equilibrium are generally equal. The proponents of the market equilibrium theory have not noticed that from a formal point of view, economic activity is equal to zero, while from common sense, economic agents are losing their motivation for activities.

The market equilibrium theory based on neoclassical analysis principles interprets the economy as a state of pursuing the greatest possible due to free competition among economic entities. Proponents of market equilibrium theory liken this equilibrium state to an optimal point, where limited resources can be used most effectively. Physicists interpret it as the termination point where energy exchange with the external environment ceases. At this point, the entire system enters a state of complete chaos. In contrast to economics, we can conclude from these explanations that when economic agents reach an equilibrium point due to free competition but have not completed more reasonable economic activities, the economy itself ceases to develop.

The economic agents in the neoclassical paradigm do not die out; like molecules in thermodynamics, they continue to move at equilibrium. For physicists, this is the haphazard motion of system components, and the system energy as a whole does not change. For economists, it is a zero-sum game of market forces that forces them to keep moving up and down the equilibrium point, where the profits of some economic agents are equal to the losses of others. Surprisingly, the advocates of the neoclassical paradigm do not notice that this interpretation is so absurd for the real economy. Unlike the physical system, the real economy consists of people and the firms they create, which collaborate to produce increasingly complex products and thus increase energy consumption. Although competition between economic agents does occur, contrary to heat exchange in the theory of physics, the game of market forces does not lead to an equilibrium point equal to zero, but rather to an increasing amount of energy consumed by a more complex system and its interaction with the environment, further and further away from the equilibrium point.

The problem is that the economy has gradually evolved into more complex and changeable production and consumption behaviors. As a living system, it has never reached an equilibrium state, and will gradually move away from the equilibrium state in the process of evolution. Economic development has the attribute of negative entropy, and it develops in a direction that is becoming increasingly complicated and less possible. When the economy deviates from the growth path and enters a state of chaos and turbulence, there may be special circumstances of retrogression. But even in this case, the economy as a permanent life system is contrary to the second law of thermodynamics. It cannot stabilize at the equilibrium point. Instead, it constantly updates and transforms the technical and institutional structures through structural crises, and "enters" into the new growth path, or to adapt to the requirements of more complex systems, it is absorbed by more complex systems. Therefore, the proponents of the neoclassical economics real economic paradigm's obsession to find equilibrium are reminiscent of the attempts of medieval physiologists to use pathological anatomy to reveal the secrets of life.

As mentioned above, the neoclassical paradigm is inapplicable because its preconditions require economic agents' spirituality, rationality, and independence. In the context of free market competition, these preconditions automatically ensure the optimal use of limited resources and the achievement of maximum possible economic efficiency. Still, none of the preconditions are consistent with the realities of the modern economy, so economic policies built on the neoclassical paradigm will never produce the desired results.

Faced with a myriad of unexplained phenomena, neoclassical theory acknowledges that "there may be loopholes in the market," but it explains them as inadequate state regulation of deviations from equilibrium. The attempt to approach this equilibrium by eliminating state deviations differs little from the widespread use of bloodletting in the Middle Ages. Bloodletting was then used as a universal treatment to cure all diseases, and this method may indeed achieve a state of sedation, but it does so at the expense of killing the organism. In the state of death, the organism would evolve according to the laws of physics, i.e., decompose into maximum entropy exactly according to the second law of thermodynamics.

The mechanical equilibrium model makes people believe in the magical property of the market's self-organization function. This property determines that neoclassical analysis cannot explain many economic phenomena, and that the economic policy recommendations based on classical analysis are exaggerated. The suggestions put forward by classical analysis always protect the interests of private capital, and sometimes even harm the interests of private capital owners, let alone protect the interests of society. After all, the important conclusions drawn from the establishment of these one-sided mechanical theories are to assume that the state does not intervene in the economy.

Just as pathologists do not treat the sick, the proponents of the neoclassical paradigm do not want to study the real economy, whose booming growth refutes the theory of market equilibrium daily. Economic thinking that revolves around the assumed properties of market equilibrium and optimization is like barbarians dancing in front of an idol for a sunny day and rain.

If the task of economic science is to formulate some proposals for economic development to improve the level of social welfare, then its object of research should not be to find the conditions for achieving market equilibrium. On the contrary, it should be to study some laws that deviate from the market equilibrium, allowing economic activity to develop in a more complex and diversified direction, and finally to develop a complete set of mechanisms.

The process of economic development and STP based on it has always been an enigma and anomaly for the neoclassical paradigm. The inability of the neoclassical paradigm to explain the phenomenon of scientific and technological progress, from which more than 90% of the growth of the GNP of developed countries originates, proves the weakness of the neoclassical paradigm science and the need to develop a new scientific paradigm. Even so, no revolution in economic science has occurred. Many proponents of the neoclassical paradigm were supported by the philosophical studies of the Academy of Scripture. The consciousness base of mainstream economic thought that for decades served as a propaganda tool to protect the interests of capitalists and their economic activity from state restrictions that would allow them to maximize their profits.

Impartially speaking, similar accusations can be made against the socialist political economy of the Soviet Union. The socialist political economy of the Soviet Union confirmed the correctness of the complex practice of socialist construction, fulfilled the function of the corresponding ideology, and never thought about applying the corresponding ideology to the practice of managing the national economy. But like all branches of neoclassical theory, such as neo-Keynesianism and neo-institutionalism, the neoclassical theory failed miserably in predicting the long-term economic development of society, including the failure to predict the collapse of the Soviet Union.

The Obsolescence of Mainstream Economic Thoughts

Mainstream economic thoughts, whether neoclassicism or Soviet dogmatic Marxism, cannot explain or predict economic development because they close themselves to the issue of the exchange of results of current economic activities. Marx answered the question of the exchange of labor results from the perspective of the "money–commodity–money" formula. He explained the economic reproduction process as capital relies on the exploitation of hired labor to possess surplus value. Marginalists answer these questions from the perspective of the law of diminishing productivity and the law of diminishing marginal utility. They believe that the exchange ratio is, on the one hand, the equivalent of the marginal productivity of labor and capital, and on the other hand, the equivalent of the marginal utility of the purchased goods.

Judging from the reasons why relevant social groups advocate the encroachment of the results of economic activities, the theories of these mainstream economic thoughts are very convincing. Still, they are completely useless for organizing such claims. Neither explanation can explain the laws of economic development, nor can it serve as the basis for formulating recommendations in economic activities.

Any theory reflects reality. Marxism, marginalism, and neoclassical theories derived from classical political economy reflect the economic conditions and the combination of production factors more than a century ago. The main factors of production at that time were capital in the form of private ownership of the means of production and the wage labor of workers who lost their ownership of the means of production. Most of the workers were farmers who later moved to cities.

Since then, the economy has changed radically, technological progress has become a major factor in economic growth, and investment in manpower has begun to exceed the investment in machinery and equipment. The main expenditure of the state is concentrated on the reproduction of human capital, which has grown from a police state (administrative state) to a socialist state. The role of creative labor in production activities has increased dramatically, business management has been transferred to professional managers, and ownership relationships have become more complicated. Mainstream economic thoughts cannot understand these changes. It has fallen into academic dogmatism. From the perspective of scientific development, mainstream economic thought has become a product of lagging behind the times.

The unreconcilable dispute between the two schools of mainstream economic thought, the dogmatic Marxist and the marginalist, is a manifestation of the outdated state of economic thought. It is like a war between two factions of economic thought, but this kind of war is not so much scientific as it is ideological. How to distribute the fruits of economic activities between labor and capital? The problem is the focus of the dispute between workers and capitalists. In fact, we should consider the third element before us. This element determines the development of the modern economy. It is scientific and technological progress. How does technological progress make contradictions no longer antagonistic? Because technological progress overcomes the influence of the law of diminishing productivity, and the increasingly diversified types of commodities and consumer preferences make the exchange of commodities not attributable to the value of the commodity, nor to the marginal utility. These classifications of commodity value and marginal utility have become empty and abstract. The collaborative work between workers who have continuously improved their education levels and capitalists who have invested in developing advanced technologies has brought about an increase in production efficiency and income by relying on knowledge rent. Knowledge rent results from the synergy between labor, capital, and science. Participants in the reproduction process distribute knowledge rent according to civil and labor laws, intellectual property protection laws, and taxation systems.

Of course, the progress of S&T can be explained from a certain angle; that is, when the degree of labor is increased to a certain level, wage growth lags behind productivity growth. From another perspective, after the marginal productivity of capital rises to a certain level, capital productivity grows simultaneously. However, this does not clarify the laws of economic development, but complicates the far-fetched explanation that as scientists, teachers, engineers, inventors, innovators, and other carriers of the knowledge economy continue to participate in economic activity, the reproduction of economic activity will no longer be relegated to the model of the two factors of labor and capital.

Mainstream economic thought, whether neoclassical or dogmatic Marxist economic thought, can be compared with the reasons for disputes when two people from the same tribe in the primitive commune divide their prey. One killed the prey, and the other made a bow and arrow. Many authors of the mainstream school of economic thought like to cite similar hypothetical examples to illustrate their opinions. Some authors of economic writings[4] even reduced everything to "Robinsonian." At the time, primitive people were fighting for his dual identity as a hunter and hunting tool maker at the same time, but all these insights were only the author's. We have an illusion that they did not expect that in primitive social relations, the psychological mechanism seriously affects the relationship between people. The psychological mechanism determines the rules for

---

4. Кларк Дж. Б. Распределение богатства. М.: Гелиос АРВ, 2000.

the distribution of necessities between each person and other people (Polshnev,[5] Le Vi-Strauss[6]). According to the law of social psychology of reproduction of clan communes, the surplus products are preserved and distributed by the big man.

The mechanism of production and distribution of material wealth in the primitive commune was not based on a rational measure of the marginal productivity of the factors of production or the labor invested, but on the psychosocial laws that governed primitive human beings who were not burdened with logical thought. Both in the mythological consciousness of ancient people and the religious consciousness of medieval societies, the production and exchange of material wealth were regulated not by a reasonable measure of marginal productivity or the price of labor, but by conventions and traditions capable of guaranteeing the reproduction of social organization and protecting the institutions necessary to manage its reproduction. The emergence of a market economy in the form proposed by modern "economics" results from destroying traditional societies and the religious worldviews associated with them. It prohibits profit and prescribes compliance with the established social hierarchy and the inherent system of production and distribution of material wealth that corresponds to it. There is no need to describe this process in this section, as historical scientific research[7] has done a good enough job. The present analysis is intended to highlight the fact that traditional economics and the Marxist, Marginalist, and Neoclassical theories based on it have all interpreted economic relations in this particular historical period since the Industrial Revolution. With the transition to a knowledge-based economy, it now appears that this historical period has come to an end.

The modern knowledge economy differs from the object of study of "economics" no less than it differs from the primitive or traditional social economy. Economic activity results in the modern knowledge economy are exchanged neither according to the law of marginal utility nor the law of price. Software products downloaded repeatedly at zero printing cost are sold at different prices, depending on the seller's free will and the buyer's social status. The share of social wealth that is shared for free is growing. The price of brand-name goods is much higher than the price of similar or even better-quality products. The diversity of goods and services far exceeds a person's ability to measure his or her objective needs and income reasonably. Advertising and artificially created images play the customary and mythical role in modern society that they did in pre-industrial times. The impact of advertising and artificial images on exchange ratios far exceeds the impact of labor inputs and marginal utility on exchange ratios.

The distribution of income is likewise no longer attributed to the marginal productivity of the factors of production. Still, it is mainly determined by the law on the protection of intellectual property, social guarantees, and monopoly effects. The main role in the monopoly effect is played by the monopoly right to issue money, which is carried out under the state and economic agents' guarantee to allocate loans for their expenses. The proceeds from the minting of money, which was marginal in the gold standard

---

5. Поршнев Б. О начале человеческой истории (Проблемы палеопсихологии). - М.: Мысль, 1974.

6. Леви-Стросс К. Структурная антропология. - М.: Изд-во ЭКСМО-Пресс, 2001.

7. Бродель Ф. Материальная цивилизация, экономика и капитализм XV-XVIII вв. М.: Прогресс, 1986.

era, became the most important source of wealth in the present era of capital trusts.[8] As mentioned above, more than a trillion dollars and euros of currency flow into the market yearly under the guaranteed obligations of the countries concerned alone. The ECB creates more purchase value at the push of a button than the value of Russia's crude oil exports[9] over a decade. The issuers of the world's currencies pump money into the economy, creating more wealth than the savings of billions of ordinary people.

The modern financial system is often referred to as the casino economy, and most transactions conducted within the system are virtual. The business of the exchange is completed by automatic devices in accordance with procedures oriented to obtain speculative profits, and speculative profits have nothing to do with the reproduction of the real economy. Most transactions are virtual transactions. Social networking services, computer games, and entertainment are gaining more weight in the consumption structure. In the high-tech field, common products are becoming cheaper and cheaper, while new products with over-consumption attributes are surprisingly expensive. On the contrary, simple and rough traditional goods are becoming increasingly expensive, and there is a growing demand for "nostalgia" services for products. For example, furniture or footwear companies will "artificially age" their products to meet capricious consumer demand.

Mainstream economic thought ignored the anomalies of dramatic growth, turned a blind eye to the qualitative changes occurring in economic reproduction, and became increasingly confined to cumbersome theories in abstract mathematical doctrines. The neoclassical paradigm is not only incapable of explaining the ongoing changes and events, but also of predicting further economic developments. The macroeconomic policies of the world's leading countries are in the hands of regulatory agencies that disregard theoretical assumptions and rely on trial-and-error methods. The global financial crisis is persistent, intensifying every seven years, and as a result, uncertainty and anxiety are growing throughout the world.

Prerequisites for the Scientific Revolution in Economics

A revolution in economic science has long been inevitable and is comparable in scale to the medical revolution of a century ago. We can compare today's mainstream economic thinking with medieval medicine, which used bloodletting to treat all diseases, and then justified the high pay by arguing a few high-falutin medical terms, regardless of the outcome. It is necessary to transition from the study of pathological anatomy and seemingly scientific transcendental philosophy to the study of the theory of the development of the social organism. The development of economic activity should become the main object of study of economic science, rather than the exchange of the results of the labor of economic activity. Accordingly, the methodology should be changed.

The economic activity development process is typically characterized by the increasing

---

8. Отырба А., Кобяков А. Как побеждать в финансовых войнах // Однако, 2014. Июнь-июль (№ 174).

9. Ершов М. Мировая финансовая система после кризиса: тенденции и проблемы развития // Деньги и кредит, 2013. № 1.

complexity and diversification of the system. Unlike the exchange theory, which seeks to find equilibrium states and to de-complicate to find universal equivalents (general equivalence), the development theory focuses on the search for complexity mechanisms that can sustain increasing reproduction within the framework of reproductive integrity. The evolution of living systems (as distinguished from non-organic systems) has a negative entropy property and evolves along the path of complexity. Since the economy is a living system, the main object of research in economic science should be the study of its developmental laws. Accordingly, the mechanisms that support the complexity of economic science and maintain its integrity and stability in the increasing diversification of economic activities and their results should also be studied.

This research direction has clear research measures/procedures under evolutionary economics. Evolutionary economics chooses to study the inherent reproduction mechanism of the economic activity process as the main research topic.[10] People have achieved impressive research results within the theoretical framework of evolutionary economics, which explains certain laws of the evolution of the economic system, including the generation mechanism and the innovation propagation mechanism. People once introduced the mathematical analysis methods of species propagation and species competition in ecology into economic science, and obtained general mathematical models of technological paths and scientific production cycles.[11]

On this basis, the above-mentioned theory of long-term technological and economic development has been developed as a continuous process of technological paradigm life cycle change. The model of economic system expansion and reproduction, which fully reflects the process of economic system reproduction development,[12] has also been studied.

Another direction of research in economic development theory is the study of system dynamics models,[13] which are based on mathematical descriptions that guarantee realistic feedback on economic reproduction. However, the feedback that indirectly reflects the reproduction of the economic system, its mobility, and the uncertainty of change is too complex and nonlinear, which was beyond the capabilities of computer mathematical modeling at that time. In the presence of better models of the expanded reproduction of the economic system, individual innovation propagation, and structural changes in economic sectors, the overall model of the systemic economic dynamics has not been established in any country so far. Due to the highly variable and increasingly diverse nature of the real economy, the possibility of building an overall model does not inherently exist.

Unlike biological systems that have evolved over millions of years and ecosystems that pursue dynamic equilibria, modern economic systems are constantly changing. In the short term, modern economic systems may converge to some hypothetical equilibrium

10. Нельсон Р., Уинтер С. Дж. Эволюционная теория экономических изменений. М.: Дело, 2002.

11. Грублер А. Инновации и экономический рост. М.: Наука, 2002; Nakicenovic N. Technological Substitution and Long Waves in the USA: The Long Wave Debate. Berlin, 1987. P. 81; Grubler A. The Rise and Fall of Infrastructures // American Economic Review, 1959. No. 49.

12. Маевский В., Малков С. Перспективы макроэкономической теории воспроизводства // Вопросы экономики, 2014. № 4.

13. Форрестер Д. Мировая динамика. М.: АСТ, 2006. С. 384.

point. Still, the constant occurrence of innovations creates bifurcation points that change the trajectory of one or several attractors that also fail to form due to the emergence of the next innovation. Synergy theory uses formal tools to model the evolution of complex systems, but modeling the evolutionary process at an abstract level can yield important knowledge about the properties of socioeconomic development.[14]

For realistic models and actual predictions, mathematical tools are not enough. We need to use a combination of man and machine to study the various situations shown by the economic system under the influence of different management.

Setting Tasks

Economic science should reveal the law of development of economic activities in the entire known history of mankind, explain the current mechanism of economic science, and predict and demonstrate the further development of current economic policies. To this end, we should clearly formulate social and economic development goals and determine the constraints that hinder their development. At the same time, the system for managing economic development should have a choice ability that can at least deal with its current and future changes.

We are not yet in a position to create a general theory of economic development. But as we all know, asking the right questions already solves half of the problem. Similar to biology, ecology, and medicine, which all study living systems, economics should not always indulge in set-in-stone formulas. If there is something set in stone in economics, it is variability and re-capacity. This property of constant change and reproduction is motivated by the essence of human nature, characterized by the creation of the self and its realization in an ever-expanding scope due to scientific inquiry. Therefore, the first question that economic science should answer is to determine the method of regulation of economic activity established by society.

The modern economy is governed by legal regulations, which are established mainly in the form of generally applicable mandatory laws, resolutions of legal bodies, and resolutions of subjects of economic activity within the scope of the above-mentioned regulations and in accordance with the will of the regulator of the regulations. The economic control system may or may not set established goals in form. In any case, the establishment of these goals is to integrate the economic interests of different social groups. These interests do not match and may conflict with each other. If the regulatory system cannot coordinate these interests to develop the economy and improve social welfare, the consequences of their interaction may be that the economy loses stability due to social changes or external influences, and the economy itself is also destroyed. Therefore, the economy (different from people) will not die, but will change according to variations in the continuously integrated social group.

History is replete with economic success stories and economic disasters. Sometimes economic miracles turn into economic disasters, and vice versa. It is surprising how few economists are interested in such attractive study topics as the birth and demise of

---

14. Капица С., Курдюмов С., Малинецкий Г. Синергетика и прогнозы будущего. М.: УРСС. 2003.

economic systems. In fact, in the last hundred years, these events have occurred only twice in Russia: after the Great October Socialist Revolution and after the collapse of the Soviet Union. Each time mainstream economic thought was as caught off guard as the economic management system, believing that such an event could not have happened.

If we take medicine as an analogy, the primary task of economic science is to consider how to maintain the health of the object of study, to study the laws of its development and degeneration, the limiting conditions that prevent it from functioning, and the conditions of its birth and demise. For economic science, specifically the study of the regeneration of economic systems, the most important issue is the study of the regeneration methods, which may be evolutionary or revolutionary, endogenous or exogenous, peaceful or violent, and creative or destructive.

The Marxist theory attempts to answer these questions based on the dialectics of the interaction between productive forces and production relations. In the process of social and economic development, a critical point of the economic cycle periodically appears, when production relations begin to hinder productive forces' development. This critical point needs to be overcome through social changes. Therefore, historical materialism explains the bourgeois revolution (transition from feudalism to capitalist relations of production) and the socialist revolution (transition from capitalism to socialist relations of production).

The catch-up development theory is based on the neoclassical economics paradigm. According to this theory, all countries following modern advanced capitalist countries have experienced the same period of liberating market forces as capitalist countries when implementing economic reforms.

However, we are witnessing the birth of an entirely new economic system in the countries of South East Asia, the existence of which was denied by conventional mainstream economic thinking. This economic system combines socialist planning and market self-organization mechanisms, state ownership of the means of production and individual ownership of the means of production, state regulation, and individual management. The system manages business activities based on the harmonious development of the interests of different social groups. Conflicts between different social groups are eliminated by working in concert and jointly developing and implementing economic development plans to improve the well-being of the people. The purpose of establishing the economic regulation system is to integrate economic interests so that everyone works for the common welfare. The subjects of economic relations within the system of economic regulation are able to perform their respective functions: private entrepreneurs expand the scale of production and increase the efficiency of production of socially necessary goods; the state provides private entrepreneurs with loans and stable economic conditions (prices, taxes, interest, regulation of foreign economic activity, etc.), access to modern infrastructure; scholars, relying on the support of the state and enterprises, constantly stimulate new flows of knowledge, and engineers put This knowledge is put into practice in new technologies, and teachers train generations of young people in accordance with the requirements of scientific and technological progress.

As noted above, Sorokin had already foreseen the emergence of a similar economic system half a century earlier, which he called the "integration system."[15] Some Soviet and American economists[16] have argued that the formation of such a system combines the advantages of capitalism and socialism and avoids the disadvantages specific to both. Still, these thoughts remain on the fringes of mainstream economic thought. Whether it was the Soviet or the US economic system, mainstream economic thought pushed both the Soviet and the US economic systems, which vainly attempted to form a world scale, to a dead end.

The US had beaten the Soviet Union in this global competition. Still, a quarter of a century on, the US lost its dominance of the world economic system, and China took over the number one position in terms of production. China, along with other emerging economies, is trying to create its own variant of the integration system, which has gradually come to dominate the world economy. In the US-centered liberal model of globalization, the aim of economic activity is profit maximization. In contrast, economic activities within the framework of the integration system align with the economic development task of increasing social welfare. Also, the liberal model of globalization and the integration system differ in their approaches to organizing international economic relations. If the US imposes full liberalization to remove cross-border obstacles on the path of expansion of its capital and enterprises, then the above-mentioned countries seek mutually beneficial cooperation in the regulation of economic activity while respecting national sovereignty.

It should be noted that mainstream thinking ignores the economic miracles of China, India, Vietnam, Malaysia, South Korea, and even Japan, viewing them as anomalies. These "abnormal phenomena" now occupy a dominant position in the reproduction of the world economy, proving its advantages in output growth and socioeconomic efficiency. Economic science has not yet been able to explain these anomalies, nor has it been possible to find why the Western European economy recovered so rapidly after the war, not to mention the astonishing development and dramatic collapse of the Soviet economy.

Methodological Basis

Any structure consists of elements, which themselves consist of elements, and so on until the fundamental element is found. The search for the fundamental element is an activity in which all science is engaged. It may be that this obsession with the search for fundamental elements is characteristic of monotheistic religious thought. It tries to attribute all observed phenomena to a root cause—the saints think the root cause is God, physicists think it is elementary particles, biologists think it is cells, economists think it is commodities—but in living systems, it is not just the elements that matter, or even not so much the elements as the connections between them. It is this connection

15. Сорокин П. Главные тенденции нашего времени // Российская академия наук, Институт социологии. М.: Наука, 1997. 350 с.

16. ждународных сравнений. М.: Экономика, 1998; его же. Десять лет системной трансформации в странах ЦВЕ и в России: итоги и уроки: научный доклад. М.: ИМЭПИ РАН, 1999; Реформы глазами российских и американских ученых / Под общ. ред. О. Т. Богомолова. - М.: Российский экономический журнал, Фонд «За экономическую грамотность», 1996.

that contains the information that determines the properties of the system. The system dies and disintegrates when the connection is broken while another element replaces the destroyed element.

For example, the connection system between nerve cells constitutes human consciousness from the physiological level. Drug anesthesia, trauma, and disease can cause loss of consciousness when these connections are broken. At the same time, the death of a single cell can be supplemented in a large range (according to some studies, this supplement can reach 2/3 of the brain content). People's consciousness at the ideological level is established through the connections between various images, concepts, and feelings. Without these connections, humans will only be able to see individual objects, they cannot build a picture of the world in their brains, and they cannot develop the world.

The same goes for economic activities. The tools and objects of economic activity are constantly changing in the production process set by related technologies. Technology determines the connection between these tools and objects and human beings. Different people may appear (resign and hire) in the organization's production process, and they enter the relationship set by technology. Therefore, to determine the law of economic activity development, we must understand the process of technological change and replacement.

Economic activity cannot be reduced to production; it is integrated with the social environment, whose inhabitants preside over, organize, and ensure economic activity and use the results of it for their own benefit. This environment consists of those with interrelationships as a result of economic activity and its results. These relations can guarantee the reproduction of economic activity with frequent changes in membership. The relations of production are determined by the system, which can bind the people in the relations of production and prescribe the forms of realization of the motives of these people's behavior. Therefore, to clarify the laws of economic development, it is necessary to understand the process of change in social institutions.

The social system regulates people's behavior to a certain extent. It makes them more willing to comply with the norms it sets, and this "willingness" is maintained through positive and negative relationships between people and society. The effectiveness of the social system depends on the degree of harmonization between the moral values of individuals and the dominant ideology. The higher the degree of coordination, the more efficient the system of production relations is determined. On the contrary, the greater the number of people who reject the dominant ideology, the less the system can support the corresponding relations of production. Thus, to understand the laws of economic development, it is necessary to consider the evolution of human value systems based on the dominant ideology. If economic science neglects the understanding of human beings, popular consciousness, and the social relations that are constantly accumulating in the relevant humanities, economic science would be reduced to the current 'economy.' The main object of economic research would be interpreted extremely simply as an emotionless economic agent or "homo economicus." This interpretation may be relevant for studying an economic system that assumes a system of individual hyper-rational entrepreneurs who are assumed to compete freely in a well-known market that does not change technology. As soon as we move away from any of the abstract situations mentioned above, all the simulation results previously obtained on such abstract situations will not be realized, and the theory built based on these simulation results will no longer be applicable to explain economic behavior and will not be able to make practical suggestions about it.

To understand the laws of economic development, it is necessary to view the economic system as a complex collection of human groups, including their ideologies, interests, and motivations for behavior related to relevant production relations, as well as the social institutions that govern these relations, and even the means and objects of production associated with certain technologies. This complex system is composed of numerous and constantly changing elements and their connections. It is typified by its essential complexity, i.e., the impossibility of reducing all its components to some basic element, the nonlinearity of interrelationships, and the uncertainty that creates difficulties in predicting and formulating practical proposals.

In summary, the central problem of economic science is the study of the interrelationships among technological change, institutional change, and ideological change. These changes may not follow universal laws, and the ways of organizing and utilizing the results of economic activity vary considerably, depending on the technical, institutional, and ideological conditions in the socioeconomic system. That is why it seems very naive for mainstream economic thought to desperately try to introduce certain universal economic laws, regardless of changes in the technical, institutional, and ideological characteristics of the socioeconomic system.

The Supporting Structure of the New Scientific Paradigm in Economics

To study the interrelationship among technology, system, and ideological changes in economics, it is necessary to clarify the laws of operation of each sub-system from the beginning. To this end, we should distinguish basic elements such as technology, system, and value and understand their changing laws. In the social sciences, relevant knowledge in the above-mentioned fields has been accumulated.

A great deal of research has been done on the laws of technology generation, diffusion, and change, and these studies have led to a series of general laws, including the well-known law of diminishing productivity. According to this law, the life cycle of any technology will reach a point from which further investment in technology development will bring diminishing returns. Like the life cycle of all living things and the cycle of the learning process, any technology cycle can be described by a logistic curve. This S-curve shows the dynamics of all the markers (production volume, market share, productivity, and product quality characteristics[17]) within a scientific production cycle.

As mentioned above, economic production activities are related through technological conjunctions, and conjunctions are a prerequisite for the synchronization of the life cycle of economic activities. The associated production complexes of the technological sphere form the complete reproduction system—the technological paradigm. Each

---

17. Сахал Д. Технический прогресс: концепции, модели, оценки. М.: Финансы и статистика, 1985

technological component of the reproduction system has a life cycle, which is described by a logical curve and goes through the stages of completeness, rapid growth, maturity, and decline. As the maturity stage of the life cycle is reached, the returns from investments in technological development gradually diminish, and this diminishing trend becomes negative with the beginning of the decline stage. Production development (due to technological conjugation) is interrelated, so the life cycle of a technological paradigm has the same logical curve form, except that the life cycle of a technological paradigm spans nearly a century.

During the maturity and recession phases of the technology paradigm life cycle, empirical data prove that development slows down and economic growth approaches its limits under resource-limited conditions. Still, these limits are breached with the emergence of new technology paradigms that remove resource constraints and allow the economy to enter a new wave of long-term growth. This process is accompanied by a depreciation of productive and human capital, a decline in production, and a depression, which in turn stimulates the flow of capital into the new technological paradigm of production.

The theory of long-term technical-economic development mentioned above as a process of continuous changes in the life cycle of the technological paradigm makes clear the laws of this nonlinear and uneven process, which appears in the form of long waves of economic quotations in the dynamic diagram of macroeconomic indicators.

Like the technological component, economic activity is guaranteed by the relations of production defined by the corresponding institutions. Institutions are also not immutable, and it is impossible to create a theory of economic development without clarifying the laws of their evolution. In the field of technical economy, as a basic analysis element, here it should be referred to as the integrity of reproduction.

The definition of the world economic paradigm was given above to analyze the laws of political-economic development, which is a complete system of interrelated institutions. These institutions ensure the current expansion and reproduction of the national economy and define the mechanisms of global economic relations. The system of institutions related to the world economic paradigm was initially formed at the level of the economy of a particular country and is being refined at the level of regional integration and world economic relations. At this time, the institutional system of the leading countries has special significance. These countries have an authoritative influence on the mechanisms of world market regulation and international economic, trade, and financial relations. The leading countries equip their peripheral economies through the above-mentioned influence, imposing on the subordinate countries the system that is in their interest. The lagging countries try to replicate the system of the leading countries, thus promoting the spread of the corresponding world economic paradigm.

Each world economic paradigm has its own life cycle, the limits of which are determined by the contradictions that accumulate within the reproduction framework that makes up the world economic system. Over time, contradictions erupted, causing increasing pressures within the system of domestic and international economic, social, and political relations, pressures that still rely on world wars for their resolution today. According to the logic of this process, world wars are initiated by countries that were leading in the old world economic order but have lost their dominant position in the current world, in order to increase regulation of their peripheral economies to improve their competitive advantage, or even to deter and weaken potential competitors. However, new dominant countries always emerge among the competitors, i.e., carriers of advanced institutional systems and production relations, thus making their economic efficiency and political power greater than that of the former dominant countries. To increase their advantage, the new dominant state tries desperately to avoid premature involvement in the war, just to join it again at the final stage and to join the victor's camp, thus occupying a dominant position worldwide.

The institutional system of the leading country in the old world economic order is linked to economic interests, which makes the institutional system of the new world economic order unable to mature in the old world economic order. The ruling elites of the dominant countries in the world economy are not interested in changes in economic methods. They have consistently refused to try to change the world economic paradigm, leading to the reproduction inertia of their old economic order. Therefore, the new world economic paradigm will not be formed in the dominant countries, but will be formed in a place that protects peripheral economic elements from direct oppression. As the world's leading countries continue to change, the system of the new world economic paradigm will continue to improve. These systems retain the existing material and technological achievements and create new opportunities for developing social productive forces.

The hypothesis of cyclical changes in the world economic paradigm, as a complete system of institutions guaranteeing economic reproduction, explains the reasons for the intermittent nature of the long-term development of the political economy. According to this hypothesis, changes in the world economic paradigm occur in discrete forms, because the dominant countries cannot change the system, and the opportunities for guaranteeing stable economic growth are exhausted. The dominant countries of the world economy tried to maintain their central position by intensifying regulation of the periphery of the world economy, which led to world wars. The transition to a new world economic paradigm was completed by the World Wars. This transition was accompanied by a change in the dominant countries and centers of the world economic development—a shift of dominance to other countries that have developed a new and more efficient system of economic reproduction.

This hypothesis reveals the underlying causes of the world war and proposes a new dialectic concept of the interaction between productivity and production relations.

While Marxism explains the formation of the Soviet socialist world system as a transition to crisis-free productive forces, the market fundamentalist doctrine sees the collapse of the Soviet Union as the feast of liberal globalization and the final formation of the world capital market. Unlike Marxism, and even fundamentalism, this hypothesis proves that there are historical limits to any institutional system and that changes are inevitable in the nonlinear and uneven development of the world economic paradigm.

The use of the concept of paradigm is intended to reflect the integrity of the reproduction of interrelated elements, i.e., mutually associated technical-productive cooperation (i.e., technical paradigm) and mutually unified systems of economic organization (economic paradigm). The interconnectedness of elements determines the synchronization of their life cycles, at least in the periods of maturity and decline, and the intermittent character of economic development, i.e., the simultaneous periodic turnover of a large number of elements and the simultaneous periodic reorganization of the interconnectedness of elements, which gives a leapfrog character to technological change (in the case of technological paradigm turnover) and political change (in the case of world economic paradigm turnover).

In this interpretation, technological change reflects a qualitative change in the components of the productive forces, while political change reflects a qualitative change in the content of the relations of production. They do not necessarily coincide, despite the obvious principle of their mutual influence and coherence. But the inertia of the relations of production is inherently higher than the technical correlates of productivity, and thus the life cycle of the world economic paradigm is much longer than that of the technical approach.

The Practical Significance of the New Scientific Paradigm in Economics

As a doctrine that articulates the cyclical changes in technology and world economic paradigms, the theory of long-term economic development explains many anomalies not recounted by mainstream economic thought. These schools of thought that constitute mainstream thought become special cases of abstract models of atrophied economic systems. Because of this, the proposals based on mainstream economic thought usually lead to the deterioration of the corresponding national economies.[18] These processes are explained scientifically within the framework of long-term economic theory, and the predictions made by long-term economic theory for the economy are realized. The new scientific paradigm developed based on the methods proposed by the long-term theory provides a reliable basis for developing methodologies for long-term forecasting of socioeconomic development, capable of anticipating the coming stages of instability of the global economic and political system and the threats lurking in the world wars. This paradigm is necessary in times of technological and world economic paradigm changes.

The discovery of the law of cyclical changes in technological approaches explains the causes of the current global crisis. It allows us to predict the formation of new technological growth paths. This discovery creates prerequisites for scientifically and rationally choosing the priority directions of STP and defining the strategy of economic overdevelopment. The strategy of advanced economic development offers the possibility of technological change, and the transition from underdeveloped countries to advanced ones, suffering from the consequences of the crisis of capital devaluation caused by the old technological production methods.

The hypothesis of the changing world economic paradigm explains the increased political tensions in the world today. Regardless of the strong will of the US to retain its leading position in the system of world economic relations, the world leading countries will change, and this process is irreversible. The system will be transformed according to the new-integrated-world economic paradigm system.

---

18. Глазьев С. Уроки очередной российской революции: крах либеральной утопии и шанс на экономическое чудо. М.: Экономическая газета, 2011. 576 с.; Обучение рынку / под ред. С. Глазьева. М.: Экономика, 2004.

The new paradigm offers promising ideas for global socioeconomic development. The US-centered liberal globalization and the dominance of multinational conglomerates associated with the Federal Reserve give way to a polycentric multicurrency system combined with market self-organization mechanisms and strategic and indicative planning regimes, dominated by a centrally regulated economy and private enterprises regulated by the state to safeguard the common interests of society. In the context of the transition to the new world economic paradigm, efficiency is substantially increased thanks to the mutual coordination of the multiple interests of operating agents, social groups, and communities. As mentioned above, economic activity in the current world economic paradigm is in the interest of those activists that maximize profit in any way. In contrast to the current world economic paradigm, the new world economic paradigm aims at increasing social welfare, thus ensuring its dominance in economic growth.

The methodology proposed above makes it easier to understand the long-term economic development mechanism, in which the stable growth phase and the qualitative change phase alternate, and the qualitative change phase appears in the form of an economic crisis. The current ignorance of these mechanisms can not only prevent these crises from occurring nor can they prevent them from evolving into world wars and revolutionary disasters. The world is currently plunged into another economic change, accompanied by the risk of a new world war. If the ruling elites of the world's leading countries understand the objective laws of economic development, the outbreak of war can possibly be avoided, and economic development will inevitably transition to a new world economic and technological paradigm. The stronger the resistance to these changes, the greater the destruction of productivity, and the higher the risk of facing a global humanitarian disaster.

There are many apocalyptic (End of the World) predictions in modern monographs. Apart from the general rhetoric about the need for self-restraint in economic development, there is little clarity on how to avoid these predictions becoming a reality. But the way out of reality lies in eliminating restrictions in the environment, food, energy, etc. The transition to a new technological paradigm has opened the era of solar energy, robotics, genetic engineering, and cellular medicine, allowing for the essential removal or weakening of these constraints. This transition is tied to old world economic paradigm regimes that stimulate antagonistic conflicts in the global production and political relations system. Adversarial conflicts in global production can create huge financial bubbles that destabilize economies, and adversarial conflicts in political relations can trigger world hybrid wars.

The rigidity of the ruling elite of the dominant state prevents the peaceful and innovative resolution of these conflicts, which eventually leads to the formation of this rigidity due to the lack of awareness of the laws of modern economic development and thus the inability to make a correct assessment of its possibilities. The principles of legal regulation of economic development, which have already been mentioned above, are needed to build the optimal configuration for economic development.

The new paradigm provides a scientific basis for the invocation of macroeconomic policy in line with the new technological path and the system of economic reproduction, and also for the development of the policy of the Russian economic overdevelopment zone. The new paradigm plays an important role in stopping the development of

American aggression into a world war, through the rapid formation of national unions, and the formation of new centers of world economic development based on the new world economic paradigm system and the new technological way of production leapfrogging growth. Russia, following in the footsteps of China, may play an important role in this process, stepping into the path of leapfrogging into the development of new technologies and the formation of a world economic paradigm.

Development Direction of the New Scientific Paradigm in Economics

The process of changes in the world economy has a catastrophic character, and this catastrophism is the result of the inability of the system of economic development management to adapt in time to the changes in the world economy. In many ways, there is no adaptation of the results to the realities of economic theory. The above has pointed out some support structures for constructing economic theory. Still, it is necessary to propose a common program, and to develop this program, first of all, it is necessary to prepare a "technical mission statement."

An effective theory of economic development should answer the question of how to ensure the stability of economic development and direct it toward the improvement of social welfare. Without discussing how this criterion is measured (or evaluated), let us take the most common indicator—gross national product (GNP) per capita, which is usually an estimate of the level of economic development. The theory of economic development should be able to argue for the best set of legal norms and regulatory regimes for economic activity to achieve the maximum rate of economic development in the foreseeable future. Since the main factor of economic development is scientific and technological progress, and the source of STP comes from the creative motivation of people, the theory of economic development should propose the necessary and sufficient conditions to increase the creative motivation of citizens to develop and realize their scientific and technological potential in order to achieve harmonious and stable economic development.

In summary, what is needed first to create a theory of economic development? It is first necessary to come up with a precise definition of its main actor (human personality). The concept of homo economicus, with its primordial motive of maximizing returns and endlessly measuring the marginal utility of consumer goods to reflect the role of man in the modern economy, is clearly no longer applicable, whether the role of man as a buyer or seller of labor, the concept of homo economicus is no longer applicable. Despite the existence of all these roles, the main driver of economic development is the person who constantly exploits his intellectual potential and possesses creativity in creating and developing new knowledge and technologies. For this purpose, he should be educated, creative, and have the necessary equipment, capital, and good conditions to work in a group with a common goal.

To adapt to the realities of modern economic activity, economic science has to use knowledge about the motivation of human psychological behavior. To realize the creative potential of the individual in economic activity, it is necessary not only to allow the person to go to the joint planning of the activity, but also to allow him to dominate the results of economic activity labor. From this point of view, the traditional economic science concept of buying and selling labor on the market is obsolete and perhaps only applicable to the lower end of the labor market, similar to the outdated view of capital as a general factor of production for the purchase of fixed assets and labor for services. The organization of high-tech production presupposes cooperative relations among its members, which are based on a common understanding of goals, methods of their achievement, and methods of distribution of results. In creative activity, mutual understanding among members is not limited to the completion of formal tasks, but rather to the resonance of labor results. This approach places certain requirements on the organizational relations of ownership of the means of production and ownership of the fruits of labor in co-productive activity.

The concept of "ownership" has been ignored or omitted from mainstream economic science. Even in the Marxist paradigm, the concept of ownership does not go beyond the ancient Roman law and the Roman trinity of possession, use, and domination. In fact, modern economic activity is based on a combination of different ownership relationships, and these ownership relationships were not written into the ancient Roman formula. In some advanced countries, the law regulates not only the rights of the owners of capital, but also the rights of workers, inventors, lenders, local and state authorities, and other subjects related to the organization of economic activity and domination of its results. Collective ownership and the right of labor collectives to participate in the management of enterprises are used more and more widely.

The new paradigm stipulates the interrelationship between economic science and legal science. The economic law system was created by the ruling elites on the premise of ensuring their own economic interests, so they were willing to interpret it as an absolute system and impose it on the entire society. Elites used various methods to persuade the public, from pressure on the media to discredit dissidents and violently to applying to rebels. Generally speaking, the failure of the ruling elite to pay enough attention to the need for change and to over-evaluate its ability to manage development with outdated methods eventually led to disasters. The ruling elites usually try to prevent the coming of revolution by combining reforms and wars to ease the tension within the corresponding economic relationship system. As a result, the socioeconomic relationship system is often chaotic and eventually collapses.

The new paradigm provides a scientific basis for the leap-forward reform of the economic law system. It can constructively resolve economic contradictions and prevent the intensification of social and political conflicts. To this end, a broad public consensus and effective decentralization procedures are required to delegate authority to institutions that aim to coordinate social and economic relations in legal norms.

Here we come to a key question, what place the economy has in the social sciences. Modern mainstream economic thought exists in an artificially created abstract vacuum, detached from the reality of human society and the other social sciences. In fact, economic activity is designed to satisfy people's needs and is subordinate to their will. In traditional societies with a religious worldview, human existence in this world was considered as preparation for eternal life and belief in saving the soul. The economy was subordinate in the hierarchy of values, and economic activity was the routine activity of endlessly repeating the production of products necessary for society's existence. The products produced were mainly considered the needs of the ruling elite. It was only after the emergence of capitalism that economic activity was aimed at the interests of the owners of the means of production and the increase of their wealth. To justify this practice in secular society, the liberal value system emerged. It embraced the arbitrariness of the individual and allowed the system of capital accumulation to be legitimized as a form of self-expanding wealth, which is still the mainstream of Western economic thought. However, this ideology is being questioned with the transition to a knowledge-based economy and society.

First, human society has reached its ecological limits, and crossing them will cause irreversible environmental degradation. This calls for appropriate limits to the liberal value system, even if these limits are inconsistent.

Second, the differences in people's income, quality of life, and ability to influence their personal and social destinies are about to reach a critical mass, beyond which a single random play by a person with access to advanced technology and sufficient wealth is enough to inflict a fatal loss on all of humanity.

Third, the function of MP is to create wealth. The nominal wealth created by trusts issued solely by debt guarantees and the issuance of world currencies has exceeded the sum of labor and capital. The amount of unsecured debt in the same currency is many times more than the total output value of major countries and the global economy.

In this way, humanity is at the mercy of a small group of people with concentrated wealth, power, and advanced technology capable of manipulating the present and future of people. Mainstream economic thought (and even sociology) largely ignores this, essentially justifying a qualitative change in the structure of socioeconomic relations due to technological progress. This change will significantly impact the state of human society until it is brought to an end by the arbitrary manipulation of individuals who were given a divine opportunity.

An in-depth study of the ideology of sustainable human development is temporarily stuck in the thinking stage of scientists, fantasists, and enthusiasts. The new scientific paradigm should provide a reliable system of coordinates for this activity. The formation of the institutional system of the integrated world economic approach has not been scientifically justified so far, and it is based on eclectic ideas that have not been scientifically justified. What is worse is that mainstream economic thinking aims to discredit this work and present the emerging new world economic paradigm system as a wreck that should be eliminated. This demonstrates the reactionary nature of the dominant paradigm of economic thought.

In the economic sciences, the ideas in Kuhn's Theory of Scientific Development are about to start a revolution.[19] A transition to a new scientific paradigm is needed in economics and the social sciences. The author hopes that this book will interest esteemed readers in joining this broad surrealist interdisciplinary discussion.

---

19. Кун Т. Структура научных революций / пер. с англ. И. З. Налетова; общая ред. и послесловие С. Р. Микулинского и Л. А. Марковой. М.: Прогресс, 1975.

References

Акаев А. А. Экономика xxi века-это нооэкономика, экономика справедливости и разума // Проблемы теории и практики управления. - 2014. -№ 11.

Айвазов А. Периодическая система мирового капиталистического развития / Альманах «Развитие и экономика». -Март 2012. -№2.

Айвазов А., Беликов В. Экономические основы цивилизационных волн развития человечества // Партнерство цивилизаций. -2016. -№3-4.

Аронсон Г. Россия накануне революции: Исторические этюды. Монархисты, либералы, масоны, социалисты. -Нью-Йорк: 1962.

Архипова В. В. Современный санкционный режим в отношении России: характеристика и глобальный аспект // Мир новой экономики. -2017. -Т. 11. -№2.

Беседа В. Попова с П. Дуткевичем. 22 идеи о том, как устроить мир (беседы с выдающимися учеными). -М.: Издательство Московского университета, 2014.

Блинов С. Ошибка доктора Кудрина // Эксперт. -2015. -№ 19.

Бодрунов С. Д. Грядущее. Новое индустриальное общество: перезагрузка. - М.: Куль-турная революция, 2016.

Богомолов О. Реформы в зеркале международных сравнений. -М.: Экономика, 1998.

Бузгалин А. В., Колганов А. И. Введение в компаративистику (Исследование и сравнительный анализ социально-экономических систем: методология, теория, применение к переходным экономикам). -М.: Таурус-Альфа, 1997.

Винслав Ю., Дементьев В., Мелентьев А., Якутин Ю. Развитие интегрированных корпоративных структур в России // Российский экономический журнал. -1998. -№11-12.

Встать в полный рост / Доклад Изборскому клубу / Под ред. С. Батчикова, А. Кобякова, С. Глазьева. 23 ноября 2014.

Волконский В. А. XXI век. Многополярный мир. Тренды и задачи истории. -М.: Книжный мир, 2017.

Выступление В. Путина на пленарной сессии клуба «Валдай». 21 сентября 2013.

Гэлбрейт Д. Деньги: откуда они приходят и куда уходят, 1975. -http: // magnetfox. com / download / 2255277 / galbraith-money- whence-it-came-where-it-went-1975-

Гельвановский М. И. Ценовая политика государства: основные направления решения проблемы // Вестник Института экономики РАН. -2011. -№2.

Глазьев С. Геноцид. -М.: Терра, 1998.

Глазьев С. Евразийская интеграция как ключевое направление современной политики России // Журнал «Изборский клуб». - 2014. -№1.

Глазьев С. Закономерность смены мирохозяйственных укладов в развитии мировой экономической системы и связанных с ними политических изменений // Наука. Культура. Общество. -2016. -№3.

Глазьев С. Информационно-цифровая революция / Доклад Изборскому клубу // Журнал «Изборский клуб». -2017. -№8.

Глазьев С. Кудрявая экономика. -М.: Политический журнал, 2006.

Глазьев С. Между Вашингтоном и Пекином // Экономические стратегии. -2015. -Т. 1. -№2 (128).

Глазьев С. Мирохозяйственные уклады в глобальном экономическом развитии // Экономика и математические методы. - 2016. -Т. 52. -№ 2.

Глазьев С. Нищета и блеск российских монетаристов // Экономическая наука современной России. -2015. -№2-3.

Глазьев С. НТП и воспроизводственные структуры в народном хозяйстве. Препринт. -М.: ЦЭМИ АН СССР, 1986.

Глазьев С. О новой парадигме в экономической науке // Государственное управление. Электронный вестник. -Июнь 2016. -Вып. 56.

Глазьев С. О практичности количественной теории денег или сколько стоит догматизм денежных властей // Вопросы экономики. -2008. -№7.

Глазьев С. Очередной документ прокризисной стратегии «мегарегулятора» (о неприемлемости центробанковского проекта «Основных направлений единой государственной денежно- кредитной политики на 2017 год и на период 2018 и 2019 годов») // Российский экономический журнал. -2016. -№5.

Глазьев С. Последняя мировая война. США начинают и проигрывают. -М.: Книжный мир, 2016.

Глазьев С. Прикладные результаты теории мирохозяйственных укладов // Экономика и математические методы. -2016. -Т. 52. -№3.

Глазьев С. Санкции США и Банка России: двойной удар по национальной экономике // Вопросы экономики. -2014. -№9.

Глазьев С. Современная теория длинных волн в развитии экономики // Экономическая наука современной России. -2012. -№ 2 (57).

Глазьев С. Социалистический ответ либеральной глобализации. -М.: АПН, 2006.

Глазьев С. Стратегия опережающего развития России в условиях глобального кризиса. -М.: Экономика, 2010.

Глазьев С. Теория долгосрочного технико-экономического развития. -М.: ВлаДар, 1993.

Глазьев С. Уроки очередной российской революции: крах либеральной утопии и шанс на экономическое чудо. -М.: Экономическая газета, 2011.

Глазьев С. Центральный банк против промышленности России // Вопросы экономики. -1998. -№1-2.

Глазьев С. Экономика будущего. Есть ли у России шанс? -М.: Книжный мир, 2017.

Глазьев С., Горидько Н., Нижегородцев Р. Критика формулы Ирвинга Фишера и иллюзии современной монетарной политики // Экономика и математические методы. -2016. -№4.

Глазьев С., Чистилин Д. Куда пойдет Россия? (Анализ предложенных программ социально-экономического развития страны) окончание // Российский экономический журнал. -2017. -№ 6.

Глазьев С. Ю. Битва за лидерство в XXI веке. Россия — США— Китай. Семь вариантов обозримого будущего. -М.: Книжный мир, 2017.

Глазьев С. Ю. Об альтернативной системе мер государственной политики модернизации и развития отечественной экономики (предложения ученых секции экономики Отделения общественных наук РАН) // Российский экономический журнал. -2011. -№ 4.

Глазьев С. Ю. О неотложных мерах по укреплению экономической безопасности

России и выводу российской экономики на траекторию опережающего развития / Доклад. М.: Институт экономических стратегий, Русский биографический институт, 2015.

Глазьев С. Ю. Снова к альтернативной системе мер государственной политики модернизации и развития отечественной экономики (предложения на 2013—2014 гг.) // Российский экономический журнал. -2013. -№ 3.

Глазьев С. Ю. «Стратегия 2020» — антимодернизационный документ // Российский экономический журнал. -2012. -№ 2.

Глазьев С. Ю. Украинская катастрофа: от американской агрессии к мировой войне? -М.: Книжный мир, 2014.

Глазьев С. Ю. Экономическая теория технического развития / Отв. ред. Д. С. Львов. -М.: Наука, 1990.

Глазьев С. Ю., Архипова В. В. Оценка влияния санкций и других кризисных факторов на состояние российской экономики // Российский экономический журнал. -2018. -№. 1.

Глазьев С. Ю., Микерин Г. И., Тесля П. Н. и др. Длинные волны: Науч. -техн. прогресс и соц. -экон. развитие / Отв. ред. С. В. Казанцев, П. Н. Тесля. -Новосибирск: Наука, 1991.

Говорухин С. Великая криминальная революция. -М.: Эрго- Пресс, 1995.

Годовой отчет Банка России за 2013 г. -http://www.cbr.ru/publ/God/ar_2013.pdf.

Грублер А. Инновации и экономический рост. -М.: Наука. 2002.

Гурвич Е., Прилепский И. Влияние финансовых санкций на российскую экономику // Вопросы экономики. -2016. -№1.

Данилов-Данильян В. И., Рывкин А. А. Воспроизводственный аспект экономического развития и некоторые проблемы управления // Экономика и мат. методы. -1982. -Т. XX. -Вып. 1.

Дементьев В. Е. Длинные волны экономического развития и финансовые пузыри / Препринт # WP / 2009 / 252-М.: ЦЭМИ РАН, 2009.

Десять лет системной трансформации в странах ЦВЕ и в России: итоги и уроки: научный доклад. -М.: ИМЭПИ РАН, 1999.

Дмитриева О. Еще раз об измененном бюджете-2009 и правительственной антикризисной программе // Российский экономический журнал. -2009. -№5.

Ежемесячный мониторинг социально-экономического положения и самочувствия населения: 2015 г. -июль 2017 г. / Под ред. Т. М. Малевой. -М.: Российская академия народного хозяйства и государственной службы при Президенте Российской Федерации, 2017.

Ершов М. В. Какая экономическая политика нужна России в условиях санкций? // Вопросы экономики. -2014. -№12.

Ершов М. Кризис 2008 года: «момент истины» для глобальной экономики и новые возможности для России // Вопросы экономики. -2008. -№12.

Ершов М. Мировая финансовая система после кризиса: тенденции и проблемы развития // Деньги и кредит. -2013. -№ 1.

Ершов М. О механизмах оживления экономики и поддержания равенства условий финансовой конкуренции после вступления России в ВТО / Аналитическая записка. 2014.

Ершов М. Об обеспечении валютной стабильности и о новых финансовых механизмах в условиях санкционного режима // Российский экономический журнал. -2014. -№ 5.

Ершов М. Экономический суверенитет России в глобальной экономике. -М.: Экономика, 2005.

Запесоцкий А. Россия между Востоком и ЗападоМ.: новый контекст старой дискуссии (к вопросу о современной теории и практике евразийства) . -СПб: Санкт-Петербургский гуманитарный университет профсоюзов, 2013.

Интеграционный барометр. -М.: Центр интеграционных исследований Евразийского банка развития, 2013, 2014.

Капица С., Курдюмов С., Малинецкий Г. Синергетика и прогнозы будущего. -М.: УРСС. 2003.

Кара-Мурза С. Г., Батчиков С. А., Глазьев С. Ю. Куда идет Россия. Белая книга реформ. -М.: Алгоритм, 2008.

Катков Г. М. Россия в 1917 г. Февральская революция. -М.: 2006.

Кейнс Дж. Избранные произведения. -М.: Экономика, 1993.

Кларк Дж. Б. Распределение богатства. -М.: Гелиос АРВ, 2000.

Клейнер Г. Б. Стратегия системной гармонии экономики России. // Экономические стратегии. -2008. -№5-6.

Кобяков А., Хазин М. Закат империи доллара и конец «Pax Americana». -М.: Вече, 2003.

Кондратьев Н. Д. Избранные сочинения. -М.: Экономика, 1993.

Кондратьев Н. Д. Мировое хозяйство и его конъюнктуры во время и после войны. -Вологда, 1922.

Кондратьев Н. Д. Проблемы экономической динамики. -М.: Экономика, 1989.

Кондратьев Н. Д. Основные проблемы экономической статики и динамики. Предварительный эскиз. -М.: Наука, 1991.

Конституция Российской Федерации. -http://www.consultant.ru/document/cons_ doc_ LAW_ 28399 / 5b9338a7944b7701fbe63f48c943e8175be16462 / .

Концепция участия России в объединении БРИКС (утверждена Президентом РФ 21. 03. 2013.).

Косикова Л. Новейшие украинские шоки российской экономики (о воздействии «постмайданного» кризиса в РУ на воспроизводственные процессы в РФ) // Российский экономический журнал. -2017. -№4.

Кудрявый В. Риски и угрозы российской электроэнергетики. Пути преодоления. 2015. -http://exergy.narod.ru/kudryavyi.pdf.

Куиггин Дж. Зомби-экономика: как мертвые идеи продолжают блуждать среди нас. -М.: Издательский дом Высшей школы экономики, 2016.

Кун Т. Структура научных революций. -М.: Прогресс, 1975.

Курлов П. Г. Гибель императорской России: Воспоминания. -М.: «Захаров», 2001.

Кьеза Д. Что вместо катастрофы. -М.: ИД «Трибуна», 2014.

Леви-Стросс К. Структурная антропология. -М.: Изд-во ЭКСМО-Пресс, 2001.

Липушкина И. Ю. Нефть Евразии: формирование общего рынка ЕАЭС. В соавт. -М.: Институт экономических стратегий, 2016.

Лукашенко А. О судьбах нашей интеграции / Известия. -17 октября 2011.

Львов Д. С. Экономическая теория научно-технического прогресса. -М.: Наука, 1982.

Львов Д. С., Глазьев С. Ю. Теоретические и прикладные аспекты управления НТП. / Экономика и математические методы. - 1986. -№5.

Маевский В. И. Реальный сектор и банковская система // Журнал Новой экономической ассоциации. -2009. -http://journal.econorus.org/jsub.Phtml?id=22.

Маевский В., Малков С. Перспективы макроэкономической теории воспроизводства // Вопросы экономики. -2014. -№ 4.

Макаров В. Л. Угроза перерождения экономики знаний под воздействием либерального рынка // Экономика региона. -2010. -№ 3.

Макаров В. Л. Социальный кластеризм. Российский вызов. - М.: Бизнес Атлас, 2010. 272 с.

Макконнелл К., Брю С. Экономикс: принципы проблемы и политика. -М.: Республика, 1992.

Макроэкономическая ситуация и денежно-финансовая политика в России / Доклад / Под ред. В. Е. Маневича и И. С. Букиной. - М.: Институт экономики РАН, 2013.

Мансуров Т. Евразийский проект Нурсултана Назарбаева, воплощенный в жизнь. -М.: Реал-пресс, 2014.

Мансуров Т. Евразийская экономическая интеграция: опыт и перспективы. -М.: Русский раритет, 2014.

Маркс К. и Энгельс Ф. Соч, т. 23. с. 10, 632. -М.: Государственное издательство политической литературы, 1960.

Мигранян А. Агрегированная модель оценки конкурентного потенциала стран ЕАЭС // Евразийская экономическая интеграция. -Ноябрь 2015. -№4 (29) .

Миндели Л. Э., Мотова М. А. Основные результаты разработки долгосрочного технологического прогноза России // Проблемы прогнозирования. -2006. -№5.

Митяев Д. А. О динамике саморазрушения мировой финансовой системы (сценарии и стратегии). Возможности адаптации и выбор стратегии для России. Сценарно-игровой доклад. -М.: Институт экономических стратегий, 2009.

Миркин Я. М. Финансовый конструктивизм. -М.: ИД «Лингва-Ф», 2014.

Моисеев Н. Н. С мыслями о будущем России. — М.: Фонд содействия развитию социальных и политических наук, 1997.

Мэнкью Г. Макроэкономика. -М.: Из-во Московского университета, 1994.

Нагорный А. Ловушка от Обамы. 2016. -https: // izborsk- club. ru / 9511.

Назарбаев Н. Евразийский союз: от идеи к истории будущего / Известия. -25 октября 2011.

Найденов В., Сменковский А. Инфляция и монетаризм. Уроки антикризисной политики. -Киев: ОАО БЦКФ, 2003.

Нанотехнологии как ключевой фактор нового технологического уклада в экономике / Под ред. С. Ю. Глазьева, В. В. Харитонова. - М.: Трованг, 2009.

Население России в 2017 году: доходы, расходы и социальное самочувствие. Мониторинг НИУ ВШЭ. Июль 2017 / Под ред. Л. Н. Овчаровой. -М.: НИУ ВШЭ, 2017.

Нельсон Р., Уинтер С. Дж. Эволюционная теория экономических изменений. -М.: Дело. 2002.

Нижегородцев Р., *Горидько Н., Шкодина И.* Институциональные основы теории финансов: современные подходы. -М.: ИНФРА- М, 2014.

Никонов В. Современный мир и его истоки. -М.: Издательство Московского Университета, 2015.

Носовский Г. В., Фоменко А. Т. Русь. Подлинная история Великой Русско-Ордынской Средневековой Империи. -М.: АСТ: Астрель, 2009.

Носовский Г. В., Фоменко А. Т. Старые карты Великой Русской Империи. -М.: АСТ: Астрель, 2009.

Носовский Г. В., Фоменко А. Т. Татаро-монгольское иго: Кто кого завоевывал. -М.: АСТ: Астрель, 2008.

Обращение Президента России к главам государств -членов Евразийского экономического союза. 18 января 2018. -http: // www. kremlin. ru / events / president / news / 56663.

Обучение рынку / Под ред. С. Ю. Глазьева. -М.: ЗАО «Издательство «Экономика», 2004.

О внешних и внутренних угрозах экономической безопасности России в условиях американской агрессии / Научный совет РАН по комплексным проблемам евразийскойэкономическойинтеграции,модернизации,конкурентоспособности и устойчивому развитию. 2014.

О ключевой ставке Банка России. Информация пресс-центра ЦБ РФ. 25 июля 2014 г. -www. cbr. ru.

Основные направления единой государственной денежно- кредитной политики на 2009 год и период 2010 и 2011 годов / Вестник Банка России. -№ 66 (1082) от 14. 11. 2008.

Основные направления единой государственной денежно- кредитной политики на 2015 г. и период 2016 и 2017 годов / Вестник Банка России. -№106 (1584) от 01. 12. 2014.

О стратегии развития экономики России. Научный доклад. -М.: Национальный институт развития, 2011.

О стратегии развития экономики России: препринт / Под ред. С. Ю. Глазьева. -М.: ООН РАН, 2011.

Отырба А., Кобяков А. Как побеждать в финансовых войнах. Альманах «Однако». -Июнь-июль 2014 г. -№ 174.

О чем мечтают россияне. Идеал и реальность / Под ред. М. К. Горшкова, Р. Крумма, Н. Е. Тихоновой. -М.: Весь мир, 2013.

Пантин В. Наиболее вероятный прогноз развития политических и военных конфликтов в период 2014-2018 гг. / Аналитический материал. 12 июля 2014 г. -newsdon. info.

Пантин В. Циклы реформ-контрреформ в России и их связь с циклами мирового развития // ПолИс. -2011. -№ 6.

Перкинс Д. Исповедь экономического убийцы. -М.: Претекст, 2005.

Перспективы и стратегические приоритеты восхождения БРИКС / Под. ред. В. Садовничего, Ю. Яковца, А. Акаева. -М.: МГУ - Международный институт Питирима Сорокина-Николая Кондратьева -ИНЭС -Национальный комитет по исследованию БРИКС -Институт Латинской Америки РАН, 2014.

Петров Ю. К формированию новой экономической модели: рестрикция бюджетных расходов или повышение собираемости налогов? // Российский экономический журнал. -2013. -№4.

Пикетти Т. Капитал в XXI веке. -М.: Ad Marginem, 2015.

Полтерович В. Механизмы «ресурсного проклятия» и экономическая политика // Вопросы экономики. -2007. -№6.

Подберезкин А., Боришполец К., Подберезкина О. Евразия и Россия. М.: 2013. -http://eurasian-defence.ru/sites/default/files/t4/4-1-1.pdf.

Полеванов В. «Бандитская» приватизация и судьба олигархов. Интервью ИА «Росбалт». -http://www.rosbalt.ru/main/2005/01/18/192666.html.

Политическое измерение мировых финансовых кризисов / Под ред. В. Якунина, С. Сулакшина, И. Орлова. -М.: Центр проблемного анализа и государственно-управленческого проектирования. Век глобализации. 2013. Вып. №2 (12) .

Поршнев Б. Оначале человеческой истории (Проблемы палеопсихологии). -М.: Мысль, 1974.

Послание Президента Российской Федерации Федеральному Собранию Российской Федерации, 3 декабря 2015 года. -http://www.kremlin.ru/events/president/news/50864.

Проханов А. Рев русской истории. 2018. -https: // izborsk- club. ru / 14935.

Путин В. Новый интеграционный проект для Евразии - будущее, которое рождается сегодня / Известия. -3 октября 2011.

Реформы глазами российских и американских ученых / Под общ. ред. О. Т. Богомолова. -М.: Российский экономический журнал, Фонд "За экономическую грамотность," 1996.

Рогов С. Место России в многополярном мире / Доклад. -М.: Институт США и Канады РАН, 2012.

Родзянко М. В. Государственная дума и февральская 1917 года революция. -Берлин: Slowo-Verlag, 1922.

Росс Дж. Китай и новый период в мировой экономике // Экономические стратегии. -2017. -№4.

Россия на пути к современной динамичной и эффективной экономике / Аналитический доклад / Под ред. А. Д. Некипелова, В. В. Ивантера, С. Ю. Глазьева. -М.: Российская академия наук, 2013.

Самуэльсон П., Нордгауз В. Макроэкономика. -К: Основы, 1995. 147. Сахал Д. Технический прогресс: концепции, модели, оценки. -М.: Финансы и статистика. 1985.

Сергейцев Т. Падение мировой сверхвласти: крымский рубеж. -М.: Однако, июнь-июль 2014. №174.

Симчера В., Соколин В., Шевяков А. К построению исторических рядов социально-экономического развития России // Экономическая наука современной России. -2001. -№6.

Смирнов Ф. Мировая финансово-экономическая архитектура. Деконструкция. -М.: ООО «Буки Веди», 2015.

Сорокин П. Главные тенденции нашего времени. -М.: Наука, Российская академия наук, Институт социологии, 1997.

Суханов Н. Н. Записки о революции. -М.: Издательство политической литературы, 1991.

Сухарев О. С. Экономические санкции: проблема оценки ущерба // Экономика и предпринимательство. -2017. -№ 8. -Ч. 4.

Сухотин Ю. В. О критериях и закономерностях социально- экономического реформирования. В кн: Экономические реформы в России. Итоги первых лет 1991-1996. ИЭ РАН. -М.: Наука, 1997.

Технологическая кооперация и повышение конкурентоспособности в ЕЭП. Доклад №10. -СПб: Центр интеграционных исследований Евразийского банка развития, ЕАБР, 2013.

Тобин Д. Денежная политика и экономический рост. -М.: Либроком, 2010.

Тоффлер Э. Третья волна. -М.: АСТ, 2010.

Трубецкой Н. С. История. Культура. Язык. -М.: ПРОГРЕСС; УНИВЕРС, 1995.

Ульянов Н. Технология на вырост // Эксперт. -2017. -№24.

Федоренко Н. П. Вопросы оптимального функционирования экономики. — М.: Наука, 1990.

Финансовые стратегии модернизации экономики: мировая практика / Под ред. Я. М. Миркина. -М.: Магистр, 2014.

Филимонов Г. Культурно-информационные механизмы внешней политики США. Истоки и новая реальность. -М.: Российский университет дружбы народов, 2012.

Фишер И. Покупательная сила денег. -М.: НКФ СССР, 1926.

Фоменко А. Т. Как было на самом деле. Каждая история желает быть рассказанной М.: АСТ, 2017.

Формирование стратегии модернизации экономики: мировая практика / Под ред. Я. М. Миркина. -М.: Магистр, 2014.

Форрестер Д. Мировая динамика. -М.: АСТ, 2006.

Фридмен М. Если бы деньги заговорили... -М.: Дело, 1998.

Фридмен М. Количественная теория денег. -М.: Эльф пресс, 1996.

Фролов К. А. Проект Украины как анти-России. Искоренение канонического православия на исторических землях Малороссии, Новороссии и Подкарпатской Руси. -М.: Алетейя, 2016.

Фукуяма Ф. Конец истории и последний человек. -М.: АСТ, 2010.

Фурсов А. Русофобия и информационная война против России. 2015 -http: // andreyfursov. ru / news / rusofobija _ i _ informa- cionnaja_ vojna_ protiv_ rossii / 2015-10-31-496.

Хантингтон С. Столкновение цивилизаций. -М.: ООО «Издательство АСТ», 2003.

Харрис Л. Денежная теория. -М.: Прогресс, 1990.

Цыпин А. П., Овсянников В. А. Оценка доли иностранного капитала в промышленности России // Молодой ученый. - 2014. -№12.

Шацилло В. Первая мировая война 1914-1918. Факты и документы. -М.: Олма-Пресс, 2003.

Швейцер П. Победа. Роль тайной стратегии администрации США в распаде Советского Союза и социалистического лагеря. Минск: 1995.

Широв А. А., Янтовский А. А., Потапенко В. В. Оценка потенциального влияния санкций на экономическое развитие России и ЕС // Проблемы прогнозирования.

-2015. -№4.

Шумпетер И. Теория экономического развития. -М.: Прогресс, 1982.

Эволюционная теория экономических изменений / Под ред. Р. Р. Нельсона, С. Дж. Уинтера. -М.: Дело, 2002.

Эволюция технико-экономических систем: возможности и границы централизованного регулирования / Под ред. Д. С. Львова, Г. Г. Фетисова, С. Ю. Глазьева. -М.: Наука, 1992.

Экономическая безопасность современной России: уроки кризиса и перспективы роста / Под ред. В. А. Черешнева, А. И. Татаркина, М. В. Федорова. -Екатеринбург: Институт экономики УрО РАН, 2012.

Эрхард Л. Полвека размышлений. -М.: Руссико-Ордынка, 1993.

Яковец Ю. Политическая экономия цивилизаций. -М.: Экономика, 2016.

Яковец Ю. В., Акаев А. А. Перспективы становления устойчивого многополярного мироустройства на базе партнерства цивилизаций: Научный доклад. -М.: МИСК, 2016.

Яковец Ю. В., Кузык Б. Н. Цивилизации: теория, история, диалог, будущее. -М.: Институт экономических стратегий, 2006.

Яковлев А., Глисин Ф. Альтернативные формы расчетов в народном хозяйстве и возможности их анализа методами субъективной статистики // Вопросы статистики. -1996. -№ 9.

Яременко Ю. В. Структурные изменения в социалистической экономике. -М.: Мысль, 1981.

2030 Чжунго: маньсян гунтун фуюй (Китай — 2030: вперед к всеобщей зажиточности) / Центр изучения положения в стране Университета Цинхуа / Под ред. Ху Аньган, Янь Илун, Вэй Син. -Пекин: Изд-во Китайского Народного университета, 2011.

"2015 Article IV Consultation with the US of America Concluding Statement of the IMF Mission." IMF, May 28, 2015.

Andersen, L., and Carlson K. "Monetary and Fiscal Actions: A Test of Their Relative Importance in Economic Stabilization." *Federal Reserve Bank of St. Louis Review*, no. 50 (1968).

Ando, A., and Modigliani F. "The Relative Stability of Monetary Velocity and the Investment Multiplier." *American Economic Review*, no. 5 (1965).

Arrighi, G. *The Long Twentieth Century: Money, Power and the Origins of Our Times*. London: Verso, 1994.

Attali, J. *Millennium: Winners and Losers in the Coming World Order*. N.Y.: Random House, 1991.

Crozet, M., and Hinz J. "Collateral Damage: The Impact of the Russia Sanctions on Sanctioning Countries' Exports. Research and Expertise on the World Economy." *CEPII Working Paper*, June 16, 2016.

Friedman, M., and Meiselman D. *The Relative Stability of Monetary Ve- locity and the Investment Multiplier in the US, 1897–1958*. N.J.: Prentice Hall, 1963.

Fukuyama, F. *The End of History and the Last Man*. N.Y: Free Press, 1992.

Grubler, A. "The Rise and Fall of Infrastructures." *American Economic Review*, no. 49 (1959).

Hammond, G. *State of the Art of Inflation Targeting*. London: Bank of England, 2012.

Herbert, S. *An Administrative Behaviour: A Study of Decision-making Processes in Administrative Organizations*. Glencoe: Free Press, 1960.

Kemp, J. *An American Renaissance: A Strategy for the 1980s*. N.Y: HarperCollins, 1979.

Maddison, A. "The World Economy: Historical Statistics." Paris: OECD, 1995.

"Main Science and Technology Indicators." Paris: OECD, no.1 (2013).

Marchetti, C., and Nakicenovic N. "The Dynamics of Energy Systems and the Logistic Substitution Model." RR-79-13 / IIASA-Laxenburg, Austria, 1979.

Nakicenovic, N. "Energy Strategies for Mitigating Global Change." IIASA-Laxenburg, Austria, 1992.

Nakicenovic, N. *Technological Substitution and Long Waves in the USA: The Long Wave Debate*. Berlin: Springer, 1987.

Obstfeld, M., Shambaugh J., and Taylor A. "Monetary Sovereignty, Exchange Rates, and Capital Controls: The Trilemma in the Interwar Period." *IMF Staff Papers* 51 (2004).

Perez, C. *Technological Revolutions and Financial Capital: The Dynamics of Bubbles and Golden Ages*. London: Elgar, 2002.

Ramo, J. *The Beijing Consensus*. London: The Foreign Policy Centre, 2004.

Russell, M. "Sanctions over Ukraine: Impact on Russia." Members' Research Service, European Parliamentary Research Service, March 2016.

Russian Federation. "2015 Article IV Consultation." *IMF Staff Country Report*, no. 15 (2015): 211.

Sidrausk, M. "Rational Choice and Patterns of Growth in a Monetary Economy." *American Economic Review* 57, no. 2 (May 1967).

Tobin, J. "Liquidity Preference as Behaviour Towards Risk," *The Review of Economic Studies*, no. 67 (February 1958).

ABOUT THE AUTHOR

GLAZIEV SERGEY YURIEVICH, Academician of the Russian Academy of Sciences (2008). He is the author of more than 400 scientific papers, among them monographs *Economic Theory of Technological Development* (1990), *Theory of Long-Term Technical and Economic Development* (1993), *Genocide* (1997), *Economics and Politics: Episodes of Struggle, Economic Theory of Technical Development, Market Training* (2004), *Nanotechnology as a Key Factor of a New Technological Order in the Economy* (2009 G), *The Strategy of Advanced Development of Russia in the Context of the Global Crisis* (2010), *Lessons of the Next Russian Revolution: The Collapse of a Liberal Utopia and a Chance for an "Economic Miracle"* (2011), *Ukrainian Catastrophe* (2015), *The Economy of the Future* (2016), *The Last World War* (2016), *The Battle for Leadership in the XXI Century* (2017), *Leaping into the Future* (2019), *Economic Development Management* (2019), *The Plague of the XXI Century: How to Avoid Disaster and Overcome the Crisis* (2020), *Beyond the Horizon of the End of History* (2021).

ABOUT THE TRANSLATOR

Zhang Yumei, associate professor and master's supervisor, is currently the chair of the English Department at Jilin International Studies University (JISU), a key provincial university in Northeast China. She is a visiting scholar of Beijing Foreign Studies University (2011–2012), a volunteer Chinese teacher at Paradise Valley Elementary School in Wyoming, USA (2015–2016), and a scholar of English language methodology at Portland University, USA (2019). The main courses she teaches are English Reading, English Linguistics, and English Education Measurement and Evaluation. She has published more than 10 academic papers on English classroom teaching and evaluation. She has presided over 5 provincial projects and participated in dozens of teaching and research programs.